THE HANDBOOK TO GOTHIC LITERATURE

The Handbook to Gothic Literature

Edited by

MARIE MULVEY-ROBERTS
Senior Lecturer in Literary Studies
University of the West of England, Bristol

First published 1998 by
MACMILLAN PRESS LTD
Houndmills, Basingstoke, Hampshire RG21 6XS
and London
Companies and representatives throughout the world

ISBN 0–333–64037–3 hardcover
ISBN 0–333–67069–8 paperback

A catalogue record for this book is available from the British Library.

This book is printed on paper suitable for recycling and made from
fully managed and sustained forest sources.

10   9   8   7   6   5   4   3   2   1
07 06 05 04 03 02 01 00 99 98

Printed in Great Britain by
Antony Rowe Ltd Chippenham, Wiltshire

For my Gothic students,
especially Sandi and Vicky,
founders of the Skeletal Society
and
To the Vampire Lovers
L. and Z.

Contents

Contents

Contents ix

Gothic Specialisms

Contents   xi

List of Contributors

Lucie Armitt, Lecturer in English at the University of Wales, Bangor

Clive Bloom, Reader in English, Middlesex University, London

Fred Botting, Lecturer in English, Lancaster University

Elisabeth Bronfen, Professor of English, Zurich University

Steven Bruhm, Associate Professor in English, Mount Saint Vincent University, Halifax, Nova Scotia

Charles Butler, Senior Lecturer in Literary Studies, University of the West of England, Bristol

Amaryll Beatrice Chanady, Professor in Comparative Literature, University of Montreal

Steve Clark, Lecturer in English, Osaka University

E. J. Clery, Research Fellow, Sheffield Hallam University

John Cloy, Librarian, John Davis Williams Library, University of Mississippi

Ian Conrich, Lecturer in Media and Cultural Studies, Nottingham Trent University

Neil Cornwell, Professor of Russian, University of Bristol

Jeffrey N. Cox, Associate Professor in English, Texas A&M University

Eric Hadley Denton, Associate Professor in English, Franklin and Marshall College, Lancaster, Pennsylvania

Madge Dresser, Principal Lecturer in Historical Studies, University of the West of England, Bristol

Sion Eirian, freelance writer, Cardiff

U. A. Fanthorpe, poet, Wootton-under-Edge

Benjamin F. Fisher, Professor of English, University of Mississippi

Michael Franklin, Lecturer in English Studies, University of Wales, Cardiff

Ken Gelder, Associate Professor and Reader in English, University of Melbourne

R. A. Gilbert, writer and bookseller, Bristol

Antonio Ballesteros González, Lecturer in English, University of Castilla, La Mancha, Spain

Iain Hamilton Grant, Lecturer in Cultural Studies, University of the West of England, Bristol

Terry Hale, Director of the British Centre for Literary Translation, University of East Anglia

Jerrold E. Hogle, Associate Professor in English, University of Arizona, Tucson

Avril Horner, Lecturer in English, Salford University

Christoph Houswitschka, Lecturer in English, University of Dresden

William Hughes, Lecturer in English, Bath Spa University College

Elizabeth Imlay, writer and publisher, Speldhurst, Kent

Darryl Jones, Lecturer in English, Trinity College, University of Dublin

Elaine Jordan, Senior Lecturer in English, University of Essex

Richard Kerridge, Senior Lecturer in English, Bath Spa University College

Sally Ledger, Lecturer in English, Birkbeck College, University of London

A. Robert Lee, Professor of English, Nihon University, Japan

T. J. Lustig, Lecturer in American Studies, Keele University

Douglas S. Mack, Senior Lecturer in English, University of Stirling

Cécile Malet-Dagréou, postgraduate student in English, Goldsmiths College, University of London

Philip W. Martin, Head of Humanities, Cheltenham and Gloucester College, Cheltenham

W. J. McCormack, Senior Lecturer in English, Goldsmiths College, University of London

Alison Milbank, writer, Cambridge

Robert Miles, Reader in English, Sheffield Hallam University

Hans-Ulrich Mohr, Technical University of Dresden

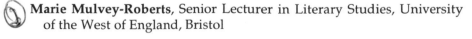 **Marie Mulvey-Roberts**, Senior Lecturer in Literary Studies, University of the West of England, Bristol

Pascal Nicklas, Lecturer in English, University of Leipzig

Graham Ovenden, artist, Cornwall

David Punter, Professor of English Studies, University of Stirling

Tina Rath, writer and postgraduate student, Royal Holloway, University of London

Faye Ringel, Associate Professor in English, US Coast Guard Academy, New London, USA

Victor Sage, Reader in English and American Studies, University of East Anglia

Neil Sammells, Dean of Humanities, Bath Spa University College

David Seed, Reader in English, Liverpool University

Helen Small, Lecturer in English, Pembroke College, Oxford

John Charles Smith, Fellow, St Catherine's College, Oxford

Allan Lloyd Smith, Lecturer in English and American Studies, University of East Anglia

Helen Stoddart, Lecturer in English, Keele University

Philip Stokes, Lecturer in Photography, Nottingham Trent University

Janet Todd, Professor in English and American Literature, University of East Anglia

Ann B. Tracy, Associate Professor in English, State University of New York at Plattsburgh

Nicola Trott, Lecturer in English, University of Glasgow

Gerry Turcotte, Senior Lecturer in English Studies, Wollongong University, Australia

William Veeder, Professor of English, University of Chicago

Mary Waldron, Lecturer in Continuing Education, University of Exeter

Alexandra Warwick, Lecturer in English Studies, University of Westminster

Thomas Willard, Associate Professor in English, University of Arizona, Tucson

Carolyn D. Williams, Senior Lecturer in English, University of Reading

Introduction

'I will read you their names directly; here they are in my pocket-book: "Castle of Wolfenbach," "Clermont," "Mysterious Warnings," "Necromancer of the Black Forest," "Midnight Bell," "Orphan of the Rhine," and "Horrid Mysteries." Those will last us some time.'

'Yes; pretty well; but are they all horrid? Are you sure they are all horrid?'

Jane Austen, *Northanger Abbey* (1818)

Jane Austen's *Northanger Abbey* has become the definitive satiric paradigm for the delusions of the Gothic reader engendering the dangers of Gothic reading. When consigned to a list of future reading in the feckless Isabella Thorpe's pocket-book, the fears generated by these *Northanger* novels, rather than being domesticated, are so positioned as to accentuate the prolepsis of redoubtable terrors.

The impulse to catalogue and classify in the spirit of Augustan taxonomy serves us with the illusion of gaining control over the otherwise uncontainable. The murky flux of the formless mass of Gothic space becomes less terrifying when confined to a handbook, particularly one that is arranged in alphabetical order. Like the horror film *The Entity*, which stars a gargantuan shapeless phenomenon that threatens to engulf the entire film set in its ever-expanding protean borders, the Gothic cultural phenomenon continues to break its boundaries. *The Handbook to Gothic Literature* sets out to delineate the contours, points of transgression, cross-over and cross-fertilisation that characterise Gothic literature and its tangential disciplines: architecture, art, film, music and photography.

The hideous progeny of Gothic literature has spawned a textual equivalent of the race of devils that Victor Frankenstein feared 'might make the very existence of the species of man a condition precarious and full of terror'.[1] Resistance to such a Gothic invasion has been mounted by a phalanx of critics in a two-pronged attack. Disarming the Gothic text by analysing it, is a variant on Wordsworth's 'We murder to Dissect',[2] which is particularly apposite when *Frankenstein* is being considered. Like Victor, who destroys the female he is creating as a mate for his creature, the literary critic dismembers and fragments the whole into customised parts. From there, follow classification and sub-division of text, author, concept, many of which are re-entered and cross-referenced under different categories such as national or regional divisions. This combination of analysis and classification underscores Gothic literature in its broad contours as well as in its idiosyncrasies. Such tactics are surety against the danger of us failing to see the Gothic castle for the gargoyles.

This book is more than an inventory of the sinister, the fantastical, and the eerie, it is a passport to what Terry Castle calls the 'hag-ridden realm of [the] unconscious'.[3] Duly labelled and arranged under headings ranging from 'The Sublime' to the 'Rosicrucian', the compendium is divided into entries that are predominantly mainstream and those that are primarily peripheral. The bifurcation of Gothic writing which tends to default along the gendered lines of female 'Terror' and male 'Horror' is included, for example, in the main section. In the second half, entries on dread-related areas such as 'The Uncanny' and 'The Grotesque' are suggestive of how 'Gothic' should not be traduced. At once an umbrella term that has traditionally covered a multitude of the fictional sinned against and sinning, the nuances of what we understand by it as a site of difference within a panoply of family resemblances, is represented in this collection.

What is Gothic literature? Is it a plot, a trope, a topos, a discourse, a mode of representation, conventions of characterisation, or a composite of all these aspects? Associated with the traditional Gothic Novel is an ivy-covered haunted ruin, a swooning heroine replete with sensibility, and a tyrannical villain, bequeathed with a lock, a key and a castle. Constituting and constitutive of anachronism and counterfeit, the Gothic plot, the proverbial textual folly, is a mirror diverting us from the Gorgon's gaze, that is, at least once removed from the source of trauma and taboo. The concoction is a dark yet familiar brew – an uneasy and eerie dialectic between anxiety and desire. A working definition of 'Gothic' and 'Gothic literature', with its polyvalency and slippage of meaning, may be gleaned from the entries aggregated here. *The Handbook to Gothic Literature* is also an index to otherness, for it captures and catalogues a way of looking at the world that is redolent of something other than itself. More perplexing still is the way in which, while trying to lock onto the Gothic co-ordinates, one can end up chasing a zero vanishing point, especially since so much of Gothic writing is preoccupied with gaps. On a pragmatic note, there will inevitably be gaps of omission particularly as Gothic culture continues to evolve. The idea for *The Handbook* was inspired by Frederick S. Frank, whose glossary of Gothic terms in his *The First Gothics* (1987) it is intended to complement. Particularly captivating are his beguiling Freudian categories as in the Beckfordian phallic genre of novels exhibiting 'Toweromania' and 'Turret Gothic', whose gendered counterparts, 'Grotto Gothic' and 'Grottophilia', are set in womb-like, cavernous environments.

As an anatomy of the Gothic world and an unholy Bible of the world's leading Gothicists, this *Handbook* purports to be introductory, referential and innovatory. Popular representations of the Gothic subsist with high cultural forms. Marginalised Gothicisms, such as 'Welsh Gothic', are represented alongside canonical Gothic writers like Ann Radcliffe (if such appended designations are not respectively tautological or oxymoronic). The Gothic writer, to misappropriate Swift in *A Tale of a Tub*, belongs to 'the Republick of dark Authors' who span the dark side of the solar ray of the Rational Enlightenment to the present day. Landmark writers that form the main contours of the Gothic landscape make up most entries. An appended list of further reading, which gives priority to 'Female Gothic' as a distinct category, includes brief bibliographies for six of the most popular writers: Horace Walpole, Ann Radcliffe, Edgar Allan Poe, Mary Shelley, Bram Stoker and Angela Carter.

Gothic life, like that of a giant poisonous plant with far-reaching tendrils, has found its sustenance by feeding off the credulities of its readers. This hot-house hybrid is constantly mutating, making new growths out of old as in its propensity for parody and pastiche. What remains consistent, according to Angela Carter, is the retention of 'a singular moral function – that of provoking unease'.[4] This inflection of Gothic as un-ease or dis-ease invites comparisons with the pathological. Having taken up residence in its host, the Gothic replicates itself throughout our culture like a virus. While resistant to the antidote of realism, it persistently conjugates with the dark side of contemporaneity, at the same time, making a textual negotiation with history. Apart from time there is place. The diaspora of Gothic writing has led to the emergence of distinct traditions in Australia and Canada and beyond. Regrettably space does not allow all the countries who have either imported or incubated Gothic cultural representations to be included here. Pragmatism dictated by undergraduate reading lists has, inevitably, restricted the entries to English-speaking countries and selected European black spots of the sinister, the uncanny and the terrible, like France, Germany and Russia.

It is to those who have created this Gothic topography, that I am most grateful. Many contributors are leading Gothicists, who have pushed back the frontiers of our understanding of the mechanisms of fear and the perverse attraction to the creeping horrors of the imagination. William Hughes has been particularly helpful as a source of reassurance and unfailingly sound advice while Macmillan's Charmian Hearne has been a most patient and understanding editor. Her fund of wisdom, insight and faith in the project, have shed much-needed light, particularly when I have felt emeshed in pockets of Gothic darkness. Neil Cornwell, Norah Crook, Marion Glastonbury, Naomi Lester, Valery Rose and my family deserve special mention for their support. Finally, I would like to thank my students for their Gothic enthusiasms and trust that this book will match up to their Gothic requirements. Though it may not contain definitive answers to such questions as 'Is Gothic literature a sub-genre of Romanticism or the other way round?', as an adjunct to Angela Carter's observation that 'we live in Gothic times',[5] the *Handbook* goes a long way in showing us where we came from and where we are going.

Bristol   MARIE MULVEY-ROBERTS

Notes

1. Mary Shelley, *Frankenstein*, ed. Johanna M. Smith (Boston: Bedford Books of St Martin's Press, 1992), p. 140.
2. William Wordsworth, 'The Tables Turned', *The Lyrical Ballads* (1798; London: Oxford University Press, 1931), p. 186.
3. Terry Castle, *The Female Thermometer: Eighteenth-Century Culture and the Invention of the Uncanny* (Oxford: Oxford University Press, 1995), p. 5.
4. Angela Carter, Afterword to *Fireworks*, in *Burning Your Boats: Collected Short Stories* (London: Vintage Random House, 1996), p. 459.
5. Ibid., p. 460.

Gothic Writers and Key Terms

Ainsworth, William Harrison (1805–82)

Ainsworth made his first venture into sensational fiction with 'The Test of Affection' (*European Magazine*, 1822), a tale that relies heavily on artificial **'SUPERNATURAL'** devices in the **ANN RADCLIFFE** mode for its effect. It was followed by 'The Spectre Bride' (*Arliss's Pocket Magazine*, 1822) and his early Gothic tales were collected in his first book, the anonymous *December Tales* (1823). All of this youthful work – which displays more enthusiasm than polish – was produced while Ainsworth was living in Manchester, where he had been born in 1805.

After he moved to London in 1824 to complete his legal training, Ainsworth took up a career in periodical publishing, although his finest work as an editor – with *Bentley's Miscellany, Ainsworth's Magazine*, and *The New Monthly Magazine* – belongs to the 1840s, by which time he had established himself as a successful popular novelist. Between 1834 and his death in 1882 he published thirty-nine novels, but while his earlier works were immensely successful he outlived his popularity and the later titles were failures.

Rookwood, his first independent novel, published anonymously in 1834, was, in his own words, 'a story in the bygone style of Mrs. Radcliffe'. It contains the standard stock-in-trade of such stories: gloomy settings, dismal vaults, and skeleton hands, with a decaying manor house and an English highwayman in place of the Radcliffean castle and Italian brigand – all of them used to great effect. His second novel of highwaymen, *Jack Sheppard* (1839), was more realist than Romantic in nature and was condemned for its idealisation of crime. With *The Miser's Daughter* (1842), in which the influence of Mrs Radcliffe can clearly be seen, he returned to the Gothic fold.

In 1848 Ainsworth published his most enduring novel, and the only one which is overtly supernatural in content, but *The Lancashire Witches* is in no sense a true Gothic novel. It *does* contain **WITCHES** and demons but its success comes by way of the author's portrayal of regional character and local topography. Throughout the 1850s and 1860s Ainsworth maintained a steady output of sound, stirring historical novels, but while supernatural episodes occasionally crept in, the Romantic elements faded away and with them his claim to be a writer of the Gothic.

R. A. GILBERT

American Gothic

American fiction began in the Gothic mode, because the first substantial American efforts in fiction coincided with the great period of British and European gothic. The examples of the British novelist William Godwin and the German romancers played an important part in inspiring **CHARLES BROCKDEN BROWN**'s early novels and the Germans similarly provided material for **WASHINGTON IRVING**'s Gothic satires. A little later **EDGAR ALLAN POE** worked in the vein of the sensationalist *Blackwood's Edinburgh Magazine*, producing tales that did not achieve the popularity he expected, largely because the literary marketplace had already moved on by the 1830s and 1840s. **NATHANIEL HAWTHORNE** fully realised the possibilities of resonance between the Gothic tradition and the American past, and **HERMAN MELVILLE** used the mode to articulate his more coded understanding of the darker underside of the new nation's optimistic surfaces. That darker note concerned in part the legacy of slavery and racial discrimination, which was to inform many subsequent fictions of **SOUTHERN GOTHIC** and is still a principal energiser of the mode, as in Toni Morrison's *Beloved*.

Another thread may be identified as the psychological possibilities of Gothicism, again a major element in Brockden Brown's novels, developed through Poe's and Hawthorne's tales and powerfully at work in **HENRY JAMES**'s ghost stories and even his major fictions. The advantage – and perhaps indeed inevitability – of the Gothic form in articulating the concerns of the unvoiced 'other' has meant that the position of the female in a predominantly masculinist culture provided another important strand in American Gothicism, instanced best by Charlotte Perkins Gilman's story 'The Yellow Wallpaper'. Recently, while the Southern Gothic tradition has modulated from Faulkner, Truman Capote and Flannery O'Connor into an exploration of the history of the racially 'othered', there can also be identified a strain of **URBAN GOTHICISM**, in the work of James Purdy, for example, or some of John Hawkes's writing, and what might be called techno-Gothic, as in Thomas Pynchon's *V* or *Gravity's Rainbow*, and finally, cyber-Gothic, in William Gibson's novels and stories. To summarise, then, although American Gothicists participated in a wider literary tradition, the circumstances of their own history and the stresses of their particular cultural and political institutions meant that a series of significant inflections determined a Gothicism that differs considerably from British or European versions.

Philip Freneau (1752–1832) struck the Gothic note early in his graveyard poem *The House of Night* (1799):

Let others draw from smiling skies their theme,
And tell of climes that boast unfading light,

I draw a darker scene, replete with gloom,
I sing the horrors of the *House of Night*.

He went on to paint a lurid picture of the death of Death himself, replete with coal-black chariot and 'Spectres attending, in black weeds array'd'. But it was Charles Brockden Brown (1771–1810) who most thoroughly founded the Gothic tradition in American fiction with his novels *Wieland* (1798), *Arthur Mervyn* (1798), *Edgar Huntly* (1799) and *Ormond*, completed in 1799. Brown's novels exploited a Radcliffean vein of explained supernaturalism, using ventriloquism, somnambulism, and the charnel scenes of plague to create his Gothic effects. William Godwin was another and more important mentor, for Brown's work is infused with rationalist precepts and is now seen to contain political implications.

Wieland begins with the mysterious death of Wieland senior, a religious fanatic consumed by a fireball in his temple of worship. His children, Clara and Theodore, convert the temple into a summer house and live in tranquility until some uncanny voices trigger Theodore Wieland's own lurking religious mania. Clara relates the terrible story of the discovery of the mangled remains of Wieland's wife and children, and realises that Theodore, in obedience to his voices, intends to kill her also. Responsibility for the whole disaster is given to Carwin, a ventriloquist who had used his strange gift to divert attention from minor misdemeanours. Clara's blaming of Carwin is itself delusional however, for the story has shown how the roots of irrationality lie deeper than mere surface causes, and indeed may involve incestuous feelings between Wieland and Clara.

Such self-reflexive subtleties are typical of Brown's novels. In *Edgar Huntly* the narrator intends to help a disturbed somnambulist, Clithero, but similarly falls victim to sleepwalking and mental disturbance, hiding papers from himself, and wandering in the wilderness of Norwalk. In one episode Huntly falls into a cave. He loses consciousness, then wakes to find himself threatened by silent Indians. Huntly kills one with a hatchet, shoots three more, and bayonets a fifth in an act of 'cruel lenity'. Covered in gore, he leaves his bayonet rifle upright in the ground as a totemic gesture. He has thus himself become savage, out of a necessity that echoes his own psychic constitution, since his own parents were butchered by Indians in an American primal scene. This adaptation of Gothic conventions to the American landscape is not simply a literary convenience but is also a significant pointer to the racial antagonism, guilt and displacement that has driven much subsequent Gothic writing. In *Arthur Mervyn* Brown effectively invented the American urban Gothic, in which the civilised city is transformed through plague into an unknowable labyrinth of horrors, and in *Ormond* he naturalised a notorious European secret society, the Illuminati, into an American urban environment.

Some of Edgar Allan Poe's work seems to follow in the mould set by Brown: the indeterminate urban situations, the nightmare intensities, but above all, the confusions of consciousness whereby the protagonist's madness destabilises narrative and setting. Like Brown fundamentally a rationalist who stops short of supernaturalism, Poe was, however, also much influenced by Romanticism, and perhaps particularly by German Romantic irony. This is demonstrated in his interest in extremes of consciousness – as in episodes of near-death states – dreamlike intensities, and an underlying macabre humour that delights in the reversal of expectations. Before Poe, Washington Allston had shown how Gothicists might theorise the darker side of the Romantic ideal in his novella *Monaldi* (1822). An American painter, and a friend of Coleridge, Allston argued in his *Lectures on Art* that the gradations between the beautiful and the sublime have a dark analogue descending to the ugly and then rising again to complete the circle. 'And in this dark segment', he claimed, 'will be found the startling union of deepening discords – still deepening as it rises from the Ugly to the Loathsome, the Horrible, the Frightful, the Appalling'. Poe's interest in precisely those qualities as the route to illumination is what raised his work above *Blackwood's Edinburgh Magazine* sensationalism and made him subsequently the darling of the French *Symbolistes*. Another influence on Poe was one of the most prolific American writers of the early period, John Neal (1793–1876), who wrote several naturalised Gothic novels between 1820 and 1840 including *Logan* (1822), a tale of hereditary family madness in the wilderness, and *Rachel Dyer* (1828), a story of the Salem witchcraft episode of 1692, which also later informed Nathaniel Hawthorne's story 'Alice Doane's Appeal'.

Other significant early Gothicists included James Kirke Paulding (1778–1860), who collaborated with Washington Irving on *Salmagundi* (1807–8), and William Gilmore Simms (1806–70), whose *Martin Faber* (1833) drew on both Godwin and Brown. James Fenimore Cooper also incorporated Gothic elements into his novels, especially in *The Spy* (1821), a story of the underside of the American Revolution, and his tale of Venetian intrigue, *The Bravo* (1831). Robert Montgomery Bird (1806–54) took up the Indian-hating theme of Brown's *Edgar Huntly* in *Nick of the Woods* (1837), an extraordinary tale of a schizophrenic Quaker/Indian killer who engraves crosses on his victims, exemplifying the potential Gothicism both of racism and of the American forests. Later, in a sensationalist and hugely successful novel, *The Quaker City; or, The Monks of Monk Hall* (1845), George Lippard took up the possibilities of urban Gothic, describing the fantastic secret underside of Quaker Philadelphia. Lippard's mixture of sensuality and radical social thought also owed much to Brockden Brown, to whom in fact he dedicated the book.

But beyond all these is the figure of Edgar Allan Poe, who developed a new economy in Gothic writing through his conception of 'unity of effect', a concern for the reading experience that left a deep impress on both American and European Gothic developments, and through his invention of the macabre detective story, which inaugurated a lasting genre. Poe's Gothic tales, such as 'Ligeia' or 'The Fall of the House of Usher', combined unspeakable frisson with a tantalising psychological complexity that continues to unfold in response to new critical discourses, whether of Jacques Lacan or of the post-structuralists. Conventionally divided into tales of imagination and those of 'ratiocination', in fact his stories of both types are examples of different strains within the Gothic, the drive towards mystery and the fantastic, and the corresponding drive towards explanation. The mystery stories invite and challenge interpretation, while the detective stories, such as 'The Murders in the Rue Morgue', incorporate elements of fantastic excess. A persistent mocking humour is to be found in these as well as in his ostensibly comic tales, reminiscent of the work of Washington Irving (1783–1859), if more savage and without Irving's more comfortable end-of-story recuperations. One of Irving's stories, in fact, 'The Adventure of the German Student', is almost exactly in the vein that Poe made his own, with its sinister celebration of what Poe called the most poetical of topics, the death of a beautiful woman, and its explanatory invocation of madness. Poe internalised the gothic nightmare, claiming: 'My terror is not of Germany, but of the soul', thus opening the way for the psychological ghost story; he also domesticated it in such tales as 'The Black Cat', a 'mere series of household events' which concludes with the animal discovered feeding off the walled-up corpse of the narrator's murdered wife. Some of Poe's work shows the effects of late eighteenth-century rationalism in its American form (which was heavily influenced by the Scottish 'Common-Sense' philosophers): the drive towards explanation and understandings of Gothic events through mental disorder, and the sense of stopping short of supernaturalism; but at the same time, he was clearly also a product of the Romantic movement, in that his tales show the compelling effects of disorder in the imaginative creation of his protagonists' worlds, without recourse to normalising narrative frameworks.

Nathaniel Hawthorne (1806–64) similarly internalised and domesticated the Gothic to explore its insights into the psychology of everyday life, and its applicability to history. In Hawthorne's hands the Gothic is *performed*: it is not allowed to direct the form of the narrative but is instead manipulated and distorted for purposes that include a recognition of its origins in destabilised personal and political situations. His tales are full of magic objects: speaking portraits, deadly shawls, broken fountains, ghostly prophecies; but these are characteristically unpacked to show their range of historical and personal meanings. The scarlet letter itself, in his novel *The Scarlet Letter* (1850) – introduced by a standard Gothic scenario, the discovery of a strange old manuscript – is an example of a totemic magic object which fascinates not so much for its strange powers as for the rich variety of meanings it is shown to contain. Similarly the fatal shawl of 'Lady Eleanore's Mantle' exudes a literal pestilence, but at the same time is an emblem of the pestilential effects of class in aristocratic isolation, and of the arrogance of beauty. Hawthorne uses mirrors, magical portraits and the effects of uncertain light to produce a mood of Gothic strangeness, rather than to develop fully Gothic narratives. In *The Scarlet Letter*, the relationship between Dimmesdale and Chillingworth echoes Poe's 'William Wilson' and Simms's *Martin Faber*, with, behind them, **MATURIN**'s *Melmoth the Wanderer*. But Hawthorne's version of the demonic investigating double is focused on the psychic cost of the Faustian bargain and its reciprocal endorsement by the victim. We find familiar Gothic figures in the magnetic and saturnine Hollingsworth of *The Blithedale Romance* (1852), the sinister monk and family secrets of *The Marble Faun* (1860), the ancestral curse of the Pyncheons in *The House of the Seven Gables* (1851), or the **WITCHCRAFT** of 'Young Goodman Brown'. In each case the Gothic elements are enlisted in the service of a heightened normality, using the extreme cases – Faustian pact, mad scientist, preternatural knowledge – to illuminate the influence of the past in the present, or the damage caused by ambition, hypocrisy, or the denial of personal truths.

These were the elements that caused Herman Melville (1819–91) to recognise a hell-fired darkness in Hawthorne's writing, in an identification that had as much to do with Melville's own needs as those of his ostensible subject. The sense of evil that Hawthorne had found buried in the puritan experience and the 'heart' that was its product was generalised in Melville's Conradian vision of a world so profoundly diabolised by the distortions of slavery and aggressive capitalism as to seem evil at its very centre. The beneficent nature hymned by Emerson and Thoreau concealed a violent rapacity that *Moby-Dick* (1851) detailed as much in man as in the sharks or the malevolent uncanny whale itself. In his novella 'Benito Cereno' (1856) Melville foreshadowed Conrad's *Heart of Darkness*, exploring the deformations of racism; and the urban Gothic novel *Pierre* (1852) investigated a tangle of incest and inherited deception that overwhelmed his narrative skills in a manner reminiscent of Hawthorne's last unfinished novels, *The Dolliver Romance*, *The Ancestral Footstep*, and *Dr Grimshawe's Secret*. What most closely links the three great American Gothicists of this period, Poe, Hawthorne and Melville, is their exploration of 'negative Romanticism', the blackness of vision when Romantic inspiration succumbs to an equally overwhelming but bleaker subjectivity.

AMBROSE BIERCE (1842–1914), who mysteriously disappeared on a trip to Mexico, never displayed a Romantic sensibility but had instead the profound cynicism often associated with the loss of illusion which was not uncommon in post-Civil War America. He mastered a particularly virulent form of satire, and produced a number of Gothic tales, collected in *Can Such Things Be?* (1893), which combine the macabre with astute psychology. His protégé, Emma Dawson, wrote **GHOST STORIES** with a powerful intermixture of sexuality, sadism, and the uncanny, collected in *The Itinerant House* (1897), which takes its title from a story about a haunted house in San Francisco, one that crops up in various locations as it is physically transplanted according to Californian practice. Mary E. Wilkins Freeman developed a similar *oeuvre*, collected in *The Wind in the Rosebush* (1903), of which 'Louella Miller' might be the best example. Louella is an ideal Victorian wife: charming, helpless, perhaps a little prone to hysteria – and the killer of six; everyone who comes near her dies. But the exemplar of female Gothic fiction in this period is 'The Yellow Wallpaper', written by Charlotte Perkins Gilman in 1892. With a menacingly sinister simplicity this story explores the prison cage created by male good intentions for the narrator, whose treatment for nervous indisposition eventually leads her to become herself the creeping figure she sees in the wallpaper of her barred room. W. D. Howells (1837–1920), (whose own daughter Winifred was subjected to the same regime: that of Dr S. Weir Mitchell), is best known as a realist writer and urbane editor, the 'Dean of American letters' as he was sometimes called. But Howells too was fascinated by the nightside and wrote several powerful ventures into the Gothic-uncanny including the stories in *Between the Dark and the Daylight* (1907) and *The Shadow of a Dream* (1890). Robert W. Chamber's extraordinary fantasy of 1895, *The King In Yellow*, invokes Ambrose Bierce's imaginary Carcosa and Hali (from 'An Inhabitant of Carcosa') to suggest the existence of a degenerate play, 'The King in Yellow', so devastating in its beauty and its depravity that a mere reading of it opens the way to corruption and death. The next year, 1896, saw Harold Frederic's story of a priest's temptation and fall, *The Damnation of Theron Ware*, which plays off Hawthornesque subjective engagement against the formal techniques of realism to produce a disturbingly skewed narrative in which Theron's seduction is paralleled by the reader's involvement.

Henry James (1843–1916), similarly regarded as a realist writer, infused his work with Gothicism, from the early stories written in imitation of Hawthorne through the last intricate novels of despair and redemption. But James's Gothicism – although not without its ghosts, as in

The Portrait of a Lady (1881) – is internalised, a Gothicism running riot in metaphor and mood rather than actualised in narrative. In *The Portrait of a Lady*, for example, Isabel is immured, not so much in a stone prison as within her husband's mind, of which she takes the measure much like some Radcliffean innocent confronting her dungeon. In *The Wings of the Dove* (1902), a palpable sense of evil is generated through the machinations of Kate Croy against the heiress Milly, culminating in a Gothicised episode in a wintry Venice; and in *The Golden Bowl* (1904) the images of entrapment and stalking produce a sense of uncanny horror in conventional domestic scenes: a bridge game, or a stroll in the gardens. Gender roles may be reversed, for the villain is as often as not female, and the innocent victim male, but the full machinery of Gothic horror is unleashed within the metaphorical structures of the texts. Two of James's most powerful stories, 'The Turn of the Screw' and 'The Jolly Corner', demonstrate the full horror of overwhelming delusion, as the governess in the first attempts to comprehend what she sees as demonic possession in her small charges, and Spencer Brydon in the second tries to confront the spectre of his *alter ego*, but finds himself defeated by its horrifying physical presence.

Although often regarded as divorced from the concerns of everyday life, James's work frequently derives its force from apprehension of the underlying structures in his society – in these tales, for example, the unspoken secret of child abuse, or the pernicious effects of *rentier* capitalism – and his ability to interrelate personal and social pressures gives his work a terrifying undertone. Edith Wharton, unfairly seen as a Jamesian realist, shared his interest in Gothic ghost stories, which in her hands often explored the unspoken territory of sexual oppression; the best are collected in *Ghosts* (1937). In a totally different vein, more related to the phantasmagoric scientism of **ARTHUR MACHEN, ALGERNON BLACKWOOD** or the **BRAM STOKER** of *The Lair of the White Worm*, **H. P. LOVECRAFT** invented a New England science-fiction bestiary conjured up in baroque prose and filled with incantatory notions of strange and terrible books, or awful knowledges shared only by the few. His obscene 'Old Ones' fantasies entwine racial stereotyping with naturalist psychology and sentimental archaic mysticism, but have little to do with the region or society afflicted by the horrors of Cthulhu.

William Faulkner (1897–1962) wrote some tales that clearly belong in a Gothic tradition, such as 'A Rose For Emily', although most of his work, like James's, would seem not to invite such interpretation. If, however, the Gothic is best described as a fiction concerned with the horrifying impress of past (and sometimes present) institutions and events, Faulkner's version of Southern history must be seen as a profoundly Gothic vision, not simply in its echoes of the form (as at the end of

Absalom! Absalom! (1936), when the mansion cracks apart like the House of Usher) but in its deeper logic, imbued as it is with entrapment and despair, flight and pursuit, the inescapability of the past in the present, or the extreme pressures of racial hostilities and a lost mythos. *Sanctuary* (1931) is an example of the **CONTEMPORARY GOTHIC**, while *Light in August* (1932) invites comparison with Godwin's *Caleb Willams*. Faulkner's world of Yoknapatawpha County is a Scott-like effort of intense re-imagination, combining the extravagance of **JACOBEAN TRAGEDY** with intense naturalistic violence. The line goes back, of course, through the Gothic passages of Harriet Beecher Stowe's *Uncle Tom's Cabin* (1851–2), to the race-generated Gothicism of Bird's Indian-hater and the first fictional encounter with Indians in Brockden Brown's *Edgar Huntly*. Faulkner's distinction, however, is to show how nothing less than the Gothic mode is able to express the reality of the South. Since his writing a whole genre of Southern Gothic has been identified, in the work of Truman Capote, Carson McCullers and Flannery O'Connor, as well as James Purdy. Recently Toni Morrison has developed Southern Gothicism from the non-white perspective, to express the atrocity of black experience in the South in *Beloved* (1987), in which the nightmare past is re-experienced through a 'spiteful' haunted house and the revenant of a murdered child. Another version of Southern Gothic has been Anne Rice's *Interview with the Vampire*, which draws upon the languid, decadent traditions of American plantation life to refresh an arguably tired European genre.

To many American writers the Gothic has come to seem the most appropriate mode for dealing with contemporary experience; its distant but all-controlling institutions, its mechanisms of alienation and destruction, and its continuing atrocities. Frequently the Gothic appears as simply one of a range of resources, like the Gothic-comedy towards the end of Vladimir Nabokov's *Lolita*, or the night scenes in John Hawkes's *The Lime Twig* or Joseph Heller's *Catch-22*. Equally it may operate at a subordinate level throughout novels that are not predominantly Gothic. Thomas Pynchon developed a form of techno-Gothic much influenced by science fiction in *V* and *Gravity's Rainbow*, and his *The Crying of Lot 49* is a controlled exercise in Gothic hysteria. Much of William Burrough's work could be described as Gothic phantasmagoria, as could a host of minor novels, like Stephen Schneck's *The Night Clerk*, or such thrillers as Thomas Harris' *Red Dragon* and *The Silence of the Lambs*. William Gaddis offers a homage to the genre in *Carpenter's Gothic*, and Susan Sontag's *Death Kit* similarly belongs to the genre. The most striking recent departure is Willam Gibson's cyber-Gothic (see **CYBERPUNK**) in the *Neuromancer* series of books, where the process of internalising that has characterised development of the Gothic mode for two centuries opens out again into a shared inner landscape created by the integration of mind and computer; a new fantastic realm operating according to the original Gothic principles. Gibson's is a fantastic reality, as much so as Maturin's, Beckford's or Hogg's, but it is driven by a disturbing new integration, no longer neurosis or religious hysteria but instead a terrifying interspace where the imaginary and the 'real' change places.

ALLAN LLOYD SMITH

Architecture *see* Gothic Revival

Australian Gothic

Long before the existence of Australia was ever confirmed by explorers and cartographers it had already been imagined as a grotesque space, a land peopled by monsters. The idea of its existence was disputed, was even heretical for a time, and with the advent of the transportation of convicts its darkness seemed confirmed. The Antipodes was a world of reversals, the dark subconscious of Britain. It was, for all intents and purposes, Gothic *par excellence*, the dungeon of the world. It is perhaps for this reason that the Gothic as a mode has been a consistent presence in Australia since European settlement. Certainly the fact that settlement began in the eighteenth and nineteenth centuries, during the rise of the Gothic as a sensationalist and resonantly influential form, contributes to its impact on the literature of Australia.

There may be other reasons for its appeal. It is certainly possible to argue that the generic qualities of the Gothic mode lend themselves to articulating the colonial experience in as much as each emerges out of a condition of deracination and uncertainty, of the familiar transposed into unfamiliar space. It is this very quality which Freud identified as the condition of the **THE UNCANNY**, where the home is unhomely – where the *heimlich* becomes *unheimlich* – and yet remains sufficiently familiar to disorient and disempower. All migrations represent a dislocation of sorts, but Australia posed particularly vexing questions for its European immigrants. Nature, it seemed to many, was out of kilter. To cite the familiar clichés: its trees shed their bark, swans were black rather than white, and the seasons were reversed. And while these features represented a physical perversion, it was widely considered to be metonymic of an attendant spiritual dis/ease.

This sense of spiritual malaise is often communicated through the Gothic mode, that is, through a literary form which emphasises the horror, uncertainty and desperation of the human experience, often representing the solitariness of that experience through characters trapped in a hostile environment, or pursued by an unspecified or unidentifiable danger. From its inception the Gothic has dealt with fears and themes which are endemic in the colonial experience: isolation, entrapment, fear of pursuit and fear of the unknown. And for each, the possibility of transformation, of surviving the dislocation, acts as a driving hope. If the Gothic is itself a hybrid form – a mode delineated by borrowings and conflations, by fragmentation and incompletion, by a rejection of set values and yet a dependence on establishment – then it is ideal to speak the colonial condition.

For many the very landscape of Australia was Gothic. To Lieutenant Daniel Southwell, one of the First Fleet arrivals, the outcrop of rocks framing the landscape of Port Jackson (now Sydney Harbour) suggested the 'charming seats, superb buildings, [and] the grand ruins of stately [Gothic] edifices'. Soon real buildings would emerge to complement the imagined ones so that by the 1840s the Gothic style was both fashionable and commonplace. In *Gothick Taste in the Colony of New South Wales* (1980), James Broadbent and Joan Kerr have argued that Gothic architecture in Australia 'was strongly associational – a symbol of a colony's maturity'. But Australia's 'maturity' – particularly in matters literary – was far from universally accepted. Australia was dismissed by many as too immature for proper history, and definitely for a Romantic literature, to exist there.

As in many countries, there was in Australia a long-running debate over the importance of realism in, and the unsuitability of Romance to, the colony's literature. For some, the idea of the Romantic was linked to Europe and its landscape and could therefore never be reproduced in the 'new' worlds since they lacked antiquity. A number of critics maintained that given this failing it was critical that other virtues be celebrated. For some, since Australia had no history to speak of, one needed to celebrate its future potential; for others, the basis for a truly important national literature could emerge only through the celebration – not an exoticising – of the local: dialect, experience, space.

Barron Field (1786–1846), the author of the first book of verse to be published in Australia, adhered to the first view, that in a land without antiquities anticipation was all. In 'On Reading the Controversy Between Lord Byron and Mr Bowles'(1823), he claimed that in Australia, 'Nature reflecting Art is not yet born; – / A land without antiquities, with one, /

And only one, poor spot of classic ground, / (That on which Cook first landed) – where, instead / Of heart-communings with ancestral relics / ... We've nothing left us but anticipation. ... / Where's no past tense; the ign'rant present's all. ...' Field may well have prefaced his poem with the epigraph 'Anticipation is to a young country what antiquity is to an old', but he nevertheless concluded his work by suggesting that the only bit of poetry to be found in the 'prose-dull land' was a ship which would carry him away – which indeed it did in 1824.

Frederick Sinnett (1830–66) suggested that Romance was inappropriate to Australian letters. Like Field, Sinnett understood that Australia could not compete with English antiquity, but that its literature of the everyday should stand on equal ground. That his view of the Romantic was largely informed by a specifically Gothic vision is made clear in an extract from his famous essay 'The Fiction Fields of Australia' (1856):

> It must be granted, then, that we are quite debarred from all the interest to be extracted from any kind of archeological accessories. No storied windows, richly dight, cast a dim, religious light over any Australian premises. There are no ruins for that rare old plant, the ivy green, to creep over and make his dainty meal of. No Australian author can hope to extricate his hero or heroine, however pressing the emergency may be, by means of a spring panel and a subterranean passage, or such like relics of feudal barons. ... There may be plenty of dilapidated buildings, but not one, the dilapidation of which is sufficiently venerable by age, to tempt the wandering footsteps of the most arrant *parvenu* of a ghost that ever walked by night. It must be admitted that Mrs Radcliffe's genius would be quite thrown away here; and we must reconcile ourselves to the conviction that the foundations of a second 'Castle of Otranto' can hardly be laid in Australia during our time.

While there may have existed a rhetorically clear line dividing the realists from the Romantics, in point of fact much writing produced in the colony blended elements of each, and it is perhaps in this way that Australia began to map out a specifically local variant of the Gothic mode, one which turned to the specifications of the domestic landscape and voice to articulate the fear and exhilaration of the colonial condition. Writers such as Marcus Clarke, 'Price Warung' (William Astley), Barbara Baynton and Henry Lawson produced detailed and localised texts anchored in the language, scenery and circumstance of their country. Though they may have insisted on the realist dimension of their work (Lawson, for example, would have been aghast to be called a romance writer), their exploration of the anxieties of the convict system, the terrors of isolated stations at the mercy of vagrants and nature, the fear of starvation or of becoming lost in the bush, are distinctly Gothic in effect – and dare one say, uniquely, originally, Australian.

That is not to deny that much early writing in Australia was derivative, or that all of it was in the Gothic style. Australia's first novel, *Quintus Servington* (1830–1), written by the convicted English forger Henry Savery (1791–1842), was a thinly disguised autobiography designed to demonstrate how his fictional equivalent was different from the general convict population. Those darker aspects of his existence are therefore subdued, and the text somehow less Gothic in nature than Savery's own life.

Not so Anna Maria Bunn's (1808–99) *The Guardian: A Tale by an Australian* (1838), the first novel printed and published in mainland Australia (*Quintus Servington* was a Tasmanian text) and the first by a woman. Though a Gothic romance, *The Guardian* manages to display impatience with this aspect of the story, so that it shifts into a range of modes, from the epistolary tale to the Comedy of Manners. Indeed, Bunn seems to hold the not uncommon view that the Gothic is somehow beneath contempt and frivolous, so that she is careful to justify its use as reflecting the immorality of her characters and their situation. Ironically, the novel is set in Ireland and Britain and refers frequently to Australia only to condemn it. Australia is a land to which graceless and incompetent individuals are exiled. As one character laments, 'All lost characters are found there.' *The Guardian* is the first of a series of dark romances which make use of a Gothic sensibility, to speak, directly or indirectly, about the Australian landscape.

Numerous Gothic romances emerged to fill a demanding interest in such texts, many derivative and flawed, others quite successful in their execution. Some worthy of note include British-born Mary Theresa Vidal's (1815–69) *Bengala: or, Some Time Ago* (1860) and the delightfully Gothic *Outlaw and Lawmaker* (1893) written by the prolific, Australian-born Rosa Praed (1851–1935). Undoubtedly one of the oddest of these numerous texts – and one of the most offensive concerning matters of race – is Edward Sorensen's *The Squatter's Ward* (1919), which perhaps mostly literally transposes the stock conventions of the Gothic tale into the Australian landscape to include a home with trapdoors and underground chambers where the master and his black servant dine.

Poised on the borderline of old and new worlds, such novels suggest much about the struggle early colonial writers faced in finding a local and useful mode of expression to speak their place. They also reveal the prejudices which framed the way many colonists saw the new world. Even the concept of Australia as a 'new' world is offensively European in its understanding, ignoring as it does the long and extraordinarily rich Aboriginal cultures which preceded European settlement.

The Gothic, however, may well have played a part in the process which reversed such views. For Marcus Clarke (1846–81), the Gothic was a way to invest Australia with a living history, by turning to detailed research on transportation and convict conditions, stories of cannibalism and rape, betrayal and suffering, as a way to frame his story of hardship and redemption enacted in an Australian landscape (as he does, for example, in his best-known work *His Natural Life*, first serialised in 1870). Even before this, Clarke had described Australia in terms which invoke a Gothic sensibility. In a famous preface to Adam Lindsay Gordon's *Poems*, Clarke said of his 'fantastic land of monstrosities' that in it 'alone is to be found the Grotesque, the Weird, the strange scribblings of nature learning how to write.'

Clarke's juvenilia reflects a preoccupation with the Gothic, including a collaboration with Gerard Manly Hopkins on an illustrated text called *Prometheus*, about a young medical student who animates a lifeless corpse. Clarke's fascination with the sensational continued to manifest itself in poems and stories with grotesque or ghostly qualities, reminiscent of Coleridge and Poe, and is most pronounced in his *The Mystery of Major Molineux and Human Repetends* (1881) and in *Sensational Tales* (1886). But it is his classic text, *His Natural Life*, which best articulates his belief that Australian history could be the subject of serious literary treatment and which began to shape a specifically Australian form of the Gothic mode, one which is predicated on the darkness and anxiety specific to the Australian experience.

That the public was slow to embrace this work suggests how reluctant many were to accept that their own history was legitimate subject matter. Many more no doubt felt that this was inappropriate material upon which to base a country's mythology. The 'stain' of convictism, it seemed, was not far enough removed. Unlike Walpole, who could invoke antiquity, or Radcliffe, who could project evil 'elsewhere' – usually France or Italy – the stuff of Australian Gothic implicated the living. The controversial publisher P. R. 'Inky' Stephensen (1901–65), for one, felt that writing should steer clear of convict subject matter since it bought into British prejudices about Australia's origins. Despite this, convictism was standard subject matter for Gothicists, from Caroline Leakey's *The Broad Arrow* (1859) to 'Price Warung's' *Tales of the Convict System* (1892) and William Gosse Hay's *The Escape of the Notorious Sir William Heans* (1919). It is a fetishising which has continued to the present day, including in Robert Hughes's *The Fatal Shore: A History of the Transportation of Convicts to Australia, 1787–1868* (1987), a work of non-fiction which has been criticised in many quarters for its Gothic 'g[l]orification' of convict hardships.

For Barbara Baynton (1857–1929), the Gothic was a way to express not only a peculiarly Australian terror, but a specifically female fear as well.

Her classic collection of short stories, *Bush Studies* (1902), delineated an entirely unromantic picture of the Australian bush. Though it may seem oxymoronic, Baynton's Gothic is intensely realist in method, describing with great detail the specificities of outback life – the arid and desolate land, the dangerous vagrants, the women besieged by nature and by men. Her stories comment on male betrayal ('Squeaker's Mate'), 'race' ('Billy Skywonkie') and male violence ('The Chosen Vessel'). Though at times melodramatic, her work makes clear that the Gothic need not be escapist, excessive or frivolous.

Many of Henry Lawson's (1867–1922) stories work in a similar fashion, refusing to romanticise rural existence. Though his *oeuvre* is not Gothic *per se*, those stories which convey the greatest sense of dread sketch the terrible loneliness and poverty of life in the Australian bush ('A Child in the Dark, and a Foreign Father'), the dangers of the everyday ('The Drover's Wife'), or the way people are either driven mad by the sere existence, or haunted by the land itself ('Rats' and 'The Bush Undertaker'). In the latter an old man disinters an Aboriginal grave and then stumbles onto the body of a dead friend – 'dried to a mummy' – and carries it home to be buried. The story is susceptible to an interesting reading of the way the Australian landscape must be stripped of its Aboriginal presence if room is to be made for its colonisers. Indeed the old man is 'haunted' by a goanna after robbing the Aboriginal grave, and he is forced to kill the totemic creature before he can bury his friend. In a phrase which recalls Marcus Clarke's, the story ends, 'And the sun sank again on the grand Australian bush – the nurse and tutor of eccentric minds, the home of the weird, and of much that is different from things in other lands.'

If the Gothic proved popular as a mode for Australian fiction in the nineteenth and early twentieth centuries, it experienced a lull until the 1970s, though extraordinary examples did emerge in the intervening decades such as Christina Stead's *The Man Who Loved Children* (1940) and Hal Porter's *Short Stories* (1940). Other notably dark tales include Kenneth Cook's terrifying account of a young teacher's experience in a country town, *Wake in Fright* (1961), a first novel which modernised Baynton's merciless renderings of outback life. Joan Lindsay's (1896–1984) curious *Picnic at Hanging Rock* (1967) managed to make the genteel world of a Melbourne ladies' college both sinister and mysterious in a novel which told of the disappearance of schoolgirls during a Saint Valentine's Day picnic in 1900. Both Thomas Keneally and Frank Moorhouse would produce novels and short story collections where the Gothic would hover always at the edges – for Keneally in novels such as *The Fear* (1965) and the controversial *The Chant of Jimmie Blacksmith* (1972); for Moorhouse, with a species of erotic-Gothic in *Tales of Mystery and Romance* (1977) and in *The Everlasting Secret Family and Other Secrets* (1980).

Perhaps the most portentous presence on the literary landscape was Nobel Prize winner Patrick White, who developed his own brand of Gothic, one which blended a metaphysical with a scatological darkness, and a scathing language which attacked what he considered to be Australia's 'dun-coloured realism'. For White, Australia was provincial in all the worst ways, and his sprawling, at times even hateful, fictions mercilessly exposed the ridiculous, the self-important, and the banal. In doing so, White also re-wrote the possibilities for Australian fiction, creating, like William Faulkner, his own language of revelation and analysis, one which proved that the suburbs could be just as chilling as the outback (though he addressed the latter in novels such as *Voss*, 1957, and *A Fringe of Leaves, 1976*).

White abhorred pomposity in all its guises and responded to such artificiality with ridicule of the cruellest order. Mrs Hunter, in *The Eye of the Storm* (1973), dies on the commode, with base puns aplenty; in *The Vivisector* (1970), Hurtle Duffield sits on an 'out dunny' meditating on the importance of art while thinking of shit and sperm, a scene which is only surpassed by his hunchback sister's efforts at stirring liquid manure in the back yard. White's characters are eaten by their dogs, beheaded, crucified; they are cannibals, transvestites, saints and idiots. In short, his world maps a psychologically Gothic terrain which is also extraordinarily physical. It is also relentlessly, though not necessarily lovingly, Australian.

The 1970s saw the emergence of a new range of voices, including those of Peter Carey and Louis Nowra. Carey's *The Fat Man in History* (1974) is filled with terrifying stories, part science fiction, part thriller, part horror tale – stories which expose the darker side of the human condition and which comment on a range of issues including the insidiousness of American imperialism. His bleakest novel, *The Tax Inspector* (1991), explores the world of child abuse; *The Unusual Life of Tristan Smith* (1994) is narrated by a three-foot-six 'monster', with a rag-doll mouth, shrivelled legs and unusual eyes which raise a shudder in all who see him.

Louis Nowra's plays *Albert Names Edward* (1975) and *Inner Voices* (1977) marked the beginning of a series of psychological explorations of the darkness which governs human interactions. Nowra would go on to write two comically bleak novels, *The Misery of Beauty* (1976) and *Palu* (1987), which focus on hybrid characters who straddle several world-views, languages or attitudes, unable ever to resolve their crises of being.

Where the Gothic literature of the 1960s and 1970s may have been dominated by male writers, the 1980s saw the emergence of major women writers who would turn to the Gothic mode not only to question the mores of Australian society, but also to comment on and condemn patriarchal values. Indeed, the Gothic has proved resilient and flexible, and as appealing to postcolonial writers as it was for their predecessors in articulating the tensions and problems of their community. Barbara Hanrahan and Kate Grenville, for example, have produced dark urban stories which celebrate damaged but vibrant heroines, victims of abuse who nevertheless rise above adversity to move triumphantly forward. Gothic texts have been produced by Janette Turner Hospital – *The Last Magician* (1992) and *Oyster* (1996); Glenda Adams – *The Tempest of Clemenza* (1996); and Gabrielle Lord – *Fortress* (1980) and *Tooth and Claw* (1983). And one of the most delightful parodies of Australian Gothic was written by Coral Lansbury in *Ringarra: A Gothic Novel* (1985).

Another prolific author in this vein is Elizabeth Jolley, whose novels have championed a voice for feminist Gothic in Australia. Quirky, eerie, even domestic in a perverse way, Jolley challenges the notion of the traditional 'heroine' of Gothic fiction, producing a long line of aged and frequently crippled figures whose selfish, at times even nasty, dispositions make them at once extremely human and oddly endearing. In novels such as *Milk and Honey* (1984) and *The Well* (1986) she re-views the familiar Australian landscape, making it uncanny through her skewed and comically perverse observations. In much of her work Jolley uses a Gothic mode to explore women's sexuality, concentrating on how the female body is made abject by patriarchy. Her strangely erotic texts deliberately 'pervert' the orthodox, suggesting new possibilities for female expression, even though she is careful to define the price which is exacted for such transgressions.

Just as earlier migrants – Marcus Clarke, for example – saw the Gothic's potential for subversion, so many contemporary migrant writers have used it to speak of their sense of exclusion and dislocation, as well as to comment on the condition of disjunction produced in a country which devalues non-Anglo-Celtic experience. For writers like Rosa Cappiello and Ania Walwicz, the Gothic manifests itself in their work as a type of scatological and linguistic excess. Rosa Cappiello's *Oh Lucky Country* offers an extended catalogue of vaginal diseases, or proclaims at length on micturition, introducing alternate though undeniable 'realities' into the dominant, antiseptic, discourse of White Australia. Ania Walwicz's prose/poetry is written in a frenetic non-standard English which flouts grammatical orthodoxy and troubles the categories of genre. Walwicz gothicises a basic experience – such as the bursting of a pipe – to recreate the sheer terror which voicelessness can generate.

In Antigone Kefala's *The Island*, the author *reverses* the characteristic positive perception of Anglo-Celtic restraint by highlighting the absurd dimension of such valued qualities. In one passage the narrator notes that Australian men can only show emotion while playing sport. At other times they are entirely inarticulate, trailing the iron chains of their Protestant upbringing across 'wet corridors in the semi-darkness of the stained glass windows and into the cafeteria where they stayed at the tables mute as statues'. East European migrants are traditionally repre-sented as loud and excessive, and yet *simultaneously* as incomprehensible and inarticulate. They are, like the orientalised Transylvanians of old, an inscrutable Gothic presence. Here Kefala uses stock Gothic iconography to reverse such prejudices.

If it is true that the Gothic has been useful for helping to establish a local Australian voice, it has also functioned as a silencing discourse for some, such as the Aboriginal people of Australia. It is not surprising that Aboriginal writers have tended not to use the Gothic mode since it has generally represented for them a disabling, rather than an enabling dis-course. In obvious terms, the Aboriginal peoples were themselves con-structed as the monstrous figures haunting the Australian landscape, spectres more frightening than any European demon, because they rep-resented a physical threat to settlers and to theories of enlightenment which believed in the civilising presence of Whites.

Charles Tompson's poem 'Black Town' (1824), modelled on Oliver Goldsmith's 'The Deserted Village', is an elegy written to lament the demise of a ten-year-old settlement which had been set up to 'civilise' the Australian Aborigines – the children of the 'lost empire' whose per-ceptions are clouded by 'Superstition's mists'. The Aborigines proved themselves unable to break 'the Gothic chain' of their heritage by not em-bracing the ill-suited farming technology of the colonisers, and by reject-ing their religious propaganda. In Charles Harpur's long Gothic poem 'The Creek of the Four Graves' (1853), the Aborigines are located as the evil darkness – 'Hell's worst fiends' – who threaten White expansion. It is a representation that is repeated in numerous poems and novels.

Aborigines also posed a greater threat to the very fiction of *terra nullius*, the obscene construction in British law which made Australia 'a land owned by no one', and therefore a place which could be claimed for the Crown (a conceit only recently overturned by the Australian High Court through the Native Title Act of 1993, more popularly known as the 'Mabo' decision). The Aboriginal presence in itself unsettled – to use the full measure of the pun – the course of Empire. In that respect, then, Aborigines had to be obliterated or absorbed through assimilation poli-cies. It is strange indeed, given the voraciousness of the European ap-petite, that it should be the Aborigines who were constructed as savage, monstrous and insatiable. In *Doctor Wooreddy's Prescription for Enduring the Ending of the World* (1983), Australia's most prolific Aboriginal writer, Mudrooroo, makes this very point. Indeed, he Gothicises the notion of the invasion by referring to the British as *num* – literally *ghosts* which haunt Aboriginal land.

Tracey Moffatt uses the Gothic mode to re-write White Australian readings of Aboriginality in two of her films, including her most recent feature-length *Bedevil* (a series of three loosely connected ghost stories). In some respects, Tracey Moffatt's films can be read within the framework of resistance film-making, resistance both to general types of racism, but also to White forms of representation. One of the objectives of her work is to interrogate the very *forms* of film-making and representation – painting, film, song, genre – and to dislodge the traditional power which is vested in both the mode and the viewer. In *Night Cries* (1990) she expands on and re-writes Charles Chauvel's 1955 film *Jedda*, a film about the dangers of assimilation. Moffatt's *Night Cries* explores the horrific effects of assimilation, by centering on the main character Jedda, and on her adoptive White mother Sarah McMann, but set 40 years in the future.

The title is written in a traditional Gothic script which makes ironic the pointed subtitle: *A Rural Tragedy*. As with Patrick White's work, Moffatt's films make clear how the everyday, the commonplace, can be the stuff of Gothic. The domestic – the sound of the music box that is fractured by the crack of a whip, the evening meal scraped across a plate by the fractured hand of an elderly woman – is truly Gothic. The set is deliberately artificial, there is no dialogue, and the soundtrack is harsh and grating. McMann is enfeebled and crippled, a metaphor for White culture perhaps; Jedda is middle-aged, impatient in her role as caretaker, and yet devastated too when her adoptive mother dies. In a spare, uncompromising film, Moffatt at once reverses the viewer's sense of the positive effects of assimilation, and brilliantly mis/uses the conventions of the Gothic to disorient and to make clear that the predatory monster – the Gothic terror – is White social policy.

Genre, of course, is comforting. It establishes order even in the midst of disorder. Genre speaks of a legacy, of a heritage, of certainty. Perhaps what is most exhilarating about the Gothic mode, and what has made it so enduring, is that unlike many other literary forms, it has been at its most exciting when least obeyed – which is ironic given that the mode is frequently dismissed for being formulaic. The history of the Gothic in Australia is the story of change and adaptation. Gothic fiction, after all, was not incorporated or exported wholesale. Rather, it was modified and grew to accommodate the climate, literary and otherwise. It is significant that Patrick White's 'Australian Writer' suggests as much in *The Eye of the Storm* when he obliquely dismisses the Romanticism of Stendhal to explain 'how he was adapting the Gothic novel to local conditions'. It is a modification which continues still.

GERRY TURCOTTE

Beckford, William (1760–1844)

On 29 September 1760, at Fonthill Splendens, William Beckford was born with a silver sugar-spoon in his mouth. His father was a womanising alderman of the same name, twice Lord Mayor of London, and friend of John Wilkes, who, with a ferocious glare worthy of Vathek, had reduced George III to a stony silence while he delivered an impromptu speech on the curtailment of freedom. Clearly the son, inheriting at the age of ten the Wiltshire estate of 5,000 acres and an immense fortune from Jamaican sugar plantations, had a lot to live up to. And living it up in virtually Oriental luxury became the pattern for the young Beckford, who gave as little thought as his father to the curtailment of freedom of his 1,000 West Indian slaves. Sweet are the uses of others' adversity, but all was not hedonism for England's wealthiest son; at five he was receiving music lessons from the nine-year-old Mozart, in his early teens he learned the principles of architecture from Sir William Chambers, and the appreciation of landscape painting from the watercolourist Alexander Cozens, rumoured to be the natural son of Peter the Great, and Mephistopheles to Beckford's Faust.

Before Beckford was twenty he revealed his precocious talent for satire in *Biographical Memoirs of Extraordinary Painters* (1780), in which invented landscape painters discovered new potentialities in the sublime and the picturesque as they vied with established artists such as Sucrewasser and Soorcrout. But his Grand Tour had not only led to a meeting in Protestant Geneva with Paul-Henri Mallet, the author of *Northern Antiquities* and champion of Gothic style, it had culminated in Venice where he had touched the fragrant hem of the gorgeous East and communicated with *bona fide* Orientals. Upon his return he employed a Mahometan tutor named Zemir with whom he translated Arabic tales (*The Story of Al Raoui* was later published in 1799) and Wortley Montagu's manuscripts, surrounded by the illuminated Oriental texts and spiced erotica of the magnificent library at Fonthill.

It was his extravagant coming-of-age and parties of 1781 which, according to Beckford, inspired the composition of *Vathek*. With state-of-the-art technical and theatrical effects courtesy of the celebrated de Loutherbourg and his newly-invented Eidophusikon, rockets, bonfires, parades and pageants, visions were conjured in Splendens Park worthy of the Giaour himself. Meanwhile the young and beautiful 'immured' themselves in the marbled Egyptian Hall, wandering hand-in-hand through labyrinthine vaulted galleries perfumed 'by the vapour of wood aloes ascending in wreaths from cassolettes placed low on the silken carpets in porcelain salvers of the richest japan'. In an exquisite delirium of intense seductiveness Nouronihar (Louisa, the wife of his cousin Peter

Beckford) and Gulchenrouz (young William 'Kitty' Courtenay) vied for his attentions, and in order that 'every sense might in turn receive its blandishments', tables of delightful viands and fragrant flowers mysteriously glided forth on concealed mechanisms.

But this was Wiltshire not Samarah and Beckford took little care to conceal his feelings for the pretty young son of Viscount Courtenay, commissioning Romney to paint the boy's portrait. Beckford was decadently dedicating himself to the creation of a public image which was to become almost inseparable from his literary achievement; Beckfordism in many respects anticipated Byronism. Both were equally fascinated by Oriental androgyny and Greek love, 'smitten with unhallowed thirst / Of nameless crime' (suppressed stanza, *Childe Harold's Pilgrimage* I). The Begum, as Beckford disrespectfully termed his mother (her Methodist strictures were to be cruelly parodied in the obscene rites and obsessive chastity of Carathis), intervened, proposing a dynastic union with Lady Margaret Gordon, daughter of the Earl of Aboyne, and the marriage was celebrated in May 1783. The following year, however, Beckford was discovered in the boy's bedroom in Powderham Castle. The scandal dashed Beckford's hopes of a peerage, driving him and his wife to the Continent.

The millionaire eccentric transformed his exotic reading into sensual reality and back again into literature. Fonthill had proved a forcing-house of Oriental Gothic and Beckford was no amateur when it came to the East; he had devoured all the central texts. From Galland's *Mille et un e nuits* and Petis de la Croix's *Thousand and One Days*, Beckford graduated to d'Herbelot's *Bibliothèque Orientale* (1697), Sale's 1734 translation of the Qu'ran, Chardin's *Travels into Persia and the East Indies* (1686), the translations and original poems of Sir William Jones, erudite works by Picart, Le Bruin, and many others.

Vathek offered decadence with endnotes and the result smelt not so much of the lamp as of blood sacrifice and smoking rhino horn. Beckford was re-creating his own Orient out of authentic materials to accommodate Gothic extremes of sensibility. This longing to extend the boundaries of intellect, feeling and egotism distinguished *Vathek* from the Enlightenment rationalism of the contemporary Oriental tale, simultaneously anticipating and stimulating the vibrant and elaborately annotated verse romances of the Romantics. A landmark in the history of European literary **ORIENTALISM**, the work was composed over as much as a year and not in a single sitting of three days and two nights, as he Romantically claimed in the *Memoirs*. Beckford had intended the first edition to be in its original French, with the present text serving as the frame for three episodes: the histories of Vathek's fellow-prisoners in the Halls of Eblis. Samuel Henley blatantly disregarded his friend's instructions, prematurely releasing his English translation as *The History of*

Caliph Vathek, an Arabian Tale, from an Unpublished Manuscript (1786) without even an authorial ascription. This betrayal, following all too close on his bereavement – in May Margaret had died of puerperal fever after the birth of their second daughter – left Beckford embittered: in angry haste he established his authorship and published the French text in both Lausanne and Paris early in 1787, *The Episodes* not seeing publication until 1912.

Beckford sought consolation in a visit to Portugal, finding atmospheric seclusion in the Gothic grandeur of a monastery and in the magnificence of a Moorish place near Cintra. Soon, however, his private *Journal* (not published until 1954) was intimately recording his sexual infatuation for well-born Portuguese youths and his desparate attempts to gain an audience with Queen Maria. He was also accumulating material for the suave travel books of his comparatively respectable old age. *Italy: with Sketches of Spain and Portugal* (1834) and *Recollections of an Excursion to the Monasteries of Alcobaça and Batalha* (1835) feature brilliant impressionistic sketches with an emphasis on the Romantic subjectivity of the accomplished and cynical cosmopolite. His earlier *Dreams, Waking Thoughts, and Incidents from Various Parts of Europe* (which Beckford suppressed upon publication in 1783 except for six copies) mingled aesthetic solipsism, wish-fulfillment, restless ennui and sardonic irony so that we can almost believe that we are following the Caliph's omnipotent eye/I across the Continent.

On his return to Fonthill in 1796, furious at his former friend Pitt's rejection of a diplomatic mission from the Regent of Portugal, Beckford directed his satire against a ministry which had suspended Habeas Corpus. His *Modern Novel Writing; or, The Elegant Enthusiast* (1796) and *Azemia* (1797), each published under a female sobriquet, burlesqued the sentimental novel and parodied the Gothic for its increasingly anti-democratic connotations. Beckford didn't need the Establishment or the *beau monde*; indulging his obsession with verticality he would elevate himself. 'Some people drink to forget their unhappiness,' he wrote. 'I do not drink, I build.' He was determined to shock, to amaze, and to dwell with his Swiss dwarf Perro in his towering folly. With the help not of Mahomet, but of that fashionable architectural apostle of the neo-Gothic, James Wyatt, and gangs of builders often working day and night, Beckford realised one of the most magnificent and potent symbols of the **GOTHIC REVIVAL**. Turner painted at least seven watercolours of Fonthill Abbey, but the three-hundred-foot tower had been jerry-built – of Scotch fir cased with stone, according to Cobbett – and a May gale of 1800 blew it down. Cobbett also deplored the overweening arrogance of Beckford's Gothic genealogical aspirations – the Abbey's heraldic motifs reflecting the claim of a hereditary link with Edward III: 'Was there ever vanity and impudence equal to these! The negro-driver brag of his high blood!' The tower was speedily re-erected for Nelson's visit, but Hazlitt was unimpressed, describing Fonthill as 'a desert of magnificence, a glittering waste of laborious idleness, a cathedral turned into a toyshop'. One is reminded of the shifting but essentially consumerist message on the magic sabre: 'We were made where everything is well made: we are the least of the wonders of a place where all is wonderful, and deserving the sight of the first potentate on earth.' For all Vathek's vaunted and Faustian pursuit of occult, esoteric, and recondite knowledge and power, his lust for the throne of the pre-Adamite kings, both the Caliph and his creator are diverted by trivia – slippers with springs, automatic knives – or obsessed with the gigantic and the miniature – the binaries of the megalomaniac toymaker.

Beckford demolished the superb Palladian Splendens in 1807, with the uncharacteristic gusto of a Philistine. Sugar prices collapsed and so did the rebuilt Fonthill Abbey tower in 1825, but by then Beckford had sold up, moved to Bath, and was busily erecting the Lansdown Tower in an original but basically Neoclassical style. There was a strong vein of self-gratification about his tower-building, hand on heart it was more fun than being MP for Wells or representing the rotten borough of Hindon, and something in Beckford envied Gulchenrouz's eternal childhood in the perpendicular inviolability of the roc's nest.

Bath's legendary recluse died prosaically of a fever on 2 May 1844, having been caught in the rain; he lies buried in the shadow of his Tower in a pink granite tomb of his own unostentatious design.

MICHAEL FRANKLIN

Bierce, Ambrose (1842–1914)

A mordant satirist, Ambrose Bierce wrote elegant short stories about war and the follies of human misperception. His importance as an American Gothicist rests not in *The Devil's Dictionary*, a collection of icy aphorisms, but in his series of **GHOST STORIES**, collected in *Can Such Things Be?* (1893). A characteristic entry from the *Dictionary* would be '*Discussion*, n. A method of confirming others in their errors', and most of Bierce's stories circle around the issue of misperception to the point of fatal error. In a typical tale of war, 'One of the Missing', Jerome Searing dies of a heart attack, having determined to outface his own rifle, which is aimed at his head while he is trapped in a ruined building. The rifle is already discharged, of course. In the ghost stories, similarly, the protagonists fall victim to their own failures of apprehension, having run up against a reality that exceeds their imagination.

Like William James, who wrote in the same period of the flow of consciousness, Bierce implies that it is not so much the truth of events that matters, but how they are perceived, and the difference that they make to the perceiver. Even quite absurd superstitious beliefs may have devastating effects, and prove to be true – in a sense. The best example perhaps is 'The Death of Halpin Frayser'. Frayser takes the wrong road in the woods, and wakes from a dreamless sleep to utter the meaningless name of 'Catherine Larue'. Next he dreams of a walk along an evil road, marked by pools and splashes of blood. He dreams that he writes a grave-yard poem, like one of his maternal great-grandfather's, and then dreams of his own strangulation, at the hands of his mother. Frayser's mangled body – and the poem – are discovered the next day on the grave of Catherine Larue. A comic detective duo in the final section of the story claim that Frayser's mother had married one Larue (later Pardee, or Branscom – with an echo perhaps of Poe's 'Murders in the Rue [Larue] Morgue'), a maniac who then killed his wife, and may have killed Frayser too. The explanation is ludicrous, and merely sends the reader back to look for a deeper internal logic in the story. But here the incestuous attachment between Halpin and his mother proves to be another red herring, along with her premonitory dream of his strangulation. There *may* be a deeper logic here, to do with excess, incest and the uncanniness of writing (Frayser dips his twig in the pool of blood to write his dream poem), but it is mocked by the ending, in which only a laugh (of the maniac, or of the author) is heard. Can such things be, indeed?

In 'The Moonlit Road' Bierce uses three distinct narrators: a son, his father, and the ghost of his murdered mother. The son walks with his father after the murder one night on a moonlit road, he turns to look at a light in a house, and when he turns back his father has disappeared. He is unable to make sense of either event, and thereafter lives a life of baffled self-pity. The father's narrative reveals that it was he who murdered his wife, in a jealous fit after thinking she had been unfaithful. Her ghost then appeared to him that night on the road, eyes fixed on his 'with an infinite gravity which is not reproach, nor hate, nor menace, nor anything less terrible than recognition'. The Biercean irony then emerges in the testimony of the ghost, who had not known who killed her and who approaches her husband in the loving hope that he will be able to see her, 'smiling and consciously beautiful'. He, of course, sees only the face of death and the strangulation marks he left on her throat. The dead, it seems, are as ignorant and helpless as the living, equally 'mad malign inhabitants' of 'the Valley of the Shadow'. Such narrative complexities and black comedy resemble the stories of Jorge Luis Borges (which name Brigid Brophy has suggested is actually the *nom de plume* of Bierce, who mysteriously disappeared in Mexico in 1914).

ALLAN LLOYD SMITH

Blackwood, Algernon (1869–1951)

Algernon Blackwood won fame as a teller of supernatural tales. Born into an evangelical Victorian family, he lived to tell tales on British radio and television, but wrote mainly during the first two decades of the twentieth century. Tales like 'The Willows', set on a waterway near Vienna, and 'The Wendigo', set in northern Ontario, show his ability to create the 'picture of a mood' that made him a special favourite of **H. P. LOVECRAFT**.

Blackwood began reading Eastern and Theosophical literature in the 1880s, and developed a strong dislike for Western scientific thinking. He left Edinburgh University after a term and spent a decade at various jobs in North America before returning to England in 1899. His beautifully written account of this period, *Episodes before Thirty* (1923), might be called 'Down and Out in Toronto and New York'.

On returning to England, Blackwood joined the Order of the Golden Dawn and began to write the sort of tales that he had told for amusement. His first book of stories, *The Empty House* (1906), belonged to the genre of the Victorian ghost story. However, his first commercial success, *John Silence, Physician Extraordinary* (1908), was a series of loosely connected tales about a psychic Sherlock Holmes who applied his esoteric studies (closely recalling Golden Dawn doctrines) to cases of hauntings and other spiritual phenomena. With *The Human Chord* (1910), Blackwood worked cabbalism as taught in the Golden Dawn into a tale about an attempt to change the earth's vibrations and bring humanity onto a new scale, a cautionary tale, nevertheless, and one that seems to have influenced Charles Williams in *All Hallows' Eve*.

Commercial success allowed Blackwood to travel and write. Out of his travels to the Caucasus, he wrote his fullest statement of a pantheistic world-view, *The Centaur* (1911), which tells the story of a solitary author probing the 'extensions of the personality'. Like much else that he wrote, the book builds on nineteenth-century ideas, especially in German Romanticism, but anticipates twentieth-century concerns. One character studies the 'Self' that can be found beyond all personality 'types' and moves from there to the 'collective consciousness of the entire Universe'. The novel is an uncanny and as yet unrecognised antic-ipation of Jungian psychology, written at a time when Blackwood was living in Switzerland.

The Great War had its toll on Blackwood, and he nearly stopped writing after the Armistice. His last novel, *The Garden of Survival* (1918), is the story of a British civil servant who finds 'the Thrill' only when he goes to Africa as a colonial administrator; only then is he able to come into contact with the beauty and goodness of his dead wife. As in novels like *The Wave: An Egyptian Aftermath* (1916) and *Julius Le Vallon: An Episode* (1916), the lovers are soul mates from an earlier life, 'washed down the ages by the waves of our own act'. Back in England, the narra-tor hears the jungle rather than the garden, and he is drawn eventually to the eternal garden state.

After the Great War, Blackwood turned to experimental theatre with the 'reincarnation play' *Karma* (1918), and to children's fiction with *Dudley & Gilderoy: A Nonsense* (1929) and *The Fruit Stoners* (1934). Most of his *Strange Stories* (1929) and other late collections were taken from earlier publications.

Blackwood dabbles in occultism of every stamp. To be sure, his Dr Silence thinks 'occultism' a 'dreadful word', but Silence uses 'spiritual alchemy' to 'transmute evil forces by raising them into higher channels'. He wards off witches and resists the powers of ancient amulets. His is deep enough 'magic' to 'know that thought is dynamic and may call into existence forms and pictures that may well exist for hundreds of years'. He is adept at 'thought-reading' and very well read, drawing upon the French magus Eliphas Lévi as well as *The Egyptian Book of the Dead*.

Like the protagonist of *The Centaur*, Blackwood wrote tales about himself, thinly concealed, and preferred the dramas of heightened mental states to the convolutions of human actions. His long story 'The Willows' is a simple tale of a night's camping among the rushes of a Danube tributary. Aside from a few disconcerting details in the river and on an island, the important events are mental, concerning the camper's perceptions of a strangely threatening force on the islands, a force associ-ated with the rustling and perhaps on-rushing willows.

Some of the *John Silence* tales are regularly reprinted – for example, 'Secret Worship', based on his experience returning to his German boarding school. But it remains a question whether Blackwood would seem 'politically incorrect' ninety years later: a classist, sexist, and racist. Silence can afford servants and can serve the poor gratis; he undoes the workings of depraved women and North Americans with traces of 'savage' or 'Red Indian' blood. Perhaps a future age will recognise that Blackwood pointed his barbs at the Victorian legacy more than any-thing, at the rational and rationalising clergyman, the money-grubbing merchant, the treasure-grabbing explorer, the jewel-loving sister, whose insensitivities help create the problems that Silence undertakes to solve.

THOMAS WILLARD

The Brontës

Anne Brontë (1820–49)
Branwell Brontë (1817–48)
Charlotte Brontë (1816–55)
Emily Brontë (1818–48)

Although the chief works of Anne, Charlotte and Emily Brontë were published after the Gothic heyday, the prolific period of their Juvenilia (c 1826–43) was contemporaneous with novels by **MARY SHELLEY**, Scott and **EDWARD BULWER-LYTTON**. Their surviving early writings, to which their brother Branwell contributed, show the influence of their wide and precocious reading, which included *Blackwood's* and *Fraser's* magazines. These printed a variety of thrilling tales and poems, and regularly surveyed the British and European literary scene. They also retailed what might be called 'horror folklore': stories of hauntings, and unexplained phenomena.

Gothic elements in the Juvenilia are represented by neurotic aristocrats, such as Branwell's Earl of Northangerland, a character prone to break out into sadism and violence. Charlotte's tales of their imaginary country, Angria, favoured high-born women in physical or moral danger, or bent on revenge, but the figure which gained ascendancy was the Duke of Zamorna, Byronic and Satanic: 'Impetuous sin, stormy pride, diving and soaring enthusiasm, war and poetry are kindling their fires in all his veins, and his wild blood boils from his heart ...' (from *A Peep into a Picture Book*, 1834). At school she once told a story to her friends which hypnotised herself: 'She brought together all the horrors her imagination could create, from surging seas, raging breakers, towering castle walls, high precipices, invisible chasms and dangers ... then a subdued cry of pain came from Charlotte herself, with a terrified command to others to call for help' (*Reminiscences of Charlotte Brontë* by Ellen Nussey, 1871). Her creations were so real to her that at times she literally saw them with, as she put it, 'irksome and alarming distinctness', and her early twenties found her still partly in thrall to her own imagination.

As she matured, Charlotte made an effort to suppress this lurid inner world, which threatened to possess her by spectral intrusion; but her attempts to cut it out from her realistic novel *The Professor* (eventually published in 1857) resulted in its rejection by publishers because it lacked 'the wild, the wonderful and thrilling'. She therefore re-incorporated it deliberately into *Jane Eyre* (1847). In this novel the hero, Rochester, lives under the curse of a mad and murderous wife, concealed in an upper story of his mansion. The book's sense of mysterious danger, reinforced by the use of dreams, visions and psychic phenomena, contributed to its extraordinary success, which persists to this day. Queen Victoria wrote 'Began reading *Jane Eyre* to my dear Albert. We remained up reading in *Jane Eyre* till $\frac{1}{2}$ past 11 – quite creepy from the awful account of what happened the night before the marriage' (*Journal of our Life in the Highlands, 1848–61*, published 1868).

Emily, too, had inhabited a strange childhood realm called Gondal. In *Wuthering Heights* (1847), she exploited the wildness, gloom and otherworldiness which had characterised her earlier Gondal poems, such as 'The Visionary'. Her power and eloquence rendered some scenes in the novel more 'horrid' than contemporary readers could stomach, and reviewers largely failed at first to recognise her genius. One wrote 'It is a compound of vulgar depravity and unnatural horrors.' In this book, however, the Gothic mode explodes into genuine greatness, and today Emily stands in the highest critical regard. Some modern readers still find the work unbearably disturbing.

Emily makes use, in her text, of the Gothic elements of buildings, rooms and enclosures, some of which literally become prisons, but she expands their use in complex structures of containment and escape, which mirror states of psychological stress and release in the characters. The development of personality in her heroine, Catherine, also goes far beyond that of her predecessors. Sandy McMillen Conger calls Catherine the 'First Gothic heroine to acknowledge the dark side of her soul'. She breaks the usual Gothic mould, with a marriage which 'does not settle conflicts, but exacerbates them. She is not simply placed between two lovers – she feels divided between two lovers.' Catherine admits that her extra-marital love is a sublime, transcendent passion, while her marital love is spiritually impotent. Somewhat more conventionally, she pays for this admission with her life.

HORACE WALPOLE said that in *The Castle of Otranto* he had attempted to 'juxtapose naturalism with romantic elements'. It can be said that the Brontës far surpassed him in this ambition. The melodrama of *Jane Eyre* is counterpointed by scenes of piercing realism, such as those at Lowood School, where the helpless girls are subjected to sadistic attacks by the headmaster. This was based on Charlotte's actual nightmarish experience at the Clergy Daughters' School. Jane Eyre herself, far from being romantically beautiful, is 'poor and obscure, and small and plain'. There seems, too, to be an absolute reality about the passage when she wanders starving on a moor. The fantasy world of *Wuthering Heights* is described through the prosaic eyes of Nelly the servant, which serves to ground it in believable narrative.

Consequent upon this technique, throughout the Brontë novels there runs an irony which enriches rather than subverts their emotional power, and enables responses at various different levels in the reader. Thus, the image of the ghostly nun in Charlotte's *Villette* (1853), despite ultimately being exploded as a hoax, contributes to the book's theme of emotional and sexual frustration. In Anne's study of degeneracy, *The Tenant of Wildfell Hall* (1848), irony clarifies the moral danger threatening a heroine trapped in marriage to a weak man who hates her.

Brontë Gothicism far transcends the mere attempt to excite: it induces a genuine sense of suffering. Well-worn motifs are infused with psychological depth and freshness. The madwoman in *Jane Eyre* is a profoundly suggestive type of the irrational. She has been seen by feminists as the epitome of female rage born of sexual repression, particularly in relation to her confinement within a secret room. The demonic behaviour of Cathy's lover Heathcliff in *Wuthering Heights* is shown to evolve from his history of deprivation. Both these books have been, and still are, continually subject to critical attention.

None of these novels can be categorised simply as 'Gothic'. For example, the influence of Classical learning, of fairy-tale, and of Judeo-Christian religion are just as much contributors to the intriguing complexities of *Jane Eyre*, while the tight pattern of vengeful and tragic relationships in *Wuthering Heights* may be compared to structures in Jacobean drama.

Branwell Brontë, though achieving almost no published work in his lifetime, became a kind of Gothic apparition in reality. He has been called 'the only Brontë to die of love'. Disappointed in his passion for a married woman, he succumbed to his inner world, and his drunken, opium-drugged figure was described by a friend: 'a mass of red unkempt uncut hair, wildly floating round a great gaunt forehead; the cheeks yellow and hollow, the mouth fallen, the thin lips not trembling but shaking, the sunken eyes, once small now glaring with the light of madness–'.

This identification with Romantic otherness was echoed by Mrs Gaskell in her *Life of Charlotte Brontë* (1857). The seemingly alien landscapes and communities of the Yorkshire moors where the Brontës lived, the gloomy-looking parsonage house overlooking the graveyard at Haworth, the tuberculosis which afflicted and destroyed the brother and sisters one after another, were reported by her to the cultured world, which, ever since, has found in the family an endlessly fascinating enigma. The Brontës' personal history has acquired almost legendary status, while in their work the Gothic tradition is seen at its most enduringly effective.

ELIZABETH IMLAY

Brown, Charles Brockden (1771–1810)

The reputation of the American Charles Brockden Brown as a Gothic writer rests on *Wieland; or, The Transformation* (1798), *Ormond; or, The Secret Witness* (1799), *Edgar Huntly; or, The Memoirs of a Sleepwalker* (1799) and *Arthur Mervyn; or, Memoirs of the Year 1793* (1799, 1800). These works are remarkable for their intensity and the breadth of their intellectual engagements. Influenced as much by Locke, Hume and Burke as by Paine, Godwin and Wollstonecraft, Brown's writing shows the productive tension of his commitments to the Enlightenment and **ROMANTICISM**.

Like **HORACE WALPOLE** and **ANN RADCLIFFE**, Brown's works often seem radically to undercut the conservatism of their avowed moral purpose. His novels tend towards closure yet their final chapters seem perfunctory and unsatisfactory. The problematic and contradictory nature of Brown's work has been attributed to its formal incoherence. Yet improvised plots and extravagant coincidences are not simply the product of Brown's hasty and careless methods of composition. The very multiplications and repetitions in his work point towards his driving concerns. Brown's most characteristically Gothic writing suspends any single commitment in favour of experiments in choice and possibility. In the work produced before and after his major phase this fruitfully exploratory quality is less evident. There is, in fact, a distinct shift from the comparatively radical positions adopted until approximately 1798 to the increasingly conservative ones espoused after about 1801. In *Alcuin: A Dialogue on the Rights of Women* (1798), Brown implicitly criticised the American Constitution by countenancing arguments for the equality of women. By 1803, however, he was a staunch supporter of the same Constitution. As magazine editor Brown attempted to remain aloof from party politics. As a political pamphleteer, however, he became increasingly disillusioned with Jefferson's foreign policy, pleading alongside Hamilton's Federalists in 1803 for the immediate and forceful seizure of Louisiana and later for repeal of the 1807 Embargo Act.

In its fascination with law, property and power, Brown's Gothic writing is rooted in a wider national debate. Gothic literature is often as concerned with the political and economic issues of its day as with the past and the 'interior' realm of psychology and imagination. Nevertheless, Brown's work is unusual in its geographical and historical specificity. America in the immediate pre- and post-Revolutionary period is always his subject.

The United States was uniquely founded on Enlightenment principles of reason and progress. It is, perhaps, the thoroughgoing demonstration of the fragility of optimistic rationalism that makes Brown's American tales distinctively Gothic. For Brown the grounds of human decisions are inevitably imperfect, the effects of human actions are always unpredictable, and moral behaviour usually conceals selfish motives. Brown is a rationalist with little faith in the power of reason, a follower of Locke without his predecessor's belief in progress. Brown's darkest insights spring from Lockean psychology. His is a world where sensory evidence is misleading and inferences from such evidence are frequently mistaken, a world in which optimistic rationalism becomes disturbingly irrational. Brown's novels show good producing evil and the rational giving rise to the irrational.

In *Edgar Huntly*, Clithero kills the villainous Wiatte in self-defence. Rather than removing evil, however, Clithero succeeds only in reinforcing it. The instrument of Wiatte's destruction becomes the tool of his revenge and the hero of the early narrative becomes the villain of its later sections: heroes and villains, in fact, are ultimately inseparable (see **HERO-VILLAIN**). Circuitries of physical resemblance link 'good' and 'bad' characters so that any stable moral spectrum dissolves. Brown's characters begin to look like the projections of each other's fears, desires and possible identities. Edgar Huntly resembles Clithero in numerous ways and Arthur Mervyn repeats or anticipates the actions of Welbeck. Indeed, Mervyn adopts new identities with all the virtuosity of Brown's impostors. He is as fascinated by power and as prone to the impulsive overriding of the barriers governing conventional social forms and private property as Brown's most sinister characters.

Change and transition are the most characteristic experiences in Brown. An almost Spenserian sense of mutability and transformation for good or ill marks virtually every page of his work. At a political level, of course, Brown's subject is the national transformation wrought by the American Revolution. At the level of plot, Brown deals with the vicissitudes of fortune and class status experienced by his central characters. But the notion of transformation is also articulated by Brown's interest in extreme or unusual states of mind and body: madness, fanaticism, clairvoyance, somnambulism, ventriloquism, spontaneous combustion and epidemic disease.

For Brown it was only generally the case that absolute honesty was a moral imperative: there were occasions when lying could promote the good. This argument leads to a corrosive perception of the nature and ethical status of representation. Brown's villains are often described as actors but his use of the theatrical metaphor is so pervasive (the world is a stage and so is the mind) that it cannot successfully circumscribe villainy. Quite the reverse. The artifice associated with villainy becomes ubiquitous: in order to unmask deceit one must practise it oneself. It is as if the existence of lies causes Brown to lose faith in the truth that lies mimic. The appearance of truthfulness thus becomes an ominous token, not of genuine honesty, but of imposture. The fact that Brown's villains are often also described as authors suggests his eventually self-cancelling suspicion of literature.

Brown's fiction is as ambivalent about the aesthetic as it is about the political. Both Arthur Mervyn and Edgar Huntly argue that writing promotes peace and order but their pens seem mostly to evoke violence and disorder. Writing here is (failed) therapy and disease, poison and (ineffective) cure. In the 'Advertisement' to *Skywalk* (his first novel, completed in 1797 – now lost) Brown maintains that fiction is rational and moral whilst simultaneously proclaiming his intention to 'enchain the attention and ravish the souls' of his readers. The Preface to *Edgar Huntly* avoids subverting its own *raison d'être* by devoting itself to contemporary American scenes instead of 'puerile superstitions and exploded manners, Gothic castles and chimeras'. It is a familiar Gothic trope: fiction denouncing fiction, romance disavowing romance. But Brown's decision, announced in a letter of 1800, to substitute in *Clara Howard* and *Jane Talbot* 'moral causes and daily incidents' for the 'prodigious or the singular' is fatal: his final two novels, both published in 1801, are generally seen as his least satisfactory. Abandoning fiction in favour of magazine editing and political pamphleteering, Brown's last remarks on literature in an 1807 issue of the *Literary Magazine and American Register* dismiss not only the props of traditional Gothic but fiction itself. 'Wild narratives of the imagination' are now completely divorced from 'real life'.

Brown's disillusion with the morality and practicalities of a literary career in America foreshadows **WASHINGTON IRVING** and **NATHANIEL HAWTHORNE**. He made significant contributions to the **ILLUMINATI NOVEL**. He democratically transformed the figure of the **GOTHIC MANSERVANT**. His interest in crime prefigured **EDGAR ALLAN POE**'s tales of detection, as did his fascination with the idea of premature burial. Brown's sense of the mutual interdependence of good and evil underlies much of Hawthorne's work. His depictions of the unreliability of sensory evidence are not surpassed until **HERMAN MELVILLE's** 'Benito Cereno'. His sophisticated treatment of doubling anticipates later Gothic writing (see **DOPPELGÄNGER; MARY SHELLEY; E. T. A. HOFFMANN**). Brown's use of ambiguity and multiple explanation for apparently supernatural events is found again in Hawthorne and the literature of **THE FANTASTIC**. His often subtle use of first-person narration anticipates the work of **HENRY JAMES**, especially 'The Turn of the Screw'. But Brown's Gothic cannot ultimately be confined to a nineteenth-century provenance. In his ability to analyse and conjure up paranoia and in his sense for the utopian and dystopian possibilities of the American experience, *Wieland* is as close to Thomas Pynchon's *Vineland* (1990) as the similarity of titles suggests.

T. J. LUSTIG

Bulwer-Lytton, Edward George Earle (1803–73)

Novelist, Member of Parliament (1831–41 and 1852–66), and Secretary for the Colonies (1858–9), his name should be given as 'Bulwer' for works written before 1843, and thereafter as 'Bulwer-Lytton' (the hyphen is often incorrectly omitted). Credited with having revived the **GOTHIC NOVEL** at a low point in its fortunes, he is nevertheless difficult to characterise simply in relation to the Gothic tradition as it was established in the eighteenth century. His own preference for the term 'metaphysical novel' is indicative of his primary interest in those areas of psychology and philosophy which escaped realist representation: supernaturalism, mysticism, and the occult. Disdainful of literature which dealt in 'the mere portraiture of outward society', he cultivated a mixed mode of storytelling which melded the Gothic with romance, Romantic tragedy, adventure-narrative, and criminal confession.

Bulwer's first published novel, *Falkland* (1827), incorporated elements of Gothic terror, but his first significant effort in the genre is to be found in the 1828 best-seller *Pelham* – a novel, ostensibly, of the 'silver-fork' or 'society' school, which gradually transmutes itself into Gothic detective fiction. Instability of genre is Bulwer-Lytton's hallmark, and – like earlier practitioners of the Gothic (**ANN RADCLIFFE** most obviously) – he delights in the frisson which can be created when seemingly mild, domestic narratives are turned into occasions for horror. He cultivated the 'grand style' (his protagonists and villains almost always regard themselves as figures of tragic stature), but he also helped to lead the Gothic away from the Radcliffean sublime to focus upon the darker aspects of ordinary life.

His fiction from *Pelham* onwards brought Gothic terror out of the past, and out of Central Europe, into the streets of crime-ridden 1820s and 1830s London. In that respect he is the direct precursor of later nineteenth-century exponents of sensation fiction, including **CHARLES DICKENS**, Wilkie Collins, and **J. SHERIDAN LE FANU**.

The eager reception of *Pelham* was followed by even more extravagant success with *Eugene Aram* (1832) and – more moderately – *Godolphin* (1833), all of which exploited the same model of 'domesticated Gothic'. It was not, however, a guaranteed formula, as the disastrous reception of *Lucretia; or, The Children of Night* (1846) proved. A dark tale of corruption, greed, bigamy, and murder which ends with its vicious anti-heroine a raving maniac, confined in a Gothic madhouse, *Lucretia* alienated even devoted readers of Bulwer-Lytton's most successful 'Newgate fiction', *Paul Clifford* (1830). It marked the end of this phase in his experimentation with the Gothic, although the same principle of generic crossbreeding can be observed in his treatment of the theme which increasingly dominated his fiction from the late 1830s: the occult.

Bulwer-Lytton's fictional explorations of **OCCULTISM** and **THE SUPERNATURAL** constitute his most innovative engagements with the Gothic. In *Ernest Maltravers* (1837) and its sequel *Alice; or, The Mysteries* (1838), jointly subtitled *Eleusiniana*, he created a protagonist of Byronic stature and Coleridgean philosophical ambition: a reclusive and world-weary student of astrology and metaphysics, whose desire to achieve a mystic union of the actual and the ideal is at last satisfied in his love for an uneducated peasant girl. The same themes are reworked to more powerful effect in *Zanoni* (1842), a novel which developed out of an earlier, fragmentary tale *Zicci* (1832). Indebted to the Faust myth and, more immediately, to Charles Maturin's *Melmoth the Wanderer*, *Zanoni* is the story of a heroic mystic who possesses the secret of immortality but who, after centuries on earth, sacrifices his powers for love of a beautiful and virtuous Italian opera singer. The late work *A Strange Story* (1862) again involves a Faustian magus, but unlike the earlier novels, it concentrates on the corruption of the human spirit by material ambition. The novel's anti-hero, Margrave, abuses his knowledge of the occult in an attempt to force a young doctor to help him find the elixir of life, and eventually pays for his sins with death and damnation. Ambitious and original though these works are, they are arguably less effective than Bulwer-Lytton's shorter supernatural fiction from this period, particularly the 1859 ghost story 'The Haunted and the Haunters' – once much-anthologised but now unjustly neglected (see **GHOST STORIES**).

All Bulwer-Lytton's writing about the occult is informed by his knowledge of **ROSICRUCIAN** lore (his grandson and biographer, the 2nd Earl of Lytton, records that Bulwer-Lytton was a Brother of the Rosy Cross and, from 1866, Honorary Grand Patron of the Order). Only recently has work on his fiction begun to take that context seriously, and to consider its role in his remaking of the Gothic tradition. The primary interest of his work for connoisseurs of the Gothic lies in its recasting of the traditional subject matter of the genre – Faustian hubris, predatory sexual desire, supernatural forces, madness, revenge – in terms which made them more immediately relevant to the concerns of early Victorian readers. At their best, his novels are highly effective in dramatising the fraught relationship between nineteenth-century materialism and idealism, utilitarianism and mysticism. The Gothic provided him with a powerful means of expressing the often irreconcilable tensions between those terms. It also enabled him to experiment more boldly with the limits of the novel form than any other writer of the 1820s and 1830s, and it established him as early Victorian England's undisputed literary master of the psychology of fear.

HELEN SMALL

Carter, Angela (1940–92)

The Gothic tradition according to Angela Carter is nothing sacred but 'deals entirely with the profane. Its great themes are incest and cannibalism. ... It retains a singular moral function – that of provoking unease' (Afterword to *Fireworks*, 1974; this, as well as the subtitle 'Nine Profane Pieces', disappeared from later editions). The relation of Carter's work to Gothic is an uneasy one. In a 1987 interview she said that she wrote *Heroes and Villains* [1969] as an exercise in Gothic because reviews of her previous fictions called them Gothic, and she didn't think they were (Stephens, *Antithesis*). One of its epigraphs is from Leslie Fiedler's *Love and Death in the American Novel*: 'The Gothic mode is essentially a form of parody, a way of assailing clichés by exaggerating them to the limit of grotesqueness.' Here she may be recognising what her work shares with the form so defined, but Gothic is just one of the anti-realistic resources she used in her parodic picaresques. They belong on both sides of the boundary between Enlightened reason and the imaginary, across which Gothic is supposed to work: they are rationally critical by fantastic means, but don't lose the magic of storytelling.

   Carter linked her kind of Gothic to tales by **EDGAR ALLAN POE** and **E. T. A. HOFFMANN**, not the short story or realist novel – to abstractions that interpret rather than 'log' everyday experience: 'Cruel tales, tales of wonder, tales of terror, fabulous narratives that deal directly with the imagery of the unconscious – mirrors; the externalized self; forsaken castles; haunted forests; forbidden sexual objects ... a system of imagery derived from subterranean areas behind everyday experience' (Afterword, *Fireworks*). Mirrors, mimicry, doubles, figure in several *Fireworks* stories: these, and other elements she describes, appear in her longer and shorter fictions. Sub-literary forms – dreams, pornography, ballads, films – have relations with high literature in her work, and also with the cultural analysis of contemporary life which she made in her essays for *New Society*: 'We live in Gothic times' (Afterword, *Fireworks*). She wanted to write-into-being new ways of living and relating, beyond those natural-ised and institutionalised, but also to write stories which the Last Person could enjoy as the last candles guttered. 'Don't fear too much; don't hope too much.'

A short list of Gothic elements in Carter's fictions:

- Death and the Maiden: Carter's first novel, *Shadow Dance* (1966), has a slashing, joking, villain-hero, Honeybuzzard, and an equally per-verse victim-heroine, Ghislaine (her name suggests 'grisly', 'ghastly' and 'slain', as well as Coleridge's medieval 'Christabel' and Geraldine). These sadomasochistic 1960s figures are reworked in much of the erotic violence of Carter's fiction, from Buzz, Lee and Annabel in *Love* (1971), to the Marquis and his bride in the title story of *The Bloody Chamber* (1979), to Mignon in *Nights at the Circus* (1984). Sadism, masochism, and their reversals, are factors in Gothic: Carter is also interested in how this structure can be dislocated. Her exercise in cultural history, *The Sadeian Woman* (1979), remembers the Gothic and the modern qualities of Sade's writing.

- Haunting: 'The Mansion of Midnight', in *The Infernal Desire Machines of Doctor Hoffman* (1972), with its sleep-walking romantic woman, is a scenario of critical-Gothic, like the vampire 'Lady of the House of Love' in *The Bloody Chamber*. Bygone cultural representations haunt all of Carter's writing, in the interests of exorcism more than nostalgia. Awakeness – being in suspense, anxious, uncertain, preternaturally alert – is a complementary factor linking Carter's writing to the Enlightenment and to Gothic fiction.

- Ruins: The old house where Marianne lives with the Barbarians in *Heroes and Villains* is burned as they leave: 'The lines of blackened statues stretched their arms forth, as if attempting to flee the fire which nevertheless engulfed them.' The more or less grandiose homes of previous times are frequently burned up (*The Magic Toyshop, Nights at the Circus, Wise Children*, 1991), or a landslide engulfs the last resting-place ('The Acrobats of Desire', in *The Infernal Desire Machines of Doctor Hoffmann*).

- Travelling heroinism: Ellen Moers coined this term for female Gothic adventures in strange territories. Carter's heroines are typically 'on the road' – Marianne in *Heroes and Villains*, 'Eve on the run again', in *The Passion of New Eve* (1977), Fevvers in *Nights at the Circus*. An associated element is:

- Entrapment and escape: The threat of pursuit, and of incarceration (in prisons, brothels, domesticity, or someone else's fantasy; see *Nights at the Circus*, or *Heroes and Villains*) are constant features of Carter's stories. Also associated are:

- Boundaries: The safety of limits and the terror of being limited. The genre itself can be reassuring: 'you know where you are, and you know exactly what stands for what'. 'Unease' may be contained, or 'where you are and what stands for what' can be unsettled, precisely because the appropriate Gothic frame is generically known. A further association would be with Kafkaesque social and psychic anxieties, such as:

- Inside/outside: One example is the frightener frightened. Barbarian Jewel wakes screaming in the night when he dreams that he is no more than the externalised fears of more civilised folk (*Heroes and Villains*). There are many versions of inside/outside anxiety, about psycho-sexual and social spaces. A parallel to Jewel would be the puppet-master patriarch Uncle Philip in *The Magic Toyshop*: his régime is transgressive, and is transgressed, by incest before the final conflagration. Both could be analogies for Carter's enthralled and mocking relation to modern Gothic.

- Over-the-top writing: In the Afterword to *Fireworks* Carter describes the Gothic style as 'ornate, unnatural', upsetting to belief in the world as fact, and this kind of style is endemic/epidemic in her writing. Landscape, atmosphere, event, are evocatively and influentially hyper-real in Ann Radcliffe's style, and Angela Carter does this sort of thing too. Only, Radcliffe calms it all down to a rational conclusion, while Carter also has a stake in the ultimate transgressions of **MATTHEW LEWIS**.

ELAINE JORDAN

Contemporary Gothic

Not until the 1960s did the twentieth century see a burgeoning of Gothic fiction comparable to the one that began in the 1790s and swept through the first three decades of the nineteenth century, though there were hints, precursors in the 1950s – for instance, Fritz Lieber's *Conjure Wife* (1952), about **WITCHCRAFT** among faculty wives; Shirley Jackson's *The Haunting of Hill House* (1959), perhaps the first modern Gothic in which the house itself is the monster; in the States, the uncommonly literary and articulate DC 'horror comics' published by William Gaines from 1950 to 1954. In the sixties, Radcliffean Gothic (see **GOTHIC ROMANCE**), foreshadowed in the fifties by Daphne DuMaurier, burgeoned first with Victoria Holt's *Mistress of Mellyn* (1960), but what soon came to be called **FEMALE GOTHIC**, characterised in cover illustration by a young female in either a cape or some degree of dishabille fleeing from a turreted structure with one lighted window, rapidly became a popular and prolific form. It was seldom, in one sense, entirely contemporary, favouring historical and especially nineteenth-century settings – costume romance.

    HORROR Gothic, the **MATTHEW LEWIS** end of the Gothic continuum, has dealt more ingeniously with its own century, making 'contemporary' a doubly apposite word. Its heightening of shock by the intrusion of uncanny threat, not into the comfortably long ago and far away but into the emphatically familiar fabric of our own lives, subverts Henry Tilney's stabilising reminder to Catherine Morland in Jane Austen's *Northanger Abbey* (1818): to consider the improbability of Gothic horrors in their own country and age. When in contemporary Gothic the horrors join us at home, stability is over. (**BRAM STOKER** in 1897, with *Dracula*'s phonographs, telegrams and typewriters, was a pioneer exploiter of modernity.)

    In Ira Levin's ground-breaking *Rosemary's Baby* (1967), which found modern equivalents for the haunted castle and the secret passage, Rosemary is impregnated with the Devil's seed during the Pope's visit to New York and, drugged, dreams of Jackie Kennedy. The powerful old witch next door is ugly in lime-green toreador pants, while the wise man from the east who arrives to worship at the demonic nativity is a Japanese with a camera. In Gary Brandner's *Walkers* (1980), set in the apartments, morgues and barrios of modern Los Angeles, the heroine, who has been warned that four consecutive zombies will attempt to kill her, is nearly undone by counting as number three a drug-crazed hippie. Stephen King pins his fiction to his time with brand names and snatches of popular songs and has remade the map of his state by the insertion of fictitious and recurring towns just a few miles up or down river from (and much resembling) known locations.

    In contemporary Gothic, supernatural threats become more richly various. In early Gothic, a wild array of ghosts and demons carry nearly the whole burden of the supernatural. Aside from John Polidori's curious novel of 1819, *The Vampyre*, neither vampires, currently so popular, nor werewolves, now a staple, get much beyond an allusion in Gothic's first flowering. Consider in contrast Stephen King's *Salem's Lot* (1975), in which nearly all the residents of a small Maine town become vampires; Robert McCammon's *They Thirst* (1981), wherein a similar fate threatens Los Angeles, in one memorable scene of which a gang of teenage **VAMPIRE** thugs drop from the ceiling of a warehouse onto a rival gang; **ANNE RICE**'s *The Vampire Lestat* (1985), in which, rather than a rock star becoming a vampire, a vampire turns rock star. Other menaces include ruthless vegetation and vegetation cults (Kingsley Amis's *The Green Man*, 1969; Thomas Tryon's *Harvest Home*, 1973), a parasitic house hungry for pain and death (Robert Marasco's *Burnt Offerings*, 1973), deadly machinations of the opposite sex (Ira Levin, *The Stepford Wives*, 1972; Robert McCammon's *Bethany's Sin*, 1980), and a variety of uncategorisable creatures, the nameless fears of our nature still nameless. Stephen King's shapechanging creature in *It* (1986) flips through monster manifestations like an index.

The most curious development in contemporary Gothic, the twentieth century's taking the monster to its collective bosom, goes beyond the sympathy elicited for Frankenstein's unhappy creature, though there is some of that – werewolves and police democratically get equal and alternating understanding in Whitley Strieber's *The Wolfen* (1978). In Chelsea Quinn Yarbro's Saint-Germain saga (beginning with *Hotel Transylvania*, 1978) the vampire hero is the most decent and attractive chap around and deserves the girl. Anne Rice, too, supplies the vampiric point of view; some are good and some are bad, just like us. Perhaps the unavoidable sexuality of vampire activity, repugnant to Dracula's victims, operates nowadays in their favour. But are these novels Gothic at all? Sometimes the monster heroes themselves are menaced by creatures sinister enough to count as the threat in an ordinary Gothic, and yet the tone is confusing. Perhaps Gothic's supernatural effects depend upon a foil of normalcy, some sane world that can be disrupted. If so, the genre may have fallen on hard times.

ANN B. TRACY

Death

Gothic representations of death are so resonant because they occur in a realm clearly delineated as other than ordinary, the supernatural realm of ghosts and spirits, of revenants and vampires, of monsters and zombies, as they also touch on torture, murder and a transgressive desire for destruction. Death becomes attractive, because it is apparently unreal, the result of exaggerated passions, revealing itself in the midst of hallucinatory delusions and involving characters that have been transposed into worlds made unfamiliar, either because they are located in some distant historical past or because the setting is from the start a phantasmatic one.

Seeking to differentiate the degree to which Gothic texts negotiate the slippery boundary between a verifiable reality and modes of perception gone awry, Tzvetan Todorov has suggested that while one of the staples of Gothic literature is the 'hesitation experienced by a person who knows only the laws of nature, confronting an apparently supernatural event', the narrative presentation of this uncertainty can be divided into three categories. The uncertainty evoked by the Gothic oscillation between reality and the imaginary can either result in faith, when new laws of nature are entertained to account for the strange phenomenon, such as the belief in the presence and power of dead spirits we find most often in tales of the marvellous but also in such tales where a character ultimately enters into blissful psychosis. Or it can result in incredulity, leaving the laws of reality intact and seeking an explanation of the extraordinary phenomena within the confines of this reality, such as the explained supernatural with which authors like **ANN RADCLIFFE** resolve the apparition of spectral voices and ghostly bodies, the staging of mysterious corpses, the insinuation of deeds of clandestine crime and violence committed in the past, asking for retribution. Incredulity, however, can also take the form of sacrificial violence to be found in **VAMPIRE** texts such as **BRAM STOKER**'s *Dracula* (1897), where the vampire-hunters stake the uncanny figure of the undead, so as to remove the uncertainty his presence had engendered among the community of the living.

Finally, Todorov offers the notion of the fantastic so as to describe a third way of narrating the interface between the imagined presence of death in life and its reality. This form of Gothic narration resides in a sustained hesitation on the part both of the characters as well as the readers towards the disconcerting events that return death to the living, while these seek to banish it to the periphery of their social world – to the graveyards at the outskirts of the cities, to the uninhabited forests and mountain peaks, to abandoned abbeys, vaults of monasteries or attics of manor houses. In this third variant it remains unresolved whether the resurrected dead are real or merely a figment of the character's deluded imagination, such as the ghosts in **HENRY JAMES**'s 'The Turn of the Screw' (1898). Or these tales enact the uncertainty whether death has successfully been locked beneath the coffin lid, the dead body replaced by an inscription on the gravestone, a commemorative portrait hung up in its place of habitation, or whether death might not always return, an anxiety we find so poignantly re-enacted in **EDGAR ALLAN POE**'s or Wilkie Collins's tales of psychic horror, and an anxiety on which the postmodern version of Gothic, the slasher and horror film, so fruitfully feeds.

Thus, even as Gothic tales render death extraordinary, they also refer to the basic fact of mortal existence, namely that the one certainty we have in life is that we must die. These stories fascinate with chilling horror, because they allow us to indirectly confront our own death, even though on the surface they appear to revolve around the death of the other. We experience death by proxy, for it occurs at someone else's body and at another site, as a narrative or visual image. The compromise they seem to offer is that, although they insist on the need to acknowledge the ubiquitous presence of death in life, our belief in our own immortality is nevertheless also confirmed. We are the survivors of the tale, entertained and educated by virtue of the death inflicted on others. Yet while Gothic tales of death may allow us to feel assured, because the disturbance played through in the narrative ultimately finds closure, as the presence of dead spirits is either recuperated in an act of mystical belief or explained away, the most resilient moments of Gothic involvement with mortality are precisely those where the reader is drawn into a phantasy scenario that hesitates between mastery over and submission before the irrevocable law of death.

To offer an example of the rhetoric gesture at stake: by mesmerising his friend at precisely the moment that death is about to set in, the narrator of Poe's 'The Facts in the Case of M. Valdemar' (1845) seeks to demonstrate his defiance of the disempowering law of mortality. As the sociologist Jean Baudrillard has argued, the phenomenon of survival must be seen in contingency with a prohibition of death and the establishment of social surveillance of this prohibition. Power is first and foremost grounded on legislating death, by manipulating and controlling the exchange between life and death, by severing the one from the other and by imposing a taboo on the dead. Power is thus installed precisely by drawing this first boundary, and all supplementary aspects of division – between soul and body, masculinity and femininity, good and bad – feed off this initial and initiating separation that partitions life off from death. Yet what is so intriguing in Poe's tale is not so much the audacity of this scientific project, as the fact that failure is written ineluctably into any successful arrestation of death. Preserving a body on the threshold between life and death is not only a duplicitous act, because by reopening the boundary between survivors and deceased the former run the risk of being infected by the latter. It is also untenable, because an artificial surmounting of death by preserving the state of liminality cannot be sustained. Asking for the boundary to be redrawn, for the hesitation between life and death to be resolved, M. Valdemar calls out in his trance 'put me to sleep – or, quick! – waken me!'

Yet the horrific scandal of the text significantly does not reside in the last image of the story, where the patient, upon being reawakened, immediately disintegrates into 'a nearly liquid mass of loathsome – of detestable putridity'. Rather, with the same breath that M. Valdemar asks to be released from his existence beyond the opposition between life and death, he speaks the disconcerting sentence of human mortality '*I say to you that I am dead*'. It is precisely in the impossibility of this linguistic utterance that the encroachment of death on life is celebrated and at the same time literally foreclosed. No human subject can speak its death to onlooking survivors, no representation can supersede the gap between a real experience of death and its verbal or visual rendition. But it is equally true that no eradication of the stain of death is possible. What the tales of gothic heroes, defying the divine law that dictates to human beings that they are mortal and therefore cannot obviate the constraint of mutability, obsessively return to is precisely this impasse. Seeking to triumph over the stain of human mortality, they break open the boundary severing life from death, only to find the phantasy of life without death return in the guise of a counter-hallucination, where their world is now exclusively ruled by the law of death. The paradigm *par excellence* of this aporetic urge is, of course, **MARY SHELLEY**'s Frankenstein. Delving among the unhallowed damps of the grave, taking his dead body-parts from vaults, charnel houses and dissecting-rooms, he seeks to give artificial birth to a new species he believes will be of excellent nature, because it is beyond mortality, but instead he produces a death-machine, bent on the total destruction of his maker's social world.

These Gothic representations of exquisite corpses, revenants, spirits or monsters articulate both an anxiety about and a desire for death. In so doing they function like a symptom, giving to the reader or viewer, in the guise of a cyphered message, the truth about his or her desire which he or she could not otherwise confront. In a gesture of compromise, concealing what they also disclose, these fundamentally duplicitous representations try to maintain a balance of sorts. They point obliquely to that which threatens to disturb the order, articulating the knowledge of mortality in a displaced, recoded and translated manner.

Of course, the thematic figurations of death in Gothic literature are legion. One finds necrophilic desire for an abundance of death, so poignantly illustrated in the scene in **MATTHEW LEWIS**'s *The Monk* (1796), where Ambrosia finds his beloved Antonia in death-like trance amongst the tombs in the vaults of the convent. One finds scenes celebrating destruction to excess, as in **WILLIAM BECKFORD**'s *Vathek*

(1786). One finds tales where characters communicate with the dead through hypnotic mediums, or do so in an act of obsessive commemoration that allows them to privilege an existence among the deceased over that amongst the living, such as in Henry James's 'Altar of the Dead'. As one also finds the counterpart, figures such as William Godwin's *St Leon* or **CHARLES MATURIN**'s Melmoth, who have drunk of the elixir of life and in their desperate desire to be redeemed into death, serve to expose the horror of a life without death. Common to all these figurations is that a duplicitous hesitation persists, because representations of death necessarily deny what they also avow, enrapturing with depictions that also disgust or terrify.

Freud coined the concept of **THE UNCANNY** (see **DAS UNHEIMLICH**) to describe moments where something disturbing that has been concealed, and as such functions like a foreign body in the psychic apparatus, suddenly emerges in the midst of what is familiar and agreeable. The uncanny comes to signify any moment where meaning develops in the direction of ambivalence until it coincides with its opposite. Inducing intellectual hesitation and undecidability, it also calls for a recuperation of the prior state of so-called untroubled normalcy. As they negotiate the boundary between life and death, this gesture of revealing the concealed, of re-installing a fusion that has been severed, subtends all Gothic representations of death.

ELISABETH BRONFEN

The Demonic

Since its outset, the **GOTHIC NOVEL** has been obsessed by the demonic in its various manifestations. Satan is the most common and singular example of a demonic presence, though others would be evil spirits, devils, ghosts and supernatural disturbances. However, the dramatic and explanatory frameworks within which presences have been placed have undergone significant changes since the eighteenth century. As Mario Praz (*The Romantic Agony*, 1933) has shown, the legacy of John Milton's gloriously superhuman and theatrical portrayal of Satan in *Paradise Lost* (1667) as a figure who 'proudly eminent / Stood like a tower; his form had not yet lost / All her original brightness' (Book 1, II. 590–2) still retained some purchase on the imaginations of early Gothic romance writers.

Perhaps with the exception of a few figures such as Zofloya (*Zofloya*, 1806) and Gil-Martin in **JAMES HOGG**'s *The Private Memoirs and Confessions of a Justified Sinner* (1824), Satanic figures do not appear as such in Gothic novels but rather certain Satanic characteristics are projected onto evil human characters. Praz cites the examples of Montoni in **ANN RADCLIFFE**'s *Mysteries of Udolpho* (1794) and Heathcliff in Emily Brontë's *Wuthering Heights* (1847) (see **THE BRONTËS**) whose sinister potential is indicated through frequent rhetorical associations with darkness (of figure and setting), chaos and destructive desires. This claim may be extended to a whole series of (male) figures such as Ambrosio (*The Monk*, 1796), Schedoni (*The Italian*, 1797) and Falkland (*Caleb Williams*, 1794) who, though human, bear, sometimes literally, an identifiably demonic stamp (see **LEWIS, MATTHEW**).

Following this, it is easy to see not only how the separation of the demonic from the ordinary and of the supernatural from the readily explicable became increasingly difficult lines to draw, but equally, how the states of confusion and doubtfulness this difficulty inspired can be read as symptomatic of more general sorts of social unease. This is partly because the move away from unmistakably diabolic figures towards portraying evil as a distinctly human potential marks the beginning of an important change of direction in the Gothic towards both internalisation and, linked to this, secularisation, so that the disturbances caused by **THE DEMONIC** become more firmly rooted in human agency. Rosemary Jackson sees the two key (and connected) registers for these changes as the Gothic's mobilisation of the Faust myth and **MARY SHELLEY**'s *Frankenstein* (1818) respectively (*Fantasy: The Literature of Subversion*, 1981). Thus whereas Marlowe had dramatised stage devils, who spectacularly punish Faust for his transgression, Romantic texts 'hesitate between supernatural and natural explanations of the devil's genesis' (Jackson, p. 54), thus offering the possibility that evil may indeed be engendered in the self. With *Frankenstein* comes a reworking of the Faustian theme of the quest for ultimate knowledge, but one from which any religious framework of reference has been removed so that it is the limits of individual human behaviour rather than the laws of God which are at stake.

One of the most influential accounts of this shift from supernatural to human explanation for disturbances to the social and natural order is Tzvetan Todorov's structuralist analysis of the fantastic (*The Fantastic: A Structural Approach to a Literary Genre*, 1973). He traces a movement within categories of fantastic occurrence from the 'marvellous' (events explained only through reference to magic or supernatural forces) to the 'pure fantastic' (which eludes explanation altogether) to the 'uncanny' (external manifestations of unconscious desires). Thus in nineteenth-century Gothic in the wake of *Frankenstein*, the demonic is frequently incorporated into dramas of dualism or divided selves, such as **OSCAR WILDE**'s *The Picture of Dorian Gray* – first published in serial form in

Lippincott's Magazine in the 1890s, or **ROBERT LOUIS STEVENSON**'s *The Strange Case of Dr Jekyll and Mr Hyde* (1886), in which Dr Jekyll's home-made drug is 'neither diabolical nor divine' and where evil is displaced from one figure onto another, recognisably the dark 'other' half of the first. Indeed, even in cases where the threat to 'the self' lies not within but is externally located in a monstrous 'other' such as a vampire, the site of conflict and possession is none the less the human and intimate one of the body (see **VAMPIRE**). Much recent criticism, therefore, has been concerned with examining the ways in which the demonic, itself a highly unstable category, may be read as a meaningful register of ongoing ideological struggles to establish and test cultural limits, with the demonic being that which breaks, subverts, or falls on the other side of a given boundary. Most frequently the stakes in these conflicts are taken to be those of gender, sexuality, class and race and in each case the demonic figure is read in terms of its unsettling of category or hierarchy in one or more of these arenas.

Whilst the demonic has continued to be a presence in these terms throughout twentieth-century Gothic, especially in popular literature and film (see **CONTEMPORY GOTHIC** and **GOTHIC FILM**), contemporary texts seem overwhelmingly preoccupied with bodily possession and spectacular disintegration. This has been visible not only in the numerous reworkings of vampire narratives, but also in *The Exorcist* (William Friedkin, 1973), *The Omen* (Richard Donner, 1976) and in literary and film versions of *Rosemary's Baby* (Ira Levin, 1967, and Roman Polanski, 1968), where possession of the body by demonic forces appears to give expression to fears of vulnerability and loss of control, yet in situations in which institutions such as the Church, the family and scientific knowledge, previously the guardians of cultural limits, are either powerless or complicit.

HELEN STODDART

Dickens, Charles (1812–70)

Early and late, Dickens's fiction is studded with Gothicism, much like a Christmas pudding comes replete with plums. Dickens's handling of the Gothic tradition, whence his fiction sprang, shows an increasing sophistication from the fairly straight terror-tale interpolated stories in *The Pickwick Papers* (1837) on to the far more subtle renderings in *The Mystery of Edwin Drood* (1870). Dickens's earliest Gothic ventures entailed much of a recognisably Gothic atmosphere and Gothic character types. 'A

Madman's Manuscript' in *Pickwick*, entails a crazed narrator, his in-nocent wife, sold to him by her money-hungry family, a stereotypical 'haunted castle' abode, murder, and motifs of concealment linked with family secrets, which were so recurrent in antecedent Gothic works. Although some have read these interpolated tales as conscious gambits to appeal to the mass market, others have interpreted them as barome-ters of the dark irrational side of life that will intrude itself into far more humorous or cheerful aspects. Such elements were to constitute import-ant parts of his novels thereafter. *Oliver Twist* (1837–8), *Bleak House* (1852–3), *The Mystery of Edwin Drood*, and other novels contain recognis-ably Gothic hallmarks in their sensationalised matters of family secrets and conflicts, frequently combined with folklore of the supernatural, often vampirism, or *Arabian Nights* features (such as brutality, violence, murder, supernaturalism) with deft artistry.

Many of Dickens's characters are presented amid circumstances that recall the literal live burials in earlier Gothic fiction. For instance, old Arthur Gride in *Nicholas Nickleby* (1838–9) would in effect entomb his hoped-for young bride within his own warped sexuality and other selfish desires. Mr Tulkinghorn, one of the more subtly rendered vampire figures, would consign Lady Dedlock to a living death by ex-posing her past, and the Smallweeds number among other characters who function in kinds of live burials in *Bleak House*. Miss Havisham in *Great Expectations* (1860–1) is doubtless Dickens's best-known victim of premature burial, to which she has volunteered herself after being jilted by her anticipated husband, but she stands as a mirror figure to what Pip might potentially have become, had his lesson in the school of hard knocks not stimulated different outlets for his self-centred impulses. Maybe the most impressive Gothic figure in Dickens is John Jasper, in *The Mystery of Edwin Drood*, Dickens's final, and uncompleted, novel, who has murderous intentions toward his nephew, Edwin Drood, because of the elder man's lust for attractive Rosa Bud. Jasper's tactics of pursuit seem, to Rosa, to partake of supernatural powers. His abilities as a mesmerist, his traits of animal magnetism, and his overall aura of evil stamp him as a descendant of many older Gothic villains.

Although others have long been credited with creating the psycho-logical novel, Dickens's fiction indicates that, had he lived some years longer, he might have won yet another accolade for himself as a psycho-logical novelist. The ever-increasing probings into the interiors of his characters, repeatedly associated in some way with his legacies from Gothic tradition, support this thesis. His terrifying characters become more frightening over the course of his literary career because they evince, more and more, characteristics that might be part of any ordinary human being's psychological makeup. There is a drift from sensationalising to centring upon emotional sensations. Perhaps the outburst of Eugene Wrayburn, in *Our Mutual Friend* (1865), concerning obscure, but unsettling events, 'Mysteries of Udolpho!' carries a freight of subtext that should not be ignored.

BENJAMIN F. FISHER

Doyle, Arthur Conan (1859–1930)

Arthur Conan Doyle was the son of Charles and Mary Doyle and was born in Edinburgh on 22 May 1859. Both families could trace their ancestors back to the Middle Ages, Mary claiming descent from the Plantagenet kings and Charles from origins in France, and both sides were ardent Catholics, the Doyles being dispossessed of their lands in Ireland because of their faith. Arthur's grandfather was the highly talented artist HB whose political lampoons graced the Regency, and all his sons seemed to possess considerable artistic gifts, Richard Doyle creating Mr Punch. Charles Doyle was unable to make a living at art and became an official of the Scottish Office of Works. He was also prone to epilepsy and alcoholism.

The young Conan Doyle finished his schooling at a Jesuit school in Austria and then went to Edinburgh University where he graduated in 1881 and signed on as a ship's surgeon on voyages to the Arctic and Africa. On his return he practised as a doctor in Plymouth and Southsea where the first Sherlock Holmes story was written.

Success as a writer came late and Doyle left medicine in his thirties. Doyle was a prodigious author, partly at least as the child of an age dominated by an obsession with print and the means of communicating to the vast literate public of the late nineteenth century through inexpensive novels and hugely popular magazines such as the *Strand*, each issue of which contained complete short stories. From 1888 to his death in 1930 Doyle produced novels, short stories, plays, poetry, two histories, books of autobiography, and ten works on spiritualism. On top of this he wrote campaigning pamphlets, dictated correspondence and managed his various business enterprises including his spiritualist bookshop in Westminster.

Of Doyle's vast output what remains proves less in quality than might be expected. The many works on spiritualism are rarely taken into account by serious scholars or readers and are usually dealt with in embarrassed tones by biographies and ignored by literary critics as intractable. At best they merely confirm the prejudices of certain spiritualist devotees. The science fiction tales, which include *The Lost World*, are now seen as amusing curiosities, enjoyable in themselves but perhaps lacking the darkly logical predictions of H. G. Wells. Doyle's forays into the supernatural tale are effective in their way but seem to lack the obsessive quality of those of **HENRY JAMES**, nor do they sustain the atmosphere of the work of **M. R. JAMES**. The histories that Doyle produced of the Boer War and the Great War were soon overtaken both by events and by the accumulations of later historians, their impartiality as histories tainted by an overly deferrential attitude towards the British cause and (despite his distrust of the old boy network) a willingness to accept the generals' line.

As with his work on recent world events, so too Doyle's advocacy of justice (especially his sustained campaigns on behalf of Sir Roger Casement and on behalf of George Edalji and Oscar Slater – both wrongfully imprisoned) was undertaken under the pressure of immediate necessity. This leaves what Doyle considered his masterworks, *Micah Clarke* (1889), *The White Company* (1891) and *Sir Nigel* (1906), which belong to a genre outdated as serious fiction even when they were written and which can be regarded as enjoyable only in terms of the limitations they labour under as minor romances rather than the status that Doyle claimed for them as works of epic seriousness.

It is upon the much more than merely literary reputation of the sixty stories of Sherlock Holmes and Dr John H. Watson that Doyle's reputation rests. Produced between 1888 and 1927, the tales were published either as complete short stories or as two-part novels, mostly in the pages of the *Strand* in Britain and a variety of magazines in America, including *Harper's*, the *American Magazine*, *Liberty* and others. The stories were then anthologised following the usual practice of the age and can be listed alongside the four novels as: *A Study in Scarlet* (1887); *The Sign of Four* (1890); *The Adventures of Sherlock Holmes* (1892); *The Memoirs of Sherlock Holmes* (1894); *The Hound of the Baskervilles* (1902); *The Return of Sherlock Holmes* (1905); *The Valley of Fear* (1915); *His Last Bow* (1917); and *The Case-Book of Sherlock Holmes* (1927).

There are very large numbers of books on Doyle and his work, including biographies by Hesketh Pearson, John Dickson Carr, Julian Symons and Pierre Nordon; Michael Hardwick has produced an excellent series of guides to the complete Holmes oeuvre; R[ichard] L[ancelyn] Green has edited a collection of newspaper letters which all discuss the great detective; the 'posthumous' messages of Doyle are preserved by the White Eagle Lodge; numerous films have used the Holmes stories as their basis, of which the series starring Basil Rathbone is the most remembered, and of the television adaptations Jeremy Brett's portrayal is currently the definitive.

Added to this there are so many versions of these tales (including a growing number of works by other writers who have borrowed characters from or enlarged upon Doyle's original conception) that enthusiasts talk of 'Sherlockiana' to describe the vast literature, both serious and ephemeral, that has come into being. It almost goes without saying that there are Sherlock Holmes societies in both the United Kingdom and the United States as well as affiliated organisations throughout the world.

Doyle as a man was peculiarly of his age, an enthusiastic imperialist but also able to admire Britain's enemies such as the Boers; a Unionist by nature and an anti-suffragette, Doyle was an advocate of divorce reform and put aside any racial prejudice to defend the rights of an Indian and a Jew. As a passionate sportsman Doyle played cricket for Middlesex (twice against W. G. Grace), boxed in his youth, played football into his forties and was a champion billiards player. A far-seeing man, he realised the dangers from submarine warfare, advocated body armour for troops in the trenches and began the first home guard unit. In his artistic inclinations Doyle was less than admiring of modernism and yet T. S. Eliot was one of his readers, going so far as to incorporate parts of 'The Musgrave Ritual' into his play *Murder in the Cathedral*.

Julian Symons comments that, 'in his work and in his personality he is the ideal representative of the Victorian era to which he belonged'.

CLIVE BLOOM

English-Canadian Gothic

Although the idea of reading Canadian literature as specifically Gothic is a fairly recent phenomenon, critics have long been struck by the sombre qualities which it evokes, qualities, moreover, which are often considered the lineament of Gothic fiction: what Margot Northey, in *The Haunted Wilderness* (1976), has called 'the dark band of Gothicism which stretches from earliest to recent times'. In *Survival: A Thematic Guide to Canadian Literature* (1972), Margaret Atwood suggests that 'the central Canadian experience is death and the central mystery is "what goes on in the coffin"'. She goes on to say that the 'tone of Canadian literature as a whole is, of course, the dark background: a reader must face the fact that Canadian literature is undeniably sombre and negative, and that this to a large extent is both a reflection and a chosen definition of the national sensibility'. In his famous 'Conclusion' to *The Literary History of Canada*, reprinted in *The Bush Garden: Essays on the Canadian Imagination*

(1971), Northrop Frye describes Canadian poetry as one 'of incubus and *cauchemar*'.

Alice Munro, for her part, has said that 'the part of the country I come from is absolutely Gothic. You can't get it all down.' Her short stories are dominated by 'Gothic mothers', and one of her best-known characters, Del Jordan, from *Lives of Girls and Women* (1971), begins her journey into literature by writing a Gothic Novel. It is in *Lives of Girls and Women* that she refers to the 'linoleum caves' of her world, a phrase which describes perfectly the domestic and ordinary, and yet no less Gothic, reality of Canadian small town experience, and one decidely framed by the female imaginary. It is a legacy with a long history in Canada, from the very first novel written by a Canadian-born writer, Julia Catherine Beckwith's *St Ursula's Convent; or, The Nun of Canada, Containing Scenes from Real Life* (1824), to the novels of Susan Swan (see, for example, *The Biggest Modern Woman in the World*, 1988, and *The Wives of Bath*, 1993).

St Ursula's Convent, as the title alone suggests, is a sensationalist romance, which attempts to eschew the Gothic influence but returns to its excesses, in a predictable novel of kidnapping, multiple weddings and flimsy historical account. From the first, Beckwith displays an allegiance to both the Old and 'New' Worlds, and this 'double vision' mediates the portrait of the country which she advances, a land 'gradually rising into notice'.

This double vision is a shared one with many colonies where its authors' allegiances may be divided between an actual or perceived homeland and their new-found space. For many Canadians this frequently translates into a sense of the inadequacies of their world. What is unusual about the Canadian experience is how long the denial of worth and history lasted. While it is not surprising that Susanna Moodie's at times Gothic *Roughing it in the Bush* (1852) should feature a character who suggests that Canada is 'too young for ghosts' – an ironic comment given the spooky nature of some of Moodie's recollections, sketches and details – it is certainly remarkable that E. J. Pratt should repeat the sentiment in 1947 in one of Canada's most famous poems, 'Can Lit'. In a much-quoted comment on the state of Canadian Literature (that is, Can Lit.), Pratt averred that 'It's only by our lack of ghosts / we're haunted.'

The phrase is remarkable not simply for the insecurity it demonstrates but also for the obvious falsity of the statement. As Atwood has observed in *Strange Things: The Malevolent North in Canadian Literature* (1995), 'the poem continues to be quoted as a still-accurate encapsulation of the flatness of the Canadian imagination. The only problem with it is that it's not true; not of the literature, at any rate. Hordes of ghosts and related creatures populate Canadian fiction and poetry.' Indeed her own work is a testament to this. Atwood has created many ghosts, for example, from the figure of Moodie in *The Journals of Susannah Moodie* (1970) haunting the Toronto landscape, to the 'ghost' of the 'pneumatic Zenia' who returns to haunt her 'friends' in *The Robber Bride* (1993). Many of her novels specifically invoke the Gothic mode, as in the parodic *Lady Oracle* (1976); others use Gothic or related devices to chilling effect, as in the futurist, speculative nightmare of *The Handmaid's Tale* (1985), the unsettling contemporary drama of *Cat's Eye* (1988) and the recent historical drama of the 16-year-old murderess Grace Marks in *Alias Grace* (1996).

If Atwood is the best-known of Canada's novelists, she is not alone in using the conventions of the Gothic Novel – or at least a Gothic style – to comment on a range of issues, from colonialism to masculine oppression. Marta Ostenso's remarkable *Wild Geese* (1925) paints a terrifying picture of prairie life and male violence. Over fifty years later, in *Obasan* (1981), Joy Kogawa manages to create a similarly tense atmosphere, though used to explore the racial discrimination which tore the Japanese-Canadian community apart during the Second World War. The story of the dispossession and incarceration of the Japanese-Canadians re-writes the idyllic sense of the Vancouver setting, and makes a lie, in particular, of the hideous notion that Canada is without ghosts.

If the Gothic has been turned to in order to speak particularly unpalatable social realities by contemporary authors, it has especially been used by women writers in Canada either to descry the racism and sexism of Canadian society, or to challenge outright the very prejudicial structures which seek to contain and control women. Marian Engel's *Bear* (1977) is, among other things, a particularly successful 'perversion' of the fairy-tale in which a woman tames the beast of masculinity to find the prince beneath. In Engel's version, set in the Canadian wilderness, it is quite clear that the actual beast – the titular bear – is far preferable to whatever mythical male might be discoverable beneath. Engel's novel is only one of many texts which push at the limits of behaviour and sexuality in order to challenge stereotypes and expectations.

Unlike nations such as Australia and the USA, Canada's literary history is dominated by women writers, many of whom turned to the Gothic mode to different extents to speak their particular sense of self and place. This is not to say, however, that male writers in Canada have been absent, nor that they have avoided the Gothic mode. To the contrary, it has proved popular throughout Canada's literary history. Major John Richardson's *Wacousta*, for example, is a classic example of colonial Gothic fiction. The novel at once articulates a sense of the strangeness of the 'New' World, and a despair at the loss of the Old. *Wacousta* (1832) is set in 1763 during the time of Ponteac's attempted capture of Britain's last remaining forts, Michillimackinac and Détroit, though it revolves mostly around a story of revenge – the 'Indian' Wacousta's embittered pursuit and persecution of Colonel de Haldimar and his family. As with so many Gothic figures, Wacousta is not what he seems; rather, he is a colonial Frankenstein's monster, the physical embodiment of the colony's own 'genetic' composition, part British, part French and part Indian, so that his struggle is metonymic of European fears of their own potential dismemberment in or by the New World space.

It is a theme pursued in another strangely Gothic text, James De Milles's lost world romance *A Strange Manuscript Found in a Copper Cylinder* (1880). More than any other nineteenth-century Canadian work, *A Strange Manuscript* disproves the common assumption that 'there are no monsters' in Canadian literature. Indeed, the novel is replete with monsters in many guises: a threatening, horrific landscape, prehistoric creatures, and a perverted human Other. Though ostensibly an account of one man's misfortunes in the world of the Kosekin people, a land situated somewhere in the Antarctic polar cap where bourgeois values have been hideously reversed, it is also a learned and at times offensively revealing example of the racism and imperialism at the heart of nineteenth-century thought.

Contemporary times have also produced a number of Gothicists, from Graeme Gibson to Timothy Findley. In a different style William Gibson created what has been termed cyber-Gothic (see **CYBERPUNK**) after he emigrated to Canada. From his position as an immigrant from the United States, located in Vancouver and observing its vigorous migration, he first began to imagine the technological terrors of globalisation which resulted in the *Neuromancer* novels.

Canada's best-known chronicler after Atwood is certainly the late Robertson Davies, whose stories and novels have always displayed a fascination with the macabre, the occult and the other-worldly. In his light-hearted collection of ghost stories *High Spirits* (1982), Davies claimed that 'Canada needs ghosts, as a dietary supplement, a vitamin taken to stave off that most dreadful of modern ailments, the Rational Rickets.' In his numerous essays, plays, and particularly in his novels – from *Fifth Business* (1970) through to *Murther and Walking Spirits* (1991) – Davies provided Canada with a rich supplement of Gothic wonders, frequently delivered in parodic form, as is evidenced in his detailed instructions for the building of Haunted Houses:

> There are countless amenities which every house needs, for literary uses, and which have been allowed to disappear from modern domestic design. The attic, for instance – invaluable for nostalgia; it is a proven psychological fact that you can't be nostalgic on the ground floor. And the cellar – admirable for murders, for knife-fights in the

dark, for the walling-up of wives who have not worn well. Your objection, I know, is that a house equipped with all these handsome comforts would be rather large. True, but when the owners have finished with it, no ingenuity at all is needed to convert it into a first-class Funeral Home. The boudoir is of ample size for a chapel, you can garage the hearse in the Secret Passage, and the oubliette provides ample, cool accommodation for Unfinished Business.

Davies's 'How to Design a Haunted House' perhaps best exemplifies the English-Canadian approach to the Gothic mode, one which distinguishes it from many other 'national' transformations, and even from French-Canadian approaches. Indeed, it is possible to say of the Québécois and French-Canadian Gothic that it draws its influence from darker sources: from legends and folk tales, to religious and political parables. The Gothic in French Canada is serious stuff, as a glance at the works of Anne Hébert or Marie Claire Blais will attest.

The Gothic in English Canada is certainly horrific, but there is also frequently an air of controlled artificiality about it, if not of outright parody, so that its practitioners seem always to be self-conscious in their use of the mode. It is as though for many it is still the case that though ghosts haunt their tales, Canada is nevertheless not legitimately Gothic – that the other-worldly is still elsewhere. This perhaps accounts for the tendency of both early and modern chroniclers to turn to Canada's 'wilderness', or to appropriate Native mythology, in order best to provide their country – and their stories – with a chilling, and 'legitimate', history, more resolutely indigenous than any transplanted European spectre could ever be.

GERRY TURCOTTE

Female Gothic

From the eighteenth century onwards, Gothic writing has been conceived of in gendered terms. Some of its earliest and most celebrated practitioners were women, such as Clara Reeve, **ANN RADCLIFFE**, Charlotte Dacre and **MARY SHELLEY**, and many Gothic tales first appeared in the pages of journals like *The Lady's Magazine*. Women's periodicals also encouraged submissions from their readers and in this way a reciprocity of female reading and writing of Gothic was established. Through the circulating libraries for the middle class, and the Gothic chapbooks for the lower classes, a new generation of women readers was able to enjoy, like Catherine Morland in Austen's *Northanger Abbey* (1818), the delights of narrative suspense: 'While I have *Udolpho* to read, I feel as if nobody could make me miserable. Oh! the dreadful black veil!' Whether the description of the devourer of Minerva Press productions as female was accurate is debatable, as men were extensive novel readers, and Austen's heroine has her male counterpart in Peacock's Scythrop in *Nightmare Abbey* (1818) who sleeps with the *Horrid Mysteries* under his pillow.

Those who have traced the Gothic to contemporary fiction are on surer ground in assuming a primarily female readership for the romances of Mary Stewart and Victoria Holt, in which a young woman, often a governess to a widower's child, flees his house and his supposed evil designs. Daphne du Maurier is linked to Ann Radcliffe in a tradition that is held to include the **BRONTËS**, Charlotte Perkins Gilman and Flannery O'Connor by this central figure of the persecuted maiden who is entrapped by a male tyrant in a labyrinthine castle. In a collection edited by Juliann E. Fleenor, *Female Gothic* (1983), the modern versions are analysed as articulations of the passage from girlhood to female maturity and socialisation in which Gothic fantasies enact escape from the all-embracing mother into individuation through sexual response. In this volume popular female Gothics are variously interpreted as sites for the safe expression of female rebellion or drugs to enforce social conformity.

The division of Gothic writing into male and female traditions is customary and usually follows the gender of the author. It distinguishes between masculine plots of transgression of social taboos by an excessive male will, and explorations of the imagination's battle against religion, law, limitation and contingency in novels such as **MATTHEW LEWIS**'s *The Monk* (1796), in which rape, murder and mortgaging of the self to the devil are variously attempted. *The Monk* is the novel praised by John Tilney in *Northanger Abbey* over the female novel of sentiment by Burney, and in preference to the girls' admiration for *The Mysteries of Udolpho* (1794). In the female tradition, the male transgressor becomes the villain whose authoritative reach as patriarch, abbot or despot seeks to entrap the heroine, usurps the great house, and threatens death or rape. Division according to a writer's gender is not, however, consistent, as Reeve, Dacre and Shelley write in the male tradition, and Ireland and **J. SHERIDAN LE FANU** in the female, while **CHARLES MATURIN** unites the two forms in *Melmoth the Wanderer* (1820).

What is also not often noticed is that the modern female form differs from the eighteenth-century romance in moving to release the male protagonist from guilt or evil purposes to allow his marriage with the heroine. Both the male and female traditions are thereby sanitised and made socially acceptable by the cancellation of any masculine threat or feminine rejection. Study of the 'classic' Gothic period is similarly poised between stressing its radical potential and its conservative ideological function. Ellen Moers in *Literary Women* (1963) described the Gothic novel as 'a device to send maidens on journeys', and this positive assessment characterises the humane approach of Margaret Doody, whose article in *Genre*, 'Deserts, Ruins, Troubled Waters: Female Dreams in Fiction and the Development of the Gothic Novel' views the form as making actual female nightmares of oppression and enclosure in a way that allows radical social protest. Although Charlotte Smith in *The Old Manor House* (1793) and Mary Wollstonecraft in *The Wrongs of Woman; Or Maria* (1798) made Gothic an overt vehicle for social and feminist critique, few recent studies attend to this ideological intervention.

Kate Ferguson Ellis's *The Contested Castle* (1989) illustrates how the Gothic revelation of the great house as a prison makes problematic the safety of the domestic sphere under capitalism at the same time as it dramatises the social relations suitable for such a society. More positively (although Ellis does allow the Gothic to have been of assistance in producing a female autonomous self), Alison Milbank's *Daughters of the House: Modes of the Gothic in Victorian Fiction* (1992) employs Benjaminesque apocalyptic to analyse an appropriation of female Gothic by male writers such as **CHARLES DICKENS** and Le Fanu as a means of radical critique of capitalism and the ideology of the separate spheres. In novels such as *Little Dorrit* (1855–7) or *Uncle Silas* (1864) the heroine's allegiance to the house is asserted through her escape from it, which reveals it, and the history-bound patriarchy that it articulates, as ruined. The Gothic heroine detects the secret power relations of aristocratic transformation while resisting, for an apocalyptic moment, the divided morality of the entrepreneurial class.

More typically, writing on the female Gothic plot reads it psychoanalytically. An influential article by Norman Holland and Leona Sherman, 'Gothic Possibilities', marks out a female alternative to the male Gothic Oedipal struggle in which the son acts to overthrow the father and gain hidden knowledge of the forbidden mother. Here the psychology of Nancy Chodorow lies behind an analysis of the Gothic plot of entrapment and escape from a labyrinthine castle as the girl's difficulty in separating from the mother when she does not have the obvious marker of sexual difference from her that the son possesses. The castle is a 'potential space' which inwardly symbolises the mother and outwardly the father, who is both feared and desired by the heroine. In this rapturous play of desire the female imagination can 'hover between radical exploration and a familiar conservative ending'.

Claire Kahane's essay 'The Gothic Mirror' similarly attends to the daughter's move towards psychic individuation, which she finds figured in Gothic writing as 'the spectral presence of a dead–undead mother, archaic and all-encompassing, a ghost signifying the problematics of femininity which the heroine must confront'. Typically, Kahane reads female characters in a novel such as *The Mysteries of Udolpho* as doubles for the heroine, so that the murderous Signora Laurentini becomes a mirror for Emily's own potential for madness and transgression. The projection onto other female figures of a heroine's repressed desires characterises Sandra Gilbert and Susan Gubar's attention to *Jane Eyre* in their *The Madwoman in the Attic* (1979), in which Bertha Mason is an avatar of Jane's rage against Rochester and illimitable desires.

Kahane's text moves to speak in sublime language as her reader delights 'in the dizzying verge of the ubiquitous Gothic precipice on the edge of the maternal blackness to which every Gothic heroine is drawn'. This is, however, again to figure the sublime in Oedipal terms of rivalry and annihilation. Patricia Yaegar, in an article not concerned with the Gothic especially but of direct relevance to it, argues for an avoidance of the Oedipal triangle in 'Toward a Female Sublime', where the aggrandising 'vertical' Romantic sublime is to be eschewed for a 'horizontal' **SUBLIME** (located in Irigaray and other French feminist theoreticians) that 'expands toward others, spreads itself out towards others, spreads itself out in multiplicity'.

This 'sublime of nearness', which does not overpower objects in an idealising triumph of the imagination but allows the other its alien character, is close to Irigaray's description of the production of true sexual difference in the non-possessive astonishment that Descartes describes as prior to the passions. For to remain hoist between the annihilating father and the all-encompassing mother is not to escape the castle but to remain within the tragic agon of the male Gothic. This cannot produce a female erotic since it is concerned with the collapse of the distance that makes desire possible, and posits as object either the Kristevan 'abjected' pre-Oedipal mother from whom one must separate in order to be a desiring subject at all, or the Oedipal father, who in incest would imprison the daughter in cycles of uncanny repetition which, in Freudian theory, have more to do with the death-drives, with *thanatos* rather than *eros*. The female Gothic in Radcliffe and her followers moves beyond the castle to search for virtue, community and a symbolic expression of the female.

The unrepresentable in the Gothic sublime is often sexual difference itself, which is a subject of general concern during the eighteenth century. The Gothic Novel's preoccupation with Milton, in forms as diverse as Shelley's Eveless and nameless Milton student in *Frankenstein* or Radcliffe's imitation of *Comus* in the temptation of Adeline in *The Romance of the Forest* (1791) are typical of a contemporary study of

Milton's presentation of sexual difference in the pre-fallen 'conversation' of the Edenic couple, which attracted a variety of interpretations, not all of them mysogynist. Adam and Eve's loss of reciprocity of feeling and sexual reponse after the Fall, in which nature itself is involved, comes to be figured obliquely in elegiac and graveyard poetry of the eighteenth century as the division between human and natural worlds, and which is only healed, momentarily, by the descent of 'Eve' (evening) in the benign undifferentiation of twilight.

In Radcliffe and Shelley one can see this melancholy compensation transfigured in Rousseauian fashion into the archetectonics of the sublime, both in the natural sublime of imaginative expansion and the Burkean sublime of the threat of annihilation within the castle that produces sexual difference. Yaegar's female sublime is asserted against Thomas Weiskel's agonistic model of the Romantic sublime, but this is different from the Gothic sublime, which articulates a pre-Romantic dialectical relation of reason and imagination. There, the other remains itself. So in Radcliffe's *A Sicilian Romance* (1790), a Duke, a Marquis and an abbot seek in vain to capture the errant Julia and to enforce their several wills and desires upon her, and in their search seize innocent strangers and invade pastoral retreats. Conversely, her governess, idly following the windings of a stream and in sublime meditation upon the landscape, hears a voice and discovers accidentally her lost pupil, whom she leaves in her seclusion. Again the same Julia is led to discover that her mother is not dead or a spectre but a prisoner, and chooses to share her mother's captivity until both are released. Others in the female Gothic are not mirrors but sharers in a subjectivity centred on the sublime, which is a social category in Radcliffe, not the preserve of a privileged individual.

Radcliffe's romances end with the heroine enjoying a virtuous Rousseauian community; Shelley makes this the home from which Victor Frankenstein flees (whose members enjoy sublime landscapes and social benevolence). *Frankenstein* charts its hero's progressive stages of rejection of the feminine 'other' from his abandonment of his 'Eve', Elizabeth, to his abortion of a female monster and the murder of both Elizabeth and Justine that occurs as a direct result of his forbidding his monster a sexual partner. The novel ends with an assertion of the power of homosocial bonds in the frozen wastes of the Arctic where there are no women. Like her later novels, Shelley's *Frankenstein* (1818) is a warning of the loss for men and women alike that ensues when the feminine other is denied symbolisation, and the female Gothic project is abandoned.

ALISON MILBANK

Frénétique School

The term *école frénétique* would seem to have been coined by Charles Nodier in 1821 in the course of the first of two articles in a conservative literary journal, reviewing a new translation (*Le Petit Pierre*, 1820) by Henri de Latouche of Christian Spiess's *Das Petermännchen* (1791). By such an expression, Nodier sought to castigate those writers who, whether in prose or verse, *'promène[nt] l'athéisme, la rage et le désespoir à travers des tombeaux; qui exhume[nt] les morts pour épouvanter les vivants, et qui tourmente[nt] l'imagination de scènes horribles, dont il faut demander le modèle aux rêves effrayants des malades'* ['flaunt their atheism, their fury and their despair across the grave, who exhume the dead in order to terrify the living, and who torment the imagination with scenes of horror the only model for which is to be found in the fearful dreams of the insane']. According to Nodier, such writers belong to neither the Classical nor the Romantic school but – in a telling phrase – to *'une école innommée'* ['an unnameable school'] which, at the reader's insistence, he intends to designate as the *frénétique* school.

Despite the not inconsiderable efforts Nodier made as a reviewer to popularise this new term, it would not seem to have caught on immediately. Indeed, it is only in the last thirty years or so that the idea has gradually established itself that some sort of *frénétique* genre existed on the fringes of French Romanticism – a genre, indeed, which it is suggested here might even be central to the movement.

Despite the terminological uncertainty, the *frénétique* tendency of Romanticism would seem to have been widely recognised at the time. Balzac, writing a decade later in his preface (generally omitted from later editions) to *La Peau de Chagrin* (1831), refers to a literature of blood and buffoonery: *'De tous côtés, s'élèvent des doléances sur la couleur sanguinolente des écrits modernes. Les cruautés, les supplices, les gens jetés à la mer, les pendus, les gibets, les condamnés, les atrocités chaudes et froides, les bourreaux, tout est devenu bouffon!'* ['From every side there arise cries of anguish over the bloody nature of modern writing. Cruelty, torture, people being thrown into the sea, hangings, gibbets, men awaiting the sentence of death, atrocities committed in the heat of the moment or cold-bloodedly, everything has become buffoonery!']. Despite Balzac's condemnation of the violent nature of contemporary writing, *La Peau de Chagrin* itself is invested with identical values. Nor is it without interest to identify some of Balzac's literary allusions: the business of men and women being thrown into the sea, for example, is surely a reference to Eugène Sue's novel, *Atar-Gull* (1831), in the course of which a sailor, after being subject to a particularly brutal beating, is set adrift on the high seas in a raft with only a dead female Negro slave for company, while the reference to a man awaiting execution is, of course, a direct allusion to Victor Hugo's *Dernier Jour d'un condamné* (1829). Indeed, by casting his net so wide in the search for examples, Balzac implies that the preoccupation with horror, far from being a marginalised aspect of French Romanticism, might in fact be a central concern.

But even as late as 1853 we find commentators – in the following example a certain Hippolyte Castille – describing French horror writing of the 1820s and 1830s as variously *'la littérature cadavérique'*, *'la littérature enragée, paradoxale et lycanthropique'*, and *'la littérature succube'*. More significantly still, Castille blames this literature of twenty or thirty years earlier as being responsible for the sense of nihilism and disillusionment which was, in his eyes, in turn responsible for the various revolutions and uprisings (in particular those of 1830 and 1848) which so marked French history in the first half of the nineteenth century.

Although it is hardly possible to hold the *frénétique* (to use Nodier's term) responsible for revolutionary upheaval in the manner that Hippolyte Castille and other conservative commentators of the epoch would have us believe, the genre was none the less deeply imbrued with revolutionary and, on occasion, counter-revolutionary discourses. Indeed, the extent to which the *frénétique* provided a cultural vehicle susceptible of accommodating shifting ideologies is perhaps the principal reason for the confusion which surrounds the genre to this day. If this is so, the *frénétique* cannot be examined without reference to its social, theological and political context – a context largely typified by lack of consensus at all levels of society. The underlying cause of this was the double trauma of the French Revolution of 1789 and the collapse of the Napoleonic Empire. In political terms, this led to the emergence of, on the right, a powerful reactionary élite (fervently Catholic and pro-monarchical) and, on the left, miscellaneous groups of Bonapartists, Liberals and Republicans. Even after Napoleon's death in 1821, it is impossible to estimate the extent of support for the restored Bourbon monarchy, how many people still believed in the supposedly-discredited Jacobin ideal of popular sovereignty, or to what degree the myths and legends of the Napoleonic Empire were still cherished. Not surprisingly, the period between 1815 and 1823 is often characterised as an era of conspiracy. A decade later, after the Revolution of July 1830, a similar state of fragmentation prevailed.

In the early 1820s, the ultra-royalists were in the ascendancy, both politically and culturally. One *frénétique* author whose work exemplifies this tendency is the vicomte d'Arlincourt. In 1821, d'Arlincourt published *Le Solitaire*, an historical novel concerning Charles the Bold but set, somewhat perplexingly, some years after his presumed death at the battle of Nancy in 1477. In the course of the novel, Charles successfully woos the virtuous Elodie, but their union calls down celestial wrath. Stendhal wrote sarcastically of the 'inversive vicount' (after d'Arlincourt's habit of changing the normal word order so as to lend his writing an historical flavour), but *Le Solitaire* was undoubtedly one of the most successful novels of the decade and marks the beginning of the French preoccupation with the Middle Ages. It is, moreover, difficult to view the novel as anything other than a refusal to accept the political rehabilitation in the 1820s of former revolutionaries represented, in this case, by Charles the Bold, a fifteenth-century usurper. In this respect, it is worth remembering that d'Arlincourt's father and grandfather (both tax-collectors) fell victim to the Committee of Public Safety during the French Revolution and that the author himself continually returned to the theme of usurpation of power throughout his literary career and long after legitimism had become a spent force.

Despite his apparent contempt for the genre, Charles Nodier contributed to the development of the *frénétique* not only as a critic but also as a novelist. In 1818, he published *Jean Sbogar*, a novel with important ideological implications concerning a bandit who passes for a nobleman. Although such a novel is obviously derivative of Henri Zschökke's *Abällino, der grosse Bandit* of 1793 (which was translated into English by **MATTHEW LEWIS** as *The Bravo of Venice* in 1805), the political dimension of the work is peculiar to France. Thus, although notionally set in Illyria, the unstable political situation which is described might just as well be that of post-Revolutionary France. Indeed, Jean Sbogar is the leader of a revolutionary movement called the *Frères du bien commun* [Brothers of the Common Weal] which would seem to espouse the basic communist tenets propounded by Babeuf, the leader of a failed left-wing coup, who was executed in 1797. The resurgence of Babouvism after 1828 possibly goes some way to accounting for the continued interest of the reading public in *Jean Sbogar* later in the century. Two years later, in 1820, Nodier was responsible for a melodrama entitled *Le Vampire*, which played with some success at the Théâtre de la Porte Saint-Martin, and had a hand in a continuation of Polidori's famous novella entitled *Lord Ruthwen, ou les Vampires*, which though written by a certain Cyprien Bérard was credited to the author of *Jean Sbogar*. Once again, a rather conventional tale is used to make a number of pronouncements concerning the rights and duties of kingship and the benefits of consensus politics: '*un roi cruel ...; un ministre qui trahit la confiance de son maître et amène des révolutions terribles ...; tous ces êtres ... ne représentent-ils pas le vampirisme?*' ['a cruel king ...; a minister who betrays the trust bestowed on him by his master and is the cause of dreadful revolutions ...; do not all these beings ... represent a form of vampirism?']. Had Louis XVIII and his successor Charles X paid more heed to such advice, French political life in the latter part of the first third of the nineteenth century might have been less marked by revolution and rumours of revolution.

Nodier's contribution to the *frénétique* around this time is interesting, amongst other reasons, for the light it throws on the manner by which French authors manipulated such texts in order to explore mainly domestic matters. As the genre became more assured, the range of issues that the *frénétique* would explore, and the formal complexity of the means by which it would do so, steadily increased.

At the height of his popularity, d'Arlincourt was known as the 'prince des Romantiques'. By the early 1830s, his legitimist political convictions were already unfashionable (though this did not prevent him from writing a series of transparently political novels dealing with the theme of usurpation in the Middle Ages). In a sense, the most representative *frénétique* author of the 1830s was Pétrus Borel (1809–59), the self-styled lycanthrope. Although Borel was considered by some of his contemporaries as a likely rival to Victor Hugo in stature, his three principal works – *Rhapsodies* (1832), a collection of poetry; *Champavert. Contes immoraux* (1833), a collection of short stories; and a two-volume novel entitled *Madame Putiphar* (1839) – sold only modestly at the time of their first appearance. Although ideological considerations are never far from the surface of Borel's writing (*Champavert*, for example, is imbrued with a political analysis which would seem to derive from the revolutionary leader St-Just), they are particularly pronounced in *Madame Putiphar*, a work which may only be read as a violent attempt to desacrilize the *Ancient Régime* by means of a sustained attack on the perceived sexual promiscuity of the monarchy. Thus, much of the novel details the unwarranted sexual advances made to the heroine by Pharaon (i.e. Louis XV) and those of his mistress Madame Putiphar (i.e. Madame de Pompadour) to the hero. The latter part of the novel describes the unrelenting persecution of the virtuous hero and heroine after they spurn the royal advances which have been made to them.

Although Borel now enjoys a considerable reputation as a precursor of the avant-garde, especially with respect to French Surrealism, it is not without interest to note that Borel's principal works would seem to have been reprinted at times of tremendous unrest. Thus, *Champavert*, first published in 1833 (shortly after the Revolution of 1830), was reprinted in 1872 (a year after the Commune), 1922 and 1948 (in other words, shortly after two world wars), and in 1967 (during a period of student unrest). The later publication history of a number of *frénétique* novels would seem to follow a similar trajectory.

Unlike the English Gothic novel, the *frénétique* has given rise to few interpretative accounts. During the first half of the twentieth century, the *frénétique* was generally viewed as almost synonymous with the **ROMAN**

NOIR, or as a slightly later French extension of a quintessentially English tradition of horror writing. Reginald Hartland even entitled his 1928 pioneering study of the genre: *Walter Scott et le roman 'frénétique': Contribution à l'étude de leur fortune en France*. Indeed, according to Hartland, Scott – together with **HORACE WALPOLE**, Clara Reeve, Mrs **RADCLIFFE**, M. G. Lewis, Maturin, and **MARY SHELLEY** – exercised a decisive influence on the genre's development. When Hartland actually attempted to provide precise examples of the mysterious spell cast by the Gothic over the *frénétique*, however, the results tended to be inconclusive. Thus, writing of the vicomte d'Arlincourt's *Le Solitaire*, he claims: 'La part de Walpole et de Mme Radcliffe est considérable et facile à distinguer' (p. 88) ['The influence of Walpole and Mrs Radcliffe is considerable and easily detected']. None the less, the only example he finds to cite of this considerable influence is the fact that the heroine is an orphan and lives – like one of Mrs Radcliffe's orphans – in an old monastery.

Although Hartland overstates the case, the *frénétique*, at least initially, did have close links with the German **SCHAUERROMAN** and the late British Gothic novel. It is hardly coincidental that Nodier should have voiced his concept of a *frénétique* literature in a review of a German horror story first translated into French in 1795, at the height of the popularity of the Gothic in France, and further developed it in reviews of translations of such works as Maturin's *The Albigenses* in 1824.

The genre rapidly found an authentically French tone, however, such that all signs of foreign influence quickly became expunged. Consequently, more recent commentators have been keen to stress the links between the *frénétique* and French Romanticism. Indeed, a number of the genre's best-known exponents – including Pétrus Borel, Charles Lassailly (whose one tremendous novel of pessimism and despair, *Les Roueries de Trialph, notre contemporain avant son suicide*, appeared in 1833), Roger de Beauvoir, Alphonse Royer, and Xavier Forneret – are generally discussed, if at all, under the slightly dismissive heading *'petits Romantiques'* ['minor Romantics']. This highlights the far from unproblematic relation of the *frénétique* with French Romanticism. Ignored and deprecated by the classical literary élite and later disowned by the French Romantic movement (who were, indeed, largely responsible for it) in the course of the struggle for ascendancy over the Classicists, the *frénétique* was doubly marginalised from the outset. In its heyday from about 1820 to 1836, however, the *frénétique* represented an important cultural phenomenon. So much so, indeed, that certain major texts of the Romantic period might properly be considered as manifestations of the genre (e.g. Victor Hugo's *Notre-Dame de Paris*, 1831; or, as was suggested earlier, Balzac's *La Peau de Chargrin*).

By 1837, the *frénétique* was on the wane in France and after that date it quickly became subsumed in the French serial novel (or *roman feuilleton*). Indeed, one of the first successful serial novels – *Les Mémoires du Diable* (1837–8) – was written by an author – Frédéric Soulié – who had begun the decade as a novelist of the *frénétique* school. After the European success of *Les Mystères de Paris* (1842–3) by Eugène Sue (another *feuilletoneist*, incidentally, who won his spurs on the *frénétique*), a number of examples of the *roman frénétique* were translated into English. These included Jules Janin's *L'Ane mort et la femme guillotinée* (1829; trans. 1851), Sue's *Atar-Gull* (1831; trans. 1841), and *La Salamandre* (1832; trans. 1845). It is perhaps not insignificant to note that the first (and almost only) critical survey in English to discuss some of the writers mentioned above (*The Modern Literature of France*, 2 vols, 1839) was by the future writer of serial fiction and Chartist G. W. M. Reynolds, who was also responsible for a translation of Hugo's *The Last Day of a Condemned Man* in 1840. It is possible that the Republican sentiments typical of *frénétique* writing in the early 1830s met with the approval of the increasingly politicised English working class in mid-nineteenth-century Britain.

TERRY HALE

German Gothic

The concept of 'Gothic' and 'Gothicism' originated in the Renaissance in Italian architectural theory. Since the beginning of the eighteenth century it has come to be used continuously in matters of taste in Britain and in the final decades in America, too. Beginning with the second edition of **HORACE WALPOLE**'s *The Castle of Otranto* (1764), it served to define a new genre, the **GOTHIC NOVEL**. Although there are manifold reciprocal correlations between the Gothic Novel in Britain and its equivalent in Germany, it is only recently that the term '*gotischer Roman*' has been accepted by German scholars working in the field of English and American literature and that the notion of a German Gothic (novel) has been – successfully – introduced by scholars like Michael Hadley from Anglo-America. Horace Walpole was an expert and opinion leader in all questions relating to the arts and their appreciation in his times, he knew what he was doing. The meanings connected with the term 'Gothic' in England were 'uncouth', 'primitive', 'medieval', 'bloody', 'highly emotional' and 'sexually more explicit than or deviant from normal'. In Germany the term '*gotisch*' had a more positive quality. It was reminiscent of an early phase of the national ancestry, the Old Germanic tribes and their migrations, whereas in Italy *gotico* referred to the Middle Ages as an epoch under the barbaric influence of Northern invaders. The Renaissance then was understood as a retrieval of the heritage of Roman antiquity. It was only with the widespread acceptance of the (neo-)Gothic style in the last decades of the eighteenth century that 'Gothic' was seen as positive, as Walpole had intended it by setting it in opposition to the Neoclassicism of his age. The categories under which what may be classified as 'Gothic literature' was discussed in eighteenth-century Germany related – in a more or less derogatory sense – to those elements of the texts which set them most obviously apart from the preceding Novel of Sensibility (*'Empfindsamkeit'*). Thus the German corollary to 'Gothic' was *'Ritter-, Räuber- und* **SCHAUERROMAN**' and it referred (a) to mediaeval knighthood and the historical element, (b) to robbers as primitive rebels against a corrupt feudal society, who live close to nature, and (c), above all, to the new momentum of an aesthetic of effect shown by all these texts, to a partly mysterious, partly excessive object world conveying all sorts of emotional thrills (*'Schauer'*).

In Germany, Gothic literature was considered an illegitimate offspring, especially in official literary criticism. Thus the first book to give a serious comprehensive overview of this composite genre came rather late: it was J. W. Appell's *Die Ritter-, Räuber- und Schauerromantik*, 1859). This book looks back upon Germany's mass-reading public around 1800 under the impression of the sweeping success of mass literature ever since, and the present mid-nineteenth-century impact of the works of Sue and Dumas in France and the rest of Europe. Appell admires those two writers but regrets their influence from a moral and aesthetic (*'taste'*) point of view. He stands within the tradition of a dichotomy of literary/artistic evaluation which separates so-called 'high-standard' from 'trivial' texts. Inadvertently, Appell provides instances which prove that such a dichotomy ignores the fact that a multiplicity of functional relations between texts across those two levels has taken place. Thus he admits that even the 'great' works of Goethe and Schiller contain *'Schauer* etc.' elements. And he points out that the early works of these writers, above all Schiller's drama *Die Räuber* and Goethe's drama *Götz von Berlichingen*, provided *the* inspiration for those mass-produced works he feels obliged to denounce. In fact, the turn towards Gothicism, i.e. the break with the literature of the Enlightenment and of sensibility, which is called **'STURM UND DRANG'** in German literary criticism, occurred mainly in drama (with the exception of Goethe's novel *Die Leiden des jungen Werthers* (1774) which had been an international success). Doubtlessly these dramas blazed the trail for the reception of the new literature, which could be produced for an extended reading public in amounts hitherto unknown. The effect of those German texts was enhanced by the reception of English literature, especially 'Ossian's' (Macpherson's) works and the renewed interest in Shakespeare's dramas (*Macbeth, Hamlet*).

Before that, the British literature of Pre-Romanticism had already been an enormous influence on **GOETHE** and Schiller. This is not surprising as the functional historical preconditions for the emergence of the German Gothic were very similar to those in Britain. This genre tries to provide 'answers' to the crisis of the early eighteenth-century ('Enlightenment') model of reality and society which, through the medium of literary texts – can be received as (1) individual (2) aesthetic experience. Significant socio-structural changes had occurred since the 1760s as the beginning Industrial Age, the American struggle for independence and the French Revolution indicate. Nature could no longer be seen as a huge machine working according to the laws of reason. The new model of reality and society which emerged from literary, artistic and cultural activities may be circumscribed as the aesthetic of the 'Picturesque and the Sublime', which saw (1) nature in the shape of landscape, and (2) history as being enacted in that landscape, as its privileged objects. And these objects were presented as offering themselves for intense psycho-physical experience, which implied the experience of a hidden transcendental sphere beyond the empirical. The Gothic Novel, which came into existence around 1790 and which became so successful with the newly emerging mass audience, strove to extend the repertoire of aesthetic detail on the one hand but, on the other hand, conventionalised and repeated it as long as it was effective. The aspect of transcendence, however, was in almost all cases, treated in terms of orthodox Christian religion.

Otto Rommel defines the German Gothic as a *'rationalistische Dämonie* (rationalist demonic)'. Typically, German Gothic Novels conclude with, at least, the suggestion of meaningful, rational forces behind all the turmoil and they advise the individual to take back his/her individualistic ambitions and live in quiet acceptance of the reasonable designs of a benevolent providential power. The authors of those texts came mainly from the Protestant states and provinces in Middle, Eastern and Northern Germany, and there they found the majority of their mass audiences, too. In terms of professional status, 71 of the 97 known authors – according to Meusel – were clergymen (22%), civil servants (20%), independent (18%), teachers (11%), academics, professors, doctors, lawyers, actors/directors (4% each), writers, booksellers (3% each), and one officer. Important preconditions for the new type of literature were the introduction of obligatory school education around the middle of the eighteenth century, improved printing techniques, and improved means of distribution, especially the new circulating libraries.

The Gothic Novel in Germany ('*Schauerroman*'), similarly to its equivalent in Britain, developed a repertoire of events, situations, props, features of landscape, character and action, which made it possible for authors and readers to share common experiences, fears and traumata. By drawing on folklore traditions, which had been retrieved through Johann Karl August Musäus's collection *Volksmaerchen der Deutschen* (1782–7) and Benedikte Naubert's and Johann Mathias Müller's *Neue Volksmärchen der Deutschen* (4 vols, 1789–93), German writers were able to do this in a particularly crass way, a fact that fascinated **M. G. LEWIS** when he toured Germany as a nineteen-year-old. He made wide use of this in *The Monk* (1796), thus triggering off a new stage of Gothicism in Britain, including a wave of translations from the most successful German writers. Another German speciality is the '*Räuberroman*', which features Gothic banditti and 'primitive rebels' (E. Hobsbawm). The most famous of these texts was *Rinaldo Rinaldini* (Leipzig, 1798) by Christian August Vulpius, the brother of Goethe's lifelong concubine. It was translated into English within 14 months of its first appearance. Equally successful was Heinrich Zschokke's *Aballino, der grosse Bandit* (1793), which was translated as *The Bravo of Venice* by M. G. Lewis in 1805. Unique to the German Gothic is also what Thalmann has called *bundesroman*, meaning novels which deal with secret societies of the Masonic type; however, mostly of a criminal nature with an emissary or a genius in the background. This sub-genre follows a pattern set by Schiller's fragmentary novel *Der Geisterseher* (1784).

Although the decisive criterion that sets the 'Gothic Novel' apart from preceding genres is the 'aesthetic of effect', as a means of relating individual experience with the new ('picturesque and sublime') model of reality and society, literary criticism has accepted several sub-divisions of this genre according to the fictional casts and environments through which this is enacted. The Canadian scholars Michel Hadley and Manfred W. Heiderich classify the German Gothic Novel as follows:

I   *Novels of Mystery*: A Rationalised Spirits; B. Secret Societies ('*Bundesroman*'); C. Purgatorial Spirits ('*Erlösungsromane*'); D. Other Spirits.
II *Historical Gothic* ('*Ritterroman*').
III *Novels of Banditry* ('*Räuberroman*').

Other popular genres, contemporaneous with but outside the scope of the Gothic, are the 'Satirical Novel' ('*Satirischer Roman*'), the 'Novel of Love and Adventure' ('*Liebes und Abenteurroman*'), the 'Novel of Character and Education' ('*Bildungsroman*'), and the 'Historical Novel' ('*Geschichtsroman*' or '*Historischer Roman*').

The most significant texts in the field of German Gothic (1790–1815) are, in alphabetical order:

Arnold, Ignaz Ferdinand: *Das Bildnis mit den Blutflecken, eine Geister-geschichte nach einer wahren Anekdote* (1800) (= category I.A); *Die doppelte Ursulinernonne, aus den Papieren des Grafen R*** mit der aschgrauen Maske* (1800) (= category I.A); *Miraculoso, der Schreckensbund der Illuminaten* (1802) (= category I.B).

Bornschein, Johann Ernst Daniel: *Moritz Graf von Protokas, das Leben eines Geistersehers* (1799); *Der Beichtstuhl, eine wahre schaudervolle Begebenheit des 18, Jahrhunderts* (1802); *Das Nordhäusische Wundermädchen, ein weiblicher Rinaldini; eine romantische Geschichte* (1802) (= cat. I.B, II, III).

Cramer, Karl Gottlob: *Adolph der Kühne, Raugraf von Dassel* (1792); *Hasper a Spada. Eine Sage aus dem 13. Jahrhundert* (1792–3) (= cat. II).

Gleich, Joseph Alois: *Jetta, die schöne Zauberin oder der Wolfsbrunn* (1797) (= cat. I.C); *Die dreyhundertjährige Wandlerin nach dem Tode oder die häßliche Schönheit* (1800) (= cat. I.C).

Grosse, Karl: *Der Genius. Aus den Papieren des Marquis C* von G** (1791–94) (= cat. I.B).

Rambach, Friedrich Eberhard (pseudonym: Ottokar Sturm): *Die eiserne Maske, eine schottische Geschichte* (1792) (= cat. II).

Schlenkert, Friedrich Christian: *Friedrich mit der gebissenen Wange. Eine dialogisierte Geschichte* (1787–8) (= cat. II).

Spieß, Christian Heinrich: *Das Petermaennchen. Eine Geistergeschichte aus dem 13. Jahrhundert* (1793) (= cat. I.D); *Die strahlende Jungfrau oder der Berggeist. Eine Zaubergeschichte* (posth. 1800) (= cat. I.D).

Vulpius, Christian August: *Rinaldo Rinaldini der Raeuberhauptmann. Eine romantische Geschichte unseres Jahrhunderts* (1798) (= cat. III).

Wächter, Georg Philip Ludwig Leonhard (pseudonym:. Veit Weber): *Sagen der Vorzeit*, 7 vols (1787–98) (= cat. I and II).

Zschökke, Heinrich: *Abällino der grosse Bandit* (1793) (= cat. III).

So far, the German Gothic Novel seems to have existed mainly on the level of mass-produced texts. There is, however, the 'high-standard author' Ludwig Tieck, who had been asked by his teacher Rambach to write the last chapter of *Die eiserne Maske*. Later, Tieck wrote the novel *William Lovell* and tales like *Der blonde Eckbert*, which use folkloristic and supernatural material but go considerably beyond Rambach's writings. Likewise, **E. T. A. HOFFMANN**'s novel *Die Elixiere des Teufels* (1815–16), which is to an extent modelled upon M. G. Lewis's *The Monk* (1795), and most of his many phantastic and uncanny writings, may be bracketed under German Gothicism. The appearance of Mephisto in Goethe's *Faust* or of Gothic elements in Jean Paul's *Titan* (1800) would make such texts also cases in point. Nevertheless, in all those last-mentioned texts there is no longer the 'rationalist demonic' of the '*Schauerroman*' but the aesthetic of what one may call 'High Romanticism', for which the Gothic now appears in the subservient role of providing (1) an inventory of objects and situations and (2) the orientation of an aesthetic of effect. The Gothic is now only an element, though still a very important one, of the high-romanticist thorough and in-depth probing of man's psycho-physical relationship with what he considers the external world: here the momentum of the Sublime and of transcendence goes beyond a 'rational-ist demonic'. In England **MARY SHELLEY**'s *Frankenstein* (1818) as well as **CHARLES MATURIN**'s *Melmoth the Wanderer* (1820) show similar aspects. They, too, are Gothic (only) in an eclectic or more indirect sense which is different from and more complex than what was written in the 1790s and up to 1815.

Around 1820 a significant decline of Gothic literature occurs, although these texts continue – with modifications and with adaptations to the expectations of the readers – to be written and read until our age. The spectrum of the novel was now more differentiated. After that date Gothic elements were still used but not as directly, and with relativisa-tions. The inheritors of the Gothic tradition are, above all, the Historical Novel, the Novel of Crime and Mystery, the Political Novel, the Phantastic Tale. The genre dominating the succession up to 1850 was the Historical Novel, a development which sprang from the Gothic mélange but which then had shaken off the supernatural effects and trappings (see **HISTORICO-GOTHIC**). It owed most of its success to Walter Scott's works. A look at these texts reveals the reasons for this change: a different sense of history had emerged in reaction to the experience of the Napoleonic era, it is part of a new model of reality and society which is a modification of the former 'Picturesque and Sublime'.

HANS-ULRICH MOHR

Ghost Stories

Ghosts, like the poor, have always been with us, although their overtly fictional appearance was fitful until the eighteenth century. Even then the ghost rarely had an agenda of its own and was most often at the mercy of an elaborate and impossible plot (as with the gigantic ghost of Alfonso in **HORACE WALPOLE**'s *The Castle of Otranto*). Once freed from the strictly Gothic embrace – a liberation that can be dated from

'Wandering Willie's Tale' in Scott's *Redgauntlet* of 1824 – the ghost story gradually evolved into the distinct form that it has retained to the present day. The essence of this form is that the plot shall revolve around the doings of the returning dead and the interaction between them and those among the living who, wittingly or unwittingly, but almost always disastrously, encounter them.

Throughout the nineteenth and for much of the twentieth century, the setting of the ghost story has often paralleled that of the **GOTHIC NOVEL**: much use is made of the gloomy, isolated and decaying country house, and of dark, misty churchyards and their heaving graves. But in structure and content it is a very different genre. The ghost story is *Super* natural: it is truly the dead who return, and there is no place for rational explanation by nature or by artifice. Nor is there any place for 'raw head and bloody bones'; the stories – if they are to succeed in their aim of bringing real fear to the reader – must work by understatement, subtly impressing the reader with a horror of the spirit. In the work of the best writers of the genre this is achieved by creating believable characters and settings: the protagonists of the stories of, for example, **J. SHERIDAN LE FANU, M. R. JAMES**, E. F. Benson or Robert Aickman could be (or could have been) our own friends and relatives.

It is also difficult successfully to sustain the necessary tension of the ghost story to the required length of a novel, and the (relatively) short story remains the most appropriate literary form for the genre – as was recognised by authors as diverse as **CHARLES DICKENS**, Elizabeth Gaskell, Hugh Walpole and Edith Wharton. Among the rare exceptions are **HENRY JAMES**'s 'The Turn of the Screw' (in *The Two Magics* (1898) and Susan Hill's *The Woman in Black* (1983)). Perhaps the latter succeeds because women are allegedly more sensitive than are men to mood and atmosphere; or perhaps not, but women have unquestionably made a disproportionate contribution to the genre throughout its history. Why this should be so remains an unanswered question. Mrs Crowe, Rhoda Broughton, Violet Paget ('Vernon Lee') and their contemporaries may have written about the margins of the visible because they were themselves on the margins of society, but this cannot be said of, for example, Violet Hunt, Elizabeth Jane Howard or Penelope Lively.

The ghost story raises other questions also; why are they written and why are they read? The simplest, but admittedly inadequate answer, is that such stories provide us with a means of evading the larger, and infinitely more unpleasant, issue of death and what may lie beyond it.

R. A. GILBERT

Goethe, Johann Wolfgang von (1749–1832)

English Romantics and American Gothics might be forgiven for homonymous confusion of Goethe with Gothic (G*th*): Goethe's mentor, Herder, once angered Goethe by playfully rhyming the etymology of his name with gods (*Götter*), **GOTHS** (*Gothen*), and excrement (*Kote*). More than most writers, Goethe wrote in tonalities, Classicism being his major key, Gothic one of his minor ones. In fact, the older Goethe was famous for referring to Classicism as healthy, Romanticism as pathological. Nevertheless, in the English-speaking world, Goethe's reception has been largely Romantic, and three works – *Die Leiden des jungen Werthers* (*The Sorrows of Young Werther* (1774), *Faust* (1808, 1832), and the ballad *Die Braut von Corinth* (1797) – have proved crucial to the Gothic agenda. Based on the Greek legend of Lamia, *The Bride of Corinth* re-introduced the female vampire into modern European literature. Werther, the title hero of the monster's favourite book, is himself a psychological Frankenstein. In his alchemical, supernatural, and otherwise illicit attempts at transcendence, Faust is the archetypal figure of 'Dark Romanticism'; the diabolical Faustian bargain – the 'choice to be damned' (Leslie Fiedler) – is at the enstaked heart of the Gothic plot.

As the chief proponent of the 1770s literary movement **STURM UND DRANG** (Storm and Stress), the young Goethe anticipated many of the features to be later associated with the Gothic and Romantic. Throughout his nature poetry, he externalised landscapes of the imagination. In *Zum SchäkespearsTag* (*Shakespeare: A Tribute*, 1771), he responded enthusiastically to Shakespeare's titanism and waved good-bye to the classical conventions of the theatre. In *Von deutscher Baukunst* (*On German Architecture*, 1772), he analysed Gothic architecture while climbing the Strasburg minster tower (despite his fear of heights). In his blockbuster tragedy *Götz von Berlichingen* (1773), he nostalgically explored the demise of a medieval world, while unleashing, down through Walter Scott, a mania for knightly sagas. His musical *Claudine von Villa Bella* (1775) set the stage for a robber and bandit mystique that persisted from Schiller's *The Robbers* (1781) to Bizet's opera *Carmen*. After 1775, Goethe settled into an extraordinarily long existence as a cultural icon at Weimar, where a visit or audience became a literary rite of passage for a steady stream of writers such as **MATTHEW LEWIS**.

Goethe's best-selling novel *The Sorrows of Young Werther* appeared in 1774 and made both author and character world-famous. Seeing no way out of a love triangle, Werther commits a well-staged suicide, choosing, in effect, the infinity of death over the limitedness of life. Not just the graveyard atmospherics, two other features ooze Gothicness. In the course of the novel, nature becomes a destructive, life-devouring monster: 'My heart is wasted by the thought of that destructive power that lies latent in every part of universal Nature ... The universe to me is an all-consuming, devouring monster.' And the novel is the missing link in a remarkable example of Gothic intertextuality. In his reading, Werther turns from Homer to Ossian – which Goethe himself translated, not yet realising the extent of James Macpherson's Neo-Gaelic, Neo-Gothic forgeries. In fact, a reading of that translation substitutes for climax in the relationship between Werther and Lotte: 'They felt their own fate in the misfortunes of Ossian's heroes – felt this together, and merged their tears.' Mary Shelley's monster shares their empathic methodology of reading, yet it awakens in the monster a self-awareness of his own lack of identity, origin, and future: 'But I thought Werter [sic] himself a more divine being than I had ever beheld or imagined ... My person was hideous, and my stature gigantic: what did this mean? Who was I? What was I? Whence did I come? What was my destination? ... I learned from Werter's imaginations despondency and gloom.' Werther's personality defines for the monster the Gothic psyche of despair.

Many of Goethe's ballads are ghost stories, the most famous of which, *Erlkönig* (*The Elf-King*, 1782), was set to pathos-intensive music by Schubert. Set against a stormy nightscape and on horseback, the ballad depicts the conversations between a fevered child, his desperate father, and the seductive invitations of death in the guise of the elf-king. The haunting ballad ends with the child dead in his father's arms (one of a wombful of dead babies in Goethe's works). In his journals, Goethe referred to the *Braut von Corinth* (1797) as his 'vampire poem'. Indeed, it is one of the seminal poetic manifestations of the **VAMPIRE** after the re-emergence of the figure from Eastern Europe (Serbia) after 1732. A dead sister returns from the grave to prevent her promised bridegroom from marrying her younger, living sister (Herder's synopsis: 'A pagan *priapises* to warm life the cold corpse of the ghost of his Christian bride'). Emphatic in its blood-sucking, the ballad is original in its explicitly erotic treatment of the vampire attack (necrophilia) and its threat of a spread of this plague unless the corpse is burnt:

Aus dem Grab werd' ich ausgetrieben,
Noch zu suchen das vermißte Gut,
Noch den schon verlornen Mann zu lieben,
Und zu saugen seines Herzens Blut.
Ist's um den geschehen,
Muß nach andern gehn,
Und das junge Volk erliegt der Wut!

From my grave betimes I have been driven,
I seek the good I lost, none shall me thwart
I seek his love to whom my troth was given,
And I have sucked the lifeblood from his heart.
If he dies, I will
Find me others still
With my fury tear young folk apart.
                              (tr. Christopher Middleton)

The ballad is expressly Gothic, too, in its setting in a world still in transition between pagan and Christian conceptions of the supernatural. It
has been widely attacked as blasphemous, and just as widely imitated,
notably in Coleridge's *Christabel* and Keats's own *Lamia*.

No matter how it is read, Goethe's *Faust* (Part I: 1790/1808; Part II:
1832) has proved his most influential work, and it suffices to list its most
cogent Gothic features. Faust's 'Gothic' study and laboratory is the
setting for heretical and alchemical experiments that include the conjuring of spirits (the Earth spirit) and the production of artificial life in the
form of a homunculus. With his own blood, Faust seals a pact with the
devil, Mephistopheles, who leads him on a supernatural journey from
witch's kitchen to witches' Sabbath. In one diabolical version that Goethe
himself ultimately censored, this *Walpurgisnacht* includes the appearance
of Satan himself, the anointing of a goat's anus with a procession of
kisses, and a 'sexual orgy'. Even uncensored, *Faust* (and the company
of spirits he keeps) is the most profound study of **THE DEMONIC** in
Western literature. Harold Bloom has called it 'the most grotesque
masterpiece of Western poetry ... a vast, cosmological satyr-play'; he
also refers specifically to *Faust II* as 'the grandest monster movie ever
directed at us ..., where Mephistopheles becomes the most imaginative
of all vampires'. The classical *Walpurgisnacht* depicts an imaginary landscape in which Goethe's imagination runs wild; he focuses not on the
Greek gods, but on a pantheon of Greek monsters: the witch Erichtho,
sphinxes, sirens, griffins, giant ants, lamiae, and the phorcyads (primeval
witches who share one eye and one tooth) among them. Even Mephisto
has his problems with Goethe's Southern Gothic: 'I have no trouble
handling Northern witches, / but these strange phantoms leave me
flabberghasted.' There is no telling what might have happened if
Frankenstein's monster had read not *Werther*, but *Faust*. While great por-
tions of Goethe's *oeuvre* and reception are classical, organic, and
scientific, his imagination is Gothic writ large.

Eric Hadley Denton

Gothic Architecture *see* Gothic Revival

Gothic Drama

While scholars have found Gothic elements in dramas ranging from Euripides to 'slasher' films, the Gothic drama proper arose, prospered, and declined in the latter eighteenth and early nineteenth centuries. The Gothic drama, while now given little attention, was at the time as popular and as powerful a form as the **GOTHIC NOVEL**, with key Gothic novelists (for example, see **MATTHEW LEWIS, CHARLES MATURIN**) better known as dramatists, and with the Romantic poets (for example, see **PERCY SHELLEY**) drawing upon Gothic plays. The importance of the Gothic drama can be seen in the fact that it first staged the powerful modern myths of the **VAMPIRE** and the Frankenstein monster (see **MARY SHELLEY**), that it offered a meeting point between 'high' and 'low' culture, and that it was in many ways the most success-ful dramatic form of its day in its ability to negotiate contemporary generic, institutional, and ideological tensions.

While there is more variety to the Gothic drama than is sometimes granted, there are some recognisably standard devices. There are almost cliché settings: the gloomy castle, the forbidding wood, the corrupt convent. There are often stereotypical characters: the brooding aristocrat, marked by some secret in his past; the young lovers, often princes or princesses in disguise; comic servants, nurses, and friars. One way of mapping Gothic plays is to see them moving from an enclosed space such as a castle, dominated by an aristocratic tyrant, into a liberated open space where the lovers can be united with the help of comic underlings. One can also see this action as a struggle between a tragic plot centring around the inward-turned villain-hero who was soon to be called the Byronic hero and a comic plot in which the villain-hero is reduced to an old man blocking the union of the young lovers. What is clear is that the Gothic drama was a mixed form, drawing upon varying dramatic types and using a wide range of theatrical techniques.

HORACE WALPOLE, credited as the creator of the Gothic novel in his *Castle of Otranto* (1764), also wrote what is generally considered to be the first Gothic drama, *The Mysterious Mother* (1768). While elements of the Gothic drama have been traced back through other mid-eighteenth-century plays such as Home's *Douglas* (1756) to the works of Otway, Southerne, and Lee, and on to Elizabethan and particularly **JACOBEAN DRAMA**, even Walpole's play produced few immediate imitators. The

Gothic drama came into its own only in the 1790s, after the publication of **ANN RADCLIFFE**'s first novel, *The Castles of Athlin and Dunbayne* (1789), had spurred interest in the Gothic, after the enlargement of London's patent theatres royal created a demand for the grand, sensationalist style of the Gothic, and after the fall of the Bastille gave standard elements of Gothic drama – the forbidding castle, the struggle between an aristocrat and a woman of apparently lower-class status, robber bands – a new ideological charge.

While the Gothic drama should not be seen as a mere stepchild of the Gothic novel, many Gothic plays were, in fact, dramatisations of novels, with *The Castle of Otranto* being dramatised by Robert Jephson as *The Count of Narbonne* (Covent Garden, 1781); with Radcliffe's novels being adapted by James Boaden (*Fountainville Forest*, Covent Garden, 1794; *The Italian Monk*, Haymarket, 1797), Miles Peter Andrews (*The Mysteries of the Castle*, Covent Garden, 1795), and Henry Siddons (*The Sicilian Romance*, Covent Garden, 1794); with Lewis's *The Monk* being staged by Boaden as *Aurelio and Miranda* (Drury Lane, 1798); and with William Godwin's *Caleb Williams* being offered by George Colman as *The Iron Chest* (Drury Lane, 1796). At the end of the Gothic drama's popularity, Mary Shelley's *Frankenstein* would be first brought to the stage by Richard Brinsley Peake as *Presumption; or, The Fate of Frankenstein* (English Opera House, 1823). Some of the best Gothic playwrights were also novelists; Matthew Lewis, for example, was the author of the extremely popular *Castle Spectre* (Drury Lane, 1797) as well as such Gothic plays as *Adelmorn, the Outlaw* (Drury Lane, 1801), *Rugantino; or, The Bravo of Venice* (Covent Garden, 1805), and *The Wood Daemon; or, 'The Clock has struck'* (Drury Lane, 1807). In many ways, it was the Gothic drama rather than the novel that defined the contemporary popularity of the Gothic and that engaged such key writers as Byron, Shelley, and Joanna Baillie.

Whatever the links of the Gothic drama to the novel, it is still important to examine it as primarily a dramatic and theatrical form, dealing with particular generic and institutional problems. The Gothic drama arose at a moment when an increase in the size of Covent Garden and Drury Lane and an increase in the competition coming from so-called 'minor' theatres forced the major theatres to seek new forms and new stage practices. There was also a crisis within the hierarchy of forms, as contemporary observers doubted whether traditional forms such as tragedy and the comedy of manners could still hold the stage. While ultimately it would be the melodrama – first introduced onto the London stage in Thomas Holcroft's vaguely Gothic *Tale of Mystery* (Covent Garden, 1802) – that would come to be the dominant form in the London theatres, during the 1790s the Gothic drama provided a vehicle for merging serious drama with popular stage techniques. The Gothic drama, particularly when it focused upon the villain-hero, the charismatic but tortured and violent aristocrat at the centre of most of these plays, seemed to offer a new kind of tragedy, but it was one that drew upon other forms (comedy, romance, opera) and that importantly drew upon new popular stage practices, particularly those linked to a theatre of sensation and shock.

Despite its both traditional and popular connections, the Gothic drama was still controversial, as can be seen in the *Anti-Jacobin's* satiric *The Rovers* (1798), which attacked the Gothic drama as undermining social, political, moral, and religious order, or in Coleridge's review of *Bertram* where he called the Gothic 'the modern jacobinical drama'. Such statements indicate the radical potential of the Gothic drama as, in the era of the fall of the Bastille, it staged over and again successful assaults upon crumbling castles and convents, icons of a decaying old regime, and as, in the era of Napoleon, it asked audiences to applaud for titanic villain-heroes. Still, in general, the Gothic drama offers a rather mixed ideological message, now sympathising with its aristocratic hero-villains as it sees their destruction as a tragic loss of power, now siding with the young lovers who escape a dying past ruled by a brooding aristocrat to celebrate a liberation from an *ancien régime* that could be identified with the Revolution itself, but finally containing both the tragedy of the villain-hero and the revolutionary romance of the young lovers within a comic movement to restore domesticity – a turn to marriage and to the traditional values often voiced by the comic servants of the plays.

This turn to traditional family structures and values as a solution to social and cultural problems suggests the ultimate victory within the nineteenth-century theatre of the domestic melodrama over the Gothic drama. As the stages came to be filled with tales of everyday woes relieved only by an adherence to a conventional domesticity, the Gothic drama turned from libertine aristocrats and liberating lovers who might overturn conventional orders, to monsters – the creature of Peake's dramatisation of *Frankenstein*, the vampire of Planché's *The Vampyre* (English Opera House, 1820) – which threaten to invade the domestic order. The sensationalism and extremism of the Gothic drama survives to this day in the horror movie, but where the Gothic drama used to evoke titanic human figures threatening to shatter traditional order, its inheritors have sought to redefine such threats as the criminal, the monstrous and the inhuman, in the face of which we gladly return to conventional roles and limits.

JEFFREY N. COX

Gothic Film

The culturally prevalent form of the modern Gothic has been manifested most strongly in film. Cinema has embraced the Gothic as a popular text, its elements continually being employed and reinvented across a myriad of productions such as *Frankenstein* (1931), *Rebecca* (1940), *The Beguiled* (1971), *The Terminator* (1986) and *Toy Story* (1995). The Gothic in film is a form that has been generically mobile, repeatedly hybridising and mutating. Attempts to present a sufficiently expansive consideration of the Gothic film have been obstructed by its omniformity, with writers consequently preferring to examine specific divisions – the Hollywood monster movies of the 1930s and 1940s, the horror films of Hammer, the cycle of 1940s persecuted-women films and the dystopian visions of tech noirs.

In 1896, a year before **BRAM STOKER**'s *Dracula*, the French trick film-maker George Méliès released *Le Manoir Du Diable*, a vampire short. In a vaulted room, witches magically appear and disappear and a cloaked figure who is able to transform from a bat, vanishes in a cloud of smoke when shown the sign of the cross. This was one of the earliest Gothic films and Méliès was to repeatedly explore the form in later productions: *La Phrénologie Burlesque* (1901), *L'Auberge du Bon Repos* (1903), and *Le Monstre* (1903).

Early cinema was drawn to adaptations of literature and stage productions, with Gothic Novels employed by a number of films. Thomas Edison's *Frankenstein* (1910) was the first attempt to film **MARY SHELLEY**'s novel. Promoted as a 'liberal adaptation of Mrs Shelley's tale', the short story presented Frankenstein successfully creating his monster through chemical mixtures and the use of a cauldron. By 1921, at least nine versions of **ROBERT LOUIS STEVENSON**'s *Dr Jekyll and Mr Hyde* had been produced by countries such as Britain, Germany, Denmark and America. **EDGAR ALLAN POE** was also popular. The French film *Le Système du Docteur Goudron et du Professeur Plume* (1912) was based on Poe's short story *The System of Dr Tarr and Professor Feather*, *The Avenging Conscience* (1914) was an adaptation of *The Tell-Tale Heart*, while Fritz Lang's film *Die Pest in Florenz* (1919) was adapted from *The Masque of the Red Death*.

Despite these films being frequently referred to as *Gothique* or *Fantastique*, a generic identity for the Gothic film was not to be established until the early 1930s, with the production of the Hollywood monster movies. *Dracula* (1931) was based on the play by Hamilton Deane and John L. Balderston, which had recently experienced a successful theatrical run. The film proved tremendously popular at the box-office and together with Universal's other Gothic horror of the same year, *Frankenstein*, was influential in establishing a new direction for the horror film. Many Hollywood monster movies followed in essentially two main production periods, 1931 to 1936 and 1939 to 1948. The number of horror films produced between these periods significantly decreased, largely through their reception in foreign markets (especially in Britain where many of these films were criticised and awarded an 'H' certificate, for 'horrific').

Universal was the most notable producer of these Hollywood horrors, although this should not overshadow recognition of the output of other major studios: MGM's *Freaks* (1932), *Mad Love* (1935) and *Mark of the Vampire* (1935), Warner Brothers' *Mystery of the Wax Museum* (1933) and *The Beast with Five Fingers* (1946), Columbia's *The Black Room* (1935), and Paramount's *Dr Jekyll and Mr Hyde* (1931) and *Island of Lost Souls* (1932). Some of the many independently produced Gothic horrors were also stirring and imaginative, such as First National's synthetic flesh horror *Doctor X* (1931), and Amusement Securities' *White Zombie* (1933).

These films removed America from the stories of horror, with the locations frequently presented as foreign: Paris for *Murders in the Rue Morgue* (1931), Egypt for *The Mummy* (1932), Austria for *The Black Cat* (1934), and Cambodia for *Revolt of the Zombies* (1936). A significant number of filmmakers working on these horror productions had fled Nazi Germany and were able to re-employ their ideas for the Hollywood monster movies. Sets were oppressive and excessive, reflecting the influence of the earlier German expressionist films. *Son of Frankenstein* (1939) is a striking example of the dramatic function of the *mise-en-scène*. Dark and brooding, the film is dominated by shadows and imposing architecture. Frankenstein's creature is discovered in a vault and revived. An assistant, Ygor, driven by revenge, uses the creature to destroy the individuals who, through an unsuccessful hanging, left him with a broken neck. The police inspector also hides a tormented past; he carries a false arm, as a substitute for the one that was ripped out in an earlier encounter with the creature.

As Rhona J. Berenstein has observed in her book *Attack of the Leading Ladies*, many of the films were promoted as Gothic romances, with love existing amidst the death and tragedy. The posters for *Dr Jekyll and Mr Hyde* (1931) described it as 'A Great Love Story', while *Dracula* (1931) which was to open at American theatres on Saint Valentine's Day, was supported by adlines such as 'The Story of the Strangest Passion Ever Known'. The films had clearly been marketed to a female audience.

The Gothic woman's film was not established until the cycle of persecuted women or women-in-peril movies of the 1940s. Repressed or paranoid, the persecuted woman is fearful of her husband's past or of an unseen malevolent male. Seeking explanations she becomes trapped in an old and gloomy building, where its mysteries only increase her fears.

The castle or secluded house which had accommodated the fiendish devices and monstrous creations of the uncontrolled scientist or aristocrat – the erotic Gothic of the villain with power – became the unknown spaces for the terrified woman. Films such as *Rebecca* (1940), *Gaslight* (1940), *Dark Waters* (1944), *Dragonwyck* (1946), *The Spiral Staircase* (1946), *The Two Mrs Carrolls* (1947), *Secret Beyond the Door* (1948), and *Caught* (1949), drew on the Radcliffean mode of the Gothic (see **ANN RADCLIFFE**), in which the feminine space, the home, is denaturalised and presented as menacing. It is only rendered familiar through the revealing of a hidden past. Locked doors are to be opened, forbidden staircases to be climbed and histories explained.

Also part of 1940s noir are Val Lewton's psychological horrors – eight films produced between 1942 and 1946, at a time when society was gripped by mortality and instability: *Cat People* (1942), *I Walked with a Zombie* (1943), *The Leopard Man* (1943), *The Seventh Victim* (1943), *The Ghost Ship* (1943), *The Curse of the Cat People* (1944), *The Body Snatcher* (1945), and *Bedlam* (1946). The stories were atmospheric and foregrounded alienation, madness and fantasy, with characters struggling to comprehend their relationship to the surrounding environment. The haunting *I Walked with a Zombie* drew on *Jane Eyre* (1847) (see **THE BRONTËS**) for its story of sexuality, sickness and voodoo in the West Indies. *Bedlam* focused its sociological horror on the sadistic control of an asylum, where an actress is committed for becoming concerned at the institution's conditions. *Cat People* featured Irena, a woman who appears to transform into a panther when sexually aroused. The poster for the film declared 'She Knew Strange, Fierce Pleasures That No Other Woman Could Ever Feel!'

These films were produced in a period when the Hollywood monster movies were in decline. By the early 1940s, audiences were repeatedly being offered horror parodies. Films such as *The Ghost Creeps* (1940), *You'll Find Out* (1940), *Spooks Run Wild* (1941), *Ghosts on the Loose* (1943), and *The Ghost Catchers* (1944) were predominantly set in haunted houses. Making the most of trap doors, sliding panels, moving suits of armour, ghostly noises and creaking floorboards, the protagonists have to endure a series of nights in residence before exposing the crooks who had used the hauntings as a cover for their operations.

A resurgence in the Gothic was not to occur until the late 1950s. The success of *The Curse of Frankenstein* (1957) led to the production of a significant number of horror films, most notably by the film's producer, Hammer. Together with a number of other independent producers – Tempean, Amicus, Tigon, Tyburn and Anglo-Amalgamated – a post-war period for the Gothic horror film was established that was to become associated with British film production.

Attacked for their explicitness and violence, these films had replaced the suspense and shadows of previous horror films with excess and colour. The acquisition by Hammer of the rights to Universal's horror films of the 1930s and 1940s allowed for the reclamation of the English heritage of Gothic literature, with adaptations of Stoker's *Dracula* (1897), Shelley's *Frankenstein* (1818) and Stevenson's *The Strange Case of Dr Jekyll and Mr Hyde* (1886). During the nineteen-year period in which Hammer produced horror films, sixteen of its productions featured Frankenstein, Dr Jekyll and Mr Hyde, or Dracula.

In Hammer's Gothic horrors, celibate male figures of authority (professor, psychiatrist, priest or archaeologist) were presented as possessing the knowledge required to defeat an evil or monstrous force. Sexual desire was an indication of an individual's weakness. Women, in particular, appeared incapable of preventing themselves from becoming victims, in the struggle between the familiar and the unknown, and the spirit and the flesh.

Hammer also produced a number of psychological thrillers. The success of Universal's *Psycho*, in 1960, inspired the production of films such as *Taste of Fear* (1960), *Fanatic* (1964) and *Crescendo* (1970). Related to the persecuted-women films of the 1940s in their construction of female-centred narratives, the productions also looked forward to the American slasher films (such as *Halloween*) of the late 1970s and early 1980s. Here, the female, having been pursued and oppressed, acquires the knowledge necessary to isolate and challenge her tormentor.

Another significant producer of Gothic films from this period was Roger Corman. Between 1960 and 1964 he released seven films adapted from the work of **EDGAR ALLAN POE**. *The Fall of the House of Usher* (1960), *The Pit and the Pendulum* (1961), *The Premature Burial* (1962), *The Raven* (1963), *The Terror* (1963), *The Masque of the Red Death* (1964), and *The Tomb of Ligeia* (1964) repeatedly focused on Poe's preoccupation with premature burial and the association of marriage with **DEATH**. The films were noted for their strong visual presentation, with *The Masque of the Red Death*, in particular, stylised through a vivid use of colour and gliding camera movements. Corman believed that this was the best method for expressing what he believed was the subconscious mind that Poe largely used while writing.

The union of surrealism and the Gothic has been interestingly explored by the director David Lynch. Prior to making his first feature film, *Eraserhead* (1976), he had lived in Pittsburgh, near to Edgar Allan Poe's home. As Lynch stated 'I lived near to the morgue. ... That was on the border of an area that was black and white, and there was conflict and such hatred it was unbelievable.' *Eraserhead*, like Lynch's subsequent films – *The Elephant Man* (1980), *Dune* (1984) and *Blue Velvet*

(1986) – contains a morbid fascination with the body and the flesh. He creates environments that are sinister and unreal, yet strangely familiar, in which the fated central characters inhabit the outer fringes of society. Birth is observed to be impure and diseased and the human form associated with abnormalities and deformities.

The creation of 'grotesques' and the social isolation of individuals is characteristic both of the **SOUTHERN GOTHIC**, a form which has been portrayed in films such as *Reflections in a Golden Eye* (1967), *Last of the Mobile Hot Shots* (1970) and *The Beguiled* (1971), and of the American rural Gothic of *Dark Night of the Scarecrow* (1981) and *Deadly Blessing* (1982). The Southern Gothic can be compared to the rarely discussed New Zealand Gothic, which can be observed in the films *The Scarecrow* (1982), *Vigil* (1984), *Trial Run* (1984), *Crush* (1992), *The Piano* (1993) and *Jack Be Nimble* (1993). New Zealand, a country which is isolated and on the 'perimeter' of the world, is known for its natural beauty. In this Eden there would appear, however, to exist an overgrown garden, in which grow images of excess and despair. The films present culturally deprived, remote communities, where industrialism is absent. Here, characters struggle against a frightening, powerful and enchanted landscape in which they are trapped and suffocated. Individuals find it difficult to communicate and can be physically or mentally disadvantaged, making their isolation even greater. A stranger or outsider, often viewed with suspicion and fear, can break the isolation and disrupt the community.

The malevolent stranger is also a theme associated with the stories of Stephen King, many of which have been adapted for film. In *Salem's Lot* (1979), *The Dark Half* (1991) and *Needful Things* (1993), an American small-town community is weakened and dismantled by an unfamiliar force. The isolated community,or home is itself presented as the sinister space in the films *The Shining* (1980), *The Children of the Corn* (1984), *Pet Sematary* (1989), *Misery* (1990) and *Dolores Claiborne* (1994), where the central characters are confined, terrorised, and mentally deteriorate. In *The Shining*, a caretaker and his family become snowbound in a vast, isolated hotel. The caretaker's decline into dementia leads him to attempt to murder his family with an axe, in a haunting pursuit through the hotel's deserted rooms and its labyrinthine corridors. A seemingly endless and twisting space, this mirrors the caretaker's tormented mind and the real maze in the hotel grounds in which he freezes to death.

The modern **AMERICAN GOTHIC** has been explored and developed in the suburban Gothic of *Poltergeist* (1982), *The burbs* (1988), *Parents* (1988), and *Edward Scissorhands* (1990), where the normality of the neighbourhood conceals death, the **SUPERNATURAL** and the monstrous. The chaos of the city was dramatically depicted in the dark **URBAN GOTHIC** *Seven* (1995), just one of the many psycho-thrillers that have been produced by Hollywood in the 1990s. A recurring theme in films such as *Pacific Heights* (1990), *Hider in the House* (1990), *Cape Fear* (1991), *The Hand that Rocks the Cradle* (1992), *Single White Female* (1992), *Deceived* (1992), and *Mother's Boys* (1994) is the penetration of the family space by an obsessive and psychotic individual. Relationships are destabilised and families appear dysfunctional. Here, a crisis exists, with the most familiar of spaces, the personal and the private, now associated with terror.

Psycho-thrillers, a development of the slasher film, are just one indication of a sustained mainstream emergence of the Gothic. The neo-Gothic is a progressive form which can be observed to occur simultaneously in the popular horror *Silence of the Lambs* (1991) and in children's films such as *The Nightmare Before Christmas* (1993) and *Toy Story* (1995).

IAN CONRICH

Gothic Novel

The Gothic Novel begins with the anonymous publication of collector, antiquarian, dilettante **HORACE WALPOLE**'s novel *The Castle of Otranto* (1764), subtitled 'A Gothick Story'. Walpole, who was also an MP, concealed himself behind layers of personae, teasingly framing the story as a fifteenth-century manuscript by one 'Onuphrio Muralto', translated by 'William Marshall, Gent.' The critics were hostile, sensing a fake, but not quite sure. The public, however, was enthusiastic; the first edition sold out in a matter of months and Walpole was prevailed upon to reveal himself as the author.

The story of *The Castle of Otranto* reveals many of the preoccupations of the later Gothic Novel. It looks back to a feudal world, in this case, medieval Italy, in which the Lord of the Manor, Manfred, the first of a long line of Gothic villain/heroes, exercises seigneurial rights over the minds and bodies of his subjects. His castle, however, as part of an ancient prophecy, appears to be haunted by a gigantic suit of armour. His obsession with primogeniture, and the inability of his wife Hippolita to provide him with an heir, lead him, on the news of the death of his sickly son, Conrad, to offer himself in a peremptory, and vaguely incestuous, fashion to his quondam prospective daughter-in-law, Isabella. Isabella, the first of a line of intrepid Gothic heroines, refuses him indignantly and flees through the subterranean vaults of the castle, taking refuge in the local monastery church. In the end, Manfred is revealed as the son of a usurper of the line of Otranto, which is represented by a young peasant of noble bearing, Theodore, who defies him and with whom Isabella has in the meantime fallen in love.

This plot encodes various obsessions of the later Gothic: the 'authenticating' pretence that the author is merely the editor of a found manuscript; the setting in medieval and 'superstitious' Southern Catholic Europe; the expectation of the supernatural; the conflation of hero and villain; the decay of primogeniture and of feudal and aristocratic rights in general, and the rise of an ambitious bourgeoisie eager to exercise individual freedom in marriage and inheritance; the focus on the victimised, but often defiant, position of women; the use of confined spaces – castles, dungeons, monasteries and prisons, to symbolise extreme emotional states by labyrinthine incarceration – all these characteristic modalities spring into being, more or less fully formed, in Walpole's tale.

But Walpole's story exhibits a contradiction between subject matter and language which is uncharacteristic of the tradition it founded. Stylistically, it is dry, witty, terse, and suffused with the rational virtues of eighteenth-century prose – it has no Romantic expansiveness, and thought it foregrounds extreme emotions, especially in the case of Manfred, its characters, generally speaking, are puppets without psychological depth and its action is screwed to a high pitch of melodrama. Walpole was personally close to the Enlightenment in France, and yet his antiquarianism and his dilettantism, beneath a humorous façade, revealed a more serious interest in neglected areas of historical scholarship and a willingness to speculate about alternative modes of awareness. In a famous account of the genesis of the tale, which proved interesting to André Breton and the French Surrealists in the 1930s, Walpole shows that he was indeed allowing his unconscious to dominate the writing process.

Mid-eighteenth-century aesthetics are built on Horace – polished, witty, decorous, and above all conscious, writing which is built on an aesthetics of product. But the Longinian aesthetics of **THE SUBLIME**, revived also in the mid-century by Burke in his *A Philosophical Inquiry into the Origin of our Ideas of the Sublime and the Beautiful* (1757), are founded on an aesthetics of process, foregrounding the affective relationship between reader and text. Burke's treatise is a blueprint for an aesthetics of terror and horror, laying down a set of conditions for the excitement of the reader's passions. The artist's task was to evoke fear, grandeur and awe in the soul of the reader.

Walpole also invented other characteristics of the genre that were to endure: his 'Gothic story' was ostensibly set back in the remote past in a age of 'superstition' when emotions were freer and manners more direct and barbarous than in eighteenth-century polite society. But as with many later Gothic novels this 'historical' content is relatively superficial, intentionally so, because the novel is essentially addressing changes of taste in its eighteenth-century audience. The expanded and expanding reading public (in large part female), despite the neo-classical strictures of the eighteenth-century establishment, craved popular entertainment, and Walpole, not without humour, was the first to provide it. The early Gothic Novels are eighteenth-century costume-dramas that play with history.

After an apparent lull of almost two decades (during which time the magazines were highly active, as Mayo has shown), the Minerva Press, backed by the new circulating libraries, began to pour out Gothic three-deckers to a formula that derived in part from Walpole, but these writers' novels lacked his comic astringency of tone. Set in the medieval past, such novels were thought of at the time as subversive or childish 'romances', according to one's point of view, and they inserted themselves, at the extreme end, into the critical debate between Novel and Romance which ran from the mid eighteenth-century to well on in the nineteenth century. By end of the 1790s, the demand for such books had grown into an addiction, as Jane Austen's famous and brilliant **GOTHIC PARODY** both of this female readership, and of male attempts to control it, in *Northanger Abbey*, (1818), proves.

The leading Gothic novelist of the eighteenth century, far surpassing her forerunners Sophia Lee and Clara Reeve in popularity and known as 'the great enchantress', was **ANN RADCLIFFE** (her style and method of the 'explained supernatural' also spoofed expertly by Austen), who kept a generation on edge with *The Mysteries of Udolpho* (1794). Two years later, **MATTHEW LEWIS**, another Whig MP, published *The Monk*, whose camp sexuality and Faustian metaphysics proved a *succès de scandale* and had to be withdrawn under threat of blasphemy after a review by Coleridge. Ann Radcliffe replied to Lewis with *The Italian* (1797), half of which is set in the dungeons of the Roman Inquisition, and the Gothic genre was fully established, recognised in particular by the **MARQUIS DE SADE**, whose judgement in 1800 that these novels were 'the necessary fruits of the revolutionary tremors felt by the whole of Europe' has proved highly influential in later critical debate, marking a tradition of linking the Gothic novel with the French Revolution.

The 1790s were a turbulent decade and the Gothic novel was a focus for various cross-currents: English antiquarianism; Whig dilettantism; German influences from the **STURM UND DRANG**; Jacobinism; **OCCULTISM** and radical Secret Societies; French Revolutionary propaganda; conservative English nationalism; anti-Catholicism; feudal nostalgia; Romantic diabolism; Godwinianism.

By 1820, thanks to the publication of parodies like Austen's *Northanger Abbey* and Peacock's *Nightmare Abbey* (1818), the influence of the Enlightenment relativism of Sir Walter Scott, and the rise of his 'historical romance', the earlier novels had begun to seem somewhat *grand guignol*.

In 1818, **MARY SHELLEY**, following in the footsteps of both her father, William Godwin (who produced two novels in the Gothic mode, *Caleb Williams*, 1794, and *St Leon*, 1799), and her mother, Mary Wollstonecraft (who also published novels influenced by the genre), brought forth what she later half-jestingly referred to as her 'hideous progeny' – one of the most famous of all the Gothic novels, *Frankenstein*.

The plot of this novel, the story of a scientist who, having exultantly discovered the secret of artificial reproduction from corpses, creates a being and then, revolted by its apparent monstrosity, morally and phys-ically abandons it, has become nothing less than a modern myth in the post-war period. Given the discovery and the use of the atom bomb, the subsequent Cold War and arms race, the developments in genetics and computers and the ethical issues raised by all these matters, this complex and ambiguously horrifying story prophetically codifies in miniature many of our contemporary concerns.

The publication of the Dublin writer **CHARLES MATURIN**'s extra-ordinary Faustian novel *Melmoth the Wanderer* (1820), which failed at the box office but was a great success in France, conventionally marks the end of the first phase of the tradition.

After 1820, the radicalism (as Kilgour has recently argued, Godwin is as much a model for the Gothic Novel as Burke), the confusion, and the anarchy of the 'old Gothick' gives way to the new conservative 'histor-ical romance' of the Waverley era (roughly 1820–37). The Minerva Press gives up the Gothic and turns to children's books. The Gothic Novel breaks up and becomes a more scattered but now permanent and widely influential aspect of literary sensibility rather than a concerted genre or movement as such: a polarisation occurs between popular forms – the **'PENNY DREADFULS'** of Reynolds and of writers like **AINSWORTH** and the popular melodrama, on the one hand (*cf*. Simpson); and, on the other, the literary tradition dominated by Scott.

Mrs Radcliffe survived into the Victorian period as a writer's writer, or a clumsy forerunner of Romanticism; but *Blackwood's Magazine* (1818–80) and Henry Colburn's *New Monthly Magazine* (1814–84) had kept alive the Gothic flame, and by the 1840s both **DICKENS** and **THE BRONTËS** were showing unmistakable signs of the influence of the Gothic. In America, **POE**, following on from Radcliffe and **CHARLES BROCKDEN BROWN**, began to produce his tales. In Scotland, defiant of the Enlightenment rationalism of Scott, **HOGG** used the Gothic conven-tion of the **DOPPELGÄNGER** – probably derived from **HOFFMANN** – to satirise the growth of evangelical Calvinism in his *The Private Memoirs and Confessions of a Justified Sinner*, and produced a truly schizophrenic text. Eventually Dickens planned a similar 'confessional' structure for his last novel *The Mystery of Edwin Drood* (1870).

By the mid-century, the Gothic Novel as a genre was apparently extinct, and the term 'Gothic', if used at all, was predominantly an architectural term (see **GOTHIC REVIVAL**). But paradoxically this diversified and underground role guaranteed its survival in the literary field. The cultural conditions in which it had first appeared – the unease about enlightenment modes of thought, about empirical science, and epistemological certainty inherited from the eighteenth-century, and the official, daylight definitions of national, and rational, Protestant culture, the criteria for 'superstition' – all these elements of late eighteenth-century cultural formation had survived, and indeed intensified in the ninteenth century. The Gothic mode had become decentred, a register available for writers of many different kinds, but its influence on Victorian writing was taken for granted, thanks to the currency of the magazines and the early immense popularity of Scott's Border Ballads.

Victorian culture, bolstered by recycled memories of Romantic poetry (for the relation between the Romantic tradition and the Gothic, see Praz), became obsessed with the escapism and utopian romance of medieval pre-industrial society, which had a symbiotic and compensatory relationship to its own growing industrialisation and urbanisation. The traditional historical themes of the Gothic, mingled with the Arthurian 'matter of Britain' and the Gothic revival in architecture, with its Catholic and anti-Catholic tensions and its claims to be a national style, reinforced the literary tradition. Many of these features are clearly evident in **BRAM STOKER**'s books at the end of the Victorian period.

Part of this currency of the mode is attributable to the Victorian pleasure in horror and darkness, and there is also a growing interest during the Victorian period in sexuality, sexual taboo and sex-roles.

The Shakespeare revival was also fully under way in the earlier eighteen hundreds and the heroic style of early Victorian acting added to the sense of a relation between theatre and the character in the novel. Dickens, in particular, employed a theatrical and melodramatic style, full of darkness, violence, and sudden horrors. Even his early comic work like *The Pickwick Papers* (1836–7), as Jackson and others have argued, owes a good deal to Gothic precedent – and later, after 1850, Dickens's London becomes a sublimely dark, disease-ridden labyrinth of courts and alleys flanking a Thames polluted and full of floating corpses. Dickens also experimented with Gothic characterisation – the symbolically 'flat' rendition of aspects of a person – in his studies of repression and criminal mentalities, frequently employing in his later work (Arthur Clenham in *Little Dorrit*, 1855–7, Jaggers and Wemmick in *Great Expectations*, 1860–1 and Bradley Headstone in *Our Mutual Friend*, 1864–5) subdued versions of the *doppelgänger* motif which Poe and Hogg had also developed.

Meanwhile, as Heilman first demonstrated, the Brontës internalised and psychologised the old Gothic, producing wild and dark accounts of the perversity of human passion, carrying on the Gothic tradition of the Satanic and Byronic Villain/Hero in the figures of Rochester and Heathcliff, set in a bleak Northern landscape of remote houses. Poe, in his magazine tales, in an intensely Schopenhauerian manner, also used the Gothic vocabulary of excess to explore an intense and suffocating inner world of psychological isolation and perversity, catalepsy and necrophilia, while at the same time using the tradition for philosophical purposes to satirise Cartesianism and parody the German Idealism which held for him such a fascination.

Precisely because it was not a concerted tradition, but a highly flexible register which could be employed as a shorthand in characterisation, setting, and narrative mode, a register which often hid itself in the respectable documentation of 'historical romance', the Gothic became a frequent sub-code in the Victorian novel. It became important for a writer to try something in this darker, affective mode, even if only a tale, only an exercise – expectations of horror, fear, anxiety and *diablerie* were strong in the audience and the mode became part of the writerly range in the nineteenth century. This period sees also the rise of new popular genres like detective and science fiction which overlap with the Gothic.

Literary history used to crystallise the later Gothic under the heading of the Victorian 'sensation school' – which included **J. SHERIDAN LE FANU**, Collins, and Charles Reade. The term 'sensation' is a reference to the physiological effect that the reading of such authors is supposed to have had on the audience, which links it directly back to the tradition of **THE SUBLIME**. The first two of these writers have undergone a revival of interest in the last ten years and now most of their works are currently available in paperback reprints. In particular, Le Fanu is seen as a major transmitter of the Gothic to later nineteenth-century writers like Bram Stoker and **AMBROSE BIERCE**. His collection *In a Glass Darkly* (1872) contains the *doppelgänger* **VAMPIRE** story 'Carmilla', which has always been a favourite of anthologists. In 1932 this story – as with several of the Gothic fictions of Poe – was made into a German expressionist film, *Vampyr*. Recent interest in lesbianism, vampirism, and perverse sexuality has revived the story, and given it currency again as a modern classic. Le Fanu's horror masterpiece, *Uncle Silas* (1864), has also been revived on stage and screen on several occasions from the 1920s onwards, while his particularly horrid chapter in *The House by the Churchyard* (1861-3), 'Narrative of a Hand', was transformed into another anthology classic, 'The Beast with Five Fingers' by W. F. Harvey. Le Fanu is prized particularly by later horror writers like **M. R. JAMES**, who edited him and on whose *Ghost Stories of an Antiquary* (1904), a leading representative of the genre in the Edwardian period, he had a great deal of influence.

Collins's *The Woman in White* (1860) owes also something to the Gothic tradition – in particular its sublime and dramatic opening scene in which a woman dressed in white is encountered wandering in a North London suburb near Hampstead Heath, having escaped incarceration. Both these writers carry on an important rhetorical tradition begun by Ann Radcliffe and developed into a sophisticated and 'modern' art by Poe with their use of the 'explained supernatural' – that of the deliberately excessive, and sometimes ironical, foregrounding of 'explanation' as a mode of their documentary façade.

The later nineteenth century sees the steady production of minor classics in the horror tradition: **HENRY JAMES**'s 'The Jolly Corner' and *The Turn of the Screw* (1898), M. R. James's collections (1904, 1911, 1919), Bram Stoker's early stories and tales, **HAWTHORNE**'s *The Scarlet Letter* (1850), Collins's *The Woman in White* and Dickens's *The Mystery of Edwin Drood* (1870). But the dominant piece of Gothic writing of this period is undoubtedly, **STEVENSON**'s novella *The Strange Case of Dr Jekyll and Mr Hyde* (1886). This narrative, which, following some of the earlier experiments of Poe and Le Fanu, presents itself rhetorically in the Gothic magazine mode as a 'Strange Case', is often viewed by post-war writers on the Gothic Novel as a rich and penetrating analysis of Victorian repression, which anticipates Freud's work on the Ego and the Id. The story of the respectable, well-intentioned Doctor and his dwarfish, murderous 'other half' has passed into popular mythology as a way of describing split personality, and contributes to the literature on the divided self in the modern period. This story too has been the subject of extensive visual representation.

The great coup of the nineteenth-century Gothic novel, however, comes at its end, with *Dracula* (1897) by Bram Stoker. This novel, together with Radcliffe's novels, Shelley's *Frankenstein*, Poe's tale 'The Fall of the House of Usher', and Stevenson's *The Strange Case of Dr Jekyll and Mr Hyde*, represents the canon of the post-Second-World-War rehabilitation of the Gothic Novel. Stoker's novel creates single-handedly the literary myth of 'Transylvania', the kingdom of vampires, portrayed as a vortex-like region of Central Europe in which the Turks were originally repelled by the Magyars. Stoker's novel sites itself along the inflammatory metaphorical axis of invasion – geographical and bodily. The novel is a *farrago* of late Victorian beliefs; it is obsessed with the nature of the unconscious; the breaking of certain sexual taboos; the loss of Empire; the degeneration of the stock (i.e. the 'blood') of Western Europe; the onset of the New Woman; the decadent reliance on Empirical Science at the expense of traditional religion.

The figure of the evil Count Dracula, the leader of the Undead, was largely ignored at the time of publication, but since the Second World War has become one of the most charismatic and visually reproduced characters in the popular tradition of the Gothic Novel, rivalling Mary Shelley's Victor Frankenstein and his Monster. Other texts from this period have been rehabilitated in the post-war period: Charlotte Perkins Gilman's *The Yellow Wallpaper* (1892), for example, a novella with Gothic overtones, has become a classic of the feminist modern tradition, re-issued in paperback. In France, Gaston Leroux produced *The Phantom of the Opera* (1911), whose monstrous version of the Beauty and the Beast fairy-tale, recast as a post-Imperial historical romance, has also gained great currency in the post-war period, being turned into a world-touring popular musical.

With the exception of the Gothic strain in the shorter narratives of Kipling, Conrad, and Wells, the Edwardian period and the 1920s and 1930s see the Gothic retreat again into the magazines and anthologies, tapping an unease about Empire which Dickens had already shown himself aware of in his last novel, *The Mystery of Edwin Drood* (1870). As Briggs has shown, the Gothic Novel appeared to decline, under threat from Modernism and the general reaction against Victorianism which took place after the First World War.

During this period, it is left to the cinema (see **GOTHIC FILM**), and in particular the directors of the German expressionist cinema, to explore new forms of re-presentation, often using the settings, motifs and plots of the Gothic novels as a framework, and thus drawing a whole generation of readers back to the novels. This German movement also provided the studio training ground for Alfred Hitchcock, whose contribution to the tradition after the war is outstanding.

This period also saw the emergence of the first of a series of unifying, explanatory critical frameworks, which seem to fit the extreme case of the Gothic Novel, in the essay of Freud on 'THE UNCANNY' (1919). This vastly influential piece of writing, which, using **HOFFMANN**'s eighteenth-century Gothic novels and stories as examples, seeks to explain the phenomena of readerly and writerly uncertainty by the unconscious projection of repressed fantasy on the part of both, brought commentary on the Gothic Novel onto a new level, a discursive field which has become part of the metalanguage of the postwar Gothic itself. Following Freud, the Surrealists also recognised the eighteenth-century English Gothic Novels as important forerunners of their own experiments with the unconscious, linking their comments to those of the Marquis de Sade already quoted.

American popular culture, which had thoroughly domesticated Freudian analysis by the end of the Second World War, found a new home for the Gothic Novel, which was marginalised during the postwar recovery period of the 1940s and 1950s in Britain. Important exceptions to this are the works of David Lyndsay, and two English Gothic Novels, between the late 1940s and 1960, the *Gormenghast Trilogy* (1946, 1950, 1959) of Mervyn Peake, and the pre-Wolfenden *doppelgänger* novel, *Radcliffe* (1963), by David Storey, a unique blend of naturalistic surface and Gothic motifs. The American interest in science and technology and the drive to demonise Eastern Europe during the Cold War period gave a new currency and availability to the shapes of Gothic fantasy, in conjunction with science fiction and detective fiction. The horror film was re-born, often deriving from magazine stories or novels of a Gothic type (like *Psycho* for example) or serving as remakes of the Gothic fictions themselves (such as the famous *Invasion of the Body Snatchers* (1956), which makes allusion to a forgotten story by R. L. Stevenson). This change, supported by the popularity of the Hammer Films in Britain, in its turn encouraged some limited underground paperback re-publication of the Gothic Novels.

After the 1960s, both genre and commentary have, in a sense, expanded in symbiosis. Or at least, they have both increased exponentially. From the late 1960s on, we have seen the growth of new markets and new readers, which parallel, but far surpass, the market expansion of the original Gothic Novels. Now, every book stall and airport bookstore has a pulp fiction section called 'horror'. The horror writer Stephen King was for a long time the world's best-selling author, and recently **ANNE RICE**, another American author, has begun to rival him with the immense popularity of her *Interview with the Vampire* (1976), which forms the beginning of a series. There are many other strands of the postwar Gothic Novel, which has evolved its own complex map.

The critical interpretation of the Gothic Novel is also evolving. The earlier dominance of psychoanalytic explanation from the 1930s to the 1950s gave way to more historical, linguistic and socio-cultural approaches. From the 1960s onwards, the growth of interest in popular culture and the rise of feminism have changed and immensely broadened the literary and critical possibilities for the Gothic. Lively international and interdisciplinary debate as to the nature of the 'subversiveness' of the Gothic Novel from the eighteenth century to the contemporary period is now under way, a debate which feeds round in a loop into the highly self-conscious fictional practice of such influential contemporary exponents as **ANGELA CARTER**, whose sophisticated collection of stories *The Bloody Chamber* (1979), a blend of fairytale and traditional sadistic Gothic, itself fully aware of the theoretical and fictional possibilities of these overlapping traditions, teases mercilessly the expectations of its would-be commentators and devotee-readers alike.

VICTOR SAGE

Gothic Revival

The revival in Britain of the Gothic, or Pointed, Style between the early eighteenth century and the later Victorian and even Edwardian periods is primarily architectural; but architecture is, as Ruskin observed, the expression of a polity, and the Gothic Revival is no exception to this rule; the continuous debates associated with its origins, definition and interpretation traverse the discourses of painting, literature, politics, religion, history, national identity, and arts and crafts.

The historicised cultivation of the pointed arch is repeatedly claimed as a national style. But the Gothic Revival is itself a contested site; by turns it is patriotic and exotic; Whig and Tory; Catholic and Protestant; rationalist and superstitious; natural and artificial; hierarchical and democratic; pragmatic and fantastic; esoteric and popular. Henry VII's chapel at Westminster, perhaps the most important single source of Gothic Revival design in the early eighteenth century, meant different things to different people. As we shall see, each new generation adds a different stress to what amounts to a complex struggle for the appropriation of the mode.

Despite, or perhaps because of, its inevitable and continuous association with pastiche, the Gothic Revival forms the basis of an English eclectic popular style which, by the late Victorian period, had become a dominant vocabulary for the organisation of public and private space. The Houses of Parliament, the Midland Hotel at St Pancras Station, the Natural History Museum, the Law Courts, Windsor Castle and the Albert Memorial, to name but a few, all owe their style in different ways to the Gothic Revival. And at the high street level, what visitor to London, Manchester, Liverpool or Birmingham does not become aware of the post-Ruskinian 'streaky bacon' style with its polychrome brick and tilework, discs of marble and bullet-mouldings, its turrets, its floriations, and capitals?

From the beginning, the Gothic had no real opposite. Reformation Britain, haunted by the dissolution of the monasteries, those 'bare ruined choirs where late the sweet birds sang', had not developed a native classical or baroque Renaissance tradition, and the Counter-Reformation style, when it came in the nineteenth century, was not baroque, but also Gothic.

Revival is notoriously difficult to distinguish from survival. Tudor architecture, a sturdy assimilation of late medieval architectural styles to some Italian influences (Walpole called it 'mongrel': see **HORACE WALPOLE**), lasted until the 1630s when Inigo Jones began the serious importation of Baroque from Italy. From then, until the 1740s, when

Walpole acquired Strawberry Hill, various forms of classicism ruled; but even so, there was still an interest in the Gothic from architects like Kent and Hawksmoor who designed the Northern Quadrangle of All Souls', Oxford, and the towers of Westminster Abbey itself. And as the antiquarian movement, driven by the need for historiographical and political continuity in post-Revolutionary England, got into full swing during the late seventeenth century, a host of local histories which contained real research into medieval buildings began to pour off the press. Thus, stimulated initially by late seventeenth- and early eighteenth-century antiquarianism, the Revival was in fact the resuscitation and reinvention of a style that was available but dormant, rather than dead.

There may thus be some broad truth in the contention that between the Henry VII chapel at Westminster and the Houses of Parliament we see nowadays, there is an unbroken tradition. But it is a tradition of historical pastiche and reinvention: both Henry VII's chapel and the Old Palace of Westminster, before the fire of 1834, had been restored by Wyatt in the eighteenth century.

In the early stages of the Revival there was a proliferation of sham or copied detail, but little or no structural principles of building. It is a commonplace to point to the hallmark of eighteenth-century Revival style as the mechanical encrustation of rococo detail – Carpenter's Gothic, plaster and stucco – on box-like villas. In some ways this situation had not changed very much by the early nineteenth century: we still find Sir Charles Eastlake in 1873 groaning about the standard of carving and craftsmanship fifty or sixty years previously. This tension between detail and structure, and the search for the right relationship between the two, was to characterise debate about the Gothic style from Walpole to Ruskin and has a profound influence on the tradition of arts and crafts.

Paradoxically, alongside the self-confessed artifice, lies the appeal of the style to nature: the more theatrical it actually becomes, the 'purer' it is claimed to be. Another persistent theme of Revival tradition, a claim made long before it was generally reinforced by Romantic aesthetics, is the relation between the pointed arch and the 'natural' world ('bare ruined choirs' are already trees in Shakespeare's sonnet). The pointed arch reproduces semiotically the *Ur-wald*. There was even one experiment in the eighteenth century which attempted to prove this proposition by 'growing' Gothic arches from wands of ash.

We can roughly distinguish five phases of the Revival: the Age of Wyatt: Strawberry Hill to Fonthill, 1747–1820; the Waverley Phase to Pugin, 1820–36; Ecclesiology, Pugin and Gilbert Scott, 1836–55; Gilbert Scott and Ruskin to Morris, 1855–72; Gothic, Art Nouveau and Modernism, 1872 and Beyond.

The Age of Wyatt: Strawberry Hill to Fonthill, 1747–1820

The term 'Gothic' is a semantic vortex, even in the eighteenth century. It usually connotes 'English'. One can dimly distinguish perhaps Whig aesthetics from Tory: from the Whig point of view, the **GOTHS** were a healthy freedom-loving set of Northern tribes from whom we descend and who succeeded in taking away the yoke of Roman imperial domination in both religious and political senses.

For Whigs, the Gothic Revival is thus a progressive sign, of the openness of the English constitution and English Common Law which evolved organically from these Goths, who became the original inhabitants (for some, they were Celts or Druids) of England. Thus, in this frame of thought, 'Gothic' connotes 'English', 'Protestant', 'democratic' and 'anti-Catholic'.

For Tory thought, on the other hand, 'Gothic' is equally 'English'; but it tends to have heraldic origins in the Anglo-Norman tradition (the architecture of which was thought of as 'Saxon' in the eighteenth century), it is Plantagenet, connotes feudalism, high Anglicanism or even Anglo-Catholicism, aristocracy, high ritual, and signifies the revival of a heroic and hierarchical vision of national religion and social organisation.

One can see the complexity of these connotations at work in a passage on architecture from **WALPOLE**'s *Anecdotes of Painting* (1762). Walpole readily opposes Grecian to Gothic but in order to make a rhetorical point about the latter:

> One must have taste to be sensible of the beauties of Grecian architecture; one only wants passions to feel Gothic. In St Peter's one is convinced that it was built by great princes. In Westminster Abbey, one thinks not of the builder; the religion of the place makes the first impression; and though stripped of its altars and shrines, it is nearer converting one to popery than all the regular pageantry of Roman domes. Gothic churches infuse superstition – Grecian, admiration.

Walpole is flirting with the 'other' here. Not everybody who read *The Gentleman's Magazine* would have agreed with this because they 'read' Henry VII's chapel with politics rather than religion uppermost in their minds. Walpole's commitment to the passions – the new values of sensibility endorsed by Burke's account of the sublime in 1757– finds Gothic architecture the perfect expression of a natural power within the observer. A mere imitation, his Cabinet at Strawberry Hill was designed to have the same effect as a Catholic chapel, causing a momentary blend of 'enthusiasm' and 'superstition' to course through the veins of the viewer. (Later, Mrs **RADCLIFFE** plays a similar game with her readers over the taboo stimulation of 'enthusiasm' which can lead to 'superstition'.) Ironically, Strawberry Hill is now a Catholic college.

Walpole's own Gothic is essentially rococo and picturesque, but his feeling for the style of medieval architecture is such that he is willing to toy with transgression in order to catch certain aesthetic effects.

The eighteenth-century gothicists were copyists who took their details from largely ecclesiastical sources and combined them eclectically in domestic settings. Batty Langley's attempt to become the Vitruvius of Gothic, his *Gothic Architecture Improved by Rules and Proportions* of 1742, despite its stress on rules, only increased the feeling of pastiche because it concentrated on (reproducible) detail, not structure. Walpole, for example, took the pillars of his garden gate from the tomb of William of Luda in Ely Cathedral, and the ceiling of his gallery from the fan vaulting in Westminster Abbey, as did the 'half-converted Jacobite' Sir Roger Newdigate at Arbury. This tendency to pastiche is partly accounted for by the fact that there were no more than a dozen churches built in England between 1760 and 1820, so architects were concerned largely with the copying, conversion, and restoration of churches rather than the building of new ones.

Walpole's favourite architect was James Wyatt, who inclined quite naturally to pastiche ecclesiastical or castellated Gothic when designing domestic buildings. Walpole passed him on to Mr Barrett, later Lord Dacre, of Lee Priory to Gothicise that house. Wyatt went on to become the restorer of Henry VII's chapel at Westminster. He tended to change the internal arrangements of old buildings in order to get a better visual and theatrical effect; Wyatt's work at Salisbury, for example, was widely disapproved of by antiquarians, but from 1796 onwards, Wyatt became Surveyor-General of the Board of Works, and George III invited him to restore Windsor Castle (1800–4); the columns, leaf capitals, and bossed vaulting were all copied direct from Salisbury and other cathedrals Wyatt was working on. Ecclesiastical Gothic interiors thus blended happily with castellated Gothic exteriors.

Wyatt is a direct link between Strawberry Hill, concerning which he was consulted, and Fonthill Abbey, which he designed for William Beckford. The difference between the two structures is an emblem of the development from the rococo beginnings to the full-blown Romanticism of the Gothic Revival: if Strawberry Hill is small-scale, comfortable and picturesque, Fonthill was sublime, huge and deeply uncomfortable: the tower was 276 ft high, the hall alone was 120 ft high, and the two north and south wings were 400 ft in length. Beckford is reputed to have hired a dwarf footman to increase the apparent height of the (30 ft) front porch when guests were arriving.

Both houses are essentially jokes; theatrical pastiche of ecclesiastical buildings, Fonthill starting out life as a sham ruined convent. But the scale of the joke had become vastly more ambitious by the time of Fonthill. Its structure was insecure, the mason, who confessed the fact to

Wyatt on his deathbed, having neglected to put in the foundations the architect had specified under the tower. The octagonal tower duly collapsed in 1825.

The development of the Revival between the two houses is marked by the advent of Romanticism, which fed off and boosted the confidence of antiquarian and archaeological researchers into the Gothic. Gray and Walpole went on the Grand Tour together as students in the 1740s and Gray's letters and the Wharton brothers' researches into medieval culture and architecture were serious and important in encouraging a new standard of analysis. Those researches also lie behind a poem of Gray's such as 'The Bard' or 'The Death of Odin' (see **GRAVEYARD SCHOOL**). Gray in his turn was a big influence on the early Blake, and Blake's paintings contain Gothic arches composed of trees, the sacred groves of the druids, thought at one stage to be Goths.

The Waverley Phase to Pugin, 1820–36

If there were no churches built during the first phase of the Gothic Revival, the second phase saw a complete change. There were rapid demographic and class changes in the early years of the nineteenth century. The industrial revolution was hotting up, cities had begun to expand rapidly from the latter years of the eighteenth century onwards. The fear of Jacobinism which became a Government reflex during the 1790s carried on into the period of the Napoleonic Wars and the alarm was such that the powerful church-going middle class persuaded the Government to pass a Bill, the Church Building Act (1818), which granted a million pounds to the building of churches in populous districts in order to contain the threat. In fact, from 1818 to 1833, it has been estimated that 6 million pounds was spent on building churches. Of the 214 churches built under the Act, 174 were Gothic. The reasons for this seem to have been economic rather than aesthetic or political: the Church Commissioners decided that Gothic was the cheapest style; and so was born the cardboard 'Commissioners' Gothic' against which the converted Catholic Pugin reacted so violently. One of the best of these churches is St Luke's, Chelsea (1819–1824), designed by J. Savage in an eclectic Perpendicular style, which is famous for the (untypically expensive) stone groined arches in the nave. Interestingly, *The Gentleman's Magazine* in 1826, though enthusiastic, regretted the choice of style, maintaining that Early English was purer and more national.

The writer's more confident tone about the history of the style – the idea that Perpendicular represents a 'degeneration' – reflects the intense antiquarian study of the early years of the century into the history and origins of Gothic style (amongst which the efforts of Pugin's father have an important place), which resulted finally in the work of a Quaker, Thomas Rickman, who had managed to stabilise some of the divergences of terminology for the styles of Gothic architecture in his *Attempt To Discriminate the Styles of English Architecture* (1819). Rickman divided buildings into Early English (twelfth century, e.g. the choir at Canterbury); Decorated (fourteenth century, e.g. the nave at York); and Perpendicular (e.g. the early sixteenth-century Henry VII chapel at Westminster). These divisions still form the basis for modern study of the subject.

Rickman also, like the elder Pugin, made an important contribution to the persistent association after 1805 between the English Gothic and the cathedrals of Normandy and Picardy, which resulted in study tours by himself and Whewell (another Protestant antiquarian driven by a desire for a more scientific tradition), and later, the painter Turner. There is an influx of more carefully drawn 'Specimens' in the period after the Napoleonic Wars (1815), when antiquarians were free once more to travel to France.

This expansion of the ecclesiastical base of Gothic style fuels both the Catholic and Anglican strains of the Revival which make up the early phase of Victorian Gothic.

The literary and antiquarian influence on the Revival was given a power-ful boost in the early nineteenth century by Sir Walter Scott. By theat-ricalising the ballad, and then later historicising the Old Gothic romance, Scott created a new tension between earnest (and sometimes rigorous) antiquarian standards of detail in the Revival and the theatrical effect of 'medievalism'. At Abbotsford, Scott created a new 'realistic' theatre of medievalism, paid for in advances from his poems and novels. In 1805, he bought an undistinguished old farm by the side of the Tweed, called Clarty-Hole, and had transformed it by his death in 1832 into a sham Gothic castle, renaming it Abbotsford – i.e. the ford of the abbots of nearby Melrose Abbey, who originally owned the land.

Sir Charles Eastlake observed in 1873 that 'it would be difficult ... to overrate the influence which Scott's poetry has had ... in encouraging a national taste for medieval architecture ...' Scott's work held a universal appeal; he boosted the Tory high Anglican nostalgia for an age of chivalry, which resulted in *The Broad Stone of Honour* (1822) – the manual for the gentlemanly ethics of the English Public Schools of the Victorian period – while, at the same time, Cardinal Newman believed that Sir Walter was the man who made the Catholic Revival possible and always included a prayer for him in his Masses. The Catholic Revival, in its turn, has a great influence on the Gothic Revival in the remarkable person of Pugin.

The young Pugin's first job was that of a superflyman at the Covent Garden Theatre, and one of his early triumphs was the sets for the ballet at the King's Theatre of Scott's *Kennilworth*, for which he painted architectural backgrounds and designed costumes. He acquired first-hand skills (as a draftsman, stage carpenter and machinist) in the engineering of stage illusion and he executed the remarkable designs for the 1831 production of Shakespeare's *Henry VIII*, work which he was to transfer directly to the architectural context in his use of Henry VIII and his wives in the King's Room at Scarisbrick Hall between 1837 and 1840. Later, this highly-developed sense of the theatrical was sometimes held against him both as an architect and as a Catholic, though it seems clear that these are the perfect (and by then even traditional) skills for the Gothic Revival architect and designer to have.

The son of a lapsed Catholic refugee from the French Revolution who was employed by the Crown Architect, Nash, to teach him the principles of Gothic, Pugin was brought up as a strict Presbyterian by his mother. But he converted to Catholicism as soon as he could get free of her in 1833. His extraordinary anti-Protestant *Contrasts* of 1836 is a turning point in the Gothic Revival. In a series of exquisitely drawn pictures Pugin contrasts the function and the beauty of many different specimens of Gothic architecture with the drab incoherence of their modern counterparts, the would-be 'functional' specimens of the debased classical style, which he detested and thought of as 'pagan'. This apparently simple appeal to the reader's eye is a brilliant piece of propaganda and the book had a massive influence on all wings of the Gothic Revival, particularly on the younger architects like Gilbert Scott, putting the Gothic style on a new footing as a serious combination of function and ornament.

Over his short life, Pugin single-handedly reorientated the relation between structure and detail. There was no aspect of building which Pugin left untouched, but his greatest gift was the ability to make exteriors look solid and unfussy, always integrating their detail and giving it technical function. Favouring the Perpendicular to begin with, in the end he settled on the Decorated style of the fourteenth century. His basic principles were those of 'revealed construction' at all levels of design. As he says in *The True Principles of Pointed or Christian Architecture* in 1844, 'The two great rules for design are these ... First, that there should be no features about a building which are not necessary for convenience, construction or propriety; second, that all ornament should consist of enrichment of the essential construction of the building.'

A huge part of Pugin's working life was consumed in the greatest architectural commission of the century, the design of the New Westminster Palace, the old Palace having been destroyed by fire in 1834. Pugin watched the fire, exultant that 'Wyatt's heresies have been effectively consigned to oblivion.' The Committee decided in 1835 that, given the site, the new parliament building should be in the Gothic or Elizabethan style, thus confirming a sense of the national character of the Gothic Revival. The plan which won the competition was Charles Barry's for whom Pugin was working as a draughtsman, but Pugin executed much of the detail of the design. Much later, passing with a friend in a boat, Pugin commented, in a resigned fashion: 'All Grecian, Sir; Tudor details on a classic body.'

From the mid-1840s until his death in 1852, Pugin was designing the interiors of the Palace. In this phase of his career, his doctrine of revealed construction also radicalised the whole arts and crafts tradition, touching ceramics, furniture, wallpaper, stonework, jewellery and precious metal-work, introducing new standards of authenticity into design through the intensity and the sheer learning of his study of medieval detail and the fluency and invention of his drawings. He believed that God's handi-work, Nature, was the source of much of the ornament in medieval deco-ration and he returned to sixteenth-century works of botany to study the structure of the original plants on which the medieval leaf and flower designs were based. His *Floriated Ornament* of 1849 anticipates both Ruskin and Morris.

Pugin had a huge impact on both ecclesiastical and domestic architec-ture. His patron was John Talbot, the Catholic Earl of Shrewsbury, and Pugin designed Alton Towers for him and Alton Castle in Shropshire. Pugin's ardent, romantic, Tory, hieratic nature mounted a polemical and radical critique of the degradation of the industrial society of his day and it is to him that we owe the idea which became currency in the later Victorian Gothic that architecture and morality, let alone ideology, are inseparable.

It was Pugin, not Ruskin, who first reformulated the Gothic Revival idea that there is an organic (natural) relation between architecture and forms of social organisation. After Pugin, the earlier revival seems sham; this is partly because he introduced genuine structural principles of building and a more accurate standard of Revival design, and partly, as we can see from his vibrant but deliberately flat interiors, because his theatrical standards were so much more ambitious than his predecessors'.

Ecclesiology, Pugin and Gilbert Scott, 1836–57

The Protestant response to Pugin came with the founding of the Camden Society in Cambridge in 1839, which gave birth to the 'science' of Ecclesiology. After the Catholic Emancipation Act of 1829, the doctrinal dividing lines between the religions had become very sensitive. Pugin had mounted a radical push in the direction of ritual. Effectively the

Oxford and Cambridge Antiquarian Societies responded by a new enthusiasm for ritual. During the next ten years, there was a steady increase in the amount of ritual details to be included in new and restored
churches, though all had to be done according to correct ecclesiological
principles. Architects were directly policed by the Camden Society.
Again the appeal is to the real as opposed to the theatrical: 'Stucco, and
paint, and composition, and graining are not out of place in the theatre
or the ballroom; but in GOD'S HOUSE everything should be real.' These
remarks show the influence of Pugin – the details of the church should
be functional and openly so.

But 'functional', in this context, is doctrinal, and there was resistance
from within the Protestant fold. Perhaps the most bitter battle was the
revival of the rood screen controversy; the old Protestantism had made
its churches in the image of what it saw as democracy, and the cutting
off of a High Altar – itself an idolatrous concept: only tables, rather than
solid altars were used in the 1830s – from the congregation, and the idea
of this division between clerisy and congregation, touched a raw political
nerve in many. By 1845, with the reaction against the Tractarians as inevitably Roman Catholic in tendency, things had moved too far in the direction of Popery and 'superstition'. As a consequence, the Camden
Society was disbanded. But the style had by then been immeasurably enriched; once more antiquarian pressure had created morphological
change, and the model for High Victorian Gothic, not only as an ecclesiastical, but also as a secular style, had been established.

But curiously there was no direct alliance between Pugin and the
emergent leaders of the Oxford movement itself, and the absorption of
his architectural ideas had been accomplished from within the Protestant
establishment. Newman was never a fan of the Gothic style, and he was
distrustful of Pugin's bigotry. Wiseman preferred Renaissance
Architecture and Keble had utilitarian leanings in architectural matters.
Hurrel Froude was obsessed by St Peter's. The Oxford Movement, from
which he had expected so much, distanced itself from Pugin, whose
alliance was with a patron from an old 'penal' Catholic family, Lord
Shrewsbury.

Gilbert Scott is an important bridge between the ecclesiastical and
secular Gothic Revival in this early Victorian period and he, as a young
architect, set about putting Pugin's principles into practice, while enthusiastically submitting his plans for churches to the Camden Society for
approval. Pugin had given a lead on domestic architecture with St
Marie's Grange, the extraordinary L-shaped house he built for himself
near Salisbury in 1835, during the construction of which, to the horror of

his builder, he refused to use any lath or plaster where they were normally employed. Authenticity consisted of a whole integrated design. As Pugin wrote to his patron: 'nothing can be more dangerous than looking at prints of buildings, or trying to imitate bits of them: these architectural books are as bad as the Scriptures in the hands of Protestants'.

Again we find similar paradoxical attacks on 'theatre' in Scott's writings on the necessary modernity of secular and domestic Gothic: 'everything which would make one feel that we are living in a house belonging essentially to a previous age, rather than our own, has a smacking more or less of *architectural masquerade*'.

Gilbert Scott and Ruskin to Morris, 1855–72

Gilbert Scott is the great populariser of the Gothic Revival. After 1847, Scott is estimated to have been concerned with 730 buildings, which included 39 cathedrals and minsters, 476 churches, 25 schools, 23 parsonages, 43 mansions, 26 public buildings, 25 colleges or college chapels. Scott insisted the style was accidentally medieval, and essentially national, and his architectural practice set out to prove this. As Clark puts it: 'Gilbert Scott stood for the ordinary man who felt an inexplicable need for pointed arches'.

In 1857, Scott published his *Remarks on Secular and Domestic Architecture, Present and Future*, which shows how this worshipper of Pugin, himself the son of a low-church Protestant parson, secularised and liberalised Pugin's principles. Gothic, for Scott, was the closest to answering the architect's constructive needs; it was the closest to nature in its ornamentation; and it was a traditional national style. Free use of the Gothic, said Scott, would create a modern style.

But Scott himself was essentially a thorough eclectic. He won a competition, to the dismay of the Camdenians, for St Nicholas's Church, Hamburg, studying German Gothic before submitting his design, which astonished the Germans and created a national fervour for the Gothic (the French also claimed the Gothic as their national style). In 1857, Scott entered a competition for two Government Offices in Whitehall. This time he created an exotic Gothic with a dash of Flemish here and a soupçon of French there. He fell foul of Palmerston, a supporter of the Palladian style, and lost a protracted dispute about Gothic versus Grecian which was debated extensively in Parliament. Scott ended up losing the competition. Frustrated and disappointed, Scott recycled the designs into the Midland Hotel, London, which he thought afterwards was 'possibly *too good* for its purpose'. What could be more impressively theatrical than this eclectic pastiche, which has been described as combining 'the west end of a German cathedral with several Flemish town halls'? Butterfield, Street, and Waterhouse may have been better technical architects than Gilbert Scott, and Burges may have created more beautiful interiors, but Scott did more than they to stamp it as a popular style, and in doing so he embodied the paradox of a 'natural theatre'.

Ruskin is the other great transmitter of Pugin's ideas to the mid-Victorians. His eloquent theories are Pugin disinfected of Catholic ideology. Ruskin was brought up in the rabid Protestant faith of his mother. The second edition of *The Seven Lamps of Architecture* (1849) contains anti-Papist diatribes aimed at Pugin and his followers, which Ruskin subsequently excised. These passages had the unconscious effect of selling much of Pugin's thought to a Protestant audience, and in doing so, advanced the Gothic Revival through his quite different commitment to medievalism, which had become the obsession of a newly-industrialised age.

Despite his contempt for the superstition that the pointed arch derived from trees, a dialectical version of this analogy, doubled to include the human subject, is in fact Ruskin's basic metaphor for the beauties of Gothic style. He added vitalism to the Gothic Revival. Ruskin's self-reflexive organicism is as inescapable as Coleridge's from which it derived, and Ruskin put this penchant for the complex and ever-present relation between natural and aesthetic form at the service of the Gothic: 'there is not a cluster of weeds growing in any cranny of ruin which has not a beauty in all respects *nearly* equal, and, in some, immeasurably superior, to that of the most elaborate sculpture of its stones. 'Here, the very difference between the human and the natural is used to justify their unity.'

'The Lamp of Truth' sophisticates but reiterates the traditional revivalist attack on shams of all description, particularly industrially reproduced detail. It says of Scott's sentimental admiration for Gothic architecture: 'Even in its highest manifestation, in the great mind of Scott, while it indeed led him to lay his scenes in Melrose Abbey and Glasgow cathedral, rather than in St Paul's or St Peter's, it did not enable him to see the difference between true Gothic at Glasgow, and false Gothic at Abbotsford.'

Ruskin also extended the reach of the Gothic in *The Stones of Venice* (1851–3) by introducing his readers to the beauties of Italian Gothic, the Venetian variety of which included Byzantine influences. It was Ruskin who did most to add details like polychromy to the vocabulary of the Gothic Revival. Ruskin assumes the structural unity of great Gothic buildings, but in practice one of the major effects of his discussions is, once again, to concentrate the minds of his readers on a theatre of detail.

In this way, he links the architecture of the Gothic Revival directly with the Pre-Raphaelites and their obsessions with relations between flat surface and detail in painting, and with the arts and crafts movement led by Morris, which has its own foregrounding of detail. All these Ruskinian obsessions came together in the Oxford Museum building, some of the details of which were designed by Pre-Raphaelites. And the detail is decorative – the high point of Gothic style, Ruskin argued, is the brief flowering of Decorated tracery in the fourteenth century. After that, the style was subject to progressive organic decay, through the French Flamboyant to the hated Perpendicular. For Ruskin, the hanging fan vaulting in Henry VII's chapel (of 1502) was a great sham because it disguised the function of the roof supports.

Morris had many connections with the Gothic Revival. He was trained as an architect in the offices of G. E. Street in the 1850s. The Red House was designed by Philip Webb, a fellow architect in the office, on an L-shaped plan after Pugin's St Marie's Grange. Street himself was, of course, trained by Gilbert Scott. In *The Stones of Venice*, the chapter on the nature of Gothic, one of the great texts of the Gothic Revival, was also one of the first things printed by Morris's Kelmscott Press. Through Morris, Ruskin's writings had a great effect on the arts and crafts movement. There is a critique of the industrial revolution which links the two men. Here, Ruskin mediates between the Revival style and Carlyle's analysis of the cash nexus and his ironic invocation of the non-alienated, organic society of the medieval period.

Gothic, Art Nouveau and Modernism, 1872 and Beyond

When Gilbert Scott's notion of Gothic had prevailed and the style had become 'popular' in all its senses, Ruskin became the opponent of the very Gothic Revival movement he had helped to strengthen in the mid-century. Ruskin recognised the irony of this in a letter to the *Pall Mall Gazette* in 1872: 'one of my principal notions for leaving my present house is that it is surrounded everywhere by the accursed Frankenstein monsters of, indirectly, my own making'.

There is some truth in this ironical claim – that Ruskin had spawned a monstrosity which eventually drove him out. In fact, much good work in the Gothic style was done after 1872 by very good architects (for example, the Town Hall, Manchester: Waterhouse, 1868–77; Glasgow University: G. C. Scott, 1870; the Natural History Museum, London: Waterhouse, 1873–80). Street's office had also trained an original talent in William Burges, the restorer of Cardiff Castle in the 1870s whose elaborately literary and theatrical polychrome interiors bridge the gap between Gothic designs from Pugin and Ruskin and the Pre-Raphaelite movement.

The real death of Gothic Revival occurred, not with Norman Shaw's Queen Anne movement of the 1880s, but with the advent of Modernism around 1900, when it became obvious that this historicised style, however electic, was rigidly ornamental and would not adapt to modern materials and new organisations of space. Modernism was also both a secular and an international movement and the Gothic Revival – despite its exportation to America, Australia and India, and its separate development in France and Germany – was tied to the idea of a national tradition.

On the other hand, the Gothic had friendlier relations with painting and with the arts and crafts movement. The cultivation of flat pattern which is a traditional element in the theatrical medievalism of Gothic interiors modulates easily into Art Nouveau. Pevsner has a classic analysis of this relationship in his discussion of Antonio Gaudí. The career of Antonio Gaudí is an emblem of what happened to the Gothic Revival. Gaudí trained as a Gothic Revivalist of an orthodox kind in the 1880s: the early parts of his extraordinary epic Temple of the Holy Family in Barcelona are extravagantly, almost parodically, Gothic and organicist. But the later façades develop through Art Nouveau and Surrealism into the final posthumous designs which are abstract, geometric and Modernist in form.

The Revival was a struggle. The propaganda for the movement was organicist, anti-machine; it stressed the use of craftsmanship and selected its materials arbitrarily. But from the outset its interest in detail also inevitably encouraged the mass production of artifical materials and artificial effects. Morris spawned another version of the same paradox – that in part he resisted industrial production, and in part he reorientated it.

Take, for example, the uneasiness of attitudes towards iron. Despite the beauty of the tracery of the Coalbrookdale Bridge, which may well have been a reminiscence of Gothic Revival forms, iron had been virtually taboo in Gothic Revival architecture since the Comissioners' churches of the early nineteenth century, when Rickman himself had used it in Liverpool in St Michael's, Toxteth.

By the 1890s, however, the knell of doom had been sounded. The Gothic style was becoming a choice, not a necessity. The Journals of Thomas Hardy are an eloquent testimony to the dominance of Gothic Revival style in the training of an architect from the 1860s onwards. Hardy himself was interested in Greek art and culture and couldn't abide what he thought of as the domination of a barbarous and affected style of building. But Hardy had his revenge on the Gothic Revival. The sub-text of his great novel *Jude the Obscure*, which presents ironically the burning ambition of an illiterate young stonemason to reach the New Jerusalem, Christminster (obviously based on Oxford), the city of his dreams, is concerned with the completely repressive social structure, encapsulated in the Gothic style, a picture which Ruskin would not have recognised until his later career when he seemed to echo it, but for quite different reasons. Hardy makes Gothic Revival architecture the perfect expression of an outdated hierarchical class system which, lost in a hieratic dream of the past, denies education and social justice to the individual citizen, whether man or woman, in the present.

VICTOR SAGE

Gothic Romance

If a term more slippery than 'Gothic' exists, that term is 'Romance'. **MATTHEW LEWIS** called *The Monk* (1796), that notoriously lewd and outrageous narrative, 'A Romance', and Joshua Pickersgill Jr described as 'A Romance' *The Three Brothers* (1803), in the climactic scene of which a baby belonging to the hero's wife is destroyed by peasants who throw it about to see whether, being black, it can fly. But **ANN RADCLIFFE** and her ilk use the term equally to describe their kinder, gentler fiction, and it is to their sort of novel that the term now usually adheres – **TERROR** Gothic, Soft Gothic, **FEMALE GOTHIC**. Such Gothic tends to have a good dash of romance in the popular understanding of the word as well as the scholarly one, while retaining the classic trilogy of necessary Gothic components – isolation, complicated setting, a threat possibly supernatural but more likely to be human and male.

The heroines of Gothic Romance are not the vaporous, swooning creatures of caricature, undone by over-sensitivity; their troubles are real. Radcliffe's Emily in *The Mysteries of Udolpho* (1794), for instance, valiantly counterfeits calmness while having a nocturnal picnic supper in the forest, storm and wolves pending, with two ruffians who 'she believes' may kill her. Her bravery is typical, though perhaps extreme. The heroines of Gothic Romance lift the black veil, go to the attic, confront the possible spectres – attempt, in short, to shed some factual light on their mysterious surroundings and find their ways out of their Gothic dilemmas. In **HORROR** Gothic, to be sure, their surroundings would be worse. Whereas in *The Monk* (1796) the unfortunate Agnes, locked in a convent charnel house, lifts in her hand a soft object that proves to be the putrefying head of a nun, in *The Mysteries of Udolpho* (1794) the terrifying object behind the famous black veil is a waxwork representation of a corpse – waxen decay, waxen worms. It has no smell, and had Emily touched it (as she does not), her fingers would not have sunk.

Is this authorial discretion the identifying note of romance? Or does the genre depend on the likelihood that the beleaguered **HEROINE** will, against all realistic odds, find her way to a happy ending? Perhaps a handful of miracles – the lucky moonbeam that falls on the trap door, the coming back clean and whole from the darkness – are a more potent distancer from the other sort of Gothic, and from the reader's world as well, than any removal in time or place.

Here, approximately, is what happens in Gothic Romance, from Ann Radcliffe and her many imitators in the 1790s and following, through Victoria Holt, and hers, in the 1960s. A young female is stripped of her human support, her mother usually dead before the novel begins, her father or other guardian dying in the early chapters. The lover (if any) who might protect her is sent away or prevented from seeing her. Depending upon the period of the novel, she may be kidnapped, or fall into the hands of an unscrupulous guardian, or go out as a governess, or marry hastily. Out in the world her troubles multiply. People want to kill her, rape her, lock her up in a convent for life, and make off with her small fortune. Her task is to defend her virtue and liberty, to resist evil, and especially to penetrate disguises – spot the plausible seeming villains, trust the suspicious looking heroes – and thereby rebuild a support system that will restore her to a quiet life. With pluck and luck she manages these near impossibilities and is rewarded with the discovery of lost relatives and/or the promise of reliable domestic love in a household of her own.

Setting is crucial for atmosphere and as metaphor. The Gothic world is melancholy, menacing, shot through with guilt and fear. But it is, despite some bizarre embellishments, recognisable as the grimmer side of the human condition, with its 'what am I doing here?' and its 'where is this anyway?' The past is mysterious, the future murky, the present full of pitfalls. Castles, no protection, are half ruined, semi-occupied by a bad lot. Their passageways and trap doors, their mysteries and apparitions, merely complicate the already tenuous situations of the heroines. In the earlier settings, Italian or Spanish, the landscapes run to mountains, chasms and heavy forests, not to mention the convents and monasteries of Catholicism (that arbitrary, sinister, un-British religion). Novelists from **THE BRONTËS** onward often favour the desolation of moors, less conducive to ambush (though there are old wells, marshes, and so on) but dramatic in their lack of shelter. Much of the action takes place in the dark.

Romance in the popular sense, the pursuit of love, though it often provides a convenient dénouement, is less of a presence than one would suppose, in part because the plots stress separation and isolation. Rather, the heroines are wracked by a longing for home, for family, for connection, and this longing – diffuse, melancholy, deep – infuses the fiction with its characteristic tone. In an inspired scene in Radcliffe's *The Italian*

(1797), the heroine Ellena paces the beach near the isolated marble house to which she has been brought to be killed, and her cowled would-be assassin Schedoni crosses and recrosses her path. The self-protective cry wrenched from her in this crisis is only superficially untrue: 'I am far from home!' she cries. 'Night is coming on!' As the villain points out, she has no home.

The motif is consistent through the decades of Gothic Romance. Jane Eyre (usually considered a step in the lineage of Gothic heroines), after wandering and starving, very nearly immolates herself in the missionary work demanded by her cousin, whose blood connection she prizes, until she is saved by the miraculous voice of Mr Rochester, who will provide a home of greater warmth. Even the dream or wraith of Catherine at the start of Emily Brontë's *Wuthering Heights* (1847) mourns, 'I've been a waif for twenty years.' The jocular description of modern Gothic Romances like Victoria Holt's *The Mistress of Mellyn* (1960) as 'Girl Gets House' is not altogether off the mark.

The home for which they long, their happy ending, is not to be bought with moral compromise. When Emily of *The Mysteries of Udolpho* stands on the brink of a happy ending, escaped from her villainous uncle-by-marriage, with her virginity and patrimony both intact, she turns away her beloved Valancourt, whose attractions thrilled a generation of readers. He has passed through a period of dissipation in Paris, and although now reformed is, in her view, ruined. He is no longer a suitable mate, and so Emily sacrifices her dreams to her standards. Only the discovery that Valancourt's dissipation was exaggerated permits a happy ending. Ellena, in Ann Radcliffe's *The Italian*, though an evil abbess is forcing her to take vows, nevertheless hesitates excruciatingly at the impropriety of being rescued by the man she loves but has not yet married; later she balks again at the indignity of marrying into his hostile family. We might remember Jane Eyre, too, who will neither marry St John without loving him, nor love Mr Rochester without marrying him. Recent heroines are comparatively flexible, but still disinclined to accept expensive gifts, stifle their opinions, or compromise their independence.

Some changes in the Gothic Romance naturally occur over the decades, though the similarities are more conspicuous. The gentility of the romances forestalls some of the dramatic changes of device evident in the tougher Gothics, which gradually give less attention to putrefaction and more to sex. In the romances, the putrefaction was always waxen and the sex always offstage.

Preoccupation with religion of an odd sort marks the early Gothic Romances but not the later ones. Heroines are not conspicuously pious in a conventional sense; indeed they are rather likelier to turn to Nature for comfort than to God. Bad nuns and monks tend to outnumber good ones, and hardened villains quail before the greater villainy of the Inquisition. But the religion of Filial Piety thrives and even protects. Matilda and Isabella in *The Castle of Otranto* (1764) hysterically assure one another that they cannot possibly love Matilda's mother Hippolita as much as she deserves. In Eleanor Sleath's *Pyrenean Banditti* (1811), the right-thinking heroine Adelaide is principally concerned, after having been robbed of her position and fortune and thrust into the hands of a loutish and vaguely criminal couple said to be her real parents, that she cannot feel the love she should feel for her new father. She assumes that she is somehow degenerate and unnatural, not that she has good taste. Her problem is solved by the revelation that the man is not after all her real father; the assumption that one must love even horrible fathers is left unchallenged. In the religion of Filial Piety, the miniature portrait is a holy medal standing for the absent parent, and the face of the parent sometimes drives off villains as a crucifix drives off vampires. In *The Italian*, for instance, the assassin Schedoni recoils at the sight of his own portrait on the bosom that he is about to poniard, and spares his niece on the mistaken premise that she is his daughter.

Heroines in the early Gothics are indisputably pretty, and although they may, like Ellena, discreetly embroider for a convent to supplement the family income, they possess aristocratic relatives. This changes after Charlotte Brontë's *Jane Eyre* (1847), though the novel itself is only marginally Gothic by Radcliffean standards. (The adventures of Romance heroines, for instance, never start in childhood except in pastiches like *Northanger Abbey* (1818).) Heroines after Jane consider themselves plain, though not always quite in her uncompromising way: they complain that their mouths are too wide, their hair too unruly, their eyes too far apart or too bold. Their possibilities are undeveloped until their heroes arrive. What is more, they are only gentlemen's daughters and, like Jane, venture out into the world to earn a living, though in the most modern of the novels the excursion is alternatively caused by an impulsive marriage to a near stranger. Thus in Victoria Holt's *Kirkland Revels* (1962), Catherine Corder marries a man who clearly feels some uneasiness about his ancient home, who takes her there and soon thereafter dies, leaving her in unexplained peril. Impulsive marriage is nearly as hazardous as being kidnapped. The great task for the most modern heroine is understanding which of the difficult or possibly villainous men around her will turn out to be the one she can trust and marry.

The metaphors of Gothic Romance still work. Though the marvellous scene in *The Mysteries of Udolpho* when Emily believes that she and her uncle are discussing the lease of her house and he believes that they are discussing her engagement, could no longer be done, only the ambivalence of the language has been lost. The struggle to acquire, not become, property, like the quest for a home and stability, is perennial. Are Gothic villains implausible? Studies tell us that we are most likely to be murdered by someone known and close to us. They tell us how often women unwittingly fall into the hands of men whose capacity for abuse they did not accurately gauge, and in what psychological labyrinths they lose the way out. 'Escapist' has long been a critically dismissive word, but we have failed to appreciate its implications. Gothic Romance may owe its devoted following and endless appeal to the most extraordinary thing that its heroines do: against all statistics and probability, they escape.

ANN B. TRACY

Graveyard School

The Graveyard School emerged in the early 1740s, with three central works: Edward Young's *Night Thoughts* (1742–5), Robert Blair's *The Grave* (1743), and James Hervey's *Meditations among the Tombs* (1745). Though they were immensely popular and widely translated during the eighteenth century, the reputation of these writers subsequently plummeted, and has yet to recover. The genre's solitary meditations on human mortality serve as an important point of transition towards **ROMANTICISM** in their unabashed egotism, absence of linguistic self-restraint, and characteristic alienation. Earlier texts such as Alexander Pope's *Elegy to the Memory of an Unfortunate Lady* (1717) and Parnell's *A Night-piece on Death* (1721) also explore the formal possibilities of melancholic complaint, but in the Graveyard School these combine with the affective stylistics, associationist psychology, and above all the aesthetics of **THE SUBLIME** developed in early eighteenth-century-criticism, producing a rhetoric of overworked surface in the service of hyperbolic declamation, staccato and aphoristic yet amorphous and endlessly self-elaborating. (The compactness and composure of Gray's *Elegy Written in a Country Churchyard* (1751) make it unrepresentative despite its overt location.) The Graveyard School's evocations of darkness, solitude, loneliness and terror are absorbed by **HORACE WALPOLE, WILLIAM BECKFORD,** and **MATTHEW LEWIS** and from there into the mainstream of nineteenth-century Gothic. In addition, André Breton's homage to Young (1924) suggests that its poetic influence survives in the surrealist line of Lautréamont's *Les Chants de Maldoror* rather than cf. Alfred Tennyson's *In Memoriam*.

STEVE CLARK

Hawthorne, Nathaniel (1804–64)

Nathaniel Hawthorne was born in 1804, in Salem, Massachusetts. The Hathornes (Nathaniel added the 'w') were an old New England family, two of whom were magistrates involved in some of the sorrier episodes surrounding witch hunting and the violent suppression of the Quakers. Hawthorne spent a solitary, bookish childhood with his sister and widowed mother before going to college at Bowdoin, Brunswick. After college Hawthorne returned to Salem where he lived with his mother until 1840, when he married Sophia Peabody. Although Hawthorne connived in the portrait of himself as an isolated artist suffering twelve years in his mother's attic, it was more than a period of lonely creativity. Hawthorne travelled widely through his native New England, researching into the local lore that would enrich his fiction. Apart from 1853–7, when Hawthorne was consul for Liverpool, and then travelling in Europe, the Hawthornes remained in New England.

Nathaniel Hawthorne was, with **EDGAR ALLAN POE**, a leading American Gothic writer of the mid-nineteenth century. But unlike Poe, Hawthorne did not write full-blooded stories in which most – if not all – the leading Gothic features might be found. As Hawthorne himself put it, he was, above all else, a writer of romances, by which he meant the tradition of marvellous, fantastic tales, as opposed to the modern 'novel' with its realistic depictions of contemporary manners. As a writer of romances Hawthorne naturally found the Gothic indispensable, but he also drew upon other genres and styles. Hawthorne eschewed overt techniques of horror and terror in favour of a more ironic mode. Nevertheless, his persistent quest to represent 'picturesque and gloomy wrongs' meant that a Gothic tone pervades his *oeuvre*.

In contriving his own brand of Gothic romance Hawthorne drew upon British, German, as well as American sources. Sir Walter Scott's historical fiction was enormously influential, as to a lesser extent was Byron, but Hawthorne also found the dark allegories of Edmund Spenser's *The Faerie Queene* a constant source of inspiration. John Bunyan's religious allegory *Pilgrim's Progress* was also important. Two American writers were crucially significant in Hawthorne's development. **CHARLES BROCKDEN BROWN**'s novels – in turn influenced by William Godwin's *Caleb Williams* (1794) – not only demonstrated that one could successfully set Gothic romances in America, but provided a fictional idiom for the Calvinist legacy both writers shared. **WASHINGTON IRVING** was even more influential. The faddish success in England of *The Sketch Book*, published in serial form in 1819–20, inspired all American writers. More particularly, the two most famous tales from the *Sketch Book* – 'The Legend of Sleepy Hollow' and 'Rip Van Winkle' – provided Hawthorne with a narrative style he was later to perfect.

After leaving Bowdoin College, Hawthorne served a long apprentice-ship during which he was – in his own words – 'the obscurest man of letters in America'. At this point there was no reciprocal copyright agree-ment between the US and Britain. Predictably, American publishers pre-ferred English authors, who they could freely reproduce, to American ones they had to pay. Unknown novelists especially found it difficult to find their way into print. For twelve years Hawthorne published tales and sketches in the magazines before a publisher undertook to produce a se-lection as a book: *Twice-Told Tales* (1837). Even then the enterprise was underwritten by a friend of Hawthorne's without his knowledge. The success of the first collection led to two more: *Mosses from an Old Manse* (1846) and *The Snow-Image and other Twice-Told Tales* (1851). But it was only after his political appointment to the post of Surveyor of the Port of Salem that Hawthorne found the means (his sacking gave him the leisure) to support the writing of a full-length romance: *The Scarlet Letter* (1850).

It was in the early tales that Hawthorne particularly applied the lessons of Irving's *Sketch Book*. As in Irving's stories, one finds a founda-tion of American lore, an easy, parabolic style, an urbane surface con-cealing psychological depths, plus a teasing, ironic approach to the supernatural. Hawthorne's brand of psychological Gothic is particularly evident in the American tales 'Young Goodman Brown' and 'My Kinsman, Major Molyneux'. Both stories are rites of passage in which a young man moves tragi-comically into adulthood. Both draw upon the ancient tradition of midnight saturnalia: in the first story, the 'hero' attends a witch's Sabbath, while in the second, a country youth on his first visit to town stumbles into a mob in the process of tarring and feath-ering Major Molyneux, the uncle the youth seeks in order to advance his fortune. The stories are explorations into the guilty psyches of appar-ently naive and innocent young men, but they are also subtle allegories of America's own, troubled, revolutionary 'coming of age'. 'The Artist of the Beautiful', 'The Birthmark', and 'Rappaccini's Daughter' are Gothic tales in the medico-scientific tradition. These stories show, not just an English, but a Germanic influence, with **E. T. A. HOFFMANN** the single most important source. Hawthorne was a great local historian; many of his tales employ supernatural and/or violent episodes from the New England past (including, obliquely, his own family's), sometimes nar-rated in a gloomy, sometimes a sportive, manner, but generally within a Gothic mode.

The Scarlet Letter secured Hawthorne's growing fame. Allegedly based on a manuscript left by a Surveyor Pue, and discovered by Hawthorne during his stint at the Salem custom-house, the story re-visits an early episode from the history of Puritan settlement in the New World. Hester Prynne has just given birth to her daughter Pearl, even though Roger Chillingworth, her husband, has been absent for some years. Hester is arraigned for adultery, and is forced to wear the letter A, all the while silently and guiltily surveyed by her adulterous partner, the Rev. Arthur Dimmesdale. The narrative focuses exclusively on the consequent suffering, endurance, and potential redemption of the central characters. At first glance the story may appear only obliquely Gothic. The supernatural is continually explained away as the product of superstitious hallucination or religious fervour. There is no central, imprisoning structure – no 'castle' nor a sense of the central characters being entrapped by a feudal past. But the romance adapts the genre to its New World setting, and in a sense the Puritans are revealed as internalising these things within themselves. The reformed, 'modern', Calvinist theology they optimistically bring to the New World eventually proves to be, in itself, a Medieval prison; the bars are the superstitious ones of fanatical faith rather than mouldering stones. The romance deals specifically with the consequence of a rigid patriarchy; the meddling, proto-scientific Chillingworth is a clear instance of the Faustian/Gothic villain; while the framing narrative – with its pretence of a discovered manuscript – takes us immediately back to the preface of the first **GOTHIC NOVEL**, **HORACE WALPOLE**'s *The Castle of Otranto* (1764).

Hawthorne's next romance, *The House of the Seven Gables* (1851), is more obviously Gothic in theme and imagery, although perhaps less so in tone. It is, as **HERMAN MELVILLE** appreciatively put it, 'dreamy'. In many respects *The House of the Seven Gables* is an American version of Walpole's *The Castle of Otranto*. The theme is the same ('the sins of the fathers'), as is the central object of contention (the ancestral house) as well as the catalyst (an ancient act of usurpation). Gothic motifs abound: a witch's curse; a mystic picture; as well as Mesmerism, Hawthorne's up-to-date version of mental invasion. The Gothic has always been concerned with the integrity of the body, and by extension, the mind; with the primitive fear of either finding ourselves cut off from others (live burial) or having others transgress our personal space, mental or physical. For Hawthorne, this potent nexus of fears, with its overtones of sado-masochism, was most vividly incarnated in the mid-nineteenth-century rage for mesmerism, the hallucinatory practices made popular by Franz Anton Mesmer. The hero of the romance, Holgrave, is an artist/writer figure as well as a mesmerist. He is, it turns out, a benevolent mesmerist; but the linkage of the two things, invading and commandeering another's mind, and art itself, remained for Hawthorne a site mustering his intense ambivalence towards his own profession. Within many of his texts, it is often the only real point of Gothic **HORROR**.

The Blithedale Romance followed in 1852. The book is based on Hawthorne's experience years earlier as a member of Brook Farm, an experiment in socialist, communitarian living. It appears to be a sly *roman-à-clef*. Zenobia, the main character, bears a few obvious resemblances to Margaret Fuller, a real-life socialist feminist who was unhappy in her love life and died by drowning (Zenobia's story in a nutshell). Whether a *roman-à-clef* or not, the present-day setting of the narrative drags against Hawthorne's natural instinct for the Gothic; even so, the Gothic does crop up, especially in the book's inset tales, in its interest in crime and redemption, and in the reworked theme of mesmerism.

Hawthorne's final, completed romance, *The Marble Faun*, appeared in 1860. As a reward for writing the presidential campaign biography of his old school friend Franklin Pierce, Hawthorne was made American consul for Liverpool, at the time a lucrative position. *The Marble Faun* represents Hawthorne's experience of Europe, but especially of Italy, where he had travelled, and where the romance is set. It is the darkest, and most Gothic, of Hawthorne's works. This is especially true of Miriam and Donatello, the European relationship Hawthorne opposes to the Americans Kenyon and Hilda. The donnée of the narrative is the most frankly supernatural of Hawthorne's givens: Count Donatello, an innocent young 'man' bearing an uncanny resemblance to the 'faun' of Praxiteles, is transformed into someone fully human through the experience of sin, guilt, and sacrifice. Set in Rome, the romance features a claustrophobic Gothic topography of crumbling palazzos, crypts and catacombs, while the central study of the Jewish Miriam and Italian Donatello represents Hawthorne's frankest depiction of the murky turbulence of sexual desire.

During his last years Hawthorne lost his artistic direction, possibly owing to the oppressive calamity of the American Civil War, which darkened his final creative endeavours. He left behind him the drafts of several romances he was unable to finish, the plot lines obsessively disappearing into a labyrinth of Gothic motifs: magical elixirs, eternal life, demonic bargains, and bloody footprints being among the more overt. **CHARLES MATURIN**'s *Melmoth the Wanderer* (1820) and William Godwin's *St Leon* (1799) appeared especially to haunt Hawthorne's last efforts. He died in 1864.

ROBERT MILES

Hero-Villain

When Leslie Fiedler claims that the 'hero-villain is indeed an invention of the gothic form, while his temptation and suffering, the beauty and terror of his bondage to evil are amongst its major themes', he is perhaps only telling half the story (*Love and Death in the American Novel*, 1960). It is true that the hero-villain necessarily bears the dual markings of both villain and victim, but, in doing so, he represents not so much a pure invention as his connection and indebtedness to a number of similar male figures including Milton's Satan, the eighteenth-century 'man of feeling', and above all, the Byronic Hero.

Byron's description of the characteristics of his eponymous hero in 'Lara' (1814) in Canto 1 is almost archetypal (see also, 'Childe Harold, I and II; 1812, and 'Manfred', 1817):

> In him inexplicably mix'd appear'd
> Much to be loved and hated, sought and fear'd;
>   (xvii, lines 289–90)

> There was in him a vital scorn of all:
> As if the worst had fall'n which could befall,
> He stood a stranger in this breathing world,
> An erring spirit from another hurled;
> A thing of dark imaginings ...
>   (xviii, lines 313–17)

Here Lara dramatises what constitutes a model combination of the 'inexplicably mixed' physical and character traits for the contradictory hero-villain figure in general. Physically he is dark and of powerful physique, and is frequently in possession of piercing eyes and an expression which indicates a mixture of contempt ('a vital scorn of all') and gloom ('a thing of dark imaginings'). As this suggests, his behaviour is unpredictable; he is moodily taciturn and violently explosive by turns. Exactly the same kinds of combinations of terms are mobilised in descriptions of more explicitly Gothic hero-villains both before and after Lara. Vathek, for example, possesses a 'pleasing and majestic figure' yet 'when he was angry, one of his eyes became so terrible, that no person could bear to behold it' (*Vathek*, 1786). Ambrosio displays 'a certain severity in his look and manner that inspired universal awe, and few could sustain the glance of his eye, at once fiery and penetrating', and is discovered during a period of his life when his 'passions are most vigorous, unbridled and despotic' (*The Monk*, 1796) (see **WILLIAM BECKFORD** and **MATTHEW LEWIS**). Whilst Melmoth's face is 'cold, stony and rigid', his voice is 'melodious' and his eyes have an 'infernal and dazzling lustre' (*Melmoth the Wanderer*, 1820 (see **CHARLES MATURIN** and **WANDERING JEW**).

These same features continue to define later more romantic hero-villains such as Heathcliff, whom Lockwood describes as having 'an erect and handsome figure, and rather morose' with a 'degree of underbred pride' and an ability to 'love and hate, equally under cover' (*Wuthering Heights*, 1847) (see **THE BRONTËS**). Even Daphne du Maurier maximises readerly suspicions when she draws on this type in her portrayal of Maxim de Winter, who is not only 'arresting, sensitive ... in some strange inexplicable way', but equally he resembles a mysteriously 'cloaked and secret', though 'Unknown Gentleman', from a portrait the narrator once saw (*Rebecca*, 1938).

Most importantly, as implied above, this contradictory personality is symptomatic of the fact that all these heroes are, in the first place, cursed by a rebellious impulse to test and transgress human social and ethical constraints. It is this consistent and fatal over-reaching which constitutes the core ambivalence of this figure; both violent, threatening and often demonic (signalled by the piercing eyes), he is yet at the same time always himself an outsider ('a stranger in this breathing world') in a state of suffering and an object of persecution (see **DEMONIC**). For these reasons the hero-villain is frequently the figure intrinsic to the social critiques of a number of texts since, as Fred Botting points out, he is rarely denounced as the cause of evil himself, but rather he 'invites respect and understanding' since 'real evil is identified among embodiments of tyranny, corruption and prejudice, identified with certain, often aristocratic, figures and, more frequently, with institutions of power manifested in government hierarchies, social norms and religious superstition' (*Gothic*, 1996). The hero-villain then, caught in a double-bind himself, simultaneously plays this contradiction out at the level of his both fascinating and destructive personality. Yet with his destruction comes readerly exhilaration, a quality to be found not only in the defiant deeds which he performs in the narrative, but also in the rich rhetoric devoted to his portrayal. As indicated above then, this exhilaration provokes not so much a condonement of wrong-doing so much as a temporary celebration (albeit a complicated and ambivalent one) of a challenging, but gloriously self-destructive maverick.

In this light it is possible to see how such characters may be read most usefully in the social and political contexts from which they emerged in the late eighteenth century. Speaking of Walter Scott's Marmion, as well as various of Byron's heroes, Marilyn Butler has noted that, as 'moody outlaws, haunted by some secret consciousness of guilt, these heroes act as a focus for contemporary fantasies' (*Romantics, Rebels and Reactionaries*, 1981). For her and other critics these figures are profoundly 'bi-partisan', in that it is Napoleon who is the real figure who crystallises their model of heroism, within which greatness and honour, though ultimately and inevitably defeat also, were secured through superior individual expertise and force of personality rather than, or despite, authority borrowed from institutions or from the collective will, both of which were fatal to the transcendental and misunderstood hero.

Each of these characteristics, however, represents a reason why the hero-villain in the Gothic serves more to throw social and sexual repression into relief than he does to demonstrate the possibility of legitimate redress or reform. For example, whilst Heathcliff may elicit our sympathy initially as he bears, 'without winking or shedding a tear', all the prejudice against his 'gypsy brat' status, including Hindley's 'blows' and Nelly's 'pinches', none the less his 'otherness' to the social, even sometimes the human, is clearly and persistently encoded in the text. Initially Nelly describes him as an 'it', and later as possessing a 'half-civilised ferocity' and as an 'evil beast', whilst Hareton calls him an 'imp of Satan', and, in a fit of jealousy, Cathy declaims him as 'an unreclaimed creature ... an arid wilderness of furze and whinstone'. Indeed the foregrounding of each of these images confirms Frank Kermode's point that Heathcliff is situated 'between' everything (the familial categories of brother and lover, categories of social class and of nature and culture, human and inhuman) but belongs to nothing ('*Wuthering Heights* as Classic'). In this respect, though the hero-villain may temporarily function as a vehicle for fantasies of unregulated desire and ambition or for sympathising with the socially persecuted, the undeniable nature of his 'otherness' (Ambrosio's closeted upbringing, Frankenstein's 'unnatural' fascination with re-animating the dead, Melmoth's demonic pact) always ultimately provides a means of distancing and disavowing his actions as unfeasible or illegitimate.

The hero-villain has also been of particular interest to feminist critics and to writers who have been especially occupied with those characters who have emerged from female imaginations; most notably characters in whom there is strong romantic investment – classically Heathcliff and Rochester (*Jane Eyre*, 1847). Elaine Showalter has used the term 'brute hero' to describe such characters in the line of Rochester who, horrified contemporary critics feared, illustrated or possibly excited dangerously masochistic or rebellious female desires (*A Literature of Their Own*, 1977). Showalter interprets these males as figures in a literary cross-dressing exercise in which 'the descendants of Rochester represent the passionate and angry qualities in their creators' (see **HEROINE**). Thus women writers, limited by social and literary conventions, are seen as being forced to project power, aggression and transgressive desire through male figures. However, such a reading, in understanding all desire in these novels as female, perhaps risks erasing the issue of gender difference and desire altogether. This would be at the expense of examining ways in which female writers might mobilise romantic hero-villains less to indulge forbidden impulses than to stage, and in doing so expose and implicitly critique, the assumptions behind patriarchal authority, especially in so far as it regulates male/female relationships, though not exclusively this domain (see Eve Kosofsky Sedgwick, *Between Men: English Literature and Male Homosocial Desire*, 1985).

Hero-villains continue to have a life in contemporary popular Gothic film and literature such as **ANNE RICE**'s vampire series, each volume of which injects the figure of the vampire, which previously it had only been possible to execrate and demonise, with heroic stature and sympathetic human qualities. Like the Byronic hero, he is forced to wander the earth in a state of permanent exile, persecuting others as a result of a condition of being which is itself the mark of his own persecution by another. This connection between the Byronic hero and the contemporary vampire is made even more explicit in Tom Holland's novel *The Vampyre* (1995). Other writers, most notably **ANGELA CARTER**, have used the type more critically and experimentally. *Heroes and Villains* (Angela Carter, 1969), as the title suggests, at once separates out the two previously combined aspects of this figure, attributing them respectively to the opposed groups of the Professors and the Barbarians, and at the same time combines them in her female hero(ine)-villain, Marianne, who has 'sharp, cold eyes and she was spiteful', whilst it is her lover Jewel who is like a 'diabolic version of female beauties of former periods'. In the fantasy, post-apocalyptic world of the novel, Carter removes, confuses and questions previously established connections between gender, and gender role and function, which operated in previous eighteenth- and nineteenth-century-versions of the Gothic.

HELEN STODDART

Heroine

HORACE WALPOLE's famous Gothic novel *The Castle of Otranto* (1764) turns upon a plot in which a vulnerable heroine, Isabella, is at the mercy of Manfred, a wicked older man. In many early Gothic novels the heroine, sometimes accompanied by the virtuous young man who loves her, is pursued across countryside and/or through subterranean labyrinths by a variation on this villain figure. She may suffer imprisonment and cruelty at the hands of her pursuer; above all, she is a potential victim of his desire. Portrayed usually in relation to contemporary notions of the proper lady, the heroine demonstrates a passive courage in the face of such danger, and her behaviour sometimes offers a clear contrast to the more energetic machinations of other women in the text. In **MATTHEW LEWIS**'s *The Monk* (1796), for example, the purity of the naive young heroine is threatened by the deeply transgressive Matilda, who has sold her soul to the devil and who aids the hero-villain in his desire to rape Antonia. Even **BRAM STOKER**'s *Dracula* (1897), a novel which unsettles conventional categories of active masculinity and passive feminity, presents a similar pattern of polarisation, offering female vampires who haunt the dreams of Jonathan Harker at one extreme and two 'heroines' who become the victims of Dracula at the other. These novels accord with Leslie Fiedler's notion of the Gothic as a genre which 'centers not in the heroine (the persecuted principle of salvation) but in the villain (the persecuting principle of damnation)' (*Love and Death in the American Novel*, 1960).

Gothic novels by women interrogate this gendering of the genre and their heroines are often a response to the cultural anxieties and dominant discourses of the time (see also **FEMALE GOTHIC**). For example, in **ANN RADCLIFFE**'s fiction, usually set in a previous age, the beautiful, sensitive and vulnerable heroines (they are often orphans or motherless) are complex products of **ROMANTICISM** and the cult of **SENSIBIL- ITY**. Thus they frequently interact with the landscape in a manner which, as Anne Mellor has argued, echoes yet is distinctive from the male Romantic writer's interest in the sublime (*Romanticism and Gender*, 1993). However, the way in which they react to moments of crisis (for example, by fainting, blushing or falling into silence) derives, as Daniel Cottom has pointed out, from a body language specific to notions of fem- ininity and sensibility current from the mid-eighteenth century (*The Civilized Imagination: A Study of Ann Radcliffe, Jane Austen, and Sir Walter Scott*, 1985). The notion that a character such as Ellena, in Ann Radcliffe's *The Italian* (1797), is therefore essentially a passive heroine, has recently been challenged by feminist readings which see her silence or refusal as a means of resistance. This resistance to coercion by, for example, a massive and corrupt institution (such as the Catholic Church) and/or a scheming, wicked older man who wishes to seduce or kill her for his own ends (Montoni, in *The Mysteries of Udolpho* (1794); Schedoni, in *The Italian*) can fruitfully be related to social changes in the eighteenth century.

The heroine's attempts to escape, Kate Ferguson Ellis has argued, indi- cate a desire to subvert a domestic ideology which was beginning to tyrannise the lives of middle-class women within a capitalist, newly-in- dustrialised society; in such a society the bourgeois home was becoming uncomfortably like the castle or prison of the Gothic text in the way it constrained its female inhabitants (*The Contested Castle: Gothic Novels and the Subversion of Domestic Ideology*, 1989). Even Jane Austen's famous 'burlesque' of the Gothic novel, *Northanger Abbey* (1818), can be read in such a way (see **GOTHIC PARODY**): Paul Morrison has suggested that the masculine surveillance of the heroine to be found in many eighteenth-century Gothic novels, is here replaced by a panoptic vision which censors and constrains women's education and social development. Thus Catherine Morland, 'in training for a heroine' between the ages of fifteen and seventeen, is subject to Henry Tilney's teasing judgement of what she reads and how she speaks ('Enclosed in Openness: *Northanger Abbey* and the Domestic Carceral'). The experience of Austen's heroine provides a complex statement not just on the perils of the imagination and the unlikelihood of **THE SUPERNATURAL** (like Radcliffe, Austen debunks ghostly terrors), but on the real horror of a society which evaluates its young women in terms of economic worth. Interestingly, much of Catherine's discomfort is due to the fact that the power of refusal accorded to Radcliffe's heroines is constantly thwarted in *Northanger Abbey* by the bullying tactics of John Thorpe and others.

Austen's novel offers a bridge between early Gothic fiction, in which the heroine is threatened by external forces, and later Gothic novels in which the drama moves more into the mind of the heroine. In *Villette* (1853), Charlotte Brontë, whilst reviving many features of Gothic fiction (for example, a foreign setting; anti-Catholic feeling; a ghostly nun), presents a subtle study of the psychological effects of repression on the mind of her heroine Lucy Snowe, who conceals a passionate nature beneath a frosty reserve. The ghostly nun who appears to Lucy Snowe several times during her time as an English teacher at Madame Beck's *pensionnat* in Labassecour is, amongst other things, a vivid metaphor for Lucy Snowe's 'buried' selves. The Radcliffean 'explanation' of the nun's presence does nothing to divest the spectre of the powerful symbolic import it comes to carry in the novel. The web of religion, nationality, class and gender which Brontë spins in *Villette* allows her to probe the problematics of identity: Lucy's negotiation of conflicting discourses and subject positions advances considerably the Gothic novel's exploration of the split self. Much of her silent suffering is related to questions concerning women's expression of sexual desire, the economic dependency of women, and cultural notions of 'femininity'.

The volatile heroine of Emily Brontë's *Wuthering Heights* (1847) demonstrates more clearly her thwarted passions by returning as a ghostly presence to haunt the dreams of Lockwood, who, significantly, sees her as a child, before the confines of womanhood closed in on her. Similarly, Jane Eyre's anguish and repressed desire find a textual expression in the character of Bertha Mason: recent feminist readings of *Jane*

Eyre (1847) suggest that Charlotte Brontë thus collapses the binary oppositions used to portray women in earlier Gothic texts into a **DOPPELGÄNGER** effect which exposes the suffocating limitations imposed on intelligent women in nineteenth-century England.

Part of the Brontës' great skill as writers lay in their ability to revitalise Gothic trappings and to create heroines whose emotional and spiritual growth is explored through the dissolution of the dividing lines between realism and Romanticism, 'masculine' and 'feminine', 'self' and 'other' (see **THE BRONTËS**). *Jane Eyre*, in particular, has captured the imagination of several Gothic writers: many novels, including Daphne du Maurier's *Rebecca* (1938) and Jean Rhys's *Wide Sargasso Sea* (1966), have been inspired by it. In these later works, the relationship between the nameless narrator and Rebecca in the first instance, and Antoinette/ Bertha in the second, offer variations on Charlotte Brontë's portrayal of a heroine haunted by another woman who is both her opposite and a hidden 'self'; in so doing they further problematise assumptions concerning the role of the heroine in Gothic fiction, particularly in relation to class and race.

Later Gothic works often present heroines similarly 'haunted': the nameless narrator of Charlotte Perkins Gilman's *The Yellow Wallpaper* (1892; also indebted to *Jane Eyre*) sees the grotesque and bulbous head of another woman in the wallpaper of the room where she is confined during a period of illness, possibly itself provoked by a husband who pathologises her state of intellectual frustration (the fact that the novel was published during a decade which saw the rise of the 'New Woman' and the campaign for suffrage both in Britain and in the United States is no accident). The frequency with which the heroine of this and other Gothic texts either appears nameless, or has several names (as in, for example, Carson McCullers' *The Member of the Wedding*, 1946, and Sylvia Plath's *The Bell Jar*, 1963) suggests that twentieth-century women writers have come to realise that the conventions of Gothic fiction offer a useful way to explore crises of identity peculiar to women, particularly those connected with the rites of passage associated with adolescence, loss of virginity, marriage and childbirth.

More recently, **ANGELA CARTER** and Fay Weldon have produced heroines within Gothic works which offer a much more robust treatment of social constructions of femininity. Weldon's Ruth Patchett in *The Life and Loves of a She-Devil* (1983), for example, transforms her physical strength into a stereotypical ideal of beauty in order to gain access to the power of the 'feminine' woman – and thus exposes, for the reader, both the economic rewards and the terrible cost of collusion with patriarchal values. In Carter's *The Magic Toyshop* (1967), Melanie, whose teenage sense of self is dominated by masculine constructs of what men desire of women, moves into a household in which the tyranny of Uncle Philip and the silence of Aunt Margaret challenge her early romantic notions of what it is to be a woman; the happiest adult relationship in this household is, in fact, an incestuous one. The short stories of *The Bloody Chamber* (1979) offer us heroines whose eroticism and sexuality are celebrated but whose complicity with voyeurism, pornography and sadomasochism raises disturbing questions about the objectification of women and the allure of the Byronic or Bluebeard hero. In the title story, the threatened murder of the heroine is foiled by the arrival of a mother on horseback (in Perrault's 1697 version, she is saved by her brothers); the ending thereby concludes the quest for the lost or absent mother undertaken by many Gothic heroines and offers a dynamic female role model. Carter's women characters may seem a far cry from Ann Radcliffe's modest young ladies, but they are the latest generation in a long line of Gothic heroines whose fates invite readers to reflect upon and query the fictional role of the heroine in Gothic writing and the social construction of 'woman'.

AVRIL HORNER

Hoffmann, E. T. A. (1776–1822)

E. T. A. Hoffmann is surely one of the most authentic, imaginative and multi-faceted artists of the Romantic Age. The meaning of the term 'Romantic' is 'romance-like', 'phantasmic'. Thus 'Romanticism' puts a strong emphasis on the imaginative in art. The scope of such an art is defined by means of a reflection on the possibilities of art, in terms of genres, media and modes of expression. Music is considered the highest form of artistic experience and knowledge. The aesthetics of the Romantic Age may be described as the aesthetic of the 'Picturesque and Sublime'. It carries to full bloom a discussion which had been going on during the eighteenth century and which had probably received its strongest impulse through Edmund Burke's *A Philosophical Enquiry into the Origin of Our Ideas of the Sublime and the Beautiful* (1757). The Sublime may briefly be characterised as the experience of transcendence in empirical, aesthetic (natural) landscape and history. In this sense, Hoffmann has proved himself not only highly creative and original as a writer of literature and essays but also an excellent draughtsman and caricaturist as well as an outstanding musician and composer. Furthermore, he has written texts which provide deep insights into the aesthetics and into the reciprocal dependencies between music, literature and the graphic arts.

Hoffmann was born on 24 January 1776 in Königsberg, the capital of Eastern Prussia, and given the first names Ernst Theodor Wilhelm. Hoffmann studied law, like his father and uncles, but he also appreciated the inspiration provided by the local cultural scene. However, no direct links are known with Immanuel Kant who taught philosophy at the university. After his exams Hoffmann became a civil servant at several law courts in those provinces of Poland which had been annexed by Prussia in the previous decades. Later (1816) he became a judge at the Superior Court of Justice for Berlin. His artistic outlook and abilities made it frequently difficult for him to succumb to the dryness of his job and the philistine and reactionary attitudes of his principals. There were several cases where he had sided openly with progressive democrats who were on trial.

After the defeat of Prussia by Napoleon and the subsequent collapse of the State, Hoffmann worked as musical director in the North Bavarian town of Bamberg and later in Dresden, Saxony (1808–13). His credentials for these positions were his work as a music instructor and the publication of several compositions. In 1810 he composed a *Miserere in B flat minor for soli, chorus, organ and orchestra* for Archduke Ferdinand of Austria, and on the title page of this score he named himself for the first time Ernst Theodor *Amadeus*, in veneration of Mozart's genius. Besides Mozart he admired Gluck, Haydn and Beethoven. Gluck's impression on him is testified by a tale entitled '*Ritter Gluck*' and his differentiated understanding of Beethoven, especially of his fifth Symphony, is expressed in the essay '*Beethoven's Instrumental-Musik*' (1813). In 1813 and 1814 he composed a fairy-tale style opera, *Undine*, which in 1816 was successfully performed in one of Berlin's leading theatres. Its scenery was designed by the famous architect Karl Ludwig Schinkel, and Karl Maria von Weber (the famous composer of the *Freischütz*) considered it one of the most ingenious pieces of their time. The opera continued to be performed for a year until the *Schauspielhaus* burnt down and the set and costumes were lost.

The appointment to the Superior Court secured Hoffmann a decent lifestyle for the first time. Meanwhile he had also become a widely read writer. Since his time in Dresden he had written a series of phantastic and grotesque tales, on which his reputation still rests. His basic theme is the complex and mysterious relationship between the worlds of the imaginative and the real. In 1814–15 he had published his tales as '*Phantasie stücke in Callots Manier*', i.e. he had classified them as bizarre facets of rococo or as '*capriccios*'. In his collection *Kreisleriana* (1810ff), which centres around Kreisler, a musical director under the threat of madness, however, he expresses a radical view of the artist's existence.

The artist is a person who is able to read the hieroglyphics of nature and thus has access to mysterious and transcendental sources of knowledge. According to Hoffmann, the artist is driven by an infinite yearning for **THE SUBLIME**. This sets him apart from the real world. Art transcends the dimension of the pragmatic. It participates in a Beyond in an elevated, spiritual as well as in an abysmal, demonic sense. In the cycle of narratives and essays entitled *Die Serapionsbrüder* (1818–21) Hoffmann defines his literary programme as the 'serapiontic principle'. It is his aim to translate his fantastic inner world into images as concrete and real as possible.

Hoffmann's final years (he died on 25 June 1822) were characterised by recurring spells of chronic illness (rheumatic fever, polyneuritis) and of quarrels with his superiors who were trying to suppress the incipient democratic movement in Germany. His fantastic tale *'Meister Floh'*, which poked fun at these measures by even quoting from law court files, was confiscated and he was severely reprimanded. With his relegation from office still imminent, Hoffmann died aged 46. Hoffmann's reputation persists to the present day. Outstanding tributes to his genius were paid through Jacques Offenbach's opera *Hoffmanns Erzählungen* (Paris, 1881; *Les Contes de Hoffmann – The Tales of Hoffmann*, through Poe's and Baudelaire's expressed admiration and, recently, through Angela Carter's postmodern fantasy novel *The Infernal Desire Machines of Doctor Hoffmann* (1972).

H.'s masterworks are

- The two novels *Die Elixiere des Teufels* (1815–16; i.e. 'The Devil's Elixirs'; this novel was inspired by M. G. Lewis's *The Monk*, which earlier had drawn heavily on German folklore and German Gothic novels), and *Lebens-Ansichten des Katers Murr nebst Fragmentarischer Biographie des Kapellmeisters Johannes Kreisler in Zufälligen Makulaturblättern* (1819–21; 'Views and Opinions of Murr, the Tomcat').
- The fantastic tales *'Ritter Gluck'* (1809), *'Der Goldene Topf'* (1814), *'Der Sandmann'* (1916), *'Nussknacker und Mausekönig'* (1816), *'Rat Krespel'* (1818), *'Klein Zaches Genannt Zinnober'* (1819), *'Das Fräulein von Scuderi'* (1819; a prototype of the detective story), *'Meister Floh'* (1822).
- The two collections (cycles) of narratives entitled *Nachtstücke* (2 vols, 1816/17), and *Die Serapionsbrüder* (4 vols, 1818–21).

HANS-ULRICH MOHR

Hogg, James (1770–1835)

James Hogg was regarded by his contemporaries as one of the leading writers of the day, but the nature of his fame was influenced by the fact that, as a young man, he had been a self-educated shepherd. The third edition (1814) of *The Queen's Wake* contains an 'Advertisement' which assures the reader that this poem 'is really and truly the production of *James Hogg*, a common Shepherd, bred among the mountains of Ettrick Forest, who went to service when only seven years of age; and since that period has never received any education whatever'. This is an accurate but incomplete account of the situation. Hogg did indeed grow up in a remote sheep-farming community where oral traditions remained strong, and his formal education did indeed cease when he was seven. Nevertheless, as a young adult he took full advantage of the excellent opportunities for intellectual development that came his way; and by the time he was writing his major works Hogg was a well-read man, at home not only in his native sheep-farming community in the Scottish Borders, but also in the literary and scientific circles of Edinburgh.

The book now generally regarded as Hogg's masterpiece is *The Private Memoirs and Confessions of a Justified Sinner* (1824). Early reviewers, reflecting the general view of Hogg's background and personality, saw it as 'an incongruous mixture of the strongest powers with the strongest absurdities'. In the 1940s, however, André Gide generated new interest in Hogg's novel when he wrote enthusiastically about its richly complex portrayal of the Devil; and since the 1940s *The Justified Sinner* has come to be regarded as one of the major Gothic Novels. In recent years, other works by Hogg have also attracted growing interest. In short, Hogg is a writer whose true stature was not recognised in his own lifetime because his social origins led to his being smothered in genteel condescension; and whose significance was not recognised thereafter, because of a lack of adequate editions. However, he now appears to be taking his place as one of the major Gothic writers; and the Stirling/South Carolina Edition of his complete works is being published by the Edinburgh University Press.

Although Hogg was regarded by his contemporaries as a man of powerful and original talent, it was felt that his lack of education caused his work to be marred by frequent failures in discretion, in expression, and in knowledge of the world. Worst of all was his lack of what was called 'delicacy', a failing which caused him to deal in his writings with subjects (such as prostitution) which were felt to be unsuitable for mention in polite literature: it will be remembered that in the *Justified Sinner*, for example, young George Colwan is killed as a result of a dispute in a brothel; and in addition the experiences of the prostitute Bell Calvert figure prominently in that novel.

One of Hogg's major novels, *The Three Perils of Woman* (1822), was felt to be particularly outrageous in its subject matter; and this text remained out of print from the late 1820s until its re-publication in the Stirling/South Carolina Edition in 1995. However, some recent critics have placed *The Three Perils of Woman* on a level with the *Justified Sinner*. Littered with corpses that have a startling tendency to reanimate, *The Three Perils of Woman* certainly has strong Gothic elements; but parody, and a concern with the nature of communication through language, also figure strongly in its rich brew.

The Three Perils of Man (1823), Hogg's remarkable version of a medieval romance, offers much Gothic diablerie at Aikwood, the castle of the wizard Michael Scott. Overflowing with vivacity and told *con brio*, *The Three Perils of Man* is increasingly coming to be seen as a highly sophisticated piece of narrative artfulness.

Some of Hogg's short stories draw on the folk traditions available to him as a child in Ettrick Forest in the Scottish Borders; for example, the haunting 'Mary Burnet' is one of his explorations of traditions of THE SUPERNATURAL, while his interest in dreams emerges in stories like 'George Dobson's Expedition to Hell'. Another strand in Hogg's writing is represented by 'Strange Letter of a Lunatic' and 'The Brownie of the Black Haggs', stories which reflect an abiding interest in abnormal psychology, and in the ways in which the mind reacts to extreme stress. One of Hogg's friends was Dr Andrew Duncan, who founded the Edinburgh Asylum in 1813, having been shocked by conditions in the old City Bedlam. Hogg's short stories originally appeared in periodicals such as *Blackwood's Edinburgh Magazine* and *Fraser's Magazine*; some of the best of them were included in *The Shepherd's Calendar* (1829), a collection republished in the Stirling/South Carolina Edition in 1995.

DOUGLAS S. MACK

Horror

Horror is often used interchangeably with terror to describe the intense emotions produced by objects of fear, whether they be uncanny or sublime, repulsive or threatening. Edmund Burke, writing on the sublime, describes the experience both as a 'delightful horror' and as 'tranquillity tinged with terror'. THE SUBLIME however, predominantly evokes feelings of terror. Linked to a sensation of awe and wonderment, to an individual's encounter with something breathtakingly incomprehensible, like the craggy, grand and gloomy mountain scenery of ANN RADCLIFFE's fiction, terror ultimately connotes an uplifting *terror* emotion, as suggested by the expression 'terrific'. Initially overwhelmed by the magnitude of the sublime object, the subject experiences a terrified release of emotional energy that stimulates an elevated sense of self and a movement of transcendence. Horror is of a quite different order of emotions: it describes a range of subjective states and objects distinct from those that surround and evoke terror. Bound up with feelings of revulsion, disgust and loathing, horror induces states of shuddering or paralysis, the loss of one's faculties, particularly consciousness and speech, or a general physical powerlessness and mental confusion. *horror* Where terror is often connected to an immediate threat, the cause of horror is far less discenible in that it involves the subject to a greater and more disturbing extent, confounding inner and outer worlds in an all-pervasive disorientation. Horror dissolves a being's sense of definite identity, a dissolution often metaphorically linked to absolute darkness and death. The sense of a dissipation of one's faculties and physical power, the vampiric draining of energy, in part explains why horror remains more difficult to dispel. Horror is evoked by encounters with objects and actions that are not so much threatening as taboo: what is least avowable in oneself, what is symbolically least palatable or recognisable, may be the most horrible. Horror appears when fears come a little too close to home.

Ann Radcliffe + terror Ann Radcliffe sharply and significantly distinguished between terror and horror: 'so far the opposite', she maintained, 'that the first expands the soul, and awakens the faculties to a high degree of life; the other contracts, freezes, and nearly annihilates them'. Terror glimpses its object and excites the imagination, thereby offering some means to escape it. Horror has nothing to do with the sublime: its object remains uncertain, lost among a general blurring of images; reciprocally, the mind is left in a state of confusion and chaos. This state is perhaps best represented by the labyrinths, dungeons or burial vaults that proliferate in Gothic fiction. Dark, clammy and disorientating spaces lead to gloomy imaginings of premature entombment and absolute separation from the world of the living. In Radcliffe's *The Italian* (1797) a prisoner being led through the labyrinthine corridors of the Inquisition's dungeons observes that 'it seemed as if death had already anticipated his work in these regions of horrors, and had condemned alike the tortured and the torturer'. As a metaphorical space, too, the labyrinth is redolent of horror and death. In *The Pursuits of Literature*, T. J. Matthias describes the dangers of what he calls 'labyrinths of literature', referring to Enlightenment philosophy as well as Gothic fictions. He describes the 'accumulated horrors' of reading such texts as producing effects of 'political death and mental darkness' in which 'my mind for a space feels a convulsion, and suffers the nature of an insurrection'. Fiction presents intolerable images that draw readers into a labyrinth of horror, losing them in a web of confusion. Maria Regina Roche, in *Clermont*, refers to 'horrible narratives' as those which lead the heroine into states of doubt and confusion, rendering her untrusting and suspicious of all those around her, particularly her father. In this way narrative draws her into the dreadful condition of utter disconnection from all that is held dear.

It is not only the soul, as Radcliffe contends in her essay, that contracts and freezes in moments of horror. Mind and body undergo convulsions and death-like torpor, as Matthias observes. For Mary Shelley, in her Introduction to *Frankenstein* (1818), 'thrilling horror' serves 'to curdle the blood', inducing effects of decomposition at a most physical and vital level. In Radcliffe's *The Mysteries of Udolpho* (1794) a horrific encounter remains an object of anxiety throughout the novel. Wandering the corridors of Udolpho at night the heroine comes across a frame draped with a black veil. On returning and drawing back the veil to glimpse what is behind it, she drops senseless to the floor. The encounter deprives her of strength, and on reflection, the horror of what was concealed behind the veil temporarily occupies her mind to the point that she loses 'all sense of past, and dread of future misfortune'. Not only left senseless and adrift, she is also rendered speechless. Indeed, so horrible was the object to which her thoughts if not her words occasionally return, that it is left undescribed for over four hundred pages. Horror, it seems, is unpresentable. Only when the actual nature of this object is discovered can the experience be recounted. The object that had 'overwhelmed her with horror' was

> a human figure of ghastly paleness, stretched at its length, and dressed in the habiliments of the grave. What added to the horror of the spectacle, was, that the face appeared partly decayed and disfigured by worms, which were visible on the features and hands.

It is not a real corpse, however, but a macabre, artificial reminder of corporeal decay fabricated by monks in order to ensure a sinner's penance.

Though partially exorcised by the revelation of its inauthenticity, the waxen image retains an aura of horror. While terror involves, as Radcliffe suggested, an imaginative aspect transcended once its object is identified, there is something about images of horror that possess the mind with more tenacity, drawing more pervasive fears from the subject than terror's immediate and temporary threat to the stability of the self. The confrontation with a dead body remains partly the cause in that the proximity and suddenness of an unexpected encounter with a mortal object provides a moment of subjective recognition in which fears of one's own mortality are released. But death alone is not necessarily evocative of horror. For Radcliffe's heroine the manner in which death is portrayed displays the significance of representation, supplementing, as it does, the first sight of the, albeit artificial, corpse with more disturbing images and associations. The images display what befalls the mortal frame after its demise. Life does not end with death but is succeeded by decay and physical corruption: the worms that crawl over and within the corpse reveal a dead body that is teeming with life; the human form becomes both the breeding ground and fodder for the lowest forms of life.

Death proceeds to absolute physical degradation. The body, whose image provides individuals with a sense of unity and integrated being, is subject to utter disintegration. Thus images of death confront imaginarily unified beings with certain horrible truths about the material human condition, truths, though never far from the surface, which are repeatedly suppressed in the course of everyday life. In *Frankenstein*, horror comes much closer to home: decomposition takes on a more subjective and uncanny form, in that it relates more fully to a novel in which the distinction between life and death constitutes the main concern. To discover the secret of life Frankenstein endures the horrors of the 'unhallowed damps of the grave' and the torturing of living animals. His most intense moment of horror comes when he animates his creation, a being he imagines as an object of beauty. His utter revulsion declares the contrary: 'the beauty of the dream vanished, and breathless horror and disgust filled my heart'. The horror is intensified: his subsequent nightmare sees his living fiancée transformed into the worm-infested body of his dead mother and culminates with the appearance of the monster, a grinning, walking corpse. The succession of horrors devastate Frankenstein, physically and mentally:

> Sometimes my pulse beat so quickly and hardly that I felt the palpitation of every artery; at others, I nearly sank to the ground through languor and extreme weakness. Mingled with this horror, I felt the bitterness of disappointment; dreams that had been my food and pleasant rest for so long a space were now become a hell to me; and the change was so rapid, the overthrow so complete!

His world turned upside down, Frankenstein cannot exorcise or escape the horror that consumes him and his family, shattering their comfortable and trusting perspective on the world.

That horror emanates from within as much as without is evinced by the devastating subjective consequences presented in the novel. Frankenstein's noble, humanitarian aspirations are bound up with baser motives and wishes, as evinced in the dream association of his fiancée and mother. His horror acknowledges desires he can barely admit: disgust and loathing continually projected onto the monster are returned to him, his own feelings, the worst aspects of his ambitions, embodied in monstrous form. In the subjective drama of the novel the monster remains the point around which subjectivity unravels: confronted by his own faults in this other shape, prevented from blaming anyone but himself for the disastrous consequences of his actions, Frankenstein's horror manifests the shame and unbearable responsibility that leave him no option but the destruction of what amounts to his double. As 'William Wilson', Poe's story of the double, attests, killing one's alter-ego constitutes an act of self-destruction.

The figure of the double opens onto that realm of experience, linked to dread and horror, called the uncanny. Evoking feelings of familiarity and strangeness, something one is both at home with and unnerved by, uncanny phenomena are, according to Freud, unhomely, **UNHEIM-LICH**: they mark the return of wishes and ideas that should have remained repressed. In Freud's essay the ambiguity that surrounds definitions of the uncanny extends to the experience itself: the double, at one stage of individual development, is linked to a narcissistic insurance against death and associated with primitive ideas about the animism of objects and the omnipotence of thoughts; it subsequently becomes a 'harbinger of death', a phantasmatic sign of the castration complex and subjection to the reality principle. The return of unconscious fantasies and anxieties is marked by familiarity, in that these are states that have been surmounted, as well as by the strangeness attendant upon a reappearance that ought, morally and rationally, to have remained hidden. Hélène Cixous's account of Freud's 'uncanny' emphasises the ambivalence it involves; for her, 'the Ghost erases the limit which exists between two states, neither alive nor dead'. The crossing of boundaries evinced by the uncanny is what is most disturbing. For Radcliffe's heroine in *The Mysteries of Udolpho* death is not preserved in its proper distant place, but held up for contemplation in the place of a picture. It is not only ghosts that display the permeability and general instability of what are assumed to be the most secure of limits. Another example Cixous offers, and one that for **EDGAR ALLAN POE** was a recurrent horror, is the idea of live burial. Premature burial, as in the experience of Gothic labyrinths, confuses life and death: 'hence the horror', observes Cixous, 'you could be dead while living, you can be in a dubious state'.

The disturbance and uncertainty of boundaries, the obliteration of the most solid distinctions between life and death, human and animal, connects horror and the uncanny in much later nineteenth-century fiction. Dracula, of all Gothic figures, best exemplifies this bond between horror and the uncanny. In the novel, Harker, a prisoner in Dracula's castle, stumbles across the Count, a picture of health at rest in his coffin, having recently sated his bloodlust. Horrified, Harker lifts a shovel to strike the vampire. 'But as I did so the head turned and the eyes fell full upon me, with all their blaze of basilisk horror. The sight seemed to paralyse me ...'. The **VAMPIRE**'s confounding of life and death, the uncanniness of the undead, remains one aspect of its strange and horrifying nature. Another moment of horror involves Harker's seduction by female vampires: 'There was a deliberate voluptuousness which was both thrilling and repulsive, and as she arched her neck she actually licked her lips like an animal.' The ambivalence of Harker's reaction testifies to the impurity underlying his revulsion; his participation offers an index of an attraction beyond the limits of avowed morality, a fascination that persists in the face of the horror. The spectacle of the doubleness of sexual identity, female sexuality in particular, is most shockingly displayed by Lucy's vampiric double: 'The sweetness was turned to adamantine, heartless cruelty, and the purity to voluptuous wantonness.'

Part of the irresistible horror of these images relates to a reversal of feminine ideals and the appearance of desire where it should not be. But it is not only female sexuality that is aroused by the vampire: horror draws desire to its limit, disclosing what should remain concealed. The animalistic associations of sexuality and the return to the body's blood begin to undermine distinctions separating human from beast. Indeed, the strange and uncanny sensations that Harker experiences in castle Dracula are linked to a general eruption of familiar and culturally suppressed ideas. Crossing and disrupting all the boundaries that separate civilisation from barbarism, unleashing the unreason, passions and desires prohibited by Victorian morality and taboos, vampires release repressed natural energies. The horror of the vampire, both its strangeness and its familiarity, its uncanny recognisability, stems from its similarity to those whose homes it enters, from the way it brings a dark and unacknowledged nature back to the surface of a decadent social world. The men in the novel have to become like the Count in order to expel him, to turn into hunters seeking his blood as they chase him from their homeland.

The horror that haunts human figures, the presentation of an animal, bodily, mortal and sexual nature they can never cast off, recurs in Gothic fiction and ghost stories. Human nature is seen to be thoroughly unstable, prone to degeneration, with physical corruption a sign of spiritual or moral decline. Degeneration, moreover, draws out the horrible proximity between primitive or beastly natures and civilised, moral human characteristics. E. F. Benson, in his short story 'The Horror-Horn', describes the cause of horror in these terms:

In form it was completely human, but the growth of hair that covered limbs and trunk alike almost completely hid the sun-tanned skin beneath. But its face, save for the down on its cheeks and chin, was hairless, and I looked on a countenance the sensual and malevolent bestiality of which froze me with horror. Had the creature been an animal, one would have felt scarcely a shudder at the gross animalism of it; the horror lay in the fact that it was a man. There lay by it a couple of gnawed bones, and, its meal finished, it was lazily licking its protuberant lips, from which came a purring murmur of content. With one hand it scratched the thick hair on its belly, in the other it held one of these bones, which presently split in half beneath the pressure of its finger and thumb. But my horror was not based on the information of what happened to those men whom these creatures caught, it was due only to my proximity to a thing so human and so infernal.

Animality and sexuality conjoin to shroud a recognisably human form with the regressive features that are perceived as diabolically inhuman. The conjunction of human shape and animal characteristics evokes horror: it is a being that refuses to remain in a symbolically established place and, shifting between animal and human features, confounds what should be a definite and absolute distinction. The confusion extends to the point that the subject of horror cannot separately recognise one or the other. The disruption of boundaries and the general ambivalence that threatens the security of human identity is often attributed to a diabolical cause.

In the nineteenth century, however, the unleashing of evil is increasingly linked to scientific experimentation. In *Dracula* the vampire is explained in religious terms as a diabolical agent, but attempts are also made to classify him in criminological terms as a recidivist and to understand his powers as chemical energies presently beyond the reach of scientific knowledge: what is horrible is not simply supernatural, but distinctly, disturbingly natural. Arthur Machen's *The Novel of the White Powder* in *The Three Impostors* (1895) describes a striking climax to physical and moral regression caused by a chemical that, through uncertain material processes, has been transformed into the *vinum sabbatti*, the potion for a witches' sabbath. A young man who unwittingly takes the drug initially enjoys a renewed, and immoral, lust for life. But at a price:

I looked, and a pang of horror seized my heart as with a white-hot iron. There upon the floor was a dark and putrid mass, seething with corruption and hideous rottenness, neither liquid nor solid, but melting and changing before our eyes, and bubbling with unctuous oily bubbles like boiling pitch. And out of the midst of it shone two burning points like eyes, and I saw a writhing and stirring as of limbs, and something moved and lifted up what might have been an arm. The doctor took a step forward, raised the iron bar and struck at the burning points; he drove in the weapon, and struck again and again a fury of loathing.

This description of complete decomposition from a solid body to a vile, oozing mass is intensified by the recognition of traces – the eyes, the limbs – that are vaguely discernible as human. The uncertainty of bodily identity testifies to a disgusting primordial formlessness, a revolting image of the decay of a being's constituent elements. Neither human nor animal, nor, indeed, mineral or vegetable, but a horrendous compost of all, the putrid mass erases all differences in a process of general corruption.

The seething, excrescent object is a *Thing* of absolute horror. The antithesis of the concrete world of solid, definite substances, the Thing that pervades horror fictions signifies a substance beyond substance that is simultaneously no longer substantial, but formless, mashed and mobile matter. In E. F. Benson's story 'Negotium Perambulans', the very Thing of human horror appears:

> The Thing had entered and now was swiftly sliding across the floor towards him, like some gigantic caterpillar. A stale phosphorescent light came from it, for though the dusk had grown to blackness outside, I could see it quite distinctly in the awful light of its own presence. From it too there came an odour of corruption and decay, as from slime that has long lain below water. It seemed to have no head, but on the front of it was an orifice of puckered skin which opened and shut and slavered at the edges. It was hairless, and slug-like in shape and texture. As it advanced its fore-part reared itself from the ground, like a snake about to strike, and it fastened on him ... it was impossible to grasp it; my hands sunk in it as in thick mud.

Tangible, but indefinitely so, the Thing remains of indeterminable shape, nature and origin. Revolting in its fleshliness, a fleshliness of the most unspeakable bodily parts, its primordial sliminess and baseness bespeaking a form of life so low, so threatening and evil, that it seems unnatural, the Thing emerges as the oozing condensation of human fears. Its liminal position situates it between worlds and of no one world: neither natural, human or diabolical, but absorbing, confounding them all in an indeterminable morass.

For all its horror, a certain fascination surrounds the Thing. Exceeding the powers of reason and understanding, refusing the symbolic boundaries that shape and sustain everyday reality, the Thing outlines the limits of the human, limits that are moral and emotional, in the evocation of horror. It signifies that which is most resistant to culture, rationality, morality and classification and, as such, mirrors, that is represents in an inverted, negative form, what in the human remains indefinable, ineffable, even, perhaps, essential. Horror constitutes the limit of reason, sense, consciousness and speech, the very emotion in which the human reaches its limit. Horror is thus ambivalently human, the feeling that preserves a sense of humanity at the very point that 'human nature' is most indefinite, most unbearable and most in danger of disintegration. Horror marks an encounter with the inhuman in its most *in*-human form.

FRED BOTTING

Imagination

A keyword in Romantic critical theory, the imagination was commonly used by the Romantics to indicate a region of experience beyond the limits of ordinary perception or understanding. In this sense the imagination becomes a little more than the capacity to 'apprehend absent things as if they were present' (Wordsworth, *Preface to the Second Edition of the Lyrical Ballads*, 1801) by the beginning of the nineteenth century where through the works of writers like Blake, Wordsworth, Coleridge, **SHELLEY** and Keats, the imagination is strongly associated with visionary insight, a state of dreamlike entrancement, epiphany or even simply bliss or 'joy'. The Romantic imagination is concerned largely with regions of psychological experience, but writings in the Gothic tradition use 'imagination' in a broader sense. **EDGAR ALLAN POE**'s *Tales of Mystery and Imagination*, for example, indicates in its title the place of these stories on the borders of human experience: these are tales of mystery, in the sense that explanations for their actions are not easy to find, and tales of imagination, in that they are frequently of no particular time or place, and more significantly, deal with the fantastic.

In one of the most famous stories in the collection, 'The Fall of the House of Usher', Poe plays on the term tellingly in the opening paragraphs:

I looked upon the scene before me – upon the mere house, and the simple landscape features of the domain – upon the bleak walls – upon the vacant eye-like windows – upon a few rank sedges – and upon a few white trunks of decayed trees – with an utter depression of soul which I can compare to no earthly sensation more properly than to the after-dream of the reveller upon opium – the bitter lapse into everyday life – the hideous dropping off of the veil. There was an iciness, a sinking, a sickening of the heart – an unredeemed dreariness of thought which no goading of the imagination could torture into aught of the sublime.

Ironically, the first-person narrator of the story announces at the start his depressed state, which is coupled with the inefficacy of the imagination: ironically, because the tale that is about to unfold tells of the most fantastic events. Poe's introduction is typical of nineteenth-century Gothic fiction in its insistent placing of the narrative in the consciousness of a 'non-imaginative' narrator, a technique probably adopted by writers to make the suspension of disbelief all the more willing. Commonsensical narrators (such as Lockwood or Nelly Dean in Emily Brontë's *Wuthering Heights* (1847) or Jonathan Harker in **BRAM STOKER**'s *Dracula*, 1897) abound (see **THE BRONTËS**). The passage also demonstrates how saturated with Romantic key-moments citations of the imagination had become, because there is at the least an allusion here to one famous Romantic imaginative moment (see **ROMANTICISM**). The depression of soul suffered in the after-effects of coming down from opium is almost certainly a reference to the loss of vision Samuel Taylor Coleridge describes in the preface to 'Kubla Khan' (1816) (or possibly to Thomas de Quincey's descriptions of the pleasures and pains of opium).

Yet this extract from Poe's story is not typical in other respects. With characteristic allusive irony, Poe sets up his tale as falling outside the province of 'normal' Gothic experience by stressing how far his narrator is distanced from the imaginative perception of the natural landscape. Far more commonly – in early Gothic fiction at least – the imaginative capacities of central characters were all-important, and their sensitivity to the landscape particularly is taken as indicative of their noble feelings. In **ANN RADCLIFFE**'s *The Romance of the Forest* (1791), for example, much is made of the heroine's imagination and sensitivity to nature, and similar qualities are attributed to Victor Frankenstein (and indeed, the monster) in Mary Shelley's *Frankenstein* (1818). Such novels are typical of Gothic writings in the Romantic period, which combine the virtues of feeling, imagination and natural innocence in heroes or heroines who suffer the misfortunes of injustice, persecution or misunderstanding.

Equally important at this time is the satirical representation of the Gothic imagination in such novels as Jane Austen's *Northanger Abbey* (1818) and Thomas Love Peacock's *Nightmare Abbey* (1818) (see **GOTHIC PARODY**). Peacock includes in his novel one Mr Flosky, a gross caricature of Samuel Taylor Coleridge whose theories of the imagination and predilection for the philosophy of Kant were well known at the time. Peacock's description of Flosky is typical of a late Enlightenment despising of the Gothic imagination as a form of regressive self-indulgence:

No one could call up a *raw-head and bloody bones* with so many adjuncts and circumstances of ghastliness. Mystery was his mental element. He lived in the midst of that visionary world in which nothing is but what is not. He dreamed with his eyes open, and saw ghosts dancing round him at noontide.

Jane Austen's heroine in *Northanger Abbey*, Catherine Morland, is portrayed as being in possession of a too impressionable imagination, having bad habits of reading in the Gothic. Although the novel is frequently cited as a satire of Ann Radcliffe's writing, this is not true in all respects, since it is an example of a pattern frequently found in Radcliffe, where the heroine's imagination leads to delusions which are exposed as such by the end of the novel.

The peculiar thrill of the Gothic imagination is famously described by Addison in The *Spectator* of 1 July 1712. There Addison expands on Dryden's description of the 'fairy way of writing', suggesting that success in this mode depends upon 'an Imagination naturally fruitful and superstitious', and further, that it is a form of writing well-suited to an English temperament characterised by way of its gloom, melancholy and propensity for 'wild Notions and Visions'. As is commonly the case, Shakespeare is cited as the great national poet, here because of his 'noble Extravagance of Fancy'. Addison concludes the essay (one of a series on the imagination) by noting how this aspect of the imaginative capacity 'makes new Worlds of its own' and creates fictions of humanity beyond nature. This acknowledgement of the imagination as a poetic faculty applied to that which is deemed to be beyond 'Nature', rather than that which is within it, makes Addison's essay an important contribution historically: it is here, in one sense, that the Gothic aesthetic of the imagination begins.

Edmund Burke, in *A Philosophical Enquiry into the Origin of our Ideas of the Sublime and the Beautiful* (1757), both modifies and develops Addison's ideas. As a thinker firmly in the tradition of Locke, Burke is in some ways more cautious than Addison, insisting, for example, that 'this power of the imagination is incapable of producing anything absolutely new'. Burke's claim is that the imagination is a re-ordering agency, essentially limited in that its ideas must derive from the senses. It is this caution, combining interestingly with some subtle psychology, that produces a distinctly modern nuance in Burke's theory. He argues that distinction, or difference, produces no great imaginative effect, but likeness, or similarity, does: 'the mind of man has naturally a far greater alacrity and satisfaction in tracing resemblances than in searching for differences: because by making resemblances we produce *new images*; we unite, we create, we enlarge our stock; but in making distinctions we offer no food at all to the imagination.' This premise means that when Burke goes on to explain the imaginative pleasure of the sublime, this pleasure is located, paradoxically, in the realm of the familiar, in rather the same way that Freud's notion of **THE UNCANNY** partakes of both the familiar and the unfamiliar.

This paradoxical combination of the extravagant and improbable on the one hand and the familiar and natural on the other is central to the development of the eighteenth-century and Romantic Gothic imagination. In **WALPOLE**'s *Castle of Otranto*, the Preface to the second edition attempts to explain the combination thus:

> It was an attempt to blend the two kinds of romance, the ancient and the modern. In the former all was imagination and improbability: in the latter, nature is always intended to be, and sometimes has been, copied with success.

In a comparable retrospective justification, Coleridge's explanation of the project of the *Lyrical Ballads*, in chapter XIV of *Biographia Literaria* (1817), this same fundamental interchange between the known and the unknown can be seen governing the theorising of the imagination:

> my endeavours should be directed to persons and characters supernatural, or at least romantic; yet so as to transfer from our inward nature a human interest and a semblance of truth sufficient to procure for these shadows of imagination that willing suspension of disbelief for the moment, which constitutes poetic faith. Mr Wordsworth, on the other hand, was to propose to himself as his object, to give the charm of novelty to things of every day, and to excite a feeling analagous to the supernatural, by awakening the mind's attention to the lethargy of custom, ...

For the early Gothic writers, the imagination was a vital concept governing the idea of composition. While later writers, such as Poe, could both defer to the idea of the imagination as a creative force and be ironic about it, the writers of the late eighteenth century used the notion of imagination as a means of legitimating their writing and characterising their art. Thus, **WILLIAM BECKFORD**, when composing *Vathek* (1786) wrote to the Rev. Samuel Henley, 'My imagination is again on fire. I have been giving the last trimmings to one episode ...' and **MATTHEW**

GREGORY LEWIS wrote in the 'Introductory Dialogue' to *Tales of Terror* (1801):

Oh! It breathes awe and rapture o'er the soul
To mark the surge in wild confusion roll,
And when the forest groans, and tempest lours,
To wake Imagination's darkest powers!
How throbs the breast with terror and delight,
Filled with rude scenes of Europe's barbarous night!

Here imagination is not only inspirational: it is the means by which a specific Gothic history is evoked.

PHILIP W. MARTIN

Irish Gothic

Some of the most important notions underlying a Gothic aesthetic can be traced to the influence of *A Philosophical Enquiry into the Origins of our Ideas of the Sublime and the Beautiful* (1757) by Irish-born Edmund Burke. His later *Reflections on the Revolution in France* (1790) deploy literary devices which might be termed Gothic, not least being that in which the idea of 'terror' calmly analysed in the *Enquiry* is projected onto the antagonist Jacobins as the badge of their iniquity. Despite this respectable base in the revolutionary years, the idea of a coherent Irish Gothic fictional tradition, commencing in the late eighteenth century, is doubtful. While the publications of the London-based Minerva Press included a good number of titles ascribed to Irish authors or evoking Irish settings, this phenomenon did not outlast the alarms of the Napoleonic period.

The familiar nineteenth-century tradition depends on the work of just three practitioners, whose working careers never overlapped – **CHARLES ROBERT MATURIN** (1782–1824), **SHERIDAN LE FANU** (1814–73), and **BRAM STOKER** (1847–1912). The work of this trio has been interpreted as stemming from some profound sense of guilt allegedly inhering in the Protestant Ascendancy class to which they have been doubtfully consigned. (None of the three came from landowning families, two were of foreign (Huguenot) background, and one of these (Le Fanu) could also boast a Gaelic ancestry, (through the Sheridans.) A more fruitful line of enquiry would examine the ways in which certain Gothic devices – notably the haunted house or ill-reputed castle – are occasionally exploited in the broader context of Irish literature in the nineteenth century and after.

Though Maturin's *Melmoth the Wanderer* (1820) is indisputably a classic of European Gothic writing, its place in an Irish literary history is more isolated. Honoré de Balzac's highly ironic sequel – *Melmoth Reconcilé* (1835) – deserves more attention than any of Maturin's other writings, with the possible exception of *Women; or Pour et contre* (1818). Little of Le Fanu's work fits the usually accepted definitions of Gothic writing, though the short story 'Strange Event in the Life of Schalken the Painter' (1839) reworks the pictorial motif initiated by **HORACE WALPOLE** in *The Castle of Otranto* (1765), and 'Carmilla' (1871–2), with its blend of vampirism and lesbianism, is a (belatedly) acknowledged source for Stoker's *Dracula* (1897).

The relation between this disconnected Irish Gothic 'tradition' and the dominant concerns of Irish writing is best described in terms (first) of social critique, and (then) of the problematics of fictional setting. In the former connection, an uncharacteristic story by William Carleton (1794–1869) underscores the point in that its focus is an incident occurring in a social class well below that usually featured in Gothic fiction. 'Wildgoose Lodge' (1830) is a tale of besiegement, narrated by a passive onlooker/participant, and ending in the destruction of a house and the death by fire of all its occupants. The origins of the story in an episode of agrarian violence familiar to the author, and the resemblance of its narrative perspective to that adopted by Maturin in the footnotes relating Irish historical incidents in *Melmoth*, serve to underscore the way in which political and fictional discourses converge in Irish Gothic.

An unexpectedly exalted context in which this convergence transposes to poetry may be identified in W. B. Yeats's progressive portrayal of the dead politician Charles Stewart Parnell as a Gothic hero. As we shall see, any Gothic inheritance which Irish literature can boast may be traceable to the mid-twentieth century rather than to the heyday of European Gothic. On the cusp of this transition, we should note how **OSCAR WILDE** (1854–1900) used Melmoth as a pseudonym after his release from prison, a detail which gives added significance to the burlesque Gothicism of 'Lord Arthur Savile's Crime' (1891) and 'The Canterville Ghost' (1891), not to mention the central, deliberately concealed device of the portrait as moral-substitute in *The Picture of Dorian Gray* (1891).

If there is a recurring point of reference for theorists of an Irish Gothic, then it is to be identified in C.R. Maturin. The rapidly shifting geographical settings of *Melmoth* might be taken as initiating a feature of the discontinuous nineteenth-century Irish tradition of Gothic outlined above – the feature of alternating locations in Ireland and Britain. These may be first detected in Le Fanu, but they take on a sharper focus in the work of a major twentieth-century Irish writer, Elizabeth Bowen (1899–1973), who has acknowledged Le Fanu's influence.

In both Le Fanu and Bowen, notions of fixed setting in either Ireland or Britain are jeopardised by a variety of means, which include Gothic devices such as the dream of reality. In the form of elusive ghosts, a Gothic presence can be detected in one or two of her earliest stories (*Encounters*, 1923), though it is more usual to identify her war-time work (*The Demon Lover*, etc., 1945) as her finest exploitation of ghostly conventions. Her late-ish novel *A World of Love* (1955) employs a batch of long-forgotten letters to introduce ghostly past presences into the action. But it is Bowen's short story 'The Happy Autumn Fields' (first published November 1944) which is crucial, not only in destablising each of two locations by insinuation of the other, but in relating present devastation to a historical past through the discovery of Victorian photographs. Having thus exploded realist conventions of fictional setting, we can proceed to read Bowen's 'The Disinherited' (from *The Cat Jumps*, 1934), with its intra-scribed confessions of murder, as a pathology of Anglo-Irish literary history.

Irish Gothic, then, is not so much an actual body of fiction composed alongside the English productions of Mrs Radcliffe and 'Monk' Lewis as it is necessary fiction mobilised by writers of the status of Wilde, Yeats, and Bowen. Quite what necessitates this later development may be difficult to identify; certainly the three cases in point differ markedly. For all that he should be congratulated on inventing Gothic comedy in some of his short stories, Wilde also drew on the violent sentimentality latent in Gothicism – his Melmoth's Christian name was Sebastian, after the martyred saint whose homo-erotic image replaces both the flesh-mask and the picture of Dorian Gray. Yeats's indirect debt to a Burkean Gothicism might be detected first in the role of terror in his quasi-philosophical system (see *A Vision*, first published 1925). But his transformation of Parnell, also regarded by some as a martyr, began in the decade of Wilde's trial, imprisonment and death; it reaches its illuminating climax in the decade of fascism with 'Parnell's Funeral' (1935) and with subsequent shorter poems on the same theme. Thus Parnell, as Gothic hero, becomes the apotheosis of a dictator otherwise too gross for direct literary celebration. In contrast, Bowen's ghosts disclose a forgotten war, the one to end all wars, and in so doing provide a means of coming to terms with the destruction of experience for which only such non-names as 'black-out', 'blitz' and 'doodle-bug' half-served.

W. J. McCormack

Irving, Washington (1783–1859)

Washington Irving grew up in a recently divided New York City, occupied by the British during the American War of Independence, and necessarily preoccupied by the violent divisions of loyalty such a war entails. He was named after George Washington by his nationalistic parents. His interest in the conflict is suggested by 'Rip Van Winkle' (1819–20), which may well be a disguised exploration of the Loyalist cause in the much disputed New York hinterland. Rip is of Dutch ancestry, and many of the old Dutch villages sided with the crown during the conflict. Afterwards, of course, they had very good reason for obscuring or mystifying their experience.

The first truly international American writer, Irving naturalised many European folktales, mostly from Germany and Spain, to create his legends of America. His style was polished and urbane, a version of Goldsmith and Addison or Steele. The themes were borrowed, perhaps, but it has to be said that they have proved among the most enduring of American legends. 'The Legend of Sleepy Hollow' (1819–20) along with 'Rip Van Winkle' seems to have expressed something important about the new American experience.

Irving's Gothicism was essentially comic, as in 'Sleepy Hollow', where Ichabod Crane is frightened by late-night ghostly tales so that his rival, Brom Bones, can terrify him with a pumpkin that appears to be a severed head. Most of the collections – *The Sketch Book* (1820), *Bracebridge Hall* (1822), and *Tales of a Traveller* (1824) – are weakened by what now seems a merely imitative urbanity, but they were immensely popular and contained the occasional Gothic gem, like 'The Adventure of the German Student'. Told by 'a nervous gentleman' in *Tales of a Traveller*, the story is of a young German studying in Paris during the Terror of the French Revolution. At the foot of the scaffold he meets a beautiful young woman of whom he has mysteriously been dreaming, in simple clothes with a black neckband decorated with diamonds as her only ornament. Wolfgang brings her to his lodgings where they swear undying love and as radical freethinkers agree to dispense with the empty formality of a marriage ceremony. In the morning he leaves to find a more suitable apartment, then returns to find her lying dead across the bed. The police are summoned, but to Wolfgang's eager query reply simply that indeed they know her, for the girl 'was guillotined yesterday'. The broad black neckband loosened, her head rolls on the floor. Irving's narrator asserts that the story is undoubtedly true, since he had it from the student himself in a madhouse in Paris. Irving is ironic about his protagonist's immersion in studies of German visionary philosophy, describing him as 'a literary ghoul, feeding in the charnel house of decayed literature', and is similarly dry about his – and the beautiful lover's – subscription to 'the liberal doctrines of the day'. His story very precisely anticipates Poe's 'Ligeia' in the description of the girl and also of Wolfgang's ornate ancient chamber as well as his reclusive disposition. But Irving's tale has considerably more political resonance in its graphic representation of the revenant as a phantom of the excesses of the Revolution, a victim implicitly of her own and Wolfgang's values, including freedom of speculation and the rejection of tradition. Irving can thus be seen to be operating as an agent of the contemporary active 'forgetting' of the American Revolution in the face of the political and social dangers posed by its European successor.

Irving, like many early nineteenth-century Americans, was influenced by the popular Scottish Common-Sense philosophy, which paid careful attention to the effects of the interpretation of sensory impressions in thought. As a result, his stories generally locate Gothic experiences in some misapprehension by an observer, and move rapidly towards the explanation of such errors. This provided him with a comic structure, while perhaps also reducing his range of Gothic effects. But his observation of the interplay between character and misinterpretation in stories like 'Dolph Heyliger' and 'The Spectre Bridegroom' or 'Wolfert Webber' made him an effective and influential satirist.

ALLAN LLOYD SMITH

Jacobs, W. W. (1863–1943)

Although best-known during his lifetime as a humorist, William Wymark Jacobs is remembered today almost solely on the strength of the macabre story 'The Monkey's Paw' (*The Lady of the Barge*, 1902). For years this much-anthologised tale was a staple in secondary school textbooks, presented as a near-perfect example of the short-story form. Its strong Gothic elements, such as stormy weather, an Eastern talisman, and a remote rural setting, along with its tight construction and effective dénouement, make 'The Monkey's Paw' one of the finest specimens of the horror story in any language.

Employment of the paw as an Indian charm introduces kismet in this yarn, which is a spinoff of the folk tale of the three wishes. When the Whites, the English family involved in the tale, tamper with preordained events by utilising the talisman, they pay dearly for their presumption. Their first wish, for money, is fulfilled by their son's employer as compensation for young White's death. The second and third are used in bringing him back to life and restoring his decomposing body to the grave. Jacobs masterfully changes the mood of the story from one of good-natured derision by the Whites regarding the paw to that of ghastly terror when they realise the extent of their error in meddling with occult matters.

As a member of the coterie of writers known as the New Humorists (who primarily produced comic sketches for periodicals destined for middle-class readers), Jacobs saw little market for his eerie material, which some critics feel is superior to his humorous work. Besides 'The Monkey's Paw', the writer early on evidenced a penchant for **THE SUPERNATURAL**. His novella *The Skipper's Wooing* (1897) included a horror story as filler, 'The Brown Man's Servant'. This terrifying tale uses such Gothic devices as a mouldy old house, an exotic Burmese villain, and a trained cobra. The piece has been compared to **CONAN DOYLE**'s 'The Speckled Band', although its component of suspense is more effective.

Jacobs's extraordinary craftsmanship is nowhere more evident than in his supernatural fiction. 'The Three Sisters' (*Night Watches*, 1914), a lesser-known tale, shows the author at his finest. Complete with a decaying family mansion, a deranged sibling, and the suggested ghost of an elder sister, the story builds to a shocking close worthy of the pen of Poe. Other fine terror tales include 'Jerry Bundler' (*Light Freights*, 1901), 'The Interruption' (*Sea Urchins*, 1898), and 'In the Library' (*The Lady of the Barge*, 1902). Several of his stories with Gothic trappings, including 'The Monkey's Paw', were adapted for the stage as short plays – notably 'Jerry Bundler' and 'In the Library'.

Unfortunately no volume of Jacobs's macabre material has yet appeared; these tales remain scattered throughout his short fiction collections and in various anthologies. Jacobs was especially skilful at suggesting supernatural themes which were explainable by psychological or natural phenomena. His fascination with crime (especially murder) adds a marked Gothic element to some of his mystery tales, such as 'The Well' (*The Lady of the Barge*, 1902) and 'The Toll-House' (*Sailors' Knots*, 1909). Despite his limited output of serious fiction, Jacobs occupies a niche in the horror genre which cannot be ignored.

JOHN CLOY

James, Henry (1843–1916)

The American writer Henry James is conventionally described as a psychological realist and certainly his great subject – the interplay of

European and American manners – as well as his devotion to formal coherence and point of view, would not usually be the hallmarks of a Gothic writer. James wrote numerous ghostly or uncanny tales including 'The Turn of the Screw' (1898), probably his single most important contribution to Gothic literature. But there is no necessary incompatibility between realism and the ghost story (see **GHOST STORIES**): the early James took his cue from Balzac and Mérimée as much as from **POE** and **HAWTHORNE**.

Nevertheless, it would be difficult to describe James as a doctrinaire realist. In transformed ways, the Gothic played a central role throughout his work. Indeed, James's whole career can be seen as an attempt to negotiate the competing claims of the Gothic and the realistic, the romance and the novel. It was, as he put it in his 1907 Preface to *The American* (1875–6), those writers who committed themselves both to the 'air of romance' and the 'element of reality' who possessed the 'largest responding imagination'. James had no unilateral attachment to romance but there is a paradoxical sense in which this in itself places him within the tradition of **GOTHIC ROMANCE**. Departing from Richardsonian novelistic conventions, **WALPOLE**'s Preface to the first edition of *The Castle of Otranto* (1764) had advocated combining preternatural events with a comparatively naturalistic treatment of character. James's handling of oppositions was immeasurably more dynamic. But Walpole's aesthetics of combination resurfaced in James's idea (put forward in an 1865 review) that 'a good ghost-story must be connected at a hundred points with the common objects of life'.

In *Love and Death in the American Novel*, Leslie Fiedler argued that James's Europe was a reinvention of the Gothic castle. From 'Travelling Companions' (1870) to 'Daisy Miller' (serialised in 1878 and published in book form in 1879) and beyond, James's European settings are certainly the precondition for a subjective adventure which is fundamentally Gothic in nature. Some would say that James's peculiar brand of late nineteenth-century Gothicism is, because psychological or metaphorical, marginal to his work. But in *The Portrait of a Lady* (1881) James's manipulation of Gothic conventions is in many ways the key to the text. His protagonist, Isabel Archer, naively sees Europe through the lens of the Gothic novel and this attitude is initially ironised. Yet, as so often in Gothic literature, the criticism of previous Gothic models sets the scene for a reintroduction of the Gothic. Isabel's problem is not that she has read too many romances but that she has not read them well enough. Unlike Emily St Aubert in **RADCLIFFE**'s *The Mysteries of Udolpho* (1794), Isabel has a terror of knowledge. It is her very resistance to lifting the Gothic veil, opening the secret door, which lands her in the dungeon of her marriage to Gilbert Osmond. Literal horror is superseded by metaphysical horror, but James shows that a de-literalised Gothic is by no means a misleading guide to reality. Whereas Emily St Aubert eventually puts the spectres to flight, Isabel's experience enables her to see the ghost of her cousin in the final pages of the novel.

James's revision of the Gothic, therefore, by no means signals his abandonment of the mode. It is true that his early studies of the double self – 'A Passionate Pilgrim' (1875) and 'Benvolio' (1875) – were not resumed until 'The Private Life' (1892), 'The Beast in the Jungle' (1903), 'The Jolly Corner' (1908) and *The Sense of the Past* (1917). A similar lapse affected his investigations of spiritual and sexual vampirism. The subject of 'The Story of a Year' (1865), 'Poor Richard' (1867), 'A Most Extraordinary Case' (1868), 'The Romance of Certain Old Clothes' (1868), 'De Grey: A Romance' (1869) and 'Longstaff's Marriage' (1878) was not again to be central to James's work until *The Sacred Fount* (1901). And James wrote no ghost stories after 'The Ghostly Rental' (1876) until 'Sir Edmund Orme' (1891), 'Owen Wingrave' (1892), 'The Way it Came' (1896), 'The Real Right Thing' (1899) and 'The Third Person' (1900). But *The Portrait of a Lady* shows that James had not renounced the Gothic even in his most devotedly naturalistic phase. In 'The Author of "Beltraffio"' (1884) and 'The Aspern Papers' (1888) he continued to explore a Gothic terrain which found increasing critical endorsement in his essays on William Dean Howells (1886) and **ROBERT LOUIS STEVENSON** (1888).

No discussion of James as a Gothic writer would be complete without mention of 'The Turn of the Screw', a superbly ambiguous novella and one of the classic first-person narratives. James described the tale as a trap for the seasoned reader, and it is certainly true that much of the subsequent (and prolific) criticism has, in its attempt to define James's narrator, a governess, as either a madwoman in the attic or an angel in the house, tended to replicate an ideological polarisation which James is himself problematising. As with *The Portrait of a Lady*, it is possible that a more fruitful reading of the text emerges from a consideration of its re-handling of the Gothic. The governess sees Bly, the country house to which she has been sent to take charge of two young children, as a 'castle of romance'. In many ways she wants to re-enact the trajectories of previous Gothic texts such as *The Mysteries of Udolpho* and *Jane Eyre*. This desire is consistently defeated by the narrative, and ultimately the governess seems less like Emily St Aubert than Radcliffe's superstitious maid, Annette, more like the tyrannical Mrs Reed in Charlotte Brontë's novel than Jane Eyre herself. As a whole, James's narrative refuses the kinds of closure (the rational explanation of apparently supernatural events, the promotion of the heroine to secure social standing through marriage) associated with early Gothic fiction.

If the closure of classic Gothic does not entirely eradicate its opening of radical uncertainties it remains true that the genre possesses a deep need for law. But James's refusal of such closure should not necessarily be taken as an acceptance of the instabilities which Gothic opens up. The use of framed narratives in many of his uncanny tales can be seen as a formal attempt to contain the Gothic. James saw the romance form as dangerously explosive and strove always to pit such centrifugal forces against the centripetal exigencies of the real. Yet he was never a simple realist. In the Preface to *The American* he wrote that 'an infallible sign of the romantic' lay in the 'rank vegetation' of power, for good or evil. Power for James was always closely associated with imaginative freedom and there is a strong sense throughout his work that those characters who seek power are implicitly seeking authorial status. Since James believed that the author was the ultimate ghost, the unrepresentable source and not the representable subject of fiction, his need to curtail his characters' quests for power (often through the use of admonitory spectral presences) was part of a commitment to representation rather than a narrow realism. Indeed, to the extent that James consistently tried to maintain his own authorial power at its fullest extent he was inevitably, as the Preface to *The American* clearly implies, perpetuating the play of romance. For this extraordinarily subtle thinker, the enclosure and revision of the Gothic was itself a distinctively Gothic strategy.

T. J. LUSTIG

James, Montague Rhodes (1862–1936)

During his lifetime, Montague Rhodes James enjoyed a formidable reputation as a Biblical scholar, translator, bibliographer, and intellectual mentor, being successively Provost of King's College, Cambridge, and of its sister foundation at Eton. His literary reputation today, however, rests primarily upon his authorship of a corpus of short fiction, published during his lifetime as *Ghost Stories of an Antiquary* (1904), *More Ghost Stories of an Antiquary* (1911), *A Thin Ghost and Others* (1919), *A Warning to the Curious* (1925), *Wailing Well* (1928), and the encyclopaedic *Collected Ghost Stories of M. R. James* (1931).

James's tales construct an almost idyllic late-Victorian and Edwardian world bounded on the one hand by the academic companionship of the College Combination Room, the library, or the cathedral close, and on the other by the country houses, seaside inns, and decaying continental abbeys frequented by scholar-gentlemen during the long vacation. Into these privileged and normally placid spaces, **THE UNCANNY**, that which is inimicable either to Anglican restraint or indeed to philosophical reasoning, is released by actions or articles seemingly innocuous in themselves – the removal of a wooden post from the ground, the casual blowing of an ancient whistle, the possession of a book or a collection of manuscripts. The gentlemen scholars, choristers, librarians and upper-middle-class families implicated in these occult dramas find, in the main, their former reliance on materialism somewhat shaken, their scepticism towards practices which might be deemed either superstitious or Ritualistic far-less binding than before their experience. The easy-going observance which popularly characterised Anglican practice then as now is called, abruptly, into question throughout these works.

For all its publication in both periodical and volume form, James's short fiction is essentially the product of an oral tradition which grew out of the comfortable, gentleman's club-like tenor of late-Victorian Cambridge. As a member of various inter-collegiate dining and discussion groups, James was encouraged to contribute not only discursive papers but original fiction also. The author maintained the oral component of these meetings in the circle which he subsequently gathered around himself at King's, a group whose composition varied across the years, but which met almost ritualistically in James's chambers after Chapel every Christmas Eve, in order to read aloud ghost stories by candle light.

Of those present, several became published authors of supernatural fiction, often utilising the scholarly or gentlemanly apparatus characteristic of James's writings. Arthur Benson, who contributed 'The House at Trehele' to the gathering on Christmas Eve 1903, for example, published two volumes of supernatural fiction, *The Hill of Trouble* (1903) and *The Isles of Sunset* (1904), during his lifetime. 'The House at Trehele' was published posthumously as *Basil Netherby* in 1927. Another member of the circle, Edmund Gill Swain, who was a Chaplain at King's between 1892 and 1905, published a collection of nine ghost stories under the title of *The Stoneground Ghost Tales* in 1912, a volume which he dedicated to M. R. James as 'the indulgent parent of such tastes as these pages indicate'. Finally, A. N. L. Munby, sometime Librarian at King's College, published *The Alabaster Hand* (1949), a collection of fourteen ghost stories, again dedicated to James.

James was, in addition to his fictional activities, a minor theoretician of occult writing, initially in his short prefaces to the two volumes of 'Antiquarian' ghost stories, and subsequently in three articles published between 1929 and 1931 in *The Touchstone*, *The Bookman* and *The Evening News*. Perhaps more significantly, James assisted in the revival of the writings of **J. SHERIDAN LE FANU** through an anthology, *Madam Crowl's Ghost and Other Tales of Mystery*, which he edited, and prefaced, in 1923.

WILLIAM HUGHES

Le Fanu, J. Sheridan (1814–73)

Joseph Thomas Sheridan Le Fanu was born in Dublin to parents of mixed origins. His father, a cleric of the established Church of Ireland, was the direct descendant of French Protestant refugees (Huguenots), though his paternal grandmother (a sister of the dramatist R. B. Sheridan) came from a background until recently Gaelic-speaking and Catholic. The novelist's mother had been a youthful admirer of the revolutionary Lord Edward Fitzgerald, and despite a streak of irrepressible conformism, sympathy for outdated radicalisms can be traced in her (Dobbin) family inheritance. None of Le Fanu's immediate forebears were owners of land on any scale; they were middle-class folk who acquired a secondary affiliation to pomp and circumstance through the holy orders of the state Church. These background details are of some importance in considering the proposition that Le Fanu's meta-narrative is the guilty confession of a callous and glutted ascendancy.

The turbulence attending Daniel O'Connell's campaign for Catholic Emancipation in the 1820s, followed by a rural 'tithe war' in the 1830s, sapped the limited material reserves of the family, who had been, since January 1826, residing in the disturbed county of Limerick. Sheridan Le Fanu studied at Trinity College Dublin between 1832 and 1836 without distinguishing himself academically. He subsequently read for the bar, but practised little as a barrister. His business interests were centred on the Dublin newspaper world. From the literary point of view, his ownership (1861–9) of the *Dublin University Magazine* (founded 1833) remains the most important of these involvements as he therein published much of the fiction for which he is remembered.

It is not easy to classify Le Fanu as a Gothic writer, without recourse to numerous derogations from the usual understanding of the term. For example, his novels from *Wylder's Hand* (1864) onwards were set in contemporary, mid-Victorian England; it makes more sense to read them as contributions to the 'sensational' school of Wilkie Collins and Charles Reade (see **SENSATION FICTION**) than as the legacy of **MATURIN**'s Irish Gothic. Nevertheless, the best of his 1860s novels – *The House by the Churchyard* (1863), *Wylder's Hand* and *Uncle Silas* (both 1864) – manage by one means or another to preserve an eighteenth-century Irish ambience in relation to which Gothic themes and tropes are clearly discernible. Moreover, the novel form did not account for all of Le Fanu's writing in the 1860s and early 1870s; on the contrary some of his most striking work is to be found in short stories, notably those collected as *Chronicles of Golden Friars* (1871) and *In a Glass Darkly* (1872). Finally, it has to be recognised that the author of *Uncle Silas* really had two careers as a writer of fiction.

The first, in the years between 1838 and 1848 principally, was given over to Irish historical fiction of the kind prompted by Walter Scott's example. Here the short story predominated, especially in the work posthumously collected as *The Purcell Papers* (1880). A **SUPERNATURAL** element is related consistently to the intrusion of Continental (usually French) influences in Irish households, a practice which uncannily relates the democratic–rationalistic legacy of the French Revolution to metaphysical agency. The exceptional story is 'Schalcken the Painter' (1839), which touches on the relationship between a Dutch artist and the triumph of Prince William of Orange (as King William III) in battles fought mainly in Ireland. One or two uncollected stories – 'Borrhomeo the Astrologer' (1861–2) and 'The Botheration of Tim Farmiloe' (same year) – sustain this high Gothic note.

The second phase sees Le Fanu as a moderately successful novelist, whose real interests appear to be channelled into the *conte* or longer tale. 'Carmilla' (1871–2) is outstanding in drawing in a subtler kind of sexual preoccupation than is usual in the nineteenth-century versions of Gothicism. This story appears in *In a Glass Darkly* (1872), a collection which impacts on later forms of popular fiction by introducing the forensic sleuth (in this case, Dr Hesselius, but *cf. Carnaki the Ghost Finder* by W. H. Hodgson, and of course, **SHERLOCK HOLMES**).

The truth is that Le Fanu is more important as an influence which affects highly diverse later developments – in **BRAM STOKER**, W. B. Yeats, James Joyce, Elizabeth Bowen, etc. – than as the author of a substantial body of achieved work. His life illuminates Victorian Ireland in ways which have not yet been fully explored.

W. J. McCORMACK

Lewis, Matthew (1775–1818)

'After Mrs **RADCLIFFE**,' wrote Hazlitt, 'Monk Lewis was the greatest master of the art of freezing the blood.' Matthew Gregory Lewis acquired his sobriquet from his most famous work, *The Monk, A Romance*, which was written (by 23 September 1794) to alleviate the tedium of the British Embassy at The Hague, where his father's influence had gained him the post of attaché. Lewis was just nineteen. Published anonymously by Joseph Bell, the first edition of *The Monk* came out in March 1796, was widely devoured, and on the whole well received; the second, later in the year, proudly announced both the author and his recent election to Parliament on the title-page: 'M. G. Lewis, M.P.' The public outcry which followed (in which Coleridge in the *Critical Review* played a role) led eventually to the 'considerable Alterations and Additions' advertised in the fourth edition, of 1798.

The Monk was completed 'in the space of ten weeks', Lewis boasted to his mother; but it was to change the course of the **GOTHIC NOVEL** in England. Although, by Lewis's own admission, it was *The Mysteries of Udolpho* (1794) that 'induced' him to 'go on with' the work, *The Monk* offers a far more unbuttoned version of Gothic than the mix of sentimental romance and explained supernaturalism which had defined the genre under Radcliffe. Lewis had the education conventional to his class, at Westminster and Christ Church, Oxford. Yet his one novel was anything but conventional. Incest and incestuous rape, murder, matricide and sororicide, all feature, together with a blasphemous identification of Satan and the Madonna, and of sexual temptation with religious devotion. Small wonder, perhaps, that De Sade took Lewis to heart (*Idée sur les romans*).

The Advertisement to *The Monk* claims a pan-European dimension for the novel, confessing a miscellany of French, Danish, and Spanish influences. Further sources were noted at the time, and have been uncovered since. But the culturally innovative link is with Germany (see **GERMAN GOTHIC**). Indeed, one reviewer noted 'Mr Lewis's ... German lust after marvellous narrative'. *The Monk*'s use of the legend of the Bleeding Nun (a plot later adapted for the ballet and stage) was the fruit of a visit to Weimar in 1792, when he met Wieland and **GOETHE**. (Although Lewis translated Part One of Goethe's *Faust* for Byron in 1817, the Monk's Faustian pact – which occurs only towards the end of the novel – derives from French and English versions of a Persian tale, the *Santon Barsisa*.)

The Monk introduces English Gothic to the **SCHAUERROMAN**, marking a decisive turn from terror, as deployed by Burke and Radcliffe, to horror, provocative of disgust and fascination in equal measure. Lewis's is a powerful representation of the demonic – indeed, the Monk's seducer turns out to be a devil in disguise – but its interest lies in conflicting forces of excess and restraint, of the insatiability of the desiring self on the one hand, and the urge to institutional conformity and hypocrisy on the other.

The novel's dramatic representation of psychic conflict – 'Ambrosio's bosom became the Theatre of a thousand contending passions' – also owes much to Shakespeare. The figure of Angelo in *Measure for Measure* (excerpted for the epigraph to chapter 1) lends itself to a compelling study in repression, and the transgressive potential of sex. From the opening scene in Milan, where the Abbot Ambrosio is observed by strangers to the city, the effect is of being inexorably drawn in, and of being denied any claim to the status of detached or dispassionate spectator.

This incitement to collusion in the contradictory movements of abhor-
rence and desire is mirrored in the critical response. That the novel was a
'pernicious effusion of youthful intemperance' 'totally unfit for general
circulation' did not prevent its being read and imitated, even by the 'fair
sex': in 1806, Charlotte Dacre (Rosa Matilda) published *Zofloya; or, The
Moor: A Romance of the Fifteenth Century*. *The Monk* was also turned into a
popular chapbook, *Almagro and Claude; or, Monastic Murder; Exemplified
by the Dreadful Doom of an Unfortunate Nun* (1803).

After *The Monk*, Lewis's writing went in two main directions: translation (mostly from the German), and drama. The two often went hand-
in-hand. *The Bravo of Venice* (1805), a rendering of J. H. D. Zschökke's
novel *Abällino, der grosse Bandit*, was in its sixth edition by 1809. Adapted
for the stage as *Rugantino*, it had a run of 30 nights, and was being
performed in the United States until 1826. In Coleridge's view, *The Bravo
of Venice* exhibits 'low thieves' Cunning', and the 'wonder of effects produced by supernatural power, without the means'. The plot follows the
adventures of one Count Rosalvo, who, banished and starving, seeks employment as a hired assassin. Grotesquely disguised, he is a savagely
successful bravo, while in his second persona of handsome stranger, he
wins the hand of the Doge's niece (the twist being that, in order to do so,
he is required to capture his own alias, the bandit Abällino).

Another German novel, translated as *Feudal Tyrants; or, The Counts of
Carlsheim and Sargans* (1806), links a convoluted plot of imprisonment
and escape to a series of memoirs. But Lewis's principal concern was the
drama. His theatrical career began spectacularly a year after *The Monk*: to
the envy of Wordsworth, whose own play had just been turned down,
The Castle Spectre opened at Drury Lane on 14 December 1797, and ran
for 48 nights. In its first three months, the play was said to have earned
£18,000; and it was being staged in England and America until 1834.
Although Coleridge found it 'a mere patchwork of plagiarism', *The Castle
Spectre* is remarkable for its melodramatic use of Gothic tableaux, notably
the appearance, to music, of a bleeding female spectre at the end of the
fourth Act.

Lewis was adept in the 'Grand Romantic Melodrama' the stage of his
day demanded. His efforts in this line began with *Rugantino* (Covent
Garden, 18 October 1805), followed by *The Wood Daemon* (Drury Lane, 1
April 1807), a Faust-cum-fairy story and musical pageant, and *Timour the
Tartar*, a spectacular with live horses and a waterfall (Covent Garden, 29
April 1811). Among his tragedies were *Rolla; or, The Peruvian Hero* (1799);
a modest hit called *Alfonso, King of Castile* (Covent Garden, 15 January
1802); *The Harper's Daughter; or, Love and Ambition* (1803), which was
abridged from Schiller's *Kabale und Liebe*, first translated by Lewis as *The
Minister*, in 1797; and *Adelgitha; or, The Fruit of a Single Error* (Drury Lane,

30 April 1807, already in four editions in book-form in 1806). Lewis also tried his hand at farce (*The Twins; or, Is It He, or His Brother?*, 1799; *The Domestic Tyrant*, 1809), and comedy (*The East Indian*, 1799, a revision of the farcical *Twins*, and itself revised as comic opera in *Rich and Poor*, 1812). *The Wood Daemon*, the story of wicked Count Hardyknute's pact with the Daemon to sacrifice a child in return for wealth and youth, and of the child's rescue, was revised as *One O'Clock! or, The Knight and the Wood Daemon, A Grand Musical Romance* (Lyceum, 1 August 1811).

The poetry which interspersed Lewis's work was often singled out for praise – by Coleridge and Hazlitt among others – and proved an exception to the general revulsion at *The Monk*: 'the beautiful ballad of *Alonzo and Imogine* ... is universally acknowledged to be a master-piece of its kind'.[8] A volume of ballads came out in 1808, and a collection of Lewis's best pieces in *Poems* (1812). *Tales of Wonder* (1801), a poorly received venture in which Scott was a collaborator, contained eight poems original to Lewis and several of his poetic translations; and four further volumes of translated fiction, and poems, were published as *Romantic Tales* (1808).

Lewis's father, with whom he quarrelled, was a deputy Secretary in the War Office; his mother, whom he provided for, left the family for the children's music master when Lewis was six. Fame gave Lewis an entrée to society, and brought him friendships with Scott (whom he met in 1798) and Byron (in 1813, and again, with Shelley, in 1816) – though, in the noble poet's private view, 'the worst parts of the Monk' were 'the *philtred* ideas of a jaded voluptuary' (*Journal*, 6 December 1813). On inheriting his father's fortune in 1812, Lewis showed a conscientiousness that belied his sensational reputation, twice visiting his Jamaican plantations to institute slave reforms (in 1815 and 1817), on the last occasion contracting the yellow fever from which he died, during the return voyage, in 1818. A fine testament to this last phase of Lewis's life is the humane, humorous, and unmannered *Journal of a West India Proprietor* (published posthumously, 1834).

NICOLA TROTT

Lovecraft, H(oward) P(hillips) (1890–1937)

H. P. Lovecraft lived and died in relative obscurity yet his widening reputation meant that by the latter half of the twentieth century he has been recognised as the most consistent and influential horror writer since Edgar Allan Poe. He was born on 20 August 1890, the son of Winfield Scott Lovecraft and Sarah Susan (née Phillips) Lovecraft in Providence,

Rhode Island, descendant of recent British immigrants down on their luck on his father's side and 'New-England Yankee' stock on his mother's. This lineage helps account for an innate Anglophilia, a conservative nature, some considerable distaste for non-Anglo-Saxons (yet he married a Jewish woman) and a demeanour and writing style (especially in letters) which suggest an eighteenth-century Tory gentleman (perhaps as compensation for his father being only a salesman).

Much of Lovecraft's antiquarianism (he referred to New York as New Amsterdam), traditionalism (as a young man he edited a paper called *The Conservative*), strange foibles (in later life he became obsessed with the temperature) and total lack of artistic drive (he refused the editorship of *Weird Tales*) may be attributed to the convergence of early fears about insanity and a retreat from the demands of modernity. Like Edward Hopper, Lovecraft was essentially a product of, and yet alienated from, his own time.

Winfield Lovecraft died in a sanitorium from a progressive and insanity-inducing disease when his son was only eight. From this date Lovecraft seems to have suffered a series of nightmares, which formed the basis for much of his fiction and which lasted until his own death. One such nightmare was the origin of the god Nyarlathotep, who combines a number of distorted features reminiscent of Lovecraft's father including, significantly, the fact that the god is the imbecilic centre of the universe and lives amid the sound of endless drumming. The original nightmare had Nyarlathotep not as a god but as an 'itinerent showman', a figure much more reminiscent of his father the travelling salesman (the slang term for which was drummer). In *The Case of Charles Dexter Ward*, it is the father who puts the son in an asylum! The influence of his father's illness on Lovecraft's writing is still a matter of much debate.

Personal material of this type reminds us that Lovecraft's art, with its bizarre war between extraterrestrial gods, was also firmly anchored in the complex social and commercial milieu of the United States. Lovecraft's work was entirely published in the popular pulp magazines which sprang up in the 1920s and flourished until the 1950s; his gods bearing many a resemblance to the titles and orders of the newly reformed Ku Klux Klan; his degenerate acolytes arousing concerns over the newer immigrants; his settings nostalgic for a more archaic and bucolic world in which money and technology had little consequence, the city was not yet a cesspool and Americans shared a common 'Anglo-Saxon' origin. This highly distorted populism also, nevertheless, included an awareness that the past was the source of a corruption inherent to the first immigrants, and the stories gain their power from this unresolved ambivalence. Lovecraft's personal neuroses (brought about by his own character traits and familial circumstances) accorded well with the rapid modernising of America itself.

The current success of Lovecraft's work may be due to the collapse in a belief in progress and technology and the substitution of interest in the occult, archaic and regressive, and the linking of these with an interest in a strange mixture of fringe ecology, New Age-ism and extraterrestrialism (see **SUPERNATURAL**) – all areas Lovecraft himself would have rejected as naive if taken seriously.

Since his death in 1937, Lovecraft's reputation has steadily increased as other writers have added their own contributions to the *oeuvre* that he created. Whilst working for *Weird Tales*, Lovecraft had already begun to co-operate with other writers in order to expand and give greater depth to the central 'mythic' structure of his stories. Most notable amongst these early collaborators was the very young Robert Bloch. Kept in print by August Derleth, who also sympathetically supplied endings for the unfinished stories, Lovecraft's bizarre and fascinating cosmography has attracted a number of writers to use his pantheon of horrific entities as a basis for their own work. Amongst such writers can be found Lin Carter, (J) Ramsey Campbell, Colin Wilson, Brian Lumley, James Wade and Gary Myers as well as film-makers such as Roger Corman and Sami and Ivan Rami (whose witty Evil Dead series filched the *Necronomicon*). Lovecraft's influence has also been felt in the world of role-play gaming, based around Cthulhu, but perhaps most unusually of all, occultists such as Kenneth Grant and Peter Redgrove have suggested that the *Necronomicon* is a 'real' book whose pages can only be read by illuminati.

Lovecraft's work consists almost entirely of short stories, but one novella, *The Case of Charles Dexter Ward*, was published during his lifetime and another, *The Lurker on the Threshold*, was completed by August Derleth. Notable stories include 'The Call of Cthulhu', 'The Dunwich Horror', 'The Horror at Red Hook', 'At the Mountains of Madness', 'Imprisoned with the Pharaohs' (under the original byline of Harry Houdini) and 'The Rats in the Wall'. George Hay has provided an excellent 'edited edition' of the *Necronomicon* (1978) and Lovecraft's correspondence has been published. Lin Carter has provided one of the first and best biographies/introductions to Lovecraft (1972).

CLIVE BLOOM

Machen, Arthur Llewellyn (1863–1947)

When it was published in John Lane's 'Keynotes' series in 1894, Machen's novella of corrupting evil, *The Great God Pan*, was widely condemned as unwholesome and degenerate. Similar condemnation of *The*

Three Impostors in 1895 labelled Machen as a writer of decadent horror, albeit a horror gloomily redolent of the Gothic rather than the ghost story (see **GHOST STORIES**).

But for all Machen's use of the stock-in-trade of this improbable variety of supernatural fiction – nameless horrors, irruptions of ancient evil, and degenerate human characters – his work succeeds, and survives, largely because of his marvellous ability to evoke the spirit of place. In both his fiction and his lyrical essays he invests with a wholly believable mystery not only his native Monmouthshire countryside, but also the streets and byways of London. It was this facility as much as the content of his stories that brought the praise and imitation of such writers as **H. P. LOVECRAFT**.

Arthur Llewellyn Jones-Machen was born at Caerleon on 3 March 1863. His lonely and introspective childhood was followed by unhappy early years in London, where he settled in the 1880s, but counterbalanced by his marriage to Amy Hogg and his friendship with the writer on occultism A. E. Waite. The 1890s proved to be his most productive period, seeing the birth of his best translations as well as his horror stories and the strange novel *The Hill of Dreams*, written 1896–7 and published serially in 1904, that is his masterpiece.

Desolated by the death of his wife in 1899, Machen left his writing for some years and took up a new career as an actor, leading to a second marriage, to Dorothy Purefoy Hudleston, and to a family. His later writing brought him greater fame – his story of the 'Angels of Mons', *The Bowmen* (1915), caused a sensation when it appeared – although it has less power and reflects his move to journalism. Towards the end of his life he returned to the themes of his early horror stories: *The Cosy Room and Other Stories* (1936) and *The Children of the Pool* (1936), but the old intensity had largely departed. Machen died on 15 December 1947, some months after his wife, but even after fifty years his powerful influence on contemporary horror fiction remains.

R. A. GILBERT

Madness

Fear of insanity is a fundamental source of terror in Gothic literature. For early practitioners of the genre it was first and foremost a powerful shock tactic: a literary equivalent to that favourite pastime of the leisured classes in London, a visit to Bedlam. Hanoverian madhouses were a legitimate source of terror – ignorance and cruelty combining in a waking

Hogarthian nightmare – and those unable or unwilling to see its inhabitants for themselves could read about its horrors in the rapidly expanding medical literature on diagnosis and treatment of the mad; in terrifying autobiographical accounts of wrongful imprisonment by men such as John Perceval, Urbane Metcalf, and John Mitford; and on occasion, in the 'mad writings' of the certified insane, like the poet James Carkesse.

The first Gothic writers were quick to exploit their contemporaries' horrified fascination with the madhouse. Descriptions of insanity in their fiction were generally highly conventional, drawing on models familiar from Augustan satire, a long ballad tradition, and Renaissance (particularly Shakespearian) drama. So, in **HORACE WALPOLE**'s *The Castle of Otranto* (1764), Manfred in his madness raves like a Jacobean revenger at the hapless peasant who witnessed Conrad's death: 'Villain! Monster! Sorcerer! 'tis thou hast slain my son!' (see **JACOBEAN TRAGEDY**). The raving bestial maniacs in **CHARLES MATURIN**'s *Melmoth the Wanderer* (1820) and countless other popular Gothic romances and tales of horror are, similarly, drawn straight from seventeenth-century drama and from Hogarth's 'Rake's Progress'. The demand for horror could strain convention to breaking-point, however. The mad nun in **ANN RADCLIFFE**'s *The Mysteries of Udolpho* (1794) has been driven insane by her lover's rejection of her. Like Shakespeare's Ophelia, she makes melancholy music, and when her madness is discovered she alludes directly to *Hamlet* and to Henry Mackenzie's sentimental reworking of the Ophelia story in *The Man of Feeling* (1771); but she pointedly lacks the innocence of the models she invokes. Her sentimental appeal to the reader is undercut by her confession that she is guilty of murder.

The forms of insanity are usually clearly gendered in early Gothic fiction. Where the mad heroines in these novels pathetically lose their wits, the male villains of Walpole, **BECKFORD**, Radcliffe, **LEWIS** and their followers are driven to insanity by vaulting ambition and uncontrollable lust (often incestuous). Their madness is little more than a cipher for immorality and evil. Although the term 'moral insanity' was not coined until the 1830s (it was first used by the Bristol physician J. C. Prichard in 1833), eighteenth- and nineteenth-century Gothic preserved the old association between insanity and villainy, and with it a great deal of confusion over how the two terms were connected. In the Gothic moral universe, madness is a fitting punishment for the guilty; but it is also the prior *cause* of evil. Only a disordered mind could plan and put into effect the acts of destruction perpetrated by a Manfred or an Ambrosio. The benevolist conviction that Man is basically good, and that evil is a perversion of God's Reason, contends here with the fear that it may be outside the individual's power to choose good over evil, reason over madness.

Evil intent and perverse desire were not the only routes to insanity. More disturbing, because less easily moralised, was the Gothic compulsion to imagine the deliberate inducement of madness in a sane man or woman. Mervyn Peake's Lord Sepulchrave, huddled on the mantelpiece, hooting like an owl (*Titus Groan*, 1946), and his Lady Cora and Lady Clarice Groan, left to die of starvation, raving mad, in a remote cell of Gormenghast Castle (*Gormenghast*, 1950), are the twentieth-century descendants of a long line of Gothic victims. The influence of the sentimental tradition on the Gothic is nowhere stronger than in its association of insanity with helpless (usually feminine) terror. Among the inumerable sufferers goaded to insanity by unremitting persecution in the English horror tradition are the nameless heroine of Matthew Gregory Lewis's monodrama 'The Captive' (1803) – so terrifying that numbers of the audience at its one and only performance were carried out in hysterics; the various maddened heroines of Charlotte Dacre's popular Gothic romances; most of the female characters in Lady Caroline Lamb's *Glenarvon* (1816); Madeline Usher in **EDGAR ALLAN POE**'s 'The Fall of the House of Usher' (1839); and Maud Ruthyn in **J. SHERIDAN LE FANU**'s *Uncle Silas* (1864). Women, when deranged by the loss of a lover or a child, or by the sexual predations of men, had an unchallenged claim upon the reader's sympathy. For a peculiarly Gothic twist to the convention, writers followed Ann Radcliffe's example in making their madwomen take the veil. From *The Mysteries of Udolpho* onwards, the insane nun stood for that peculiar amalgamation of deranged passion and obscurely ritualised penance which the English Protestant imagination persisted in associating with European Catholicism.

The sentimental-Gothic drama of female madness through persecution had a powerful alternative current. While many writers were content to leave the reasons for their heroines' persecution obscure, others turned more deliberately to the Gothic mode as a means of exposing social injustice. Feminist fiction, from Mary Wollstonecraft's *Maria; or, The Wrongs of Woman* (1798) onwards, has appropriated Gothic convention in order to articulate the writers' angry protest against the subjection of women. Among the numerous descendants of Wollstonecraft's tale are Charlotte Brontë's *Villette* (1853), Charlotte Perkins Gilman's *The Yellow Wallpaper* (1892), Leonora Carrington's *The House of Fear* (1988), Antonia White's *Beyond the Glass* (1954), Doris Lessing's *The Four-Gated City* (1969), and Marge Piercy's *Woman on the Edge of Time* (1979). All are fiercely condemnatory of the medical profession's attempts to control women's minds. Though there are powerful examples of male writers using the Gothic to similar ends, 'psychiatric Gothic' continues to be most strongly represented by women's writing.

For all its claim to have probed unshrinkingly the dark regions of the psyche, eighteenth- and nineteenth-century Gothic fiction was often surprisingly reluctant to depict the inducement of male insanity through terror. Until the very end of the Victorian era, popular Gothic novels dealt overwhelmingly in the familiar literary types of male insanity: the raving bestial maniac, the deranged scholar, the poor fool. They dallied with the reader's fear that the male hero would be driven to insanity, but they rarely brought the threat to fruition. **JAMES HOGG**'s bizarre Scottish tales of paranoia and persecution (notably the 'Strange Letter of a Lunatic', 1830) are rare exceptions, and – though indebted to Gothic precursors – they stand apart from the main tradition in English. Even nineteenth-century 'asylum fiction', explicitly concerned with the high incidence of wrongful incarceration in mid-Victorian Britain, used Gothic forms loosely and, often, irreverently. Henry Cockton's *Valentine Vox, the Ventriloquist* (1840), Samuel Warren's *Ten Thousand a Year* (1840–1), and Robert Surtees's *Handley Cross* (1843) all mined Gothic literature for comic effect in imagining the horrors of a private asylum. Even Charles Reade, the leading practitioner of 1870s asylum fiction, though he depicted the mid-Victorian asylum as a grotesquely Gothic madhouse in *Hard Cash* (1863), refused to imagine the destruction of his hero's sanity.

In this context, **EDGAR ALLAN POE**'s contribution to the Gothic cannot be underestimated. His explorations of the psychology of fear (most famously 'The Fall of the House of Usher', 1839, and the masterly short story 'The Pit and the Pendulum', 1843) opened out the Gothic to the subjective examination of mental breakdown. Freed from sentimental convention, Poe's fiction introduced new possibilities for thinking and writing about male – and female – madness. As Bradford Morrow and Patrick McGrath argued in their introduction to *The New Gothic* (1991), he is the single most important figure in linking the eighteenth-century's elaborately fantastic dramas of persecution (its 'crumbling fungoid castles and clammy vaults') to the twentieth-century's concern with the terrors of the mind: hysteria, neurosis, paranoia, dementia, perversion. With the exception of J. Sheridan Le Fanu, Poe found few serious followers in fiction until the very end of the century, when **BRAM STOKER**, **ROBERT LOUIS STEVENSON** and **HENRY JAMES** began to revive the Gothic heritage in line with the findings of contemporary psychology, psychiatry and psychoanalysis. Theories of multiple personality, new interpretations of hysteria, and above all the dissemination of the Freudian concept of the unconscious, brought new energy and new urgency to an investigation of psychopathology which Gothic fiction had long claimed as its special province.

Although it is tempting to see twentieth-century Gothic as a direct translation of modern theories of the mind into imaginative literature, the genre has fiercely maintained its tradition of resistance to medical psychology as a source of 'explanation'. 'New Gothic' writing (by Stephen King, Emma Tennant, Patrick McGrath, Kathy Acker, and others) engages with topical medical concerns (bulimia, 'suburban neurosis', AIDS), but it has remained firmly within the Gothic tradition in rejecting any reassuring conviction that the mind is fully accessible to science, to understanding, or to sympathy. Retaining the unfashionable concept of 'evil', and reviving ostensibly outmoded forms of supernaturalism, New Gothic has fashioned for itself a vocabulary in which madness can still be imagined as terrifyingly incommunicable, outside all normative modes of moral or medical interpretation.

Even within the Radcliffean tradition of the 'explained supernatural', Gothic madness has always raised, albeit spectrally, the problem of interpretation. Like other closely-related genres – **SENSATION FICTION**, asylum fiction, **HORROR** fiction – the Gothic plays on its readers' recognition that the boundary between sanity and insanity is hard to define and harder to defend. Often that precariousness has extended to the reception not just of the fiction itself but of its writers and readers. When Ann Radcliffe left England to travel, after the publication of *The Italian*, rumours circulated that the strain of her Gothic imaginings had driven her insane, and that she was destined to live out the remainder of her days in an asylum. Such stories abound about Gothic writers. Distrust of the genre is equally evident in the fears of eighteenth- and nineteenth-century doctors that reading Gothic fiction would undermine the mental health of young women; and in the concern of Jane Austen and her contemporaries to teach the reader to resist the dangerous seductions of the genre. In modified forms, such anxieties still influence the reception (and the marketing) of Gothic literature today. The logic of this concern about what effect horror fiction will have on its writers and readers has attracted considerable literary critical attention in recent years. Taking their lead from D. A. Miller's 1986 essay on sensation-fiction, writers on the Gothic have become attuned to the knowingness with which the genre exploits deep-seated fears within its culture: anxieties about the stability or instability of that culture's definitions of gender, class, race, health, power, justice. Like sensation fiction, Gothic literature plays on its readers' anxieties, dramatising their most intimate fears without fully articulating what it is doing; and in producing the symptoms of anxiety or (in more full-blooded Gothic vein) horror, terror, panic, it prevents the reader interpreting and assuaging those fears. In short, it 'hystericises' the reader, allowing him or her the frisson of being in a state of mind perilously close to madness, with the security that – even if the narrative refuses to provide a safe ending – the book can be put down and subjected to rational consideration.

The Gothic fascination with dramatising the production of madness also goes some way towards explaining its attraction for another school of criticism. As Shoshana Felman and Mary Jacobus have argued, Gothic literature is necessarily alert to the difficulties of interpretation. Its heroes and heroines, driven to madness (or close to it) in their desperate attempts to make sense of contradictory signs and patterns, can seem comparable to the readers of Gothic fiction, trying to make sense of a disorienting text. Post-structuralism has found, in Gothic fiction, an ideal set of case-studies for the practice of reading more generally. If reading Gothic is different, in this analysis, from any other act of reading, it is because the Gothic has explored, more persistently and more innovatively than other genres, the degree to which the reader's confidence in his or her interpretations is liable to be shaken.

HELEN SMALL

Maturin, Charles Robert (1780–1824)

Born in Dublin (25 September 1780) of Huguenot descent, Charles Robert Maturin was brought up in comfortable and advantageous surroundings (his father worked for the Irish Post Office). In 1795 he entered Trinity College, from which he graduated in 1800 as a classical scholar. In 1803, fulfilling family wishes, he was ordained minister and appointed to Loughrea's curacy. There, he met and married Henrietta Kingsberry. In 1806, he was transferred to St Peter's, Dublin, where he stayed until his death. Although in an affluent neighbourhood, Maturin's income was too small to support a growing family. He turned to writing, probably his true vocation, hoping it would provide much needed additional earnings.

In 1807, Maturin published *Fatal Revenge; or, The Family of Montorio* under the pseudonym of Dennis Jasper Murphy, at his own expense. In spite of weaknesses, the novel already announced some of the major themes which Maturin would fully exploit later: human fears, guilt, revenge, persecution, fanaticism, and what he called the 'midnight darkness of the soul'. In Father Schemoli he introduced the double figure of the **WANDERING JEW** and Faust, later incarnated at their best in Melmoth.

The following year, Maturin published *The Wild Irish Boy*, under the same conditions. Urged by financial difficulties, he had decided to write about Ireland, expecting his choice would satisfy the public's taste. Yet the novel was poorly received. Maturin later admitted not enjoying writing it. Moreover, his apparent fascination with sexual taboos as well as with **THE SUPERNATURAL**, the irrational and the diabolic, was endangering his relationship with the Church and already compromising his chances of advancement.

In 1809, a charge of embezzlement was unjustly brought against Maturin's father, who lost his profitable position. Until he was proved innocent and reappointed, the Maturin family was plunged into extreme poverty. This dramatic turn of events marked the intensification of incessant financial worries which were to haunt and torment Maturin for the rest of his life. In 1810, all chances of escaping from ruin were obliterated: Maturin had provided security for a relative (his brother, most likely) whose debts were transferred to him. He declared: 'the only real evil of life is coming fast on me – horrid actual want is staring me in the face'. Not surprisingly, the theme of poverty pervades all his works. The Walbergs' fate especially, in *Melmoth the Wanderer*, seems to echo, uncannily, that of the Maturins. To guarantee additional income, Maturin started tutoring and boarding students, but his role as a teacher never satisfied him. He went back to writing.

The Milesian Chief, Maturin's best novel so far, was published in 1812 under the same pseudonym. It enabled him to exploit Ireland's history, traditions and culture, and to explore the 'obscure recesses of the human heart' – one of his favourite themes. His views of patriotism, war, religion and love, as well as his ambivalent feelings towards his country, were divulged more openly too. In December, Maturin started a life-long correspondence with Sir Walter Scott, who had positively reviewed *Fatal Revenge*, and became his literary adviser, encouraging friend and loyal confidant.

In 1814, Maturin sent Scott the manuscript of a drama, *Bertram; or, The Castle of St Adolbrand*, which, after some revision, was referred to Lord Byron. In May 1816, it was produced at Drury Lane, with Edmund Kean in the leading role. *Bertram's* success, both on stage and in print, was far beyond Maturin's expectations. The character of Bertram (more strongly depicted in the text than on stage, to his disappointment) driven by uncontrollable passions and demonic forces towards revenge, self-destruction, murder, and driving his former love to **MADNESS** and **DEATH** thrilled audiences. Maturin had won his first literary victory: he consequently revealed the authorship of his previous works. Unfortunately, this further increased, irreparably, the conflict between himself and the Church.

However, encouraged by such financial success, he wrote another drama, keeping Edmund Kean in mind. *Manuel*, produced at Drury Lane in March 1817, failed miserably. Kean was blamed – he offered a very poor performance indeed – but Maturin conceded it was a bad play. The

strange, heterogeneous combination of theatrical genres, incredible im-
probabilities in the plot, and the lack of a likable hero, contributed to its
downfall. Once again, Maturin's attempt to suit the public's taste rather
than following his own inclinations, had failed. Moreover, Samuel
Coleridge's spiteful diatribe against *Bertram*, which he denounced for its
subversive, immoral and 'Jacobinical' tendencies, made life much harder
for Maturin the clergyman and writer. The money earned from the play
had dwindled away: it paid debts and was spent extravagantly – for a
while, Maturin indulged in dandyism, living above his means. By 1818,
his financial situation was on the verge of collapse.

Women; or, Pour et Contre was published that same year. This uncon-
ventional love story offered a good study of the psychological and physical nature of amorous passion and of its destructive power. Maturin also
successfully analysed Evangelicalism, its hypocrisy, and the unnecessary, devastating denial of one's humanity. He wrote realistically and
sensitively, displaying an insightful knowledge of human nature.

Not convinced that drama was not his medium, Maturin wrote
Fredolfo, produced at Covent Garden in 1819 and performed once. It was
his final attempt as a playwright. Actors were dissatisfied, and so was
the audience. The villain's murderous violence and treachery infuriated
them. Paradoxically, *Fredolfo* is better than *Bertram* owing to Maturin's
skilful portrait of the 'wakeful demon' in man. He demonstrates how
thin the line between good and evil often is, and how repression easily
results in cruelty, sadism, violence and death. Such an uncompromising
position sparked the unfounded idea that Maturin was going insane – an
idea somewhat reinforced by the publication of his masterpiece, in 1820.

Thanks to *Melmoth the Wanderer*, Maturin's name has survived as
Melmoth joined the ranks of Byron's Manfred, Goethe's Faust, Milton's
Satan, and Molière's Don Juan. Five tales, structured in a chinese-box
fashion, unfold the exceptional and supernatural destiny of Melmoth the
outcast, who is granted a 150 year life extension for selling his soul in exchange for knowledge forbidden to man. The novel combines Maturin's
favourite themes: religious persecution and fanaticism (his anti-
Catholicism finds its best expression here), man's evil and inhumane potential, madness, the corrupting and destructive nature of society and
the inevitable failure of love. It offers a wide variety of settings (Ireland,
an Indian island, an English madhouse, a Spanish monastery, the
Inquisition's headquarters) and memorable characters (Monçada,
Stanton, Immalee, Walberg, Elinor). Written forcefully, convincingly,
with the full commitment of its author, *Melmoth* is an exceptionally
captivating work.

In 1824, *The Albigenses*, a historical novel about the Catholic crusades
against the Albigenses in thirteenth-century France, was published.

Maturin's financial situation was worse than ever. His health declined rapidly, owing to long hours of work and little sleep (he always wrote at night). He died on 30 October 1824, an isolated, depressed and poverty-stricken man. He is remembered for an interesting book of *Sermons* and works which offered the unique and dark vision of a cruel, inhumane world characterised by the disintegration of moral values, the perversion and sadism of religion, and the omnipotence of Evil.

CÉCILE MALET-DAGRÉOU

Melville, Herman (1819–91)

Melville's more or less first-ever publication was nothing other than a canny piece of Gothic, the two-part 'Fragments from a Writing Desk' published in the *Democratic Press and Lansingburgh Advertiser* for 4 and 18 May 1839. Juvenilia as it may be, its young swain's pursuit of a beautiful, veiled deaf-mute treads a nice line between seriousness and spoof. Whichever the case, Melville shows an early familiarity with the legacy of 'Monk' **LEWIS, HORACE WALPOLE** and Mrs **RADCLIFFE**.

The literary career proper, however, took shape with *Typee* (1846), and its sequel *Omoo* (1847), South Seas romances which purported – not a little disingenuously – to be the 'unvarnished truth' of Melville's own sea-wanderings in the Pacific. Adventureliness there is in profusion, but also signs of a darker, altogether more concealed world, a Paradise Flawed. Cannibalism hovers threateningly. Rites and sacrifices, even the tattooing, contribute to a kind of Marquesan/Tahitian Gothic. Is Tommo/Typee, the narrator, bound for elysium or inferno, in heaven or hell? None of which did anything but further intrigue an early readership quick to pronounce Melville the season's hit in being the latest American mariner-turned-writer.

Mardi (1849), his next 'romance', strikes a yet more consciously Gothic note, the world as encyphered, mysterious, endemically and deeply other. Begun as though again Pacific island-odyssey, it quickly becomes a kind of self-conscious (and so unleavened) Spenserian–metaphysical allegory centred in the narrator's quest for his white goddess Yillah, and for her nemesis, the dark Queen Hautia. That it failed as much in sales as in imaginative design hardly surprises. The literariness intrudes, the philosophy looks all too newly acquired. Almost inevitably his publishers called him back to what Melville grumblingly designated his 'cakes and ale' fiction. Yet the upshot, two narratives also drawn from his seafaring, once again was not to be without its own touches of Gothic.

Redburn (1849), based on his youthful crossing from New York to Liverpool and back at the age of nineteen, contains a gallery of horrors, from the sight of a sailor seized by *delirium tremens* (and to whose bunk the neophyte hero is then assigned) to the mean, tubercular Jackson who tyrannises the crew and dies splattering his heart's blood over them, and from a Liverpool dockside of paupery and starvation to an outbreak of fever in steerage on the return journey. *White-Jacket* (1850), the world as imaged in the man-of-war *Neversink*, bound on a journey from Peru round Cape Horn to Rio and then to America, contains similar components: the caul-like jacket which nearly causes the narrator's death when he falls overboard, the flogging episodes, the gargoyle figure of Surgeon Cadwallader Cuticle, and the closed 'Articles of War' command of Captain Claret, a likely first silhouette of Ahab in *Moby-Dick* (1851).

But it was with his great centrepiece, his 'hell-fired' whale-hunt, that Melville came to be thought a virtuoso of Gothicism. For *Moby-Dick* deploys its own working components in the genre, an ever-elusive phantasmal whale ('ubiquitous in time and place'), a Faustian New Englander of a captain in Ahab, the *Pequod* as a world-ship as eclectic and polyglot as any, and Ishmael as the classic 'isolato' narrator. Each, too, is bound upon a journey which transposes the search for sperm-oil into a still larger quest for the vexing, endlessly cross-plied, 'light' of all truth. It is a quest that takes them through hell-fires ('The Try-works'), sea-fury ('The Three-Day Chase'), the Lear-like stomp and fury of Ahab ('The Symphony') and the final, hubristic sinking of ship and crew with only Ishmael to bear narrative witness ('The Chase – Third Day').

Ahab himself, over-reacher, revenger, manichean, might virtually be the Gothic **HERO/VILLAIN** *in propria persona*. Hidden from view until the *Pequod* is out to sea, heard only through the ominous tap of his peg-leg, tortured by his sense of what the whale has done to him and what 'hidden' powers it signifies, he believes the false prophesy of Fedallah, his secret Parsee, and dies roped and dragged to his death by the dream of a victorious last confrontation. His affection for Pip, the black boy driven to near-madness by his fall overboard, his Shakespearean talk, his necromantic blessing of the harpoons, and his deafness to all appeal from Starbuck and the other Mates, indeed all call up Lear. As his own Old Testament name implies, and for all that he 'has his humanities', Ahab becomes the murderous idealist, a ruined and ruinous monarch. Emily Brontë's Heathcliff notwithstanding, can nineteenth-century Gothicism be said to have produced a fiercer incarnation?

Mid-way into writing, *Moby-Dick* Melville published his 'Hawthorne and His Mosses', ostensibly an encomium to the **HAWTHORNE** of 'Young Goodman Brown' and the other New England tales of *Mosses from An Old Manse* (1846). But in seizing upon 'those short, quick probings at the very axis of reality' and the 'blackness in Hawthorne', he as much speaks of, and to, the dynamics of his own art. Not only was *Moby-Dick* so indicated but also *Pierre* (1852), which followed, a Gothic text indeed whose shift of scene from country to city and assiduously reflexive story of the writer as 'fool of truth' suggests life to be a *huis clos*, a fatal labyrinth and incarceration. As Pierre Glendinning dies in his prison-cell, would-be redeemer of his own father's fathering of an illegitimate daughter, and with his intended wife and half-sister to hand, the scene calls up vintage Gothic horror – though, as always with Melville, with just a suspicion of hoax. The spirit of Mrs **RADCLIFFE** may so accompany that of, say, a Thomas Love Peacock and the mock-Gothic of *Nightmare Abbey* (1818).

Melville's stories, in turn, sardonic, often dazzlingly concentrated and elusive, work their own Gothic seam. Three from *The Piazza Tales* (1856) in particular signify: 'Bartleby, the Scrivener' (1853), with its portrait of life blanched and drained by Wall Street's materialist ethos; 'The Encantadas' (1854), based on Melville's experience of the Galápagos Isles, as a larval, Dantean hell; and 'Benito Cereno' (1855) as a world turned upside-down, a slave-ship whose black insurrectionists mimic their own former enslavement and which probes the unconscionable stain of Empire as a power-system of human ownership and servitude.

With *The Confidence-Man* (1857), a Mississippi ship-of-fools 'masquerade' told as a dawn-to-midnight river sailing, Melville closed his public story-telling account. The novel's ending, inside a cabin whose solar lamp is fading, also draws on a suitably Gothic impetus: the world as illusion, chimera, a dark-hued *As You Like It* of cynical plays and players. There remains other Melville, to be sure, notably the poetry of *Battle-Pieces and Aspects of the War* (1865), which contains its own Gothic vision of America's fratricide in pieces like 'The Apparition' and 'Malvern Hill', and *Clarel* (1876), a massive quest-for-faith verse epic whose Holy Land setting and pilgrimage take on any amount of Gothic shadow.

But the 'inside narrative' which most has been given posthumous rehabilitation is *Billy Budd, Sailor* (1888–91). Its triangle of 'phenomenal' men includes 'welkin-eyed' Billy, 'starry' Captain Edward Vere, and the 'surcharged' John Claggart – a shipboard Judas or Iago whose naming of the foretopman as mutineer may indeed be due to 'the mystery of iniquity'. In the setting aboard a British man-of-war during the Napoleonic Wars, and in which Billy will go to his death as martyred innocence, the master-at-arms in Melville's novella offers a glimpse of his last Gothic figure, no less than a villain fated to despoil Eden.

A. ROBERT LEE

Monstrosity

In eighteenth-century aesthetic and moral criticism the word 'monster' signified ugliness, irrationality and unnaturalness. The antithesis of neo-classical values of harmonious and unified composition, a monster was deformed, irregular and disproportionate (features associated with the terrific and awe-inspiring immensity of **THE SUBLIME**); in moral terms it implied works that transgressed the codes of reason and morality, presenting excessive and viciously improper scenes and characters.

Applied, often indiscriminately, to romances and novels as well as examples of Gothic architecture, monsters appeared to be on the increase in the latter half of the eighteenth century: **M. G. LEWIS**'s *The Monk* (1796) was attacked in a review for being a monster, that is for representing and encouraging every type of improper, depraved and licentious behaviour. Indeed, the numerous evil aristocrats, monks and quasi-paternal figures – the staple villains – display the characteristics of monsters throughout Gothic fiction of the period.

As a composite term for a range of negative and anti-social features, monster, none the less, served a useful critical and moral function, outlined by Alexander Pope in his *Essay on Man* (1733–4): 'Vice is a monster of so frightful mien. / As, to be hated, needs but to be seen' (ll. 217–18). As visible demonstrations of vice, monsters displayed – and cautioned readers against – indulgence in improper behaviour, thereby emphasising the benefits of virtuous conduct and signalling the proper – disgusted – reaction to examples of vice. However, the proliferation of monsters (in the shape of romances, Gothic novels and the villains therein) that occurred in the course of the eighteenth-century rendered the line between virtuous and vicious figures less clearly distinguishable: monsters evoked a wider monstrosity that disrupted systems of classification and value.

The monstrous disclosure of the instability of systems of moral and aesthetic meaning produced ambivalent monsters, best evinced in **MARY SHELLEY**'s *Frankenstein* (1818). Imbued with Romantic sympathies for the outcast and rebel, the novel presents a humane and suffering monster, less a figure of vice and transgression and more a victim of monstrous social exclusions. Indeed, blurring the boundaries between good and bad, human and monster, the novel interrogates prevailing value systems to the extent that monstrosity becomes uncannily pervasive, an effect of and intrinsic to the sphere of the human.

FRED BOTTING

New Gothic *see* Contemporary Gothic

Nightmare

The common meaning of nightmare (a frightening dream) is frequently evoked in the use of such dreams in Gothic fiction where they are often prescient. The origin of the word is in folklore, which variously supposes the bad dream to be accompanied by a stifling feeling in the sleeper's chest, or uses the word simply to refer to this discomfort. Versions of this mythology suppose that the pressure on the chest is caused by an incubus who squats there, or indeed a female monster, or succubus (hence 'mare') conjuring the dreams in the sleeper's mind. In Fuseli's series of paintings and drawings of the subject (such as *'The Nightmare'*, 1782 and *'An Incubus Leaving Two Sleeping Girls*, c. 1793) the phenomenon of the nightmare is overlaid with the iconography of eroticism: the painting entitled 'The Nightmare' depicts a grim incubus on the stomach of a muslin-clad supine young woman lying on a bed, whose expression and attitude are suggestive of post-coital bliss rather than distress; the drawing/watercolour version of the sleeping girls (1810) is clearly indicating lesbian sexuality. In all versions, Fuseli's 'nightmare' comprises a literalising version of the term, for his visiting incubus is brought to the scene by a horse. In the pictures of the two girls, the horse is seen through an open window galloping away with the incubus on its back; in versions of 'The Nightmare', the horse's head, somewhat absurdly, pokes through the curtains behind the bed. The painting was brilliantly parodied in Richard Newton's etching 'A Night Mare' (1794).

In its sense of a distressing or disturbingly prescient dream, nightmare is a common device in Gothic fiction, where it also refers to a state between sleeping and waking, or indeed, death and life. The use of nightmare or dream as a fictional or dramatic device to figure the future or provide an allegorical reading of the plot is – of course – not restricted to Gothic writing, and is widely found in the literature of many cultures. Yet nightmare has a particular place in what might be called the mythology of the Gothic imagination, for alongside the nightmares in the text, there are those which mark its beginnings. **WALPOLE**'s *Castle of Otranto* (1764), for example, had its origins in a dream the author experienced at Strawberry Hill, his Gothic residence. Writing about this in a letter of 9 March 1765, Walpole records 'I thought myself in an ancient castle ... and that on the uppermost bannister of a great staircase I saw a gigantic hand in armour. In the evening I sat down and began to write, without knowing in the least what I intended to say or relate.' **ROBERT LOUIS**

STEVENSON's *Dr Jekyll and Mr Hyde* (1886) was allegedly inspired by a nightmare he experienced at Skerryvore.

  MARY SHELLEY, perhaps most intriguingly of all, marks the moment of the monster's creation in *Frankenstein* (1818) with a nightmare, and complements this in a preface which describes the beginnings of the novel in terms of a waking dream: 'When I placed my head on my pillow I did not sleep, nor could I be said to think. My imagination, unbidden, possessed and guided me, sifting the successive images that arose in my mind with a vividness far beyond the usual bound of reverie.' Preface and text become entangled, as the account of the inspiration for the novel corresponds almost exactly with the demon of Frankenstein's creation which is to haunt him: 'He sleeps; but he is awakened; he opens his eyes; behold the horrid thing stands at his bedside. ... I opened mine in terror. The idea so possessed my mind, that a thrill of fear ran through me, and I wished to exchange the ghastly image of my fancy for the realities around. ... I could not so easily get rid of my hideous phantom; still it haunted me.' Mary Shelley's concern in this novel with creativity and transgressive progeniture finds the device of nightmare or disturbing dream particularly useful in figuring the intense conflict between creative inspiration and responsibility for the created object.

PHILIP W. MARTIN

Occultism

Occultism and its components, the occult sciences, stand in the same relation to ordinary knowledge as the occult has traditionally had to the manifest, the secret to the obvious, the esoteric to the exoteric. The old distinction survives in some medical terms like 'occult bleeding' long after chemists stopped talking about the 'occult qualities' and physicists stopped speaking of magnetism as an 'occult attraction'. Etymologically, the word 'occult' means 'concealed' and is unrelated to 'cult', which means 'worship'. However, Gothic literature makes a cult of the occult. Novelists like **EDWARD BULWER-LYTTON** (1803–73) and Charles Williams (1886–1945) were affiliated with esoteric societies. What they learned there differed considerably from modern science but had just as much claim on people's imagination at a time when Eastern doctrines were being assimilated and Western roots being reclaimed, when Christian orthodoxy was being challenged and reinforced.

  The occult sciences were outmoded science, based on such ancient schemata as the four qualities (hot, cold, moist, dry) and their combinations in the four elements (fire, air, earth, water), the four humours (blood, choler, phlegm, bile) and the four temperaments (sanguine, choleric, phlegmatic, melancholy). Poets continued writing about these discredited concepts because they found little inspiration in the periodic table or the medical handbook; they also persisted in talking about sunrise and sunset long after the Copernican revolution, realising as poets had all along that the cosmos would be inhuman if not seen in human terms.

As viewed from a pre-Copernican perspective, the traditional occult sciences form a hierarchy reaching from alchemy (concerned with the terrestrial world) to astrology (concerned with the influences of the celestial bodies) and cabbalism (concerned with the 'super-celestial' or archetypal world). The magician may try to understand the divine workings of the universe, using a natural or white magic, or to influence the course of events to personal ends through a malefic or black magic. The distinctions between black and white were relatively late and open to debate, varying from author to author. But by taking account of the occult ideas in the novels of Charles Williams, we can see where occultism enters the otherwise traditionally Christian world of a rather Victorian novelist in the early twentieth century.

Williams describes a four-level world that reaches from Heaven to Hell and includes both the fallen world and the unfallen world of Eden and the New Jerusalem. Heaven is the source of everything else, and the cosmic struggles occur there – notably in *War in Heaven* (1930), which takes its title from *Paradise Lost*, Book V. Hell is basically private, and *Descent into Hell* (1937) describes the despair and isolation that await those who will not bear each other's burdens. The world of the original creation is a world of Platonic ideas, corresponding to the knowledge that Adam had when he named the creatures; it is envisioned at the close of *The Place of the Lion* (1931), which C. S. Lewis liked especially, and is approximated with Tarot cards in *The Greater Trumps* (1932). The world of the new creation is called the City in *All Hallows' Eve* (1944) and, like Blake's Golgonooza, contains all true acts of the imagination and all doers of true acts. The false actors dominate the fallen world with promises of a better life, but that world is a place of threatening race riots (in *Shadows of Ecstasy*, 1933) and global war (in *All Hallows' Eve*), a deadland from which Williams's characters must either rise or fall.

Dissatisfaction with the everyday world is what gets things going in Williams's novels and the action leads to the test of character. The villains are inevitably those who seek a selfishly personal salvation; they are damned to their own personal fates, like the Satanic book-publisher in *War in Heaven* and the false messiahs in *Shadows* and *All Hallows*. The heroes are ordinary people who get caught in larger processes and do extraordinary things to help others, most frequently the victims of Satanic spells and potions (*War*) or other forms of psychic invasion. The occult practices cover the full spectrum, from alchemy and multiplying of the stone in *Many Dimensions* (1931) to the grail quest in *War* and from angelology and Tarot in *Place* and *Greater Trumps* to cabbalism and thaumaturgy in *All Hallows*. The villains reason that, if knowledge is power, hidden knowledge is especially powerful. They kill to keep their secrets (*War* begins as a murder mystery) or steal (*War, Many Dimensions, Greater Trumps*) or deceive followers (*Shadows, All Hallows*). The victims are sensitive people, often women but also Africans (*Shadows*), Gypsies (*Greater Trumps*) and children (*War, All Hallows*), whose basic goodness is a source of power for the selfish. The rescuers are smart enough to learn about the forces they are up against and to recognise the need for divine intervention. They become Grail knights in *War*, but succeed only when they have the aid of Prester John, the mysterious figure from the East. There are scary cults in these novels, including some presided over by charismatics who are centuries old (*Shadows, All Hallows*). But the cults are always perversions of real worship because they are cults of the Superman, not of all people and their God. The real worship, the true *cultus*, turns out to be the affirmation of life that only unselfish people can make.

Williams gives an ironic turn to occultism, then, by showing up occultists as the selfish fools they sometimes are. His plots are technically comic because they end on a happy note, the evil uprooted, the good made better. Williams satirises ordinary society when he shows tradesmen vying to profit from the alchemical *multiplicatio* in *Many Dimensions*, but he is harsher on the over-reaching magicians. Other novelists take different stances, of course. Aleister Crowley, who may have served as a model for at least one of Williams's villains, devotes more of his *roman à clef, The Moonchild*, to showing up rivals than to describing the creation of the homunculus. Clive Barker, who brings the war in Heaven to a California town in *The Great and Secret Show*, has foolish heroes as well as foolish villains. But one of the most thoroughgoing occult fictions of recent years, Umberto Eco's *Foucault's Pendulum* (1989), is a comic masterpiece, the very word *pendolo* being a *double entendre*. The villains in the piece are old-order occultists, determined to realise an ancient quest. The heroes are editors trying to profit in the occult book business and discovering that everything they publish seems to fit together. They are nearly made victims of their knowledge, like some of the old alchemists whose texts are quoted as epigrams, but outwit their adversaries thanks to a double background in the Italian Resistance and personal computing. The motive force behind the novel is the human desire to make sense of a seemingly senseless world, specifically to find order in a chaos of esoteric teachings. The moment we think we understand it all, we risk being thrown from the heights of contemplation into a pit, with **POE**'s pendulum swinging dangerously near.

THOMAS WILLARD

Orientalism

The sensational reception which greeted publication of *Les Mille et une nuits* (Paris, 1704–17) demonstrated that the recondite materials of scholarly Orientalism might be transformed into a literary model and a popular craze, an aesthetic which was to prove as tenacious as it was ubiquitous. Antoine Galland, an Arabist who had completed and published d'Herbelot's *Bibliothèque Orientale*, offered an elegant and judiciously censored translation, tempering the erotic and intensifying the exotic. The East had always connoted expensive consumer items from silks, spices, and sandalwood to porcelain, coffee, and tea; European familiarity with these colours, textures, and scents was complicit in the voyeuristic invasion of the fragrant and forbidden space of the serail, where conspicuous consumption entailed appealingly abominable debauchery. Lady Mary Wortley Montagu, one of the few Westerners ever to enter a Turkish harem, in attempting to convey the magnificent luxury is drawn into materialistic computations – the Sultana's 'whole dress must be worth above £100,000 sterling' – where the cost of each sable ('£200 English money') is exactly twice the price of a handsome slave girl.

> This is but too like (says you) the Arabian tales: these embroidered napkins, and a jewel as large as a turkey's egg! – You forget, dear sister, those very tales were writ by an author of this country and (excepting the enchantments) are a real representation of the manners here. (To Lady Mar, 10 March 1718)

The intertextuality of excess also reinforced the juxtaposition of sexuality and violence; the very frame of *Les Mille et une nuits* underlines the contemptuous misogyny and capricious cruelty of the Oriental despot. Such Eurocentric stereotypes were reinforced in both genuine and pseudo-Oriental fiction. While Shahrazad evades death through her skills as a narrator, Anaïs the heroine of Zulema's story (told by the Persian Rica to a lady of the French court), in Letter 141 of Montesquieu's *Persian Letters* (1721), is less lucky and much luckier. Instantly killed for daring to reproach her tyrannous husband, she is wafted to a celestial palace where a seraglio of beautiful men make love to her with devoted and inexhaustible expertise. By placing an Oriental in Europe (a device also used by Voltaire and Goldsmith) Montesquieu defamiliarises and satirises Western society, here attacking the prurience of the French aristocrat, while comparing sexual experience and Paradisical prospects across the divides of culture, religion, and gender.

The Oriental stereotypes of diabolical scimitar-wielding Saracens, muskily lascivious princesses, and a heaven of kohl-eyed houris were as old as the crusades and the Charlemagne romances, and if we acknowledge that Gothic also is rooted in pre-novelistic Romance (which itself, according to Thomas Wharton's *History of English Poetry*, 1774–89, originated in the Near East) it is not difficult to locate points of intersection. Certainly there was a significant overlap as the Oriental and the Gothic continued to encode the alien and the other in terms of both external threat and internal corruption.

It is a distorting simplification of literary and cultural history that Europe looked Eastwards or backwards to escape an exhausted classicism and a moribund rationalism. Although the Orient conventionally represents decadence, despotism, and savagery, by a species of Enlightenment re-orientation Confucian China was considered by Voltaire and the *Philosophes* as a haven of sobriety, reason, and tolerance. A similar ambiguity and breadth of reference was enjoyed by the term Gothic, connoting, on the one hand, rude and tasteless barbarism, Catholic medievalism, and Norman yoking, or the 'democratic' cultural and political traditions of Celt and Saxon, Protestant and nationalist virtues, on the other.

Scholars and poets were also beginning to appreciate that the Oriental and the Hellenic were by no means binaries, as they considered the implications of discovering that Homer, the earliest Greek philosophers, and the Hebrew patriarchs had studied in Egypt. Pope, in the Preface to his translation of *The Iliad* (1715), argues that the 'unequalled fire and rapture' which makes Homer's epic 'a wild paradise' reflects both the sublimity of the Scriptures and 'the Spirit of the Orientals'. Eastern languages had been studied merely as an adjunct to Old Testament exegesis, but the pioneering *De Sacra Poesi Hebraeorum Praelectiones* (1753) of Bishop Robert Lowth encouraged viewing the Bible as a work of Oriental literature. Later in the century German biblical criticism developed these ideas, and Eichhorn, in his *Commentary on the Apocalypse of John* (1791), reads the Book of Revelation as a dramatic Oriental poem based on the fall of Jerusalem, arguably a species of eschatological and apocalyptic Gothic, the sublimity of which appealed to Coleridge as the subject for an 'anti-classical' epic.

Ancient and modern, classical and Oriental came together in the contemporary Arabic nomads whose culture and manners reminded

travellers of those portrayed in Homer. In 1772 Sir William Jones's pane-
gyric on the Arabs revealed a more Gothic aesthetic, celebrating in his
'Essay on the Poetry of the Eastern Nations' a primitive but dynamic
culture of untutored bardic genius, noble savagery, and resistance to
tyranny; their poetry reflecting an invigorating and heroic version of the
pastoral out of Arabia Felix. His translation of the pre-Islamic *Moallakát*
(1782) introduced the West to Bedouin boasting of their prowess in
hunting, fighting, feasting, and invading maidens' howdahs.

WILLIAM BECKFORD had imbibed the rugged exoticism of *Moallakát*
(as the fourteen references in Henley's notes make clear) and with its
grotesque company of dwarfs, giants, genii, eunuchs, mutes, and afrits,
Vathek (1786) marks the apogee of Gothic Orientalism. Extravagance of invention and narrative hyperbole were associated by current theories of
environmental determinism with sultry climes as surely as Asiatic luxury,
the source of Oriental debauchery, decadence, and despotism. Straddling
the Oriental tale and the Gothic novel, the text was a landmark in both
genres. Vathek is a Mahometan Faust whose psychological and physical
existence is mirrored in the vibrant depiction of interior and exterior landscapes – the paradisical idyll, the tower of pride, the yawning abyss, and
the subterranean Hall. This Arabian tale created a nuanced aesthetic of
evil with rich Oriental and Occidental resonances.

Meanwhile in London and later in Calcutta Sir William Jones was ap-
plying to both poetry and philology scientific techniques which were to
establish the foundations of modern Oriental scholarship, discovering
similitude rather than otherness, comparing Firdausi with Dryden, Hafiz
with Anacreon, the *Mahábhárata* with the *Iliad*. Jones's enormous
erudition had a pervasive influence upon the developing genre of the
Oriental verse tale, enabling Landor, Southey, Byron, and Moore to root
their Romantic subjectivity in scholarly, annotated objectivity.

Walter Savage Landor's *Gebir* (1798) and Robert Southey's *Thalaba the
Destroyer* (1801) mark the metamorphosis of the Oriental tale into the
Romantic verse narrative. Both poems employ contemporary Gothicism
to underline the decadence and decay of once-magnificent civilisations in
differing responses to the republican historical analysis of Volney's *Les
Ruines* (1791). In Landor the reader is treated to malign magic, moonlight
incantations, and an underworld compounded of immense space and
intense confinement; Southey provides a similarly Gothic combination
of desire and terror in the sensual domains of Aloadin and the demonic
cavern of Dom-Daniel. Thalaba is haunted nightly by the 'vampire-
corpse' of Oneiza who counsels despair; this Oriental ghoul had marketable potential as was evidenced by Byron's *The Giaour* (1813), Mary
Shelley's *Frankenstein* (1818), and John Polidori's *The Vampyre* (1819).

In *The Curse of Kehama* (1810) Southey overcompensated for his 'flatter-
ing misrepresentation' of Islamic culture by delineating Hinduism as the

epitome of Oriental Gothic, a monstrous mire of blood-drinking sacrality, a charnel of demonic and self-immolating devotees. The Preface refers to Hinduism as 'that mythology which Sir William Jones had been the first to introduce into English poetry', but Southey's hostility to the religion allied him to the Evangelical missionaries and Anglicists gaining ground in India. Jones's translation of the Sanskrit play *Sacontala* (1789) had entranced German Romanticism into seeing India as the holy land of Europe's childhood, and his own *Hymns to Hindu Deities* (1784–8) had used Pindarics and Deist sonorities to portray a dignified and decorous Hinduism. Southey, afraid of being swamped by the Oriental elements which Jones had claimed would revitalise Western culture, Gothicised the subcontinent.

The power of *Kehama* impressed the young **SHELLEY**, but his enthusiasm for the Gothic Romanticism of Sydney Owenson's (Lady Morgan) novel *The Missionary* (1811), in which the confrontations between the Catholic priest Hilarion and the Hindu priestess Luxima create an infinitely more sympathetic picture of Hinduism, drew the poet closer to Jones's position. Shelley's immediate empathetic response was his 'Zeinab and Kathema' (1811–12), in which Zeinab, a Kashmiri maiden, is abducted from her idyllic home by 'Christian murderers' and shipped to England where she turns to prostitution and rebellion. Kathema buys passage on an English frigate to pursue his search, and on a dark December evening collapses on a wild heath. When he wakes the moonlight reveals he has been lying underneath the naked decomposing gibbeted body of Zeinab; he mounts the gibbet, twists a chain around his neck and hangs himself beside her. Shelley's recourse to Gothic to express the intensity of his contempt for a corrupt and corrupting society anticipates the ending of *The Revolt of Islam* (1817), where the lovers Laon and Cythna are chained and burnt at the stake by the tyrant.

Philhellenism and pederasty had drawn Byron close to the Orient, and the heroes of his Oriental tales are to some extent, like himself, Gothic villains turned Turk, burdened with a guilty secret. The Giaour, a non-Muslim outsider, is loved by Leila, a slave; when her master discovers this, she is sewn into a sack and thrown into the sea. Byron was particularly aware of this punishment as a Gothic signifier of the arbitrary male power to silence woman, as he had rescued a girl from a similar fate at Piraeus.

Orientalism had come a long way in the century between Pope's gibe at the hack who might 'turn a Persian tale for half-a-crown' and the advance of £3,000 to Tom Moore for *Lalla Rookh* (1817). Political meanings continued to be concealed beneath Oriental allegories, and by the late 1820s the Oriental had displaced the Gothic as representing the Other.

MICHAEL FRANKLIN

Penny Dreadfuls

From its birth the **GOTHIC NOVEL** in Britain was the prerogative of the upper and professional classes: when one volume of a multi-volume novel cost more than the average weekly wage, the literate artisan was denied access by price. But the mechanisation of printing in the early nineteenth century enabled enterprising publishers, such as Edward Lloyd and John Dicks, to produce cheap popular fiction in a form that satisfied the demands of the poorer majority of an increasingly literate population.

This was in no sense 'literary' fiction; while the Romantic setting and content of the typical Gothic tale was retained, extended descriptive passages made way for a constant succession of sensational events described in lurid terms and with an excess of hyperbole that mirrored the popular theatre of the day. Novels of this kind appeared in serial form: either in the columns of the burgeoning periodical press, or independently in illustrated – and interminable – weekly parts, which from their price and content gave rise to the generic term the 'Penny Dreadful'.

Its fortunes rose as those of the Gothic Novel declined – its heyday was the 1840s and 1850s – but the staple fare of both was much the same: crime, vice and **THE SUPERNATURAL**. The Penny Dreadful, however, had a further agenda. Most of the stories were written for the people and of the people: **'STURM UND DRANG'** allied to folk tradition with a liberal helping of radicalism. The Chartist G. W. M. Reynolds (1814–79) was among the most prolific writers of Penny Dreadfuls and many of his novels, e.g. *Mysteries of London* (1844–8) and *Mysteries of the Courts of London* (1848–56), portray the nobility as vicious and depraved.

The authors of the Penny Dreadfuls were, for the most part, journeymen writers who supplied what their public wanted. Thus Thomas Peckett Prest (1810–79) produced shocking crime in the form of *Sweeney Todd, the Demon Barber of Fleet Street* (1846–8; originally entitled *The String of Pearls; or, The Sailor's Gift*), and supernatural **HORROR** with *Varney the Vampire; or, The Feast of Blood* (1847–9), while Reynolds supplied, *inter alia, Wagner the Wehr-Wolf* (1847), and the equally prolific J. F. Smith (1803–90) turned out historical romances to order – of which *Black Bess; or, The Knight of the Road* (1863–8) is perhaps the best.

Changing popular tastes, in terms of style if not of content, led to the gradual demise of the Penny Dreadful but it survived into the 1890s by diluting the excess of blood and horror and adapting itself to a juvenile readership – pre-eminently in the 'Jack Harkaway' romances of Samuel Bracebridge Hemyng. It could not prolong its life indefinitely, however, and by the end of the Victorian era it had passed away.

R. A. GILBERT

Poe, Edgar Allan (1809–49)

Although Poe has often been credited for it, he did not invent the Gothic tale. Many of his first reviewers, moreover, lamented that he had taken up a passé mode when his fiction began to appear. Nevertheless, Poe's name is inextricably entwined with literary Gothicism, and he did alter its courses. He spoke explicitly for himself, and implicitly for many other good Gothic writers, when in the Preface to his first collection of short stories, *Tales of the Grotesque and Arabesque* (1839–40), he countered the charges of excessive 'German', or what we now call 'Gothic', elements that critics deplored in his fiction: 'If in many of my productions terror has been the thesis, I maintain that terror is not of Germany, but of the soul, – that I have deduced this terror only from its legitimate sources, and urged it only to its legitimate results.' In other words, Poe explored terror where it originated and functioned: in the mind. His haunted minds reveal far more art than do those in many another Gothic tale where the mainstay is a thrill at sheer gut level.

Poe's greatest love was poetry, a natural for one captivated mainly by the Byron–Shelley spell, and secondarily by the verse of their contemporaries whose pursuits tended toward Gothicism, witness Walter Scott, whose earliest poems derive from German horror balladry, not to mention numerous lesser writers. Poe's poetry early displayed his predilections toward, and some sophisticated handling of, Gothic tropes. *Tamerlane* (1827) indicates his informed treatment of the prototypical Gothic hero. Tamerlane is blighted by thwarted love, and he consequently emerges as one motivated by fiery passions and tyrannical conduct. Echoes of Scott's *The Lay of the Last Minstrel* (1805), Byron's *Manfred* (1817) and *Childe Harold's Pilgrimage* (1812–18), the Tamburlaine plays of several predecessors, including **MATTHEW LEWIS**, the Eblis episode in **WILLIAM BECKFORD**'s *Vathek* (1786): all these and much more make *Tamerlane* a natural heir to their Gothicism. No matter that Poe's pagan Asiatic warlord's making a dying confession to a Catholic priest is anachronistic.

Poe's Gothic art shows to far greater advantage in shorter poems: 'Bridal Ballad', 'The Coliseum', 'Sonnet – To Silence', 'Lenore', 'The Lake', 'The Raven', 'Ulalume', 'Dream-Land', and 'Annabel Lee' offer representative examples. In such works, Poe, like many of the British Romantics who immediately preceded him, transformed what had been essentially descriptive landscapes into a geography of the imagination, and those interior worlds were fraught with far more nightmares than comforting dreams. 'Dream-Land' depicts experiences 'Out of SPACE – out of TIME', and thus it prepares for later works by Poe in which the perimeters of human experience are often distorted, at once holding out effects of

Gothic thrills for thrill's sake and plausible psychological horrors. The speaker turns inward to a region of weird mindscapes when the 'heart whose woes are legion' threatens to overwhelm him. Within this dream world, amidst vastnesses of flowing waters, great valleys, mountains constantly toppling, and fiery skies, supernatural visitants like ghouls and 'ghosts', 'Sheeted Memories of the Past –', help to enrich the fantasy.

Such later successes as 'The Raven', 'Ulalume', and 'Annabel Lee' evolve from these and other earlier poems in theme and form. Poe repeatedly stated that the most poetic of all themes was the death of a beautiful woman, and the trio named dramatise events inspired by dead young females. To some extent, these maidens are analogous to the ghosts whose conduct influences the courses of the protagonists. 'The Raven', in its insistent rhythms and rhymes, produces monotony deliberately calculated as enchantment for both protagonist and readers. For the speaker, weary from poring over books of magic, such technique may serve as the calling up, possibly inadvertently, of a haunting presence symbolised by the bird. For readers, the technique offers hypnotic lures into a world of nightmare fantasy. As the speaker drifts from a being in reasonable command of his emotional faculties ever further into an unsettling obsession that seems sure to destroy his rationality, rendered forcibly by means of the shadow enshrouding him as the poem concludes, the raven alters from a seemingly innocuous bird into a creature from the netherworld – geographic and emotional – whose destructive powers seem to multiply until he represents the very devil figure that folklore has long perceived in him. We might detect similarities between the 'drizzly November' in the soul of **HERMAN MELVILLE**'s Ishmael, in *Moby-Dick* (1851), and the 'drear December' background for Poe's protagonist. Allusions to the beloved maiden Lenore, now dead, the subsuming of intellectuality by non-rational forces, as the raven mounts the bust of Pallas, and the acceleration of darkness as the 'radiant' maiden fades and the raven takes over, combine with the notions earlier established – that the speaker tenants a chamber (his mind) that increasingly haunts him – to reinforce a drama of a disintegrating mind. The growing sense of that debilitating condition, set forth with an indirectness and hesitancy, enhanced by the repetitions in rhyme and phrase, further enervates the speaker. Here indeed is a Gothic story in dramatic verse.

Likewise, the haunting episode in 'Ulalume' occurs fittingly on Halloween night, as the speaker and his Psyche, a counsellor connected with light (perhaps the glow of a mind formerly at ease), traverse a partly familiar, partly strange, pathway. Ulalume and her lover have indeed been star-crossed, as is borne out by the astrological lore – of sexuality and war – that bodes ill for the living travellers as they wander through inauspicious surroundings rife with hints of imminent eruption. In

'Ulalume' we may be witnessing a debate between the male and female sides of a self that has grown dangerously out of touch with reality. The melancholy speaker and the 'graveyard' (see **GRAVEYARD SCHOOL**) aspects from earlier Gothicism gain a new life of artistic functionalism. 'Annabel Lee' moves us from situations of death-in-life to what may be actual death. The demise of his beautiful young Annabel may be presented in lilting tones in order to hint that that tragedy has deranged the speaker, rather as the emotional destruction of Shakespeare's Ophelia leads to her plaining song. We are left to wonder whether we have been listening to a necrophiliac or to an actual ghost.

Poe subsequently tried his hand at other literary forms, among them *Politian*, a fragmentary verse drama. Several scenes appeared in the *Southern Literary Messenger* during 1835–6, doubtless because of need for additional copy, and Poe only grudgingly consented to reprint them in *The Raven and other Poems* (1845) to fill out that book, as if he had become ashamed of this early, fumbling work. Based on the famous Beauchamp-Sharp 'Kentucky tragedy' of 1825, a triangular affair of sensational psycho-sexual proportions that culminated in the murder of the seducer, suicide of the wronged woman, and execution of the murderer, her husband, who recovered from attempted suicide to be hanged. Set in sixteenth-century Rome, with characters whose classical names derive from Poe's knowledge of ancient writings, *Politian* bears all the trappings of the Gothic plays (see **GOTHIC DRAMA**) that proliferated during the wake of the **GOTHIC NOVEL** craze of the 1790s and continued to be popular well into the nineteenth century. *Politian* is interesting as a literary curiosity, but little more. Its characters and dialogue are wooden.

Short fiction allowed Poe his greatest successes, however, and from first to last in that form his bonds with Gothicism are unmistakable. Poe sought in fiction writing the financial security that his verse had not achieved. To meet the demands of the marketplace for fiction, he undertook a course of intensive independent study in the successful Gothic story, so to speak, quickly mastered the rudiments of such marketable fare, and thereafter produced the works that have brought him lasting fame. Like many another young writer, in his exuberance over an evident ability to fashion what he thought likely to sell, Poe soon turned to mocking what writers of terror tales, himself included, turned out as staple wares. His propensities for satirising and parodying Gothic horrors have contributed to continual divergences in critical opinions.

Poe's work came to the notice of a group selected to judge a literary contest sponsored by one of the mammoth weeklies in vogue during the 1830s and 1840s, the Baltimore *Saturday Visiter*, in 1833. Poe's tale 'MS. found in a Bottle', was awarded the prize for fiction, followed by publication in the *Saturday Visiter* in October 1833. That event brought about his friendship with John Pendleton Kennedy, a recognised man of letters of the day, and Kennedy's good offices led to Poe's embarking on what would be the first of several editorial assignments that brought attention to the periodicals for which he worked.

Simultaneous with these kinds of recognition, Poe revealed the scheme for what, had it appeared as he initially conceived it, would have been a highly sophisticated book, a frame-narrative centred in a pretentious literary organisation, with much of its content connected to Gothic elements. 'Tales of the Folio Club', the title generally used for this project, numbered as its members caricatures of renowned fiction writers, who were to read tales that in many respects would have been comic takeoffs from or 'quizzes' of their models. Sir Walter Scott, Horace Smith, Lady Morgan, N. P. Willis, and even Poe himself, figured in this august gathering. Many of the tales incorporated humorous motifs of gluttony and alcoholism, mirroring the proclivities of the Folio Club constituents themselves. Each club member would have presented a tale fashioned in his own manner, followed by debate as to its merits, give and take so constructed as to ridicule pomposity in contemporaneous literary criticism. Finally, one disgusted participant was to have seized the manuscripts and hastened with them to a publisher in order to expose the follies of the enterprise. Unfortunately, because of publishers' rejections, this book never appeared; Poe dismantled it to sell individual stories to gift books and magazines. Early reviewers divined comic impulses at work in the stories as they appeared singly, but without the Folio Club context such comic purposes were obscured, and so they have remained.

'MS. found in a Bottle', for example, might well be a a supernatural story and a drunkard's tall tale, as might 'The Assignation' (originally entitled 'The Visionary'), 'Bon-Bon', 'Metzengerstein', 'Silence – A Fable', and 'Shadow – A Parable'. 'Lionizing' and 'King Pest' may in part mime the disruption occasioned by the theft of the manuscripts. All are marked by what may seem like clumsy stylistics and particularly stilted dialogue. If these were calculated as deliberate techniques involving intoxication and gluttony, however, they allow us to apprehend a subtlety in Poe's fiction that had not been present, or that had not been so artistically wrought, by many earlier Gothicists.

The Narrative of Arthur Gordon Pym (1837–8), Poe's novel written at the behest of James Kirke Paulding, which has won increasing critical attention and respect in the last forty years, is in all likelihood an outgrowth of the 'Tales of the Folio Club', with exaggerated horrors, violence and brutality, natural or supernatural (or apparently supernatural), expressed in rhetoric that resonates with the same indecisiveness, repetition, and tall-tale qualities found in the earlier drunkards' tales, all related by the typical Poe narrator, a self-centred, emotionally overwrought and anxiety-ridden character.

The shorter fiction, however, is usually cited for giving Poe repute as one who transformed shop-worn Gothic plots, settings and characters into the stuff of modern literature, most notably as it portrays the mind under agonising pressures. The notion that one may easily distinguish one body or type of Poe's fiction from another pales when we recall that the detective story as we now know it, as well as science fiction, are actually results of Poe's experimental Gothicism. 'The Murders in the Rue Morgue' (1841), for example, stands as a work of 'explained supernaturalism' because its seemingly otherworldly atrocities prove to be the activities of an orangutan. Likewise, the circumstances in 'The Mystery of Marie Roget' and 'The Purloined Letter' (1845) could, with few alterations, be moved wholly into territories of the supernatural. Just so, as regards science fiction. Thus they typify the hoaxes which their author was wont to perpetrate upon his readers for purposes of testing their alertness. The weird world of Roderick Usher and his odd tastes and pursuits have been discovered to originate in medical knowledge and terminology ('Nervous Fever', symptom by symptom) of Poe's day. 'The System of Dr Tarr and Professor Fether', as well, derives from scientific explorations in treating insanity during Poe's time, although its surface drift might readily lull us into suspecting that supernatural agencies dictate the action. Kindred underpinnings enliven 'The Masque of the Red Death', explicable as plausibly in terms of Prospero's illusory wish to evade realities that link life with time and death as it is a horrific tale that is only rhetorically above much other scary storytelling by Poe's contemporaries.

The renowned tales about women – 'Berenice', 'Morella', 'Ligeia', and 'Eleonora', along with 'The Fall of the House of Usher' and 'The Assignation' – take us as certainly as does 'The Masque of the Red Death' into parables of unintegrated selves, as they do into claptrap haunted castles tenanted by perishing frail ones who are cardboard rather than fully realised characters. Poe subtly manipulates Gothic conventions in theme and form to symbolise the dangers that lurk when the potentially creative, nurturing, and sexual female principle in the self is repressed by the ill-informed, fearful, and thus destructively aggressive, male principle. Again Poe pushes close the borders of melodramatics and psychological depths, but the palm must be given to the latter. Interestingly, that generally overlooked tale in such discussions, 'The Assignation', is Poe's first rendering in fiction of his death-of-a-beautiful-woman theme, well framed within implications regarding creativity (in art and human sexuality) rendered in a poetic prose that leads us to ponder gender issues as much as the occurrences in the subsequent tales of this type have done for many readers. A supernatural aura seems to hover over this tale until its startling conclusion conveys another message.

The other overlooked, or ignored, tale about women, 'Eleonora', suggests (because it was Poe's last with this theme) that the narrator's second love relationship brings about an integrated selfhood; thus the visitation from Eleonora's spirit is understandably beneficent, in contrast to the horrors occasioned by the 'returns' of the females or their influences in the previous tales. We could also, in such contexts, preceive in the conclusion to *The Narrative of Arthur Gordon Pym*, which breaks off as he comes upon a mysterious white, shrouded giant figure, the culmination of young Pym's quest for selfhood and maturity. The white figure, that is, may symbolise a feminine presence essential to complete the development and maturity of the self.

One could continue to enumerate tales from the Poe canon that transfuse new vitality into Gothic veins: 'The Black Cat', 'The Tell-Tale Heart', 'William Wilson', 'The Cask of Amontillado', 'The Pit and the Pendulum', 'Hop-Frog', 'Mesmeric Revelation', the apocalyptic colloquies, 'Some Words with a Mummy', 'The Premature Burial'. 'The Sphinx' – and many more. Forbidding worlds and equally eerie inhabitants of such worlds are haunting in their presences. In all of them we encounter kindred speech patterns and singular actions among the characters. Haunted castles of the mind rather than antiquarian descriptions of architectural ruins come to the fore. Not for idle purposes do the bridal chamber in 'Ligeia' and the mansion in 'The Fall of the House of Usher' respectively resemble a coffin and a human head. Nor are the journeys in 'William Wilson', 'The Pit and the Pendulum', or 'The System of Dr Tarr and Professor Fether' circular, and largely interior, as a consequence of any inartistic repetitiveness on Poe's part.

Form and content coalesce beautifully in all of these tales, but 'The Fall of the House of Usher' stands out as Poe's most significant creation in Gothicism, and therefore it warrants extended consideration. The tale may profitably be read as the narrator's journey into the depths of self; there he confronts horrors devolving from disparateness between appearance and reality. The uninviting, vague country he has passed through *en route* to the House of Usher may be suggestive of his own emotional uncertainties. He approaches the Usher mansion, representative of his own head or mind, with much reluctance, as if he is afraid to step inside himself. This hesitancy is emphasised by the halting, stumbling prose in the opening paragraphs. Once he decides to enter the house, he leaves behind his horse, the servants, and the family physician, symbolic perhaps, respectively, of sexuality, everyday living, and a spirit of scientific rationalism.

In this interpretation, Roderick has indeed been a childhood companion, one whose own unstable identity, yet one so tightly knit to that of his twin, Madeline, symbolises the storyteller's own condition. Instability is evident in matters related to physical and psychological aspects of life, and thus the 'house' of Usher offers us multiple significances. If the Ushers' own debilitated organic and mental health results from incest, Roderick's repressed sexuality (manifest in the 'illness' of Madeline, which may point to thwarted sexual and other nurturing and creative impulses), or whatever else 'bad blood' may include, we need not doubt that it frightens the narrator, who figuratively beholds the situation within his own self in its female and male components in the Ushers and their house. The narrator has, of course, voluntarily entered this head–edifice, to sojourn for a time, and in so doing he shows his kinship with the all too curious protagonists from previous Gothicism, who inevitably step into the very places they should most likely avoid. Like the knight in 'Eldorado', Poe's most upbeat poem, this explorer seeks to know life's mysteries; unlike that traveller, however, this visitor to the House of Usher finally flees in terror, without any trace of his once condescending stance toward Roderick. He is given a lesson in the consequences of unbalancing the self, once again rendered in terms of gender upsets.

No wonder, then, that he had not known sooner about Madeline; his and Roderick's companionship had been that of adolescents. Even at this point, his reaction to her (and what she represents) is one of astonishment and anxiety, as if he cannot readily admit the female potential in his own makeup. That Madeline should overcome her weaknesses in order to return to Roderick, and that in such a return she may perform as a vampire figure, is a natural way of dramatising the evils of repression. Here, all femininity is subsumed because Roderick (and the narrator) fear this part of personality, and yet they are fascinated by it such that it is delineated in terms of a twin relationship. If the narrator finds in the Ushers reflections of his own psycho-physical makeup, then Madeline's 'malady' is as undeniably as much of his own making as it is of Roderick's. That bonding shows in his reponses to Roderick's artistic endeavours and hypochondria; they repell him yet he toys with them. Thus he is as responsible for the decay and downfall of the house-head as they. He is left at the close of the tale suffering from the same 'lights-out' symptoms as those that make 'The Haunted Palace', Roderick's own poem, so appalling. Like Roderick, this character has succumbed to the fear of fear itself – and the fear originates in his own warped psyche.

We ought also never to pronounce exclusively on the comedy or sobriety in these, or other Poe works, although zealots have argued for one or another kind of interpretation as the more significant. 'Ligeia' and 'The Fall of the House of Usher' have been read as wholly serious fictions (variously involving autobiography, psychology, race, gender, and Marxism) and, with equal validity, as parodies of the excesses to which Gothicism is often prone, indicative of how easily the horrific may slip into the amusing. Keeping company with these works are 'The Raven', an early poem, 'The Sleeper', 'The Cask of Amontillado' (horrifying, yet not without sardonic humour), 'The System of Dr Tarr and Professor Fether' and 'Silence – A Fable'. All force us to consider carefully the possibilities for horror and humour embedded within their frameworks. Terrors are there, whether those aroused by murder, violence, animal aspects of human nature, or just a sense that appearances are slipping away to leave us confronting unpleasant realities. Perhaps the concomitant comedy is suggestive of motivation toward laughter to forestall weeping at such recognitions, of tendencies to laugh, or to try to laugh, away our fears. Such tactics makes us leave many of Poe's creative works with thoughts that we have been witnessing dramas of irreparably fragmented selves.

The close resemblances between Poe's tales and poems remind us that in the former, as in the latter, he manifests a well-nigh Keatsian art in appealing to our sensory perceptions, inviting us to walk a tightrope between external and emotional experiences. Not without forethought does Mr Blackwood in 'How to Write a Blackwood Article' exhort the Signora Psyche Zenobia, aspirant writer of popular fiction: 'Sensations are the great things after all.' Poe's creative work merges sensations and things, making comprehensible the weight he so often gives to physical description as the means of entrance into corridors of the mind or as symbols of those corridors. Poe also realised the virtues of keeping his Gothicism terse; by means of that practice he created Gothicism that still carries an impact while that fostered by scores of other Gothicists has faded, because length makes it boresome. As a precursor of writers from **HERMAN MELVILLE, CHARLES DICKENS, HENRY JAMES, ARTHUR MACHEN**, M. P. Shiel, Edith Wharton, William Faulkner, Flannery O'Connor, **ANGELA CARTER**, and Stephen King, plus hosts of others who have turned out occult, crime, and science fiction, Poe is not to be ignored.

BENJAMIN F. FISHER

Postcolonial Gothic

Countries which might generally be described as postcolonial (Canada, USA, New Zealand, Australia, Africa, the Caribbean, and so on) have produced a range of distinctive Gothic narratives. It would be possible to claim 'magic realism' as Gothic, for example: it is a genre associated primarily with Latin America and the Caribbean which unsettles the constraints of both colonial structures and realist conventions through magical irruptions and bizarre occurrences. A hitherto-familiar Gothic narrative may also be re-written through a postcolonial context. The marginal but disturbing Creole Jamaican character Bertha Mason in Charlotte Brontë's *Jane Eyre* (1847) became the focus of Jean Rhys's *Wide Sargasso Sea* (1966), for example. More spectacularly, aspects of Brontë's narrative were relocated wholesale to the Caribbean in Jacques Torneur's marvellous horror film *I Walked with a Zombie* (1943).

Postcolonial nations can re-animate the traumas of their colonial pasts to produce Gothic narratives. Ghost stories can certainly be built around this process – as in the Steven Spielberg film *Poltergeist* (1982), which has a settler family pay the price for occupying a house built upon an Indian burial ground. Re-animation can occur in other ways, too: for example, the mobilising of 'traditional' indigenous beliefs in retributive spirits in a modern South African context for Richard Stanley's film *Dust Devil* (1991) or in a contemporary Australian setting for Sam Watson's novel *The Kadaitcha Sung* (1990). But postcolonialism can give rise to a more ambivalent relation to colonial events and race relations, and this, too, generates Gothic narratives. The Aboriginal film-maker Tracey Moffatt's *BeDevil* (1992) represents Australia as a place full of ghostly 'effects', which unsettle or bemuse Aborigines and white settlers alike. In this sense, they work to bring an otherwise divided nation together. But postcolonial Gothic narratives usually remain caught somewhere *in between* reconciliation and difference. The postcolonial place is partly familiar, and partly unfamiliar – partly resembling home ('New Caledonia', 'New England', and so on) and yet also evoking something quite unrecognisable and strange. Many postcolonial Gothic narratives exploit the uncanny features of this predicament.

KEN GELDER

Radcliffe, Ann (1764–1823)

Ann Radcliffe was born on 9 July 1764 in London, the only child of William Ward and Ann Oates. Her parents resided in the commercial district of Holborn, and were involved in 'trade'. In the 1780s the family moved to Bath, where Ann met William Radcliffe, an Oxford graduate and law student. They married in 1787, in Bath, but shortly afterwards moved to London where the couple resided until Ann's death in 1823.

Ann Radcliffe's literary career spanned eight short, but highly productive, years. In 1789 she published *The Castles of Athlin and Dunbayne* and in 1790 *A Sicilian Romance*, both respectfully, if moderately reviewed. *The Romance of the Forest*, published in 1791, made her reputation. The £500 she received for *The Mysteries of Udolpho* (1794), and the £800 for *The Italian* (1797), made her one of the highest paid novelists of the decade. In addition to her five romances Ann Radcliffe produced, in 1795, a travel book describing a journey down the Rhine made with her husband the previous summer, during a lull in the fighting with France. Border difficulties meant the Radcliffes were unable to cross into Switzerland, their intended destination. A distant glimpse was all Radcliffe had of the Alpine sublimity which had figured so prominently in her novels. In compensation the Radcliffes toured the Lake District, in search of domestic sublimity, and this, too, is included in the travel book.

In 1797, at the age of only thirty-three, heralded as the unrivalled mistress of her own brand of romance, Ann Radcliffe suddenly stopped publishing. Radcliffe had always been reclusive; she now withdrew into impenetrable obscurity, only broken on her death by the posthumous publication in 1826 of her final works, *Gaston de Blondeville*, a novel, and *St Alban's Abbey*, a metrical romance. Virtually all of the biographical information we have comes from a single source, her husband William. He wrote a substantial entry on his wife for the *Annual Biography and Obituary for the Year 1824*, and closely briefed Thomas Noon Talfourd, who appended a biographical memoir to *Gaston de Blondeville*.

In his Introduction to the novels of Ann Radcliffe (1824) Sir Walter Scott advanced a position that was to become a commonplace of nineteenth-century Radcliffe criticism: 'Mrs Radcliffe, as an author, has the most decided claim to take her place among the favoured few, who have been distinguished as the founders of a class, or school.' For much of the twentieth century Radcliffe's reputation has suffered from an inadequate appreciation of the justness of Scott's judgement. And without a just understanding of Radcliffe's achievement one cannot understand fully the history of the Gothic novel, for hers was a decisive contribution.

Two prejudicial interpretations have especially distorted her reputation. First, her use of the explained supernatural, where apparent mysteries are finally resolved into physical causes, has been taken as evidence of conservative, eighteenth-century rationalism. Early Gothic writing has traditionally been seen as a form of dark Romanticism. To judge Radcliffe a conventional rationalist is therefore to see her, not as a member of the Gothic avant-garde, but as an anti-Gothic, anti-Romantic, reactionary. In effect, this reading removes Radcliffe from the leading edges of 1790s literary culture, and places her among the backward looking, trailing fringes.

Secondly, Radcliffe has been judged a timid female novelist. This prejudice is really a reworking of the first. What lies behind it is the assumption that the male Gothic (the line of writers stretching from **HORACE WALPOLE, WILLIAM BECKFORD, MATTHEW LEWIS,** through **CHARLES MATURIN** and **JAMES HOGG** to the Americans **HERMAN MELVILLE** and **NATHANIEL HAWTHORNE**) represents the true Gothic strain. Male Gothic texts have been deemed more transgressive, and therefore more 'Gothic', for a variety of reasons: they do not explain the supernatural, which leaves their texts open-ended and irresolute; they are frank, rather than coy, about sexual violence; and they frequently pit a rebellious subject against a meaningless and/or diabolical cosmos. Mrs Radcliffe, with her unscathed heroines, explained mysteries, and behind-the-times Burkean terror, appeared to be doing no more than sprucing up the old-fashioned eighteenth-century sentimental novel with genteel terror tactics, thus holding back, rather than advancing, Horace Walpole's 'experiment'.

But this, emphatically, was not how Radcliffe's contemporaries saw it. Radcliffe's models were fresh in readers' minds. The reviews repeatedly made mention of the 'tradition' in which Radcliffe was working: Horace Walpole's *The Castle of Otranto* (1764); Clara Reeve's *The Old English Baron* (1778); Sophia Lee's *The Recess* (1783–5). William Hazlitt, reviewing the situation in 1818, explicitly contrasts Radcliffe with her Gothic progenitors, concluding that her models were 'dry', 'meagre' or 'dismal', and that only in her work did Walpole's experiment come truly to life. To return to Scott's terms, she was not re-cycling other writers' props. On the contrary, she was the founder of her own school of fiction. As Scott elsewhere characterises her, she was 'the first poetess of romantic fiction'. She was, as the general public had it, 'the Great Enchantress'.

There were a number of factors at work in twentieth-century misconceptions of Radcliffe. One was simple unfamiliarity with literary history. Many of the 'male Gothic' works Radcliffe was judged against appeared after her *oeuvre* was in the public domain. These writers may have reacted against her, but in many respects she made them possible. Another factor was a common tendency in early twentieth-century criticism to approach literary texts as product rather than process, as finished artefacts to be synoptically reviewed, and analysed. Such an approach is bound to lead to a reading of Radcliffe where the mysteries are all explained, where one is left with prosaic, lifeless props, incapable of generating either effect or meaning. But that is not how her public read her. Although some reviewers took her to task for overdoing the explained supernatural, others expressed their appreciation of her unrivalled mastery at generating surmise in her readers, at (as Coleridge put it) 'escaping the guesses' of her readers. The suggestions that arise, in the process of reading, are as much a part of the thematic *gestalt* of a Radcliffe text as the final explanations.

The clearer picture we now have of Radcliffe's achievement is mainly owing to the pioneering work done by feminist critics. By stressing the rival claims of the **FEMALE GOTHIC** they have counterbalanced the prejudicial reading inherent in the privileging of the male Gothic, but more than that they have re-taught us how to read Radcliffe. The basic premise of the 'female Gothic' is that it encodes displaced expressions of female experience. It is in the surmises and suggestions arising from apparent supernatural events that these displaced expressions are to be found. To uncover the 'female Gothic' is to return to reading Radcliffe as process.

In its obituary notice, the *Gentleman's Magazine* (very much a mainstream publication) proudly noted that Radcliffe's novels had been translated into the main European languages, to England's glory. Her influence has been incalculable, not only on the Gothic, but on the novel in general, and not only in Anglo-American culture, but far beyond. As the psychoanalytic critics Leona Sherman and Norman Holland influentially put it, 'the image of the woman-plus-habitation and the plot of mysterious sexual and supernatural threats in an atmosphere of dynastic mysteries within the habitation has changed little since the eighteenth century ...'. Radcliffe was the primary architect of this enduring plot, and it reaches 'down' to Mills and Boon and Harlequin romance, through **THE BRONTËS**, and outwards to France, where her reputation has been unswervingly high, and to Russia, where novelists such as Dostoevsky freely acknowledged their debts. When Keats was preparing to write his Gothic tale 'The Eve of St Agnes' (1820), he wrote that he was going to draw upon 'mother Radcliff' [sic], where we should read 'mother', not as a patronising epithet, but as 'matrix', the generic source all post-Radcliffean Gothicists drew upon.

Early Works

Although Radcliffe's first two novels – *The Castles of Athlin and Dunbayne* and *A Sicilian Romance* – may be seen as 'prentice work, they also reveal Radcliffe quickly discovering her true subject while forging her recurring plot structures.

The Castles of Athlin and Dunbayne features usurpation, a foundling, and providentially restored order. As such, its plot reaches back through *The Old English Baron* to Walpole's *The Castle of Otranto*, and beyond that, to Shakespeare's late romances. A two-fold conflict advances the plot. Malcolm, the wicked Baron of Dunbayne, has designs upon Mary of the Castle of Athlin, designs to which Mary and her brother Osbert are implacably opposed given that Malcolm has murdered their father. Meanwhile, Mary has fallen in love with Alleyn, an apparent peasant, an alliance Mary's family find unthinkable, given their sense of feudal caste. Malcolm is a usurper; the true heir to Dunbayne is in fact Alleyn, left as a foundling after Malcolm had murdered Alleyn's father and incarcerated his mother and sister. Malcolm is eventually vanquished; the truth comes out; and the true social order is restored with Mary and Alleyn's marriage. The Scottish setting, the medieval time frame, the providential intervention, and the focus on male protagonists, are all elements destined to disappear from Radcliffe's *oeuvre* (apart from the posthumous material). But there is also much that was to become familiar, such as the nature worship of the protagonists, a taste for the sublime and the picturesque, and a disposition to melancholy, superstition and a sense of the phantasmal nature of everyday life.

In her next novel, *A Sicilian Romance*, all the main features of the Radcliffe plot come sharply into focus. A young noble woman, Julia de Mazzini, is imprisoned within the family castle by her father who has arranged a marriage with a highly disagreeable, but rich duke, more his than his daughter's age. Julia takes flight, has many adventures, is assisted on several occasions by her lover Hippolitus, before, through sheer accident, discovering her mother who has been entombed in the bowels of the family palazzo by her father. Mazzini is poisoned by his new, younger 'wife', after catching her in the act of infidelity; and with his death the way is cleared for the heroine to marry Hippolitus, the man of her choice.

This simple plot description conceals a number of profound changes. First, Radcliffe has moved her historical setting forward, to the dawn of the Enlightenment, which affords a contrast between Mazzini's old-fashioned feudal values, such as primogeniture and arranged marriages, and a younger generation conditioned by sensibility and romantic love. In *A Sicilian Romance*, dawn breaks upon a backward, feudal order; which is exactly how sympathisers with the French Revolution saw contemporary events. Radicals contrasted a modern family unit, based on love, choice and mutual respect, with a dysfunctional, feudal one exclusively devoted to enhancing the patriarchal house. It was a contrast between an old and a new order, between the aristocracy and the middle class; and according to radical rhetoric, the new would sweep the old away. *A Sicilian Romance* embodies this radical rhetoric, only disguised as the late sixteenth-century shift from the medieval to the modern, from the repressive manners of the *ancien régime* to a new bourgeois sensibility.

Although Radcliffe's romances move progressively forward in time, each one being set later in history, all implicitly contain this contrast between the feudal and the modern. *A Sicilian Romance* changes in other, equally significant ways. The central figure is now a heroine; and while her lover endeavours to help her, he often proves ineffectual, or is missing during key episodes, which provides the heroine with the opportunity to take the initiative in spite of her best efforts to obey decorum, and remain passive. In *The Castles of Athlin and Dunbayne* the heroine is ineffectually helped by her mother while being persecuted by an older man who is the antithesis of her absent father. *A Sicilian Romance* rearranges these elements, in that the heroine is now persecuted by the father, while the mother is missing. This, too, is a structural change which recurs in the rest of Radcliffe's fiction, although the father figure usually turns out to be an uncle, or is only (as with Montoni in *the Mysteries of Udolpho*) a legal rather than a biological father. This change both sharpened the patriarchal overtones of the medieval order Radcliffe's heroines are in flight from, and introduced an element feminist critics especially have read as an essential component of the female Gothic: a search for an absent mother (read figuratively as a quest for identity made problematic by a cultural effacement of the maternal).

The Mature Romances

Although the structure of the Radcliffe plot was largely fixed in *A Sicilian Romance*, Radcliffe's subsequent romances introduced technical innovations which deepened and complicated her works. Her landscape descriptions – so important to the emotional texture of her narrative – also grew more nuanced. This holds especially true of her deployment of **THE SUBLIME** and picturesque, landscape modes crucial to Romantic poetics. In particular, though, her succeeding works witnessed alterations in her attitude towards sensibility, which can be read as a barometer registering the changes in political atmosphere which so characterised the 1790s, as public sympathy towards the French Revolution broke into turbulence in consequence of the Terror. Where *A Sicilian Romance* sees sensibility as an unproblematic, and welcome, aspect of modern manners – as the natural index of the growth of civil society – her later romances are defensive and protective on the issue, especially given the tendency of conservative critics to add **SENSIBILITY** to the list of the causes of revolutionary violence. Radcliffe did not simply invent a Gothic formula, and then recycle it; her work constantly changed, in response to its own internal dynamic, and to the rapidly changing literary and political scene.

   The Romance of the Forest introduces several important technical features. The heroine, Adeline, relates her history to the wife of La Motte, her benefactor. The introduction of a first-person narrative deepens Adeline's characterisation, for we are entitled to ask what Adeline's style of narration, with its idealisations and omissions, says about her. At a later point, Adeline, exploring behind an arras, encounters a secret passage leading to a dungeon where she discovers a manuscript apparently relating a tale of imprisonment and murder. It turns out that this is the narrative of her father, who has been murdered by her uncle, the very Marquis de Montalt presently planning (unwittingly) the incestuous rape of his niece. The document solves the mystery of Adeline's identity, while restoring her usurped property rights. As Adeline's discovering of the manuscript is hedged round with the supernatural it remains open whether the manuscript actually exists, or is just fantasised by Adeline. Indeed, the whole episode may be read figuratively as the scene of female writing, something done secretively (behind the arras), prone to creating idealising, escapist romance, but nevertheless productive of a narrative disclosing clues as to the heroine's/writer's identity.

Thematically, *The Romance of the Forest* is significant for its introduction of La Luc, modelled on the Savoyard priest from Rousseau's *Emile*. As the epitome of sensibility La Luc affirms Radcliffe's liberal sympathies; at the same time, his depiction is part of a larger project whereby Radcliffe endeavours to give her texts complexity by weaving into her narratives allusions and references to contemporary aesthetic values, visual, literary and philosophical. Radcliffe is not a naive writer, but one finely attuned to the aesthetic discourses of her time.

The device of the explained supernatural is given its fullest, most sophisticated expression in *The Mysteries of Udolpho*, Radcliffe's most famous novel. Emily, the heroine, is taught by her father that true sensibility lies in resisting its excesses, such as supernatural terror. Although Emily learns to rein in her sensibility, two linked episodes continually undermine her mental discipline: her recollection of the body glimpsed behind the veil in Udolpho, and her father's secret manuscript, into which Emily has transgressively glanced. The final explanations reveal that the 'body' is a waxen image and the manuscript horrors a reference to her aunt's murder. Earlier, Emily had falsely surmised that the image was the corpse of Laurentini, hidden behind the veil after Montoni had stripped her of her property. Although false, this surmise truly represents her situation, that Montoni will discard her once he has acquired the titles to her lands. As such, Montoni is a nightmare version of the patriarchal order, one in complete contrast to the benevolent world promised by her father where Romantic love finds a true basis in civil society. But this pillar of belief is also undermined when Emily's feverish sensibility construes her father's manuscript as relating her own illegitimacy. The novel ends with Emily reassured as to her father's probity and the possibility of a civil, patriarchal society. In the interim, the surmises arising from her superstitious fears prompt a more balanced, complicated view.

In *The Italian* Radcliffe turned to the Inquisition as a means of introducing new varieties of terror. With its robust Protestantism *The Italian* may give the impression that Radcliffe had jumped on a xenophobic, nationalist bandwagon. But as always with Radcliffe, a closer look reveals subtleties. In many respects the novel represents Radcliffe's final reassessment of sensibility, one undoubtedly prompted by Matthew Lewis's sensationalist, voyeuristic satire in *The Monk* (1796). A key element of sensibility was faith in the morally improving nature of scenes of 'virtue' in distress – typically, a young woman on the verge of being outraged. The problem with this, though, was that it represented the female body as a delectable object of the male gaze (the latent eroticism of which De Sade was more than happy to exploit). *The Italian* effectively turns the tables by subjecting the hero to the effeminising gaze of the patriarchal Inquisition. Radcliffe's earlier novels had embraced the early radical trust in sensibility as a means of revolutionising modern manners, thus hastening the arrival of a truly civil society. Radcliffe did not turn her back on sensibility, but she did become more sensitive to aspects of power embedded within sensible, aspects deftly explored in the last novel she published in her lifetime.

ROBERT MILES

Rice, Anne (1941–)

Christened Howard O'Brien after her father, who had been an unsuccessful writer, Anne Rice was brought up in the Irish Catholic quarter of New Orleans. As a cultural crossroads with its traditions of voodoo and Creole Catholicism, it provided her with a Gothic cityscape that became the template for her fictional vampire-ridden cities. Childhood walks in cemeteries, where bodies were buried in vaults and crypts above the ground, were to inspire Rice to re-create her own superterranean inhabitants of a metropolis of death. Having been educated at the Holy Name of Jesus Convent, she considered becoming a nun. Eventually, she decided to pursue her interest in the afterlife by choosing another form of the cloistered life, this time, as a writer of **VAMPIRE** fiction.

By expanding upon a short story, she produced her most famous novel so far, *Interview with the Vampire* (1976), which was turned into a Hollywood block-buster in 1994. This was the first of *The Vampire Chronicles*, which was followed by *The Vampire Lestat* (1985), *Queen of the Damned* (1988), *Tale of the Body Thief* (1992) and *Memnoch the Devil* (1995). The main character, the vagabond vampire Lestat de Lioncourt, is based on the poet Stan Rice, whom she married in 1961. Other novels dealing with occult themes include *The Witching Hour* (1990), *The Mummy* (1989),

Lasher (1994), *Taltos: Lives of the Mayfair Witches* (1994), *Servant of the Bones* (1996) and *Violin* (1997). Less supernatural and more sublunary departures are *The Feast of All Saints* (1979), about the miscegenation of the New Orleans *gens de couleur libre*, and *Cry to Heaven* (1982), which is concerned with the castrati of eighteenth-century Venice. These novels are a postcolonial foray into the exoticism of European decadence and degeneracy, which contrasts with her fiction produced under the sobriquet of Anne Rampling, through which Rice exploits the glossy and commercialised erotica of contemporary California. Using the cryptic *nom de plume* of A. N. Roquelaure, she has also produced a pornographic variation of the fairy-tale 'Sleeping Beauty' in the sado-masochistic trilogy: *The Claiming of Sleeping Beauty* (1983), *Beauty's Punishment* (1984) and *Beauty's Release* (1985).

What all Rice's novels share is a preoccupation with eroticism and gender. Not only are her vampires androgynous beings, but her fascination with androgyny and homo-eroticism is evident from her preference for writing from a male point of view. Having described herself as a 'Gay man writing in a woman's body', Rice claims that the child vampire Claudia in *Interview with the Vampire* 'is the embodiment of [her] failure to deal with the feminine. She [Claudia] is a woman trapped in a child's body. She's the person robbed of power.' Based upon her daughter Michelle, who died of leukaemia, Claudia represents not only a literary necromancy, but is also the undead agency for the exorcism of her bereavement.

Vampirism is employed elsewhere as a metaphor for other threats to corporeal integrity, such as AIDS and drug dependency. Rice's mother, who died from an alcohol-related illness, once set her bed alight while in a drunken stupor. A fear of fire is endemic among many of Rice's vampire characters, for whom mirrors, garlic and crucifixes are passé. While these vampires continue to represent the proverbial outsider, their author, on account of her modish popular success, has now been exiled from the cultish margins into the commercial mainstream.

MARIE MULVEY-ROBERTS

Roman Noir

As early as 1927, James R. Foster suggested that the English Gothic Novel as developed by authors such as Mrs **RADCLIFFE** was highly indebted to the French sentimental adventure tale of the preceding sixty years. If this is the case, the term *roman noir* should be perceived not merely as a synonym for English Gothic fiction in French translation but also as an independent genre in its own right, though one which later accommodated such a vast body of foreign literature in translation that its own identity and origins became obscured. The term should also be distinguished from the later *FRÉNÉTIQUE* SCHOOL.

According to Foster, although Richardson remained an important influence during the latter half of the eighteenth century, English novelists were increasingly drawn to incorporate more melodramatic elements in their works following the example of the Abbé Prévost (1696–1763). This influence has two aspects: first, the treatment of love, which, although English writers softened the sensuality, is presented in terms of an intense and impetuous passion; secondly, the use of marvellous and moving incidents such as shipwrecks, piracy, abduction, incredible coincidence, robbery and, of course, THE SUPERNATURAL.

Although Prévost's first three novels were translated into English in the 1730s, almost immediately following their French publication, it is perhaps not insignificant that as late as 1786 Charlotte Smith was responsible for an English version of the *Histoire de Manon Lescau* (1731). Similarly, Foster sees Sophia Lee's *The Recess* (1783–5) as largely based on Prévost's *Le Philosophe anglais: Histoire de Cleveland* (1731). Indeed, Foster goes so far as to claim: 'The novel [*The Recess*] is evidence that the author's cleverness lay in the ability to imitate exactly rather than to leave the imprint of her individuality on the re-worked material. The substance and manner of *Cleveland* is here reproduced so unchanged that a detailed description of *The Recess* is unnecessary.' At least one contemporary French commentator spotted the resemblance however, and Harriet Lee, the author's sister, later admitted that '*Cleveland*, written I believe by the Abbé Prêvot [is] the first novel of the type Sophia chose to write.'

Prévost's own French imitators – particularly Mme de Tencin, Baculard d'Arnaud, Mme Riccoboni and Mme de Genlis – also enjoyed a sizeable English readership. The work of Baculard d'Arnaud (1716–1805), which is often designated by the term *drame monacale* (literally, monastic drama) because of the frequency with which his ill-starred lovers find themselves imprisoned in such settings, was frequently translated. The novella *Varbeck* (1774) – in which Warbeck purposefully throws away a battle and falsely confesses he is an imposter for the sake of love – was adapted into English by Sophia Lee as *Warbeck, a pathetic tale* in 1786. Likewise, Clara Reeve's *The Exiles; or, Memoirs of the Count de Crondstadt* (1789) has been claimed to be founded on two stories by Baculard d'Arnaud. The French influence on English Gothic fiction may be more substantial than even this might suggest, however, if one looks further afield to material such as Gayot de Pitavel's *Causes célèbres* – a multi-volumed collection of criminal cases which began publication in 1734 – in whose pages even Mrs Radcliffe is said to have sought inspiration.

Although Foster is generally correct in his analysis, his remarks none the less require nuancing. Male critics have often accused women writers of possessing an imitative gift rather than a creative one. This is particularly relevant with respect to the so-called 'borrowings' of Sophia Lee. While the earlier French tradition of sentimental melodrama, or *roman noir*, does indeed overlap with the English Gothic tradition, it is none the less essential to bear in mind that each is the product of a different cultural system. When cultural appropriation occurs – whether by means of a writer making use of an element or elements from another writer's work or in the form of translation (itself not only a selective process but also one in which different cultural encodings are possible) – it is generally motivated in some way. Thus, the question is not so much who borrowed what from whom, but why and how was the material modified. (See Venuti, 1995, for an exemplary reading of I. U. Tarchetti's translation of Mary Shelley's 'The Mortal Immortal' into Italian.)

Take the case of Sophia Lee's *The Recess* and Prévost's *Cleveland*. The hero of Prévost's novel is the illegitimate son of Oliver Cromwell and, as such, is raised out of sight of the world in the cavern of Romeny Hole. After the death of his mother, he makes for France whence he sets sail for Jamaica and undergoes a number of exciting adventures amongst the Indians. Returning to France, a group of fanatical priests try to convert him to Catholicism and his reason deserts him under the weight of all his misfortunes. Finally, the novel is prolonged by an account of the relationship between Cleveland's daughter Cécile, and the Duke of Monmouth. Each of these elements, and more besides, do indeed find a corollary in *The Recess*. Thus, the title of Sophia Lee's novel refers to a subterranean retreat where Matilda and Ellinor, the children of a secret marriage between Mary Stuart and the Duke of Norfolk, are forced to spend their early years out of reach of the vindictive Elizabeth I. Matilda later clandestinely weds the Earl of Leicester, who is subsequently murdered in France where the couple have sought refuge from 'the savage hand of Elizabeth'. Matilda is then kidnapped and taken to the plantations of Jamaica where she gives birth to a daughter called Mary. Ellinor, meanwhile, has fallen in love with the Earl of Essex. The imprisonment and execution of Essex unbalances her reason, and there is a most effective scene in which she appears in the bedchamber of the dying Elizabeth who mistakenly believes that she is being haunted by the ghost of her former victim. Ellinor expires, and Matilda and Mary settle in Richmond. James I is by now on the throne, and Mary is betrothed to the Prince of Wales who dies before the alliance may be formalised. Even the death of Cécile of chickenpox finds a parallel in Mary catching the same disease (although she eventually dies of another cause).

Despite these similarities in the plot of *The Recess* and *Cleveland*, there are also major changes and omissions. Historical settings are not chosen haphazardly or merely as a convenient source of local colour but usually fulfill a metaphoric function even if this is not always easy to define with respect to a particular work. Thus, the decision to move the action from the time of the Protectorate back to the late Tudor period is a crucial one. Indeed, it is to change the entire ideological emphasis of the work. Prévost's novel, despite its intrinsically romanesque features, is framed within much wider early eighteenth century religious and philosophical debates (including one concerning the nature of civil government). *The Recess*, on the other hand, while attacking the abuses of absolute monarchy, would seem to suggest time as a major factor in the dissolution of political animosities. In this sense, the location of the subterranean recess where Matilda and Ellinor spend their childhood is perhaps significant for we are informed that it is to be found in the precincts of 'the Abbey, which might rather be called a palace; it was erected upon the ruins of a monastery destroyed at the Reformation, and still was called by the name of St. Vincent'. Equally significant is Sophia Lee's decision to change the gender of the victims of oppression in her novel. Even on the narrative level, it is interesting to note that the author does not eschew the epistolary form popularised by Richardson. If sentimentality was a product of the political and social climate of the eighteenth century, it none the less takes different forms in Britain and France.

Harriet Lee once referred, with some justification, to *The Recess* as 'the first English romance that blended interesting fiction with historical events and characters, embellishing both by picturesque description'. Not surprisingly, it eventually found its way into French translation. Indeed, during the years of the French Revolution and the Napoleonic Empire, the English **GOTHIC NOVEL** was almost as popular in France as in Britain. Clara Reeve's *The Champion of Virtue* (1777) and *The Old English Baron* (1778) both made their way into French in 1787. In the course of the following three decades practically every English Gothic novel of any distinction would do likewise. Although Mrs Radcliffe's *The Romance of the Forest* (1791) was not translated until 1794, in the course of the next three years French editions appeared of not only *The Castles of Athlin and Dunbayne* (1789) and *A Sicilian Romance* (1790) but also of *The Mysteries of Udolpho* (1794). Indeed, such was Mrs Radcliffe's popularity in France towards this period that publishers were vying with each other to bring out translations of her novels. Thus, there are two French translations of *The Italian; or, the Confessional of the Black Penitents* (1797): one, by the Abbé Morellet, conventionally entitled *L'Italian, ou le Confessionnal des Pénitents Noirs*; the other, by Mary Gay, as *Elénore de Rosalba, L'Italian, ou le Confessionnal des Pénitents Noirs* (both 1797).

Some further idea of the extent and duration of Mrs Radcliffe's popularity in France is indicated by the number of works falsely attributed to her. These include *Les Visions du Château des Pyrénées* of 1809 (in fact, Catherine Cuthbertson's *The Romance of the Pyrenees*, 1803); *Le Couvent de Sainte Catherine, ou les Mœurs du XIIIème Siècle* of 1810 (original unidentified); *La Fôret de Montalbano, ou le Fils Généreux*, 1813 (a translation of another work by Catherine Cuthbertson) and the Baron de Lamothe-Langon's *L'Hermite de la Tombe Mystérieuse, ou le Fantôme du Vieux Château*, 1816. Needless to say, **LEWIS**'s *The Monk* (1796) was another frequently reprinted title in French translation. As late as 1820, publishers were competing with each other over **MATURIN**'s *Melmoth the Wanderer*. Hardly had the novel been published in Britain before two French translations appeared: one, as *L'Homme du Mystère, ou Histoire de Melmoth le Voyageur*, by Émile Bégin; the other, as *Melmoth, ou l'Homme Errant*, by Jean Cohen.

Although the reception of the English Gothic novel in France was charted by Alice Killen as early as 1920, the ideological factors underlying this phenomenon have passed largely unremarked. Indeed, reading accounts by literary historians of the French vogue for the Gothic it is frequently possible to forget that it occurred during one of the momentous periods in French history. The question remains as to whether the genre was perceived in precisely the same manner in France as in Britain or whether the different audiences involved (and the specific subcultural groups which comprise each of those audiences) used such texts in order to explore and redefine their own identities.

Some indication of the manner in which ideological messages – messages of a radically different nature from those to be found in English works of the same period – were encoded into French popular fiction at this time is to be found in novels such as *Pauliska, ou la perversité moderne* (1796) and *Le Cimetière de la Madeleine* (1800). Michel Foucault would seem to have been the first author in recent years to draw attention to Reveroni Saint-Cyr's *Pauliska*. The novel recounts the vicissitudes suffered by Pauliska, a beautiful young countess, during her attempted flight from a Poland which is being sacked by the Russians. The book's most recent commentator, Béatrice Didier, has not failed to see a parallel between such a plot and Marie-Antoinette's abortive flight to Varennes. Appropriately enough – since Saint-Cyr himself would seem to have been involved with drawing up plans to defend the Tuileries and save Louis XVI – Pauliska is aided by a young army captain, Ernest Pradislas, devoted to her service. Indeed, the entire novel may be seen as an elaborate attack on Enlightenment thought. Scientific rationalism, for example, is ridiculed in the form of Baron d'Olnitz, Pauliska's principal persecutor, who believes that love, like rabies, may be injected into a person's veins in the form of a serum. At another point, Pradislas is captured by a society of female *philosophes* extending from Madrid to Saint-Petersburg – obviously intended to represent the system of Masonic lodges which many royalists held responsible for the dissemination of Enlightenment ideas – and made to participate in a bizarre experiment intended to demonstrate the purely physical nature of the male sex drive. This experiment proves something of a failure since a member of the sect promptly falls in love with him and they contrive to escape together.

   J. F. Regnault-Warin's *Le Cimetière de la Madeleine* opens with a description of the narrator's solitary promenade through the Tuileries at nightfall towards the Champs-Élysées. As he passes across the Place de la Révolution – which seems to him to be still *'fumante de sang'* ['reeking with blood'] – a firework display catches his attention. The Place de la Révolution, which only reverted to the name of Place de la Concorde in 1830, was where Louis XVI was executed in 1793. The firework display, on the other hand, is suggestive of the celebrations to mark a military victory, and the narrator falls into a brown study during which he foresees the end of the Napoleonic era, still some fourteen years distant. From the Place de la Révolution he makes a short detour to the Church of the Madeleine, the last resting place of many of those who died during the French Revolution: *'Vergniaud, muet, semble avoir pardoné Robespierre; et un petit ver fait sa pâture du cœur d'un roi de France!'* ['Vergniaud, dumb, seems to have pardoned Robespierre; and a tiny worm feeds off the heart of a king of France!'] There, after being besieged by a crowd of hideous ghosts covered in blood, he faints. When he regains consciousness, he meets the Abbé Edgeworth de Fermont who over the course of the next eleven nights – in a manner more than reminiscent of Edward Young's *Night Thoughts* (1742–5) – proceeds to recount the last days of Louis XVI whom he served as chaplain and accompanied to the guillotine. The precise historical details – or, more importantly, the historical misreadings that the author proposes (such as Philippe Égalité's attempts to force Marie-Antoinette to marry him) – need not concern us here except in so far as they represent a conscious effort of the author to settle an old royalist score concerning Orleanist political manoeuvrings (Gillet, 1992).

   Pauliska, ou la perversité moderne and *Le Cimetière de la Madeleine* are imbrued with a royalist political agenda far removed from the concerns of British Gothic novelists and demonstrating the extent to which domestically produced genre fiction may be ideologically encoded. Further evidence of this process at work may become available when researchers start to focus their attention on the strategies employed by translators in the preparation of their manuscripts for publication. Charles Baudelaire, the principal translator of **EDGAR ALLAN POE** as well as a poet and critic in his own right, was apparently the first writer to comment in public that Cohen's 1821 translation of *Melmoth* was abridged by as much as a quarter. More significantly, the passages which had been most subject to censorship – or rather, presumably, self-censorship – were those of a particularly anticlerical nature. Following the Restoration of the Bourbon monarchy in France in 1814, and especially in the immediate aftermath of the assassination of the Duc de Berry by a fanatical Republican in 1820, the country fell into the grips of a rigid and reactionary Catholicism. One manifestation of this, as far as publishing was concerned, was that an official list of proscribed works was drawn up. Although consisting in the main of works by *philosophes* such as Voltaire and Diderot, the net was cast wide enough to include books such as Lewis's *Le Moine* and Balzac's *Le Vicaire de Ardennes*. Cohen presumably decided to proceed with precaution when tackling such issues as Maturin's attacks on the Jesuits, the Catholic Church and the Spanish Inquisition in the pages of *Melmoth*. The spectre of Jesuitism – the order had been expelled in 1757, but during the Restoration members were secretly encouraged to teach in schools and even allowed to open schools of their own – would continue to haunt France throughout the nineteenth century, with serial novels such as Eugène Sue's *Le Juif Errant* (1844–5) doing little to calm matters, and one cannot help but speculate that this goes some way to accounting for Maturin's prolonged popularity in France.

Although much work remains to be done concerning the identity of the translators of Gothic fiction into French, the social class of these may not only be indicative of the fact that the clergy and minor aristocracy had the necessary language skills to undertake such a task and were forced to look to translation as a means of earning a living, but may also suggest that such fiction corresponded to their own ideological agenda. Equally, however, a number of translators of the period signed themselves (if at all) more modestly than a certain Baronness Caroline d'Aufdiener, *née* Wuinet, '*agrégée à plusieurs académies étrangères*' who translated *Le Couvent de Sainte-Catherine* in 1810 (Lévy, 1974). Changes in the social composition of the literary marketplace in Revolutionary and post-Revolutionary France, and the ascent of those of more humble origins, necessarily affect translation practices. A great deal of detailed research remains to be done with regard to the *roman noir*.

TERRY HALE

Romanticism

In its literary-historical sense, Romanticism is a broad term used to cover the writings of the period 1789–1830 which share certain general characteristics including a high valuation of emotions and subjectivity, a trust in the power of **THE IMAGINATION**, an interest in the psychology of perception, autobiographical writing, and a veneration of 'Nature' as an organic entity continuous with the mind or as a region of innocence and simple values. In its more popular usage, Romanticism refers to an attitude of mind that is escapist, idly speculative or gripped by the features of romance (love, disguise, imprisonment, chivalric quest). In the eighteenth century, this kind of romance was relegated to a position of inferiority by the writers of novels. Samuel Richardson, for example, in a famous defence of the novelist's art included in a letter (5 October 1752), exclaimed, 'do you think I am writing a Romance? Don't you see that I am copying Nature?' As the **GOTHIC NOVEL** often utilised the subtitle 'A Romance' it was readily stigmatised as a genre unworthy of serious attention. This tendency was countered by writers such as **WALPOLE** (*The Castle of Otranto*, 1764) and Clara Reeve (*The Old English Baron*, 1778), both of whom defended the Romantic Gothic in the prefaces to their novels on the grounds that it was able to combine the virtues of 'Imagination' and 'Nature'; the fantastic and the real. 'Romantic', in the eighteenth century, is a term that is strongly contested: for Walpole and Reeve it denotes a new aesthetic combination as the term metamorphoses to denote a new imaginative power; to more conservative critics, 'romantic' is commonly used to describe a frivolous condition, or a kind of writing thought to be irresponsibly improbable. In its modern sense, however, Romantic is used almost exclusively as a generic term.

Romanticism and Gothicism are inter-related in many ways. Like the Gothic, Romanticism has a pronounced interest in the idea of a 'Northern' tradition that runs counter to the neo-classical 'Southern' tradition that was so prominent in the art forms of the eighteenth century, and since the Renaissance, has represented a conventional way of legitimating specific literary, architectural and artistic traditions. Gothic develops as a counter-tendency to this tradition in the eighteenth century, and British Romanticism, certainly, takes a number of its aesthetic tenets from that counter-tendency. William Blake, for example, regarded by many as the first of the Romantic artists, shows a pronounced interest in Northern medieval (Gothic) architectural forms in his paintings and engravings, and his poetry and prophetic writings employ a syntax and a vocabulary that also suggest a strong 'Gothic' influence. The mode of James Macpherson's Ossianic poems, for instance (the Ossianic poems were supposedly transcribed from ancient Gaelic manuscripts), is evidently an influence in Blake, and these poems were also admired by many Romantic writers. The *Lyrical Ballads* (1798) by Wordsworth and Coleridge, a work often cited as marking the beginnings of English

Romantic poetry, is strongly indebted to the ballad revivalists of the eighteenth century, such as Thomas Percy, who published his popular and influential *Reliques of Ancient English Poetry* in 1765. Later Romantic poets also showed a pronounced interest in continuing this 'Northern' lineage: Byron's *Childe Harold's Pilgrimage* (1812–18) and Keats's *The Eve of St Agnes* (1820) are two important examples. Closely allied to this Gothic appropriation of a Northern past is the Romantic interest in primitivism: Gothic primitivism tends to claim the northern 'barbaric' past as being the source of indomitable British liberty; Romantic primitivism sometimes operates similarly, but has a more important manifestation in the developed interest in the primitivist or pre-civilised 'natural' states of noble savages, isolated rustics and children.

In addition to this genealogical link with the Gothic, Romanticism's writers regularly engage with the Gothic idiom. Works such as 'Christabel', *Remorse*, 'The Ballad of the Dark Ladie' (Coleridge); *Manfred* (Byron); *Frankenstein* (**MARY SHELLEY**); *Zastrozzi* (**PERCY BYSSHE SHELLEY**); *Eve of St Agnes* (Keats) are unequivocally Gothic in style, while novelists such as **CHARLES MATURIN** (*Melmoth the Wanderer*) and **JAMES HOGG** (*Confessions of a Justified Sinner*) are claimed as canonical writers by critics of either movement. Romanticism shares Gothic's sustained interest in the borders of human experience: as the range of Gothic motifs produces a symbolic language capable of representing repressed desire, or an obsessive fascination with taboo, so Romanticism takes an interest in that language for its own fascinations with the disturbing power of imaginative or psychic activity. Coleridge's interest in the imagination is a relatively simple example of how the Gothic supernatural was harnessed for the Romantic cause. Speaking of the making of the *Lyrical Ballads* in chapter XIV of *Biographia Literaria*, he explains the interest he and Wordsworth shared in writing poetry dealing with supernatural events:

> the incidents and agents were to be, in part at least, supernatural; and the excellence aimed at was to consist in the interesting of the affections by the dramatic truth of such emotions, as would naturally accompany such situations, supposing them real. And *real* in this sense they have been to every human being who, from whatever source of delusion, has at any time believed himself under supernatural agency.

If reality is dependent on an authentic state of mind, and not on a cognitive grasp of an external verifiable state of things, then Romanticism's enthusiastic endorsement of the imagination is simultaneously a licence for the legitimacy of Gothic delusion as a source of extended vision or emotional experience.

In addition to Romanticism's embracing of the Gothic imagination, there are some areas of Romantic writing in which the power of imagination or vision is figured by way of specifically Gothic features. Thomas de Quincey's *Confessions of an English Opium Eater* (1822), for example, describes the visions induced by opium by way of the notion of phantasmagoria. Of the first stage in opium-induced hallucination, de Quincey writes:

> I know not whether my reader is aware that many children, perhaps most, have a power of painting, as it were, upon the darkness, all sorts of phantoms; in some, that power is simply a mechanic affection of the eye; others have voluntary, or a semi-voluntary power to dismiss or summon them ... In the middle of 1817, I think it was, that this faculty became positively distressing to me: at night, when I lay awake in bed, vast processions passed along in mournful pomp ... at the same time, a corresponding change took place in my dreams; a theatre seemed suddenly opened and lighted up within my brain, which presented nightly spectacles of more than earthly splendour.

De Quincey also makes use of the notion of distorted perspective, induced particularly by a sense of the diminution of the human form or its scale of perception in the presence of the gigantic, a device used in Gothic forms (for example in *The Castle of Otranto*, 1764) and in the sublime. He recalls that each night he would sink into a depthless abyss, and he likens the sense of progressive infinity he encounters there to the 'vast Gothic halls' in Piranesi's *Carceri d'Invenzione* (*c.* 1745). In de Quincey we can find a fusion of Romantic and Gothic interests: the architecture and the scenery of his opium dreams are frequently Gothic, while the analysis he applies to his visions and the significance he attaches to them as psychological events are specifically Romantic.

Romanticism therefore offers examples of texts that use Gothic as elements in a pastiche (Coleridge's 'Ancient Mariner' is another example) but we can also find more sustained exercises in Gothic here. Byron's drama *Manfred* (1817) is perhaps the most emphatic Gothic–Romantic text, combining an exuberant participation in Gothic scenery and effects with an introspective brooding Romantic hero. The drama owes much to the Gothic theatre of the period, from which it derives many of its features and mannerisms. Mary Shelley's *Frankenstein* (1818) also shows a strong dependence on Gothic conventions, particularly in its narrative technique, in its exploration of the themes of parenthood and persecuted innocence, and its employment of the alpine **SUBLIME** (also used by Byron in *Manfred*). *Frankenstein* and *Manfred* both have their origins in discussions between Mary Shelley, Percy Bysshe Shelley, Byron and John Polidori in 1816, and it is therefore no coincidence that both texts combine a strong Gothic mode with an examination of the Romantic ego. While Byron's drama shows some willingness to sustain that ego by way of its melodramatic presentation of the hero's noble death, Mary Shelley's novel is much more sceptical, and Victor Frankenstein's obsessive ambitions are consistently subjected to critique.

Lastly some mention should be made of Romanticism's most frequently cited **GOTHIC PARODIES**, Jane Austen's *Northanger Abbey* (1818) and Thomas Love Peacock's *Nightmare Abbey* (1818). Austen's novel is a satirical representation of the follies of reading Gothic romances: the heroine, Catherine Morland, an enthusiast of Mrs Radcliffe's novels, is made to look foolish by deluding herself that General Tilney, her host at Northanger, is a criminal. Although this work is commonly regarded as being in parodic relation to the Gothic Novel, it does not really parody Gothic conventions, so much as condemn, in an entirely conservative way, the diseased imagination that the romance supposedly incites. Even so, *Northanger Abbey*'s relation to the Gothic Novel is more complex: the broad shape of the novel conforms to the shape of the Radcliffean novel, wherein the dénouement is structured around the dissipation of mystery and the disproving of delusions or illusions. Further, there is a way in which Catherine Morland's deluded identification of Tilney as a villain is right, for his class bigotry is villainous, and his behaviour in this sense, tyrannical. Austen's adroit manipulation of her novel's relation to the Gothic form is particularly subtle in these respects, and moves beyond the set of relations commonly supposed within the terms of parody. Peacock's novel is unequivocally parodic, not so much of the Gothic form itself (in which Peacock shows sustained interest elsewhere) but of Romantic enthusiasm for what the author identifies as Gothic extravagance. Some of the major Romantic figures appear in the novel (Shelley as Scythrop, Byron as Mr Cypress, Coleridge as Mr Flosky) and each is pilloried for the Gothic humours they exhibit: Shelley for his enthusiastic indulgence in 'metaphysical romance and romantic metaphysics'; Byron for his morbidity; Coleridge for his visionary mystifications. Peacock's hugely enjoyable and irreverent portrayal of Romanticism in this novel is at the same time a perceptive analysis of its genealogical roots in Gothic.

PHILIP W. MARTIN

Russian Gothic

'Russian Gothic' as a term has not until recently enjoyed a great deal of currency in critical studies of Russian literature. The word 'Gothic' is commonly used in connection with, in particular, Fedor Dostoevsky: in the case of early works of the 1840s, such as *The Double* and *The Landlady*, which may correctly be said to be Gothic; or of the later and more famous novels, which may include Gothic elements or traces (from *Crime and Punishment*, 1866, to *The Brothers Karamazov*, 1880). Otherwise, what might have been termed Gothic in Russian literature has tended, with rare exceptions, to be submerged under the blanket heading of 'Russian Romanticism' or '**THE FANTASTIC**'. There is, for example, no entry under 'Gothic' in many a Western reference book to Russian literature, while even *The Concise Literary Encyclopedia* (vol. 2, Moscow, 1964) runs to only a very brief entry under '**GOTHIC NOVEL**' ['*Goticheskii roman*']; likewise, *The Modern Encyclopedia of Russian and Soviet Literatures* (vol. 9, Gulf Breeze, 1989) has little over half a page on the subject. This situation may be partly explicable in terms of the vicissitudes of the Soviet period, during the worst times of which even 'Romanticism' and 'Dostoevsky' were dirty words and critical energies were certainly not to be expended on **THE SUPERNATURAL**! Furthermore, the burgeoning of interest in Gothic as a literary style, even in the West, is still comparatively recent.

Even the Raduga Publishers' (Moscow) anthology entitled *Russian 19th-Century Gothic Tales* (one of the most fruitful sources available in English translation) seems to have acquired that title for its English-language version by chance (the Russian title being given as *Fantasticheskii mir russkoi povesti*, 'The Fantastic World of the Russian Novella'). This particular volume, published in 1984, includes a range of stories extending from Antonii Pogorelsky and Orest Somov in the 1820s to Vladimir Odoevsky's 'The Living Corpse' (published 1844, but dated 1838) and A. K. Tolstoy's early vampire story *The Vampire* of 1841. The early works of Dostoevsky apart, this period just about reflects the heyday of this style in Russia. Mikhail Lermontov and Nikolai Gogol are also represented; Gogol's *The Nose* is problematic, residing more plausibly within the realm of pure psychological fantasy, but *The Portrait* clearly belongs. Included too is Russia's one undisputed masterpiece in the genre, Alexander Pushkin's *The Queen of Spades* (1834), as well as works by a number of minor figures (Mikhail Zagoskin, Osip Senkovsky and the poet Evgenii Baratynsky). The blurb to this collection, which has no general introduction, refers to 'enchanting flights of imagination, vivid imagery borrowed from folk tale and legend, grotesque fantasy and utopian dreams of a distant, happy future'. While all this may have a certain amount in common with Western definitions of the Gothic, we may prefer to stress alternative features – old castles, hapless maidens, wicked relatives and mysterious revenants – as more characteristic of the genre.

Apart from an input from folklore, and such other native medieval literary genres as the Kievan, Novgorodian and Muscovite chronicles and saints' lives, Russian Gothic derives from an amalgam of European influences: the English **GOTHIC NOVEL**, the influential tales of **E. T. A. HOFFMANN** and the French *fantastique* tradition, together with the more contemporaneous **FRÉNÉTIQUE SCHOOL**. Various non-literary sources coming through both Russia and the West can also be pin-pointed, such as the alchemical and esoteric traditions (see **CABALISM** and **HERMETISM**). A particularly Russian element, though drawn from the all-pervading influence in Russia of German Romanticism, is the concept of *dvoemirie* (or philosophical dualism). *Frankenstein* (1818) too has its Russian connections and Odoevsky reviewed **MARY SHELLEY's** *The Last Man* (1826). **CHARLES MATURIN's** *Melmoth the Wanderer* (1820) had an impact on both Gogol (in *The Portrait*) and Dostoevsky (see in particular *The Brothers Karamazov*). Dostoevsky, for that matter, had imbibed **ANN RADCLIFFE's** novels while still a child. Parallels can be drawn too with **EDGAR ALLAN POE** (who was admired by both Odoevsky and Dostoevsky, as well as, subsequently, by the French and Russian Symbolists), while Russian literature, like its Western counterparts, proceeded with the approach of the fin de siècle to embrace Gothic elements within its own Symbolist movement. A twentieth-century revival emerged, even from a Soviet literature officially dominated by socialist realism, most notably in the writing of Mikhail Bulgakov. Furthermore, all kinds of reinvigorations, including Gothic elements, are to be found in the works of the 'alternative prose' writers of the post-Soviet era.

However, if we return to the period referred to above, from 1825 to 1844, we find that these dates almost exactly span the creative career of Prince Vladimir Odoevsky (1804–69), the writer from whose pen issued what is arguably the most impressive body of genuine Russian Gothic writing: this included some of the stories contained within his *magnum opus*, the philosophical frame-tale *Russian Nights* (1844), and several independent novellas, most notably perhaps his 'dilogy' *The Salamander* (1841) and *The Cosmorama* (1839), as well as a number of shorter stories, such as 'The Ghost' (1838: see Minto, 1994). However, Odoevsky's reputation in this area is only now beginning to receive due critical attention, both in the West and in Russia. Only recently, for instance, has it come to light that Odoevsky's stories 'The Improvisor' (from *Russian Nights*) and 'The Sylph' (1837) were plagiarised (via a French translation of the 1850s) by the Irish-American fantastic writer Fitz-James O'Brien (1828–62). Odoevsky's tales collectively run to the full gamut of occult and Gothic paraphernalia, from folkloric trappings and magical effects, including the suspension of time and place, through supernatural arson and spontaneous human combustion, to the walking dead. He also specialised in proto-science fiction and anti-utopia, as well as in fiction of artistic delirium, a kind of manic *Küenstlernovelle*: tales based on Piranesi and

Beethoven, plus his remarkable pseudo-biography of Johann Sebastian Bach (see *Russian Nights*).

An early imitation of the Gothic in Russian was 'Bornholm Island' (1794), a story by the sentimentalist writer (and subsequently historian), Nikolai Karamzin. In poetry, Gottfried Bürger's ballad of the return of the demon-bridegroom, *Lenore* (1774), itself virtually an archetype of German romanticism, was transposed into multiple Russian versions by Zhukovsky and, more freely, by Pushkin and Lermontov (notably the latter's narrative poem *The Demon*, 1829–41). Pushkin's remarkable achievement in the same genre, *The Bronze Horseman* (1833), featuring the famously animated statue, also deals in part with Gothic motifs. The Decembrist writer Alexander Bestuzhev (better known under his exile pen-name 'Marlinsky') introduced the Gothic into both his contemporary and historical tales of adventure, while in the 1830s such features were commonly found in Gogol's Ukrainian and St Petersburg cycles and in the folkloric stories of Alexander Veltman. However, Gogol's major prose work, *Dead Souls* (1842), is not – the resonance of its title notwithstanding – in any recognisable sense a Gothic novel. The city of St Petersburg (subsequently Petrograd/Leningrad), it should certainly be remembered, took on a powerful Gothic-type mystique of its own in Russian literature: from Pushkin onwards, throughout the nineteenth century and into the twentieth, in stories by for instance Evgenii Zamiatin and Daniil Kharms, right up to the contemporary period, with Andrei Bitov's novel *Pushkin House* (1978). Now that the city's original name has been restored, who can doubt that further works in that tradition will be written?

Lermontov, by the end of his all too brief literary career (in 1841), left two intriguingly unfinished prose pieces in the Gothic mode (*Vadim* and '*Shtoss*'). His prose masterpiece, *A Hero of Our Time* (1840), retains only vestigial Gothic features. Pushkin's major contribution to fiction of this type, *The Queen of Spades*, can be read as a Gothic tale *par excellence*, or as **GOTHIC PARODY** or, indeed, given that it is an example of the pure fantastic, in a number of yet further ways (see Cornwell, 1993; Leighton, 1994). A. K. [or Aleksei] Tolstoy (a cousin of the famous Lev Tolstoy) wrote vampire stories in the 1840s, notably *The Vampire* and *The Family of the Vourdalak* (see Frayling, 1992). Other writers to turn their hand to this style include Nikolai Leskov and Aleksei Apukhtin. Ivan Turgenev, normally renowned as one of the founding fathers of Russian realism, also wrote several ghostly or fantastic tales, including 'Phantoms' (1864) and the late story 'Clara Milich' (1883). Dostoevsky returned to a fantastical mode in his late short works of the 1870s, notably 'Bobok' and 'The Dream of a Ridiculous Man' (both in their different ways partial reworkings of Odoevsky's 'The Living Corpse'). Madness was a frequent ingredient (and possible resolution), manifesting itself at times through the phenomenon of 'the double', in Russian ghostly or fantastic tales from Pushkin, Gogol and Odoevsky, through Dostoevsky and Vsevolod Garshin (*The Red Flower*, 1883), to Anton Chekhov's one and only exercise in the Gothic mode, 'The Black Monk' (1894).

Dvoemirie made a vigorous return to Russian literature in the literary production of the Symbolist period, which emphasised demonism and the Eternal Feminine within a poetics of decadence. The turn of the century also saw fiction and drama of a fantastic nature from Leonid Andreev and Gothic elements featuring in the prose of several of the leading Symbolist poets: notably Andrei Bely, Valerii Briusov and Fedor Sologub. Bely, best known for *The Silver Dove* (1911) and his modernist masterpiece *Petersburg* (1913 and 1922), is, like Dostoevsky before him, far too complex a figure to be pigeon-holed as a Gothic novelist, although more than a modicum of this tradition, among much else, is to be found within his fiction. Closer to mainstream Gothic, with its intrusions of **THE UNCANNY** and **THE DEMONIC**, comes Sologub's acclaimed novel *The Petty Demon* (1907), though less successful is his fantasy trilogy *The Created Legend* (1914). Briusov approached the Gothic in several of his shorter stories and in his historical novel of **WITCHCRAFT** in Renaissance Germany, *The Fiery Angel* (1908). An entertaining example of the exploitation of the traditions of the novel and the fantastic is also to be found in a little-known and untranslated novel entitled *The Travels and Adventures of Nikodim the Elder* (1917), written by an obscure writer called A. Skaldin.

In the Soviet period, Gothic traits in fiction were revived or preserved amid the experimental writings of the 1920s, notably in the Hoffmannian plotting which characterised the stories of Veniamin Kaverin (one of the members of the early post-Revolutionary literary group who styled themselves 'The Serapion Brothers', after **E. T. A. HOFFMANN**'s expansive frame-tale of that name). The *chef d'oeuvre* of fantasy of the Soviet period, though, was undoubtedly Bulgakov's spectacular *The Master and Margarita* (written 1928–40, published first in 1966–7 and in full only in 1973 – its publishing history is almost a Gothic saga in itself), a multi-layered novel of historiographic metafiction, replete with diabolism, magic and rich satirical humour. Thereafter such elements were only to be found confined within science fiction (see in particular the inventive novels and stories of the brothers Arkadii and Boris Strugatsky, written in the post-Stalin period), until the fantastic (and officially unpublished) prose fiction of Abram Terts (in reality the progressive literary critic Andrei Siniavsky) pointed the way to the dissident revivals and renewed experimentalism witnessed in the last quarter of the twentieth century. Russian émigré fiction retained intermittent Gothic tendencies, for instance in certain of the works of Vladimir Nabokov. These took on a new lease of life in the work of writers of the 'Third Wave' of emigration, from the 1970s: in one story by Zinovy Zinik, speculation even revolves around 'a comparison between the English eighteenth-century Gothic novel and the phenomenon of the third wave of Russian emigration'. According to Zinik, the 'other world' was behind a Gothic iron curtain: 'we regard those over there as living corpses. They regard us as phantoms.'

There is as yet no satisfactory full study in any language of Russian Gothic, even of its most obviously fruitful nineteenth-century phase, although a number of detailed limited or specialised studies have been undertaken by Russian scholars.

NEIL CORNWELL

Sade, Donatien Alphonse, Count (known as Marquis de) (1740–1814)

The Marquis de Sade is a marginal figure in the Gothic tradition. He is perhaps better seen as a joint-inheritor of the genre of sentimental and didactic fiction that begins with Samuel Richardson, and as the most ferocious critic of its benevolist vision of human nature. He did, however, deliver himself of a famous judgement on eighteenth-century Gothic writing, in a prefatory essay to the collection of stories *Crimes de l'Amour*, entitled '*Idée sur le roman*' (translated as 'Reflections on the Novel'):

> This genre was the inevitable product of the revolutionary shocks with which the whole of Europe resounded. For those who were acquainted with all the ills that are brought upon men by the wicked, the novel was becoming as difficult to write as it was monotonous to read; there was nobody left who had not experienced more misfortunes in four or five years than could be depicted in a century by literature's most gifted novelist. It was therefore necessary to call upon hell for aid in the creation of titles that could arouse interest, and to situate in the land of fantasies what was common knowledge, from mere observation of the history of man in this iron age.

This was the most eloquent linking by a contemporary of the Gothic boom of the 1790s with the French Revolution, and historicist critics have not failed to develop the insight when interpreting the novels of the period.

The same essay shows that by the late 1790s, Sade was an avid reader of the work of **MATTHEW LEWIS** and **ANN RADCLIFFE**. But while he praises the 'brilliant imagination' of Radcliffe, he dislikes her device of the 'explained supernatural', and rates Lewis more highly. As a dogmatic atheist himself, Sade eschewed any hint of the metaphysical in his own fiction. Where he does seem to subscribe to the conventions of Gothic writing is in his depiction of 'virtue in distress', constantly, not to say monotonously, showing scenes of the persecution of helpless females and youths. The acts of rape, torture and mutilation to which his fictional victims are subjected in *Justine; or, The Misfortunes of Virtue* (1791) and *The 120 Days of Sodom* (not published until 1904) go far beyond anything in the works of Lewis or the more sensational German novelists. However, even in this respect there is a vital difference in kind, for while in most Gothic fiction of the time, horror and suffering is ultimately redeemed by a providential outcome, in the fiction of Sade it generally reinforces a materialist thesis propounded at length by the most villainous characters, that crimes are committed in accordance with natural laws. Sade has, of course, lent his name to the psychopathological condition of 'sadism', involving sexual pleasure derived from cruelty. The term was first introduced in the *Dictionnaire universal* (1834), and became a scientific category in the writings of Krafft-Ebing and Freud.

The outline of Sade's life is simply told. He was born into a position of wealth and privilege, but after having made an advantageous marriage, he began to show signs of his sexual proclivities, and his strong-minded mother-in-law arranged for his committal to prison by arbitrary *lettre de cachet* in 1777. He was to remain in prison, with only brief respite, until his death, and it was there that he completed the majority of his literary works.

If the pattern of Sade's career is relatively straightforward, the writings and their posthumous reputation are paradoxical. The libertinism he advocated is cognate with 'liberty', yet sexual freedom as he portrays it is invariably decked out in the Gothic trappings of incarceration and tyranny. In the nineteenth century he remained a powerful underground influence, but in the twentieth century Sade has been openly championed first by the Surrealists and then by the intellectual avant-garde in France, including notably Georges Bataille and Roland Barthes. For post-structuralist theory, his work has represented the acme of transgression in thought and language, and even the revelation of a 'truth' beyond the contradictions of Western metaphysics. His literary influence has broadened as the works become more readily available: can any current writer in the Gothic mode avoid it? But a link with one of the best known exponents of twentieth-century Gothic deserves special note. In 1979 **ANGELA CARTER** published *The Sadeian Woman*, a polemical appropriation of Sade to the cause of feminism, and in the same year brought out *The Bloody Chamber*, her collection of dark fairy-tales, clearly written in dialogue with Sade.

E. J. CLERY

Sado-Masochism

With reference to the works of the **MARQUIS DE SADE**, the nineteenth-century Viennese sexologist Richard von Krafft-Ebing suggested in his *Psychopathia Sexualis* that a sexual perversion in which satisfaction is gained by virtue of inflicting suffering and humiliation upon others should be called sadism. Over the years this designation has also come to be used in reference to the infliction of violence and aggression, whether or not this is accompanied by sexual satisfaction. Evoking the work of the French author Sacher Masoch, Krafft-Ebing in turn suggested that the opposite sexual perversion, in which satisfaction is contingent upon being the victim of suffering and humiliation, should be called masochism. This can involve physical pain induced by pricking, bastinado, flagellation, strangulation, or the playing through of painful phantasy scenes revolving around the enactment of servility, corporal chastisement and guilt.

From the onset of his work on instincts and perversions, Sigmund Freud emphasised that sadism as an active and masochism as a passive posture enlacing pain with pleasure are the two faces of a single perversion, although the one aspect may be more strongly developed than the other. At the same time he also emphasised that while these two terms could not be studied in isolation, it was equally true that the underlying contrast between activity and passivity extended beyond the question of sexual perversion, proving itself to be among the universal characteristics of sexual life. As such, the polarity reappears in psychoanalytic theory in the opposition between phallic and castrated, as well as in the opposition between masculine and feminine.

In his discussion of infantile sexual development, Freud posits an originary sadism, manifesting an urge to master, where the exersion of aggression is not yet connected to any sexual pleasure. Masochism is, then, a reversal of activity into passivity, where the subject turns its sadistic urge round upon its own self, and it is only at this point that pain collides with sexual excitation. In this second stage the subject either inflicts suffering on himself or has pain inflicted upon him by another person. As a third stage brings about another turning round of the masochistic position, sadism finally emerges in the sexual sense of the word. However, because in both the second and the third phase the duplicitously pleasurable pain requires the phantasied identification with the other person, Laplanche and Pontalis insist that 'sexuality's intervention in the process is correlated with the emergence of the intersubjective dimension and of phantasy.'

Within Gothic literature phantasy enactments of sado-masochism can be found in the intersubjective conflict, the domination–submission played through in narratives where political institutions are shown to inflict violence on their subjects, notably the scenes of torture in novels by **ANN RADCLIFFE, MATTHEW LEWIS**, or **CHARLES MATURIN**. But they can also be found manifested in the register of intrasubjective conflict, where characters enact the struggle between a sadistic super-ego as representative of the law and a masochistic ego as representative of forbidden pleasures, by suffering from guilt, self-punishment or self-purging, notably in novels by **CHARLES BROCKDEN BROWN, HERMAN MELVILLE** or **JAMES HOGG**.

ELISABETH BRONFEN

San Francisco Gothic

In the last three decades of the nineteenth century, the Bay Area of northern California was home to a loosely configured group of popular writers who are almost entirely forgotten today. Yet their best Gothic tales possess considerable power and their science fiction stories are among the first in the genre.

AMBROSE BIERCE is the principal figure here. His Gothic tales constitute one of the premier achievements (still largely unappreciated by scholars) of Gilded Age fiction; his influence on and encouragement of Bay Area writers was considerable.

Two Gothicists whom Bierce supported with particular enthusiasm are Emma Frances Dawson (1839–1923) and W. C. Morrow (1854–1923). Dawson is arguably the West Coast's foremost woman of letters in this period, yet she is so lost to history that no entry for her appears in the Welsley *Notable American Women* volumes. In addition to considerable musical talent, Dawson managed to live by her pen (often precariously) as a translator of texts in five languages, a poet, and a writer of Gothic tales. These were collected in 1897 in *An Itinerant House and Other Tales*. Bierce said of Dawson: 'to her it [San Francisco] is a dream city – a city of wraiths and things forbidden to the senses ... a city where it is never morning, where birds never sing, where children are unknown'. Whether Bierce is correct that *An Itinerant House* 'is a work of supreme genius', its best tales ('An Itinerant House', 'The Second Card Wins', 'Are the Dead Dead?', and the prize-winning 'etching', 'The Night Before the Wedding' where the last of several points of view is a watch dog's!) will amply reward attention.

This is even truer of W. C. Morrow's best work. A long-time journalist and influential teacher of writing, Morrow like Dawson published in the

West's leading periodicals. His Gothic collection *The Ape, the Idiot, and Other People* (1899) was well-received by East Coast and British reviewers, but attracted little popular attention. Morrow's best tales, 'The Monster-Maker', 'The Queen of My Twelve Little Devils', 'His Unconquerable Enemy', and 'The Removal Company', indicate how contemporary his sensibility was. He shared with **ROBERT LOUIS STEVENSON**, a concern with aberrant science and abnormal psychology; with **CONAN DOYLE**, a fascination with the detective figure; and with Bierce and the whole Gothic tradition, a determination to explore the damaging perversities of that most sacred of nineteenth-century institutions, The Home.

In addition to more minor writers (Yda Addis, Anna M. Fitch, N. C. Kouns, R. D. Milne, Annie Lake Townsend), the Gothic tradition in the Bay Area was enriched by two major figures known chiefly as 'Naturalists' – Jack London ('The Red One,' 'Batard', *The Sea Wolf*) and Frank Norris (especially *McTeague*).

WILLIAM VEEDER

Scottish Gothic

The Union of 1707 between Scotland and England produced a new multi-nation state, Britain. The wedding that was the Union did not create any noticeable crisis of national identity in the larger and more powerful partner, England: for most English people, 'England' and 'Britain' were for all practical purposes synonymous terms. For the smaller, weaker, and allegedly more 'primitive' partner, however, the Union produced a situation in which the Scottish national identity was felt to be slipping away, like sand through the fingers. Walter Scott (1771–1832) wrote on this subject in the Introduction to his collection of traditional ballads, *Minstrelsy of the Scottish Border* (1802–3).

> In the notes, and occasional dissertations, it has been my object to throw together, perhaps without sufficient attention to method, a variety of remarks regarding popular superstitions, and legendary history, which, if not now collected, must soon have been totally forgotten. By such efforts, feeble as they are, I may contribute somewhat to the history of my native country; the peculiar features of whose manners and character are daily melting and dissolving into those of her sister and ally. And, trivial as may appear such an offering, to the manes of a kingdom, once proud and independent, I hang it upon her altar with a mixture of feelings, which I shall not attempt to describe.

Scottish Gothic, like many other aspects of post-Union Scottish culture, draws some of its specifically Scottish nature from a desire to collect, to polish, and to re-create the traditions (including the 'popular super-stitions, and legendary history') of pre-Union Scottish culture. An impulse of this kind lies behind, for example, the Ossian poems of James Macpherson (1736–96), and also animates such poems by Robert Burns (1759–96) as 'Tam o' Shanter' and 'Halloween'. Similarly, the fictions of Scott often seek to adjust to the Union by carving out an accepted place for Scotland in a new, composite British national identity.

The German Romantics were read with particular interest in Scotland, because their raw energy was thought to offer a way forward for Scottish writing. Germany, like Scotland, was perceived as being a country lacking an advanced and cultivated literature; but this very defect could be turned to advantage, as it allowed space for the fresh and uninhibited exploration of new areas of experience. Henry Mackenzie's essay on the German theatre, read before the Royal Society of Edinburgh on 21 April 1788, helped to spark strong enthusiasm for **GERMAN GOTHIC** in the Scottish capital. Carried along by the tide, the young Walter Scott and some of his friends set about learning German: and Scott's early career as a writer featured the publication of translations from the German, in-cluding 'William and Helen', a version of Bürger's 'Lenore' (1774); and a translation of **GOETHE**, *Goetz of Berlichingen* (1799). This German-inspired interest in Gothic also resulted in Scott becoming a contributor to **M. G. LEWIS**'s *Tales of Wonder* (1801); and Gothic elements are like-wise present in *Minstrelsy of the Scottish Border*. Recent critics, notably Ian Duncan and Fiona Robertson, have focused on the continuing import-ance of the Gothic in Scott's mature writings.

Edinburgh's interest in German Gothic is also a factor in *The Private Memoirs and Confessions of a Justified Sinner* (1824), a major Gothic novel by Scott's friend and contemporary **JAMES HOGG** (1770–1835). Various critics have seen the influence of **HOFFMANN**'s *Die Elixiere des Teufels* in Hogg's masterpiece; and a translation of *Die Elixiere des Teufels* by Hogg's friend R. P. Gillies was published in Edinburgh by William Blackwood in June 1824, the month in which *The Private Memoirs and Confessions of a Justified Sinner* also appeared. In the 1820s, *Blackwood's Edinburgh Magazine* (with its 'Horae Germanicae') was an important point of contact between German literature and the English-speaking world; and the new genera-tion of Scottish writers, establishing themselves in the 1820s, carried on the interest of the Scott/Hogg generation in German Romanticism. For example, John Gibson Lockhart (1794–1854), a leading light in *Blackwood's*, translated Schlegel; and Thomas Carlyle (1795–1881) was translating and corresponding with Goethe, and writing on Hoffmann, while still based in Scotland in the 1820s. Lockhart's German interests emerge in the Gothic elements in his novel *Reginald Dalton* (1823), and elsewhere.

Towards the end of the nineteenth century, the Gothic elements in the writings of Scott and Hogg were influential in the fiction of **ROBERT LOUIS STEVENSON** (1850–94). Thus, there is a Scots-speaking narrative voice in Scott's 'Wandering Willie's Tale' (from *Redgauntlet*, 1824): in this short story of the supernatural, Wandering Willie's gudesire attends a banquet for the dead, in Hell. The Scots narrative voice of 'Wandering Willie's Tale' finds an echo in Stevenson's 'Thrawn Janet' (1887), and in 'The Tale of Tod Lapraik' (from *Catriona*, 1893). Similarly, the re-emergence of the Master's living body from the grave in Stevenson's novel *The Master of Ballantrae* (1889) echoes the re-emergence of Davie Duff's living body from the grave in Hogg's *The Three Perils of Woman* (1822), a novel full of corpses that refuse to lie down. Equally, Hogg's *Private Memoirs and Confessions of a Justified Sinner* connects with the diabolism and fraternal conflicts of *The Master of Ballantrae*; and Hogg's novel also connects with the concern with doubleness that lies at the heart of Stevenson's *The Strange Case of Dr Jekyll and Mr Hyde* (1886).

In such things as its Darwinian focus on the monkey-like Hyde, Stevenson's short novel embodies concerns that were widespread in *fin-de-siècle* Europe. However, the Scottish roots of *Dr Jekyll and Mr Hyde* are also important, not only in the Hogg-like concern with doubling, but also because of an implied reference in the text to the Burke and Hare murders in Edinburgh in the 1820s. Jekyll's scientific experiments, which advance knowledge but also release evil, are conducted in a laboratory that had formerly been a dissecting theatre; and this calls to mind the Edinburgh dissecting theatre of Dr Robert Knox. Knox's work as a dissector advanced scientific knowledge; but it also released evil through the activities of Burke and Hare, who began to murder tramps and prostitutes in order to keep up their lucrative trade in supplying dead bodies to Dr Knox. The short story 'The Body Snatcher' is another example of Stevenson's interest in the moral dilemmas posed by the scientific researches of Dr Knox.

DOUGLAS S. MACK

Shelley, Mary (1797–1851)

The dominant image of the Frankenstein monster is the clanking, bolted Boris Karloff, who is belied by the more naturalistic representation of the creature in the frontispiece to the revised 1831 edition of Mary Shelley's novel *Frankenstein*. The monstrous brood of her creation has found its way into cinema, popular fiction and critical theory by taking literally her

injunction in the 1831 Introduction to 'go forth and prosper'. The proliferation of the monstrous body is the anxiety that afflicts the mad scientist
hero, Victor Frankenstein. Not only does his career allegorise the way in
which science may be taken over by its metaphors, it also demonstrates
how men can lose control of the monsters that they themselves create.

Shelley's iconic status as a Gothic novelist rests primarily on her
first novel *Frankenstein*, which was published anonymously in 1818.
Contemporary critical attention tended to focus on the author as a disciple of her father, William Godwin, who had also written a Gothic fiction,
St Leon (1799), to whom the novel was dedicated. Once her identity was
known, she attracted interest as the wife of **PERCY BYSSHE SHELLEY**,
whom she had married in 1816 and who provided her with a prototype
for her eponymous hero, Victor. Recently, there has been a shift towards
acknowledging Mary Shelley not only as the daughter of Mary Wollstonecraft, but also, like her fictional monster, as more than the sum of
her parts. Now she is being recognised as a distinguished writer in her
own right and not just as a creative conduit for these family relations.

Increasing attention is being given to Shelley's writings other than
Frankenstein, which include five novels, one novella, two travelogues,
more than two dozen short stories, two mythological dramas and a
plethora of letters, essays, poems and reviews. Apart from the witch, Fior
di Mandragola, in her historical romance *Valperga; or, The Life and
Adventures of Castruccio, Prince of Lucca* (1823), the apocalyptic nightmare
in the futuristic *The Last Man* (1826), the incest taboo explored in her
novella *Matilda* that was completed in 1819, and the essay 'On Ghosts'
(1824), a quintessence of Gothic material may be found in her short
stories. These include three stories published in *The Keepsake*; the alchemical 'The Mortal Immortal: A Tale' (1833), 'The Evil Eye' (1829) and
'Transformation' (1830), which is an adaptation of Byron's unfinished
poetic drama, *The Deformed Transformed* (1824). The incomplete 'Valerius;
the Reanimated Roman' of 1819 concerns the rebirth of a body without a
soul, while 'Roger Dodsworth: The Reanimated Englishman' (1826) is a
spoof about Godwin and suspended animation. Both are minor variations on *Frankenstein*. In this, her major novel, Mary Shelley charts the
destructive outcome of Victor's creation of a monstrous being from
corpses in a calculated attempt to 'speak to the mysterious fears of our
nature, and awaken thrilling horror – one to make the reader dread to
look round, to curdle the blood, and quicken the beatings of the heart'
(Introduction, 1831).

The first three-volume edition was followed in 1823 by a two-volume
reprint that had been arranged by Godwin. It appeared shortly after
Richard Brinsley Peake's stage adaptation entitled *Presumption; or, The
Fate of Frankenstein*, which Shelley had seen performed in August 1823.

For the third edition, of 1831, she made extensive revisions and expanded the introduction. While it has been customary to regard this final edition as the definitive text, some recent critics and editors, such as Marilyn Butler, favour the 1818 edition as the more radical and less sentimental version. What is generally regarded as the greater determinism of the later edition has had the effect of exonerating Victor as a Romantic over-reacher.

Shelley's remaining novels, *Valperga*, the historical *The Fortunes of Perkin Warbeck* (1830), and the contemporary *Lodore* (1835) and *Falkner* (1837), with their fashionable settings, are case studies of well-meaning individuals, who are overwhelmed by their own delusions or by the destructive ambition of others for power. An early formative influence was the book that Godwin wrote for Mary and her elder stepsister Fanny Imlay, which was a *Life of Lady Jane Grey* (1806), whose obedience to her parents' wishes led her to the scaffold. Coincidentally, Fanny's life also ended tragically when, on 9 October 1816, she took an overdose of laudanum. Like Victor's creature, who is also on a trajectory of self-destruction, she had felt neglected by her family. Later that year, Percy's first wife Harriet, who had been deserted by both lover and husband, committed suicide by drowning in the Serpentine. Her death facilitated the marriage of Percy and Mary, who eloped to the Continent in 1814. They were accompanied by Mary's half-sister Jane (later 'Claire') Clairmont and recorded their journey in their *History of Six Weeks' Tour through a Part of France, Switzerland, Germany and Holland* (1817).

Death, mutability and abandonment are the Gothic themes that permeated not only Shelley's life but also her fiction. Even her birth precipitated the death of her mother approximately ten days after from puerperal fever. Years later she would lie next to Wollstonecraft's grave at St Pancras Churchyard reading her father's *Essay on Sepulchres* (1809). Having presented her with this textual *memento mori*, it is appropriate that Godwin elected to be buried next to Wollstonecraft. It was on this hallowed burial ground that Mary Wollstonecraft Godwin and P. B. Shelley conducted their transgressive courtship.

Since P. B. Shelley's boyhood interests had extended to carrying out necromantic experiments in a graveyard and raising the devil in a chemistry laboratory, it is not surprising to find Victor embracing a synthesis of magic and science. Neglecting domestic affections, most notably his family and fiancée, Elizabeth, his retreat into grisly researches is a Dantesque descent into a hellish underworld of grave-robbing and charnel houses. Body-snatching was rendered obsolete a year after the publication of the third edition of *Frankenstein* by the 1832 Anatomy Act, which made available for dissection the unclaimed bodies of paupers. The topicality of this legislation may be why the blasphemy of Victor's nefarious activities has impacted less on the modern reader than on Shelley's contemporaries. The monstrosity of his creation is predicated upon the dilemma that, despite the choicest parts having been selected, only a divinity can harmonise the whole. The way in which Victor deserts the creature he creates, who out of revenge seeks to destroy his creator, is evocative of both John Milton's *Paradise Lost* (1667), from where the epigraph to the novel is taken, and Shelley's own experiences of paternal neglect. The way in which her Romantic scientist retreats to his laboratory bears similarities with how P. B. Shelley sought the solitude of the Romantic poet and how Godwin withdrew from the family by retiring to his study after his marriage to Mary Jane Clairmont in 1801. Mary's reputed dislike of her stepmother fanned her romantic and excessive attachment to her father, which found expression in her novella *Matilda*. The plot, concerning the imagined incestuous relationship between a father and daughter, was a subject that Godwin found to be 'disgusting and detestable'. Until 1959, *Matilda* remained unpublished.

P. B. Shelley's neglect of his paternal obligations exacerbated the difficulties Shelley experienced with childbirth. In 1815, her prematurely born illegitimate daughter died after only 11 days of life. In 1816, she gave birth to William, probably named after her younger half-brother, who lived his short life nomadically, crossing Europe three times in a carriage. His untimely death, three years later, is foreshadowed in *Frankenstein*, when the creature murders Victor's young brother William, and pins the blame on the family servant, Justine Moritz, who is wrongly executed for the crime. Shelley suffered another bereavement when her infant Clara Everina died a year after her birth in 1817. The only surviving child was Percy Florence, who was born in 1819.

According to some modern feminist psycho-biographical critics, Shelley projected herself as the progenitor of 'monstrous' births through Victor and his monstrous creation. In her 1831 Introduction, she describes how in a waking dream the dead are brought back to life by a 'pale student of unhallowed art' (see **NECROMANCY**), while in her *Journal* entry for 19 March 1815 she records, 'Dream that my little baby came to life again that it had only been cold, and that we rubbed it before the fire, and it lived.' The images of fire and reanimation are evocative of *Frankenstein*'s subtitle, *A Modern Prometheus*, which refers to the legend of a transgressive mortal, who stole fire from heaven. Prometheus is a metonym for the spark of masculine creativity, and is also the begetter of a creation myth, whereby inanimate clay figures are revitalised. The profanity of Victor's Prometheanism is represented by this act of solitary male propagation, which produces the proverbial scientist's brain child. Not only does Victor dispense with both a life-giving God and a nurturing mother, but he also subjugates female nature through masculinist science.

As regards Shelley's authorial creativity, the sense of her own birth being monstrous must have impelled her to expiate her matricidal guilt through the novel, at the same time, exorcising her own bereavement as a mother. Indeed the imagery of hideous procreation is spawned by **WILLIAM BECKFORD** in the note he wrote on the fly-leaf of his own copy of the first edition, where he damns it as 'perhaps, the foulest Toadstool that has yet sprung up from the reeking dunghill of the present times'. A long time after its female authorship had been revealed, which accentuated the mixture of fear and loathing, astonishment and admiration with which the novel was received, Mary had felt obliged to explain in her later Introduction, 'How I, then a young girl, came to think of, and to dilate upon, so very hideous an idea?' (1831).

The idea may have taken root when, as a girl, she stayed in Dundee in Scotland for nearly two years with the family of the wealthy merchant William Baxter. The impetus for completing the novel is thought by Butler to have arisen from the interest of Shelley and her husband in current debates between the schools of vitalism and materialism as to the creation of life, experiments in galvanism on executed criminals and a general vogue for automata. A version of the genesis of the novel that is more romanticised in every sense appears in the 1831 Introduction. Here may be found the now familiar account of the ghost-story-telling episode held in 1816 near Geneva, which took place between the Shelleys, Byron, and his physician, John Polidori, at Villa Diodati on the shores of Lake Leman. The suggestion had originated with Byron after he had read stories contained in the *Fantasmagoriana* (1812), which had been translated from the German of Friedrich Schulze and Johann Apel's *Gespensterbuch* (1811–12) (see **GERMAN GOTHIC**) into French. Even though an English translation entitled *Tales of the Dead* was published the following year, it was the French version that was circulated around the villa. Shelley extended her original ghost story, which is no longer extant, into a novel. Its epistolary narrative frame consists of a series of letters sent by the Arctic explorer Captain Robert Walton, to his sister Mrs Margaret Walton Saville, whose initials are shared by Mary Wollstonecraft Shelley. The narrative voice is later appropriated by Victor and then by his creature, who remains nameless.

There are echoes of other voices in the text, such as John Milton, John Locke, Jean-Jacques Rousseau and **GOETHE**. Aside from the polyphonic, the composition of *Frankenstein* incorporates a monstrous patchwork of intertextuality. Victor's scientific ingenuity with the decomposing parts of corpses is reflected in Mary Shelley's literary ingenuity in recomposing various corpora into the body of her own monstrous text. Other readings by critics see the novel as a chilling protest against class oppression, an allegorical warning of the Terror of the French Revolution, a Malthusian dystopia born out of the fear of a monstrous growth in population; and Victor's creation is a mirror-image of colonisation, since, in wanting to shape the world anew, he plunders the old. The fear of breeding a race of monsters leads him to destroy the female mate he has created for his creature by dismembering 'the thing' he has put together. The perception of both creature and mate as subalterns, who are sub-human, is integral to the process of colonisation and the concept of 'thingification'. Once it was known that the author was a woman, the novel became a trope for the monstrosities produced by the female imagination as a source of patriarchal anxiety. In the light of its overt pedagogic, epistemological and metaphysical concerns, P. B. Shelley as Mary's ventriloquist is justified in declaring 'I have not considered myself as merely weaving a series of supernatural terrors' (Preface, 1817).

Apart from functioning as a skull and cross-bones morality tale or as a foray into embryonic science fiction (see **GOTHIC SCIENCE FICTION**), which had been galvanised by contemporary scientific debates, *Frankenstein* can also be read as Gothic travelogue. Travel-writing was a genre to which Shelley returned in *Rambles in Germany and Italy in 1840, 1842, and 1843* (1844), where she wrote about her travels with her son. Prior to that, she had devoted herself to editing her husband's poems, published in 1839, and his essays, letters, translations and fragments that appeared in 1839 but with 1840 written on the title-page.

The death of P. B. Shelley in 1822 and of Byron in 1824 had made them, for Shelley, 'the people of the grave – that miserable conclave to which the beings I best loved belonged' (*Journal*, 15 May 1824). Premature death was a Romantic contagion that struck down so many in her circle. Identifying herself in her *Journal* as 'The Last Man', she dramatises this sense of desolation in her third novel. The bleak mirage of the extinction of the human race by an unrelenting epidemic of the plague, reduces *The Last Man* to a nadir of nihilism. What takes it beyond Gothic terror is the way in which it challenges high Romantic ideals. Inevitably this culminates in the terminal failure of art, which can no longer be redeemed by the imagination. In response to this pessimistic vision, many contemporary reviewers were scathing. *The Wasp*, for example, retitled the book *The Last Woman*, while the *St James Gazette* exulted in its portrayal of the author as 'The Last Woman' having no-one with whom to talk.

Before she died, in London, of a brain tumour at the age of 53, Shelley significantly chose to be buried with her parents at St Pancras. After her death, her daughter-in-law, Lady Jane Shelley, decided to have her buried instead in the graveyard at St Peter's Church in Bournemouth, near her son's new family home, Boscombe Manor. As it transpired, this was a far-sighted decision, since the cemetery Shelley had chosen was dug up in 1868 to make way for St Pancras Station, which was designed appropriately in the style of the Victorian **GOTHIC REVIVAL**.

While Lady Shelley made sure that the bodies of Godwin and Wollstonecraft were exhumed and then reburied in Bournemouth, she left the second Mrs Godwin unceremoniously behind. Unfortunately, the rector of St Peter's refused at first to bury the disinterred bodies, which represented an unholy trinity of heretical authors. Encamped outside the locked iron gates of the cemetery, Lady Shelley ensconced herself in her carriage in front of the hearse and refused to budge until the rector relented. Wishing to avoid a scandal, he eventually permitted a gravedigger to lower the coffins into their grave. These sepulchral proceedings were conducted with a Frankensteinian fervour, aptly marked by no religious rites. For many devotees, there has been an omission that continues to this day, which outweighs the absence of any funeral service. Even though Wollstonecraft was acknowledged on her gravestone as the author of the *Vindication*, there is no mention on the tombstone of Mary Wollstonecraft Shelley that she had ever been the author of *Frankenstein*. For that recognition, one must step outside the boundaries of the consecrated ground to the outside of the churchyard wall, where the plaque proclaiming her authorship has been exiled.

MARIE MULVEY-ROBERTS

Shelley, Percy Bysshe (1792–1822)

Percy Bysshe Shelley had early and abiding passions for alchemical science, ghost-raising, and horror-rituals. At preparatory school, he was a devotee of the Minerva Press, and especially admired **RADCLIFFE**'s *The Italian*, **LEWIS**'s *The Monk*, and Charlotte Dacre's *Zofloya*, all of which enter into the short Gothic fictions he published in his last term at Eton and first term at Oxford, *Zastrozzi, a Romance* (spring 1810) and *St Irvyne; or, The Rosicrucian* (December 1810 [1811 on title-page]).

Zastrozzi is a mock-Minerva novel, with stock Gothic names and characters (though the villainous Machiavel and suffering hero may be seen as each other's antitype). The *Critical Review* for November 1810 judged it, in cliché gothic, as 'one of the most savage and improbable demons that ever issued from a diseased brain'. More perceptively, the *Gentleman's Magazine* for September 1810 noticed that 'the denouement ... is conducted on the principles of moral justice'. With its epigraph from Milton, *Zastrozzi* shows already the themes of rebellion and revenge, and of a superior, humanitarian code, which run all the way to *The Cenci* (1819).

Early Gothic works include: a lost horror tale called *The Nightmare*, which Shelley wanted Fuseli to illustrate; *The Wandering Jew*, a verse melodrama co-written with his cousin Tom Medwin; the Chattertonian 'Ghasta; or, the Avenging Demon ...', one of the pieces in *Original Poetry by Victor and Cazire* (published anonymously with his sister, September 1810, and hastily withdrawn for plagiarism of 'Monk' Lewis); *St Irvyne*, an unstable mix of alchemy, free love, and crimes of passion; and *Zeinab and Kathema* (1810–11), in imitation of Southey's *Thalaba the Destroyer* (1801).

Shelley's manipulation of the Gothic ranges all the way from pranking and pastiche to the profoundest speculation. In this latter sense, Gothic or occult elements and episodes merge into his interminable questioning of secret sources and powers: the opening of *Alastor*, where the narrator 'makes "his bed/In charnels and on coffins ... forcing some lone ghost ... to render up the tale/Of what we are"'; or the *Hymn to Intellectual Beauty*, where Platonism and Gothicism uncannily coincide ('While yet a boy I sought for ghosts ...'); or the Zoroastrian summonings of *Prometheus Unbound* and *Hellas*.

Peacock recorded Shelley's deep responsiveness to the Gothic American novelist **CHARLES BROCKDEN BROWN**, 'remarkable for the way in which natural causes were made to produce supernatural effects'. Shelley cultivated a power of suggestion over others as well as himself, a power he designated as 'natural magic' (note to *Hellas*): most famously, there were the horror sessions with Jane Clairmont at Church Terrace in 1814; the ghost stories, partially recorded by Shelley, which were sparked by Byron's book of German *Fantasmagoriana* in 1816; and (another Villa Diodati episode) the recitation of *Christabel* which induced Shelley's vision of a woman with eyes instead of nipples.

NICOLA TROTT

Southern Gothic

If America's Southern Gothic claims any one founding text, it has to be **EDGAR ALLAN POE**'s 'The Fall of the House of Usher' (1839). The eye-like windows, the fissured walls, the miasmic tarn, the decay, and the nerve-wracked artist protagonist, all hint of the psychic abyss. But another dimension has equally been thought to hold. The Usher Mansion, Roderick and Madeline's brother–sister love, and even the *symboliste* resonances of the unfolding story, also yield a long-supposed perfect Gothic image of 'The South', the Deep South, that is, shot through with brooding family darkness and a deeply inward sense of the past as burden.

'Usher', accordingly, has served as at once prophecy and emblem of the defeat brought on by the Yankee North ('The War Between The States' or simply 'The War', as the Civil War was known to supporters of the Confederacy). Not least in this configuration is the haunting legacy of slaveholding with its built-in phobias about insurrection and miscegenation. Likewise, and for all its Antarctic exploration setting, Poe's only completed novel, *The Narrative of Arthur Gordon Pym* (1837–8), has also been taken for an oblique version of Southern Gothic – especially the tribal black figures set in a white landscape, the strange cyphers, and the final glimpse of a numinous, all-white supreme being.

'Gothic' Poe, then, has had several lives, foremost, and rightly, that which acts on his own cue of 'I write a Gothic not of Germany but of the soul.' Such, too, was perpetuated in the French translations of Baudelaire and Mallarmé. But his identification as a maker of the Gothic South has never been far out of view, a region of shadow, narcissism, and perhaps above all, lost glory. Here, indeed, was another kind of American 'house' replete with its ghosts, inverted desire, and gentility of a kind whose later incarnations would run as variously as Margaret Mitchell's 'Gothic' confection, *Gone With the Wind* (1936), and Tennessee Williams's sexual melodrama, *Cat On A Hot Tin Roof* (1955).

Nor was Poe the only early nineteenth-century Southerner with a taste for Gothic. Its traces are to be found in John Pendleton Kennedy's Virginia sketches, *Swallow Barn* (1832), and William Gilmore Simms's novel of Indian-warfare, *The Yemassee* (1835). Mark Twain, too, who began life as the Missouri-raised Samuel Clemens, for all his better-known claim as America's major satiric humorist, shows his own Gothic inclinations, whether in the cave scenes and last, desperate inhumation of Injun Joe in *The Adventures of Tom Sawyer* (1876), or the delirium tremens and drowning of Pap Finn in *The Adventures of Huckleberry Finn* (1884), or the *cauchemar* scenarios of later work like *What is Man?* (1906) and *The Mysterious Stranger* (1916). **AMBROSE BIERCE**, although born in Ohio and an ex-Union officer who saw Sherman's March on Atlanta, belongs in similar company, most of all on the basis of cryptic, Southern-set pieces like 'An Occurrence at Owl Creek Bridge', 'A Horseman in The Sky' and 'Chicamauga'.

In the creation of his 'Yoknapatawpha County' and other fiction William Faulkner would confirm that Southern Gothic still had plenty of staying power. Stories like 'A Rose for Emily' (1930), with its spare, alarming portrait of a spinster's necrophilic love and revenge, or 'Dry September' (1931), with its beautifully paced account of a racial lynch-drama, carry their own confirming hallmarks. The novels, equally, albeit with a knowing enough irony, point in the same direction. *The Sound and The Fury* (1929) offers the riven, incestuous Compson menagerie. In *As I Lay Dying* (1930) Addie Bundren wishes a nothing if not Gothic journey to the burying-ground on her family. *Sanctuary* (1931) contains a figure of rare sexual malevolence and darkness in Popeye. Joanna Burden's descent into nymphomania and religiosity in *Light in August* (1932) turns on its own kind of sexual Gothic. In *Absalom, Absalom!* (1936), the brute, white-supremacist killing of Joe Christmas by Percy Grimm could not be more chilling. Faulkner's use of Gothic as a sense of place is to be seen in his rendering of ancestral Southern wilderness in 'The Bear' and other sequences of *Go Down, Moses* (1942).

Faulkner, in turn, has anything but wanted for Southern successors. Flannery O'Connor, despite a famous gibe that she found New York as Gothic as anything in her own native Georgia, holds a special niche. From out of a mainly Bible-Protestant, small-town and country South, hers is a Catholic vision of comic-ironic redemptions, be they of egoists caught off-guard or of 'nasty-nice' women, as she called them, hoist by the petard of their own respectability. Characteristic stories include 'A Good Man is Hard to Find', in which the murderer, known as The Misfit, might almost be on a mission of Christian purgation; 'Parker's Back', whose title-figure seeks the face of the martyred Christ in his own tattoo; 'Revelation', with its mocking inversion of Mrs Turpin's expected heaven; or 'The Enduring Chill', whose intellectual-humanist hero, the very figure of *ennui*, finds himself mocked in the final, descending image of the Holy Ghost. Southern Gothic is given similar play in her two novels. *Wise Blood* (1952), in which Hazel Motes, an obsessional and bigot, literally blinds himself in hopes of seeing God, offers a dark, parabular comedy of divine madness. *The Violent Bear It Away* (1960) tells a tale of Georgia-style prophets and prophecy, a Book of Revelation involving homosexual rape and, again, a complex dialectic of spiritual sight and blindness.

In Carson McCullers's fiction, Southern Gothic takes on a yet more explicit sexual character; notably *The Heart is a Lonely Hunter* (1941) as centred in the androgynous and adolescent girl, Mick Kelley, who finds herself in company with other misfits in her small-town Southern world, drawn to the deaf-mute John Singer; *Reflections in a Golden Eye* (1941), set on a Southern army-post, and which takes a more violent turn into racial murder, homosexual love, and self-mutilation; *The Ballad of The Sad Café* (1951) with its disjunctive love-triangle; and *Clock without Hands* (1961), which depicts 'race' in the South as a violent and ongoing baroque.

Gothic as somehow always integral to Southern writing has much persisted – granted a fair margin of definition. The gallery includes Eudora Welty's *Robber Bridegroom* (1942) with its contrasts of frontier and dream violence; Truman Capote's *Other Voices, Other Rooms* (1948), a portrait of hothouse Southern family, languor and paedophilia; William Styron's *Lie Down in Darkness* (1951), with its Faulknerian echoes of a doomed Tidewater, Virginia dynasty; Robert Penn Warren's *The Cave* (1959), which depicts an entrapped victim made subject to exploitative reportage; James Dickey's *Deliverance* (1970), in which a weekend hunt-saga in an unspecified South is made over into the stuff of nightmare; and Bobby Ann Mason's *In Country* (1985), with its tale of Vietnam as inner trauma and accusation carried over into 1980s Kentucky.

Yet another kind of Gothicism is to be met with in African-American writing, from Jean Toomer's 'Harlem Renaissance' lush, blood-imaged Georgia in *Cane* (1923), to William Demby's portrait of a young black boy caught in the racial dead-end of a West Virginia hill town in *Beetlecreek* (1950), to Ishmael Reed's witty (and nothing if not postmodern) pastiche of 'The Old South' as Gothic in *Flight To Canada* (1976).

A. ROBERT LEE

Stevenson, Robert Louis (1850–94)

Amid Stevenson's many writings (from travel accounts and adventures for boys to historical novels and South-Sea allegories), there is a very clear 'Gothic period': the early to middle 1880s. After his marriage to Fanny Osborne in San Francisco, Stevenson returned to his native Scotland in 1881. There, during stays at Pitlochry and Braemar (Summer 1881) and Bournemouth (1884–7), he wrote the tales 'Thrawn Janet' and 'The Body-Snatchers' and the longer stories 'Markheim' and 'Olalla'. These latter pieces were finished by late 1885, and that was the autumn in which, after a 'fine bogey' nightmare, he wrote the *Strange Case of Dr Jekyll and Mr Hyde*, published as a 'shilling shocker' in January 1886 to brisk sales in Britain and America and a spate of dramatic adaptations starting in 1887. True, the 'Gothic' elements of quasi-haunted old houses, ghostly figures of past or present guilts, and struggles between the personal regressions and class-conscious drives in the self do appear sporadically in other Stevenson works, some of them from the same decade: *Treasure Island* (1883); *Kidnapped* (Summer 1886); *The Master of Ballantrae* (1889). But it is the five blatantly 'horrific' tales from 1881 to 1886 that have become Stevenson's genuinely 'Gothic' corpus and show the unique contributions he made to this hybrid genre. These pieces reveal the ways he focused the Gothic form on the modern self torn between psychological and social forces pulling it towards the ancient, rural, superstitious past *and* the rapidly changing, more secular, increasingly urban present.

Stevenson's interest in Gothic writing was probably spurred by Fanny's penchant for 'crawlers', as well as a sense that they would sell nicely in short fictional forms. Yet the Gothic's roots were already entangled for Stevenson with the 'devil in disguise' stories from the Covenanting tradition of Scottish Presbyterianism (see **SCOTTISH GOTHIC**). These were among the tales first told to him by his staunch Covenanter nanny back in the upper middle-class Edinburgh house in which he was raised. It may have been the 'respectable' veneer and conventional Christianity of his family that Stevenson later found hypocritical after his bohemian college or tramp-artist years and his increasing religious scepticism. Yet he always retained, as W. E. Henley said, 'something of the Shorter-Catechist' that made him keep recalling the stark good-and-evil dualisms of folk characterisations and mixing them in with his complex portraits of people who wrestled with conflicting moral positions, much as he did.

One result is 'Thrawn Janet', a flashback story told in Scotch dialect to explain the condition of a moorland minister who has become both a bible-beating scourge of sinners from the pulpit and a 'scared' and 'uncertain' person in private. The flashback seems to take the folk position that his one-time housekeeper Janet, nearly drowned by local women for suspected witchcraft, was possessed by the 'black man' in her twisted ('thrawn') condition after that assault on her – but her penultimate state, hung up by a nail in the minister's haunted manse, perhaps by herself or the 'man', leaves the reader and the preacher bedevilled as to whether her 'possession' was socially or supernaturally imposed on her.

'The Body-Snatchers', in turn, is itself told mostly in flashback to account for a stormy encounter at a village tavern between a local drunkard, Fettes, and a well-dressed physician from the city, Wolfe Macfarlane. The narrator discovers that both were once students of, and the providers of bodies for, the esteemed dissector 'Mr K——' of Edinburgh, for whom they gradually became accomplices in urban murder as well as country grave-robbing. Though written in some homage to *Frankenstein* (see **MARY SHELLEY**), this story is haunted most obviously by the actual 'Burke and Hare' scandal of 1828, where two Edinburgh 'resurrectionists' were found to have murdered sixteen people for a Dr Robert Knox, who was, like Stevenson's Macfarlane and K——, never proven guilty himself. The most Gothic element of this story, though, is Macfarlane's and Fettes's final digging-up in a 'rustic graveyard' of a shrouded farm-woman's body. As they drive off, this figure horrifically transmutes itself into the reunited corpse of 'Mr. Gray', a mysterious, lower-class crony of Macfarlane's in Edinburgh whom Macfarlane had killed and brought to Fettes and K——for dissection. Gray is an early version of Hyde, an amorphous 'small' blend of the 'pale and dark' and of 'refinement' and the 'vulgar'. He has 'remarkable control over Macfarlane' and is thus his secret, unrespectable, class-shifting *alter ego* who must be eliminated to preserve Macfarlane's pose of respectability, yet must haunt him and Fettes as the embodiment of their multifarious, suppressed, and money-hungry 'night life'.

The fluidity of class-postures and states of being (the shades of gray) with which this figure threatens those closest to him becomes the basic 'spectral other' in Stevenson's other forays into the Gothic. After all, it combines the 'devil in disguise' with Stevenson's sense of the bourgeois self as wafted between contrary cultural incentives towards 'free movement' and restraint. In 'Markheim', the title character kills and begins to rob a pawnbroker only to be haunted at once by a 'lump of terror' whose 'outlines' appear to 'change and waver' even as they show 'a likeness to himself'. Like much of the *Strange Case of Dr Jekyull and Mr Hyde*, this moment echoes **JAMES HOGG**'s highly Scottish *Private Memoirs and Confessions of a Justified Sinner* (1824), most of all the shifting likeness/un-likeness of Gil-Martin, the hero's natural/supernatural 'other'.

The **EDGAR ALLAN POE**-ish narrator of 'Olalla', meanwhile, long resists his growing sense, reminiscent of 'Ligeia' and 'The Fall of the House of Usher', that the ravishingly beautiful woman he has found in a Spanish Gothic castle is the latest member of a werewolf- or vampire-like race born from the degeneration of an inbred family back towards the conditions of the beasts. He feels the pull of this atavism precisely in the potentially shape-shifting beauty that seems to deny it and so plays out the late nineteenth-century fear, post-Darwin and pre-*Dracula* (see **BRAM STOKER**), of humankind as threatened by *de*volution in its evolution, whatever religious emblems we use to keep that de-formation at bay.

When the lawyer Utterson sees Stevenson's Hyde as 'troglodytic' in *The Strange Case of Dr Jekyll and Mr Hyde*, then, he is speaking to the deep fear of regression to a violent animality in us that soon appeared again in reactions to the 'Jack the Ripper' murders, so associated with the book, in the London of 1888. But Utterson's view, like that of all the interpreters who try to explain and deny the shape-shifting main character through-out most of the book, is but one 'pinning down' among many that strive to arrest the greatest terror in that novella, the one that has been building in Stevenson's Gothic since 1881: the haunting possibility, as Jekyll finally confesses, that the supposedly coherent human being is a 'polity of multifarious, incongruous, and independent denizens' looking backwards and forwards for meaning. This polymorphous perversity is something that a Covenanter's *or* a bourgeois doctor's concept of 'black and white' may try to contain (as Jekyll does in splitting, then in killing himself), but it will not be stilled completely, particularly not in the class and style-crossing, and thus **URBAN GOTHIC**, hybridity of Jekyll's London home.

Ultimately, and at the climax of Stevenson's 'Gothic' period, Hyde is not a primitive beast but, as Utterson notes, 'an impression of deformity without any nameable malformation', mixing 'timidity and boldness'. In being the 'othered' de-formation of any of the forms possible for us or inside us, he points to the myriad differences from ourselves within ourselves, a particular kind of secret at the heart of the 'respectable' houses in the aging and class-climbing city. Stevenson's Gothic thus gives us one of the strongest representations we have of that horror in our modern being whereby our 'identities' are really based on a fluidity of potentials that we keep trying to, but cannot, beat down and deny.

JERROLD E. HOGLE

Stoker, Bram [Abraham] (1847–1912)

The reputation of Bram Stoker rests today almost exclusively upon his authorship of *Dracula*. In his lifetime, however, Stoker was better known as the Anglo-Irish manager and biographer of the London actor Sir Henry Irving, than as the author of eleven novels, three volumes of short stories, and a vast corpus of largely uncollected short and serial fiction, biography and criticism.

Of Stoker's eleven novels only five – *Dracula* (1897), *The Mystery of the Sea* (1902), *The Jewel of Seven Stars* (1903), *The Lady of the Shroud* (1909) and *The Lair of the White Worm* (1911) – may be regarded as unequivocally Gothic. However, two of the author's collections of short stories – *Under the Sunset* (1882), a collection of moral tales ostensibly for children, and the posthumous *Dracula's Guest and other Weird Tales* (1914) – draw perceptibly on Gothic motifs. The remaining novels, with much of the uncollected short fiction, can be classified essentially as romances, which at times embody elements of the adventure story and the **GOTHIC NOVEL**. There is, however, a fairly consistent complex of themes and issues, most notably gender and race, which informs the full range of Stoker's fiction, and whose discourses may be traced throughout his writings. Stoker's recension of the Gothic is thus one in which the apparent preoccupations of a segment of the British middle classes are channelled through conventions such as the Gothic Hero and Heroine, the quest for treasure or for knowledge, and the theme of abduction, in order to produce a series of tense fictional scenarios in which the strength of one or more discourses may be both fictionally tested and arguably verified.

Modern critical studies of Stoker's writings have been largely psycho-biographical in approach, and have focused attention onto *Dracula* at the expense of the author's other works. In addition to this, Dracula – the character – has become the epicentre of a modern cultural myth of which *Dracula* – the novel – is but a small component. Taken within its nine-teenth-century context, however, *Dracula* provides a clear demonstration of how Gothic motifs yield to contemporary discourses throughout the author's fiction. Recent scholarship has associated the distinctive pallor, hairy palms and rank breath of the **VAMPIRE** with popular signifiers constructing the masturbator in Victorian culture. Thus, the isolation and introspection of the Gothic **HERO-VILLAIN** have been reworked into the signification of what was termed the 'solitary vice'. This reworking displaces somewhat the nature of the sexual threat traditionally posed by the Gothic Hero. Dracula, like **ANN RADCLIFFE**'s Montoni, hovers menacingly in the theoretical ground between seducer and rapist. But the consequence of his attack is arguably a debasement not of the indi-vidual but of the race. The popular eugenics of Victorian commentators such as William Acton insist that the masturbator not only destroys himself, but blights his descendants also. The signification of the indi-vidual thus begins to embody a whole series of related racial issues con-cerning not merely the potential decadence of the race from within, but also the eugenic risks apparently posed by other racial groups – in particular those that come, like Dracula himself, from the East.

This racial script may be seen, equally, to co-exist with the physiolo-gical and symbolic resonances of blood in *Dracula*. The text's representa-tions of the secretion, depletion and transfer of blood participate in a metonymic complex in which the alleged racial qualities encoded in blood are enhanced, diluted, corrupted or transferred. These encodings in turn map over further issues of gender and of class, although these latter are often exposed more directly in Stoker's other writings. The combination of Western racial bloods in *Dracula*, whether literally (as in the various acts of transfusion), or figuratively (as in the alliance forged around Van Helsing's leadership), thus conveys not just the apparently inevitable triumph of Western stock over less developed or 'degenerate' opposition, but the superiority also of the moral, intellectual and emo-tional qualities culturally encoded in the blood signifier.

The theme of racial alliance is repeated in *The Mystery of the Sea*, al-though here an English hero is romantically partnered with an American heroine in opposition to a Spanish nobleman. Set against the background of the Spanish–American War of 1898, the novel describes the search for a hoard of gold – treasure from the Spanish Armada of 1588 – concealed on the Scottish coast by an ancestor of the Spaniard. This latter detail, in conjunction with the American heroine's explicit familial descent from Sir Francis Drake, allows a contemporary political conflict to be reconfigured as a matter of historical, racial and religious significance. The apparently straightforward pattern of oppositions between the hero, Hunter, and Don Bernardino, the Spaniard, is, however, disturbed by the Gothic content of the narrative. Hunter possesses the gift of prophetic second sight. It is this faculty that permits him to perceive the potential sexual dangers vested in a classic Gothic abduction plot involving the heroine, Marjory Anita Drake. In responding without reservation to Hunter's plea for assistance, the Spaniard becomes acceptable within the complex of discourses that meet in the character of Hunter. The common standard of chivalrous masculinity that links the two characters, it appears, is more powerful than personal, class or national interests.

The Jewel of Seven Stars is exceptional among Stoker's Gothic novels in that it contains no obvious racial script. The novel describes an attempt to resurrect the mummy of an Egyptian sorcerer-queen, Tera, at the turn of the twentieth century. Two versions of the work appeared in the author's lifetime. The first concludes with the deaths of all but the narrator, Malcom Ross, when the attempted resurrection is thwarted by a violent storm. The second, published in 1912, structures the resurrection as a clear failure, and concludes with a marriage between the narrator and the heroine, Margaret Trelawny. The plot lends itself immediately to the obvious Gothic themes of both blasphemy and the search for forbidden knowledge. However, the novel embodies also a subtle reworking of the **DOPPELGÄNGER** motif through the Egyptian cosmology of the *Ka* or spiritual double, by means of which the narrative structures the possession of Margaret by the personality of her physical double, Queen Tera.

The Lady of the Shroud marks a return by the author, albeit with some irony, to the theme of vampirism. The novel describes the experiences of a British adventurer who inherits a Balkan castle in the early years of the twentieth century. The hero, Rupert Sent Leger, wins the trust of the local people, leading them finally to victory against a Turkish aggressor. The narrative concludes with a festival of Balkan solidarity, in which a political union is concluded between the various warring states, under the benevolent eye of King Edward VII. Stoker skilfully combines this political script with what appears to be a conventional vampire plot. A number of ironic references within Rupert's narrative, however, suggest that the alleged female vampire he encounters is in fact a living person fully cognizant of the signification of literary and mythical vampirism. The 'vampire' is finally revealed as the daughter of the hereditary ruler of the region, shortly before she is kidnapped by Turkish brigands. Rupert's rescue of her concludes with the public recognition of the marriage contracted between them in secret some time earlier. Her name, Teuta, has an obvious racial signification.

Stoker's final novel, *The Lair of the White Worm*, adapts the British folk legend of the Laidley Worm, constructing the White Worm of the title as a massive serpent capable of taking female form. The Worm is ultimately destroyed with explosives detonated by the Australian hero, Adam Salton. It has been suggested that the human personification of the Worm, Lady Arabella March, represents an assertive and predatory womanhood unacceptable to late Victorian and Edwardian morality. Though Lady Arabella, like Queen Tera, is physically destroyed, it is worth recalling the fate of several of Stoker's non-supernatural heroines. Marjory Anita Drake and Teuta are both assertive and self-confident: both are chastened by a kidnap ordeal, after which they submit willingly to the traditional female marital role of passive partner. It would seem that, if a universal standard of masculinity is presumed in the behaviour of chivalrous males of all classes, then there is a related standard of restraint and passivity embedded in the author's fictionalisation of the female.

One biographer has suggested that Stoker's later writings exhibit signs of sexual guilt, a consequence of the author having allegedly contracted syphilis around the turn of the century. While this remains a tempting hypothesis for a critical establishment frequently preoccupied with sexual symbolism, it must be stated that the death certificate – with its enigmatic conclusion, 'exhaustion' – is far from conclusive.

WILLIAM HUGHES

The Sublime

In classical oratory the adjective 'sublime' was applied to the high or elevated style of discourse. In 1674, as part of the neo-classical project of seventeenth-century French culture, the poet and critic Nicholas Boileau translated a key Greek text, *Peri Hupsous* ('On the Sublime'), dating from the first century, and wrongly but consistently attributed to Longinus. From this point onwards the concept of the sublime enjoyed a central position in European aesthetic debate until well into the nineteenth century. Power is seen to be of the essence of the sublime style, which literally 'moves' or 'transports' its hearers. One of Longinus's rare references to the Hebrew scriptures is Genesis 1:3, 'And God said, Let there be light; and there was light.' This is an example of absolute power in which word and effect are one, but also of another way in which Longinus foreshadows the development of the sublime in England in his attention to the rhetorical effect of natural forces. Thunder and lightning are both figures for the oratorical sublime and also sublime in their own right: 'Nature impels us to admire not a small river "that ministers to our necessities" but the Nile, the Ister, and the Rhine.'

In John Dennis's essay *The Grounds of Criticism in Poetry* of 1704 this list of the terrible in nature is extended to include supernatural beings and witchcraft. His stress on enchantments and the wild creation is a British development and makes possible a defence and justification of English literature against the cavils of classical critics. This is important for the **GOTHIC NOVEL**, which wishes to situate itself not in a novelistic tradition but in that of 'romance', and refers repeatedly to Shakespeare, Spenser and the Jacobean dramatists. Samuel Monk's important study of eighteenth-century British theories of the sublime argues that the term became in the early part of the century a repository for all the emotions and literary effects unacceptable to the dominant neo-classical virtues of balance, order and rationality. In the writings of Dennis, John Baillie and even Addison there can be traced a growing emphasis on sublime emotion and the passions of enthusiasm, terror, horror, joy and melancholy. This tendency culminates in Burke's attempt, in his *A Philosophical Enquiry into the Origin of our Ideas of the Sublime and the Beautiful* (1757), to found a psychology based on Locke, for the sublime passions, that would be particularly influential on the Gothic Novel.

Burke, unlike some contemporary aestheticians, locates the sublime purely in terms of fear, the source of which is the 'king of terrors' himself – **DEATH** – and a sense of possible threat to the subject's self-preservation. The threat must not be direct else pleasure or 'delight' cannot be extracted from the experience. In this way Burke provides a psychological justification for the Gothic tale of terror. More clearly than Addison, Burke makes the decisive (and particularly British) move of *Patriarchal* separating entirely the sublime from the beautiful. The latter is a social category, including all the regular and soft qualities that Burke considers feminine. These, like Longinus's ministering small rivers, delight but do not overpower, whereas the sublime is always 'some modification of power' that works against our will. The transcendent is notably absent from a work that locates the sublime viscerally in direct relation to the play of sense stimuli upon the body. The *Philosophical Enquiry* is 'sensationalist' in the manner of much Gothic fiction where bodily affect is the main theatre of meaning (see **GOTHIC BODY**). Such novels can be read as primers of Burkean sublime stimuli such as obscurity, vastness, difficulty, infinity, darkness with sudden lights, magnificence, succession, and so on.

In the second half of the century critical interest turns, in the writings of Edward Young, Alexander Gerard and the Warton brothers, to the writer as sublime in studies about the nature of imagination and literary genius. Lord Kames's extensive treatise *Elements of Criticism* (1762) followed a broadly Burkean line but removed desire from the sublime by separating the disinterested aesthetic appreciation of an object or landscape from its practical use or enjoyment. With Thomas Reid's attempt to locate the sublime in the mental qualities of its creator a way opens up from Humean empiricism to Kantian idealism. Kant's *Critique of Judgment* (1790) sees sublime pleasure as disinterested because it seeks no knowledge of the object. In Kant the sublime becomes a capacity of thinking in the human subject which enables it to rise above its physical limitations, after an initial check to its vital forces. Although it is unlikely that any Gothic authors of this period knew Kant, one does, however, find in Gothic of the turn of the nineteenth century a dialectic between the Burkean model of endangered subjectivity, and what one might interpret as a Kantian or idealist belief in the power of the mind to 'sublime', to rise victorious over opposition to desire or imagination's reach.

The Gothic practitioner who reacts most creatively to sublime theory is **ANN RADCLIFFE** who, while largely Burkean, in a posthumously published essay moved to differentiate horror from terror: 'terror and horror are so far opposite that the first expands the soul and awakens the faculties to a high degree of life; and the other contracts, freezes and nearly annihilates them'. An example in her fiction would be the terror Emily St Aubert feels in *The Mysteries of Udolpho* (1794) before the uncertain secrets of the black veil, and the horror at discovery of what she believes is a dead body, and which causes her to fall senseless. This distinction is crucial for Radcliffe's revision of Burke in the terms of the **GRAVE-YARD SCHOOL** of meditative poetry, in which melancholy registers the experience of living in a true 'paradise lost' in which the relation with the natural world is awry, as are social relations. As in the poetry, which Radcliffe quotes extensively, her heroine will cultivate pensive evening meditation in which 'the silence and grandeur of solitude impressed a sacred awe upon her heart, and lifted her thoughts to the GOD OF HEAVEN AND EARTH.' This sublime establishes both human distance from the creator but also its kinship, so that the subject refinds herself through her position as creature in a sublime creation.

The movement from the 'soft and glowing' to 'sacred awe' is from the beautiful to the sublime in Burkean orthodoxy but one should not assume a simple elevation or dilation of the heroine's consciousness, for she is still wrapt in a 'melancholy charm' and her elevated thoughts present the divine as textually different, in capital letters. The mountains, ruined themselves by the Fall of man according to Bishop Burnet, stress the lost character of human existence. In Thomson's *The Seasons* (1726–30) melancholy leads to 'all the social offspring of the heart', and Radcliffe's novels, like those of Rousseau, create communities of virtue where the sublime can be shared, and the loss of plenitude admitted and healed. From this one can see why Radcliffe views horror as nugatory. The quasi-corpse behind the black veil filled up the gap in comprehension between the subject, Emily, and the world outside her. It stopped any liberatory potential in her thoughts by its morbid physicality. Terror of the unknown allows loss in the melancholy sublime to be figured as absence, whereas horror baulks the imagination and confirms a material secularity.

Charlotte Dacre explores the movement from terror to horror in her popular *Zofloya; or, The Moor of Venice* (1805). In a final transfiguration that reveals his power Zofloya seems to take the natural sublime into himself: 'Common objects seemed to shrink in his presence, the earth to tremble at the firmness of his step; now alone his native grandeur shone in its full glory, not eclipsed by but adding to the terrible magnificence of the scene.' Dacre's work is very alert to the natural sublime but it is an aesthetic powerless against the demonic control of a Satanic universe. Indeed, the moment of infernal metanoia in her heroine, Victoria, occurs as she pretends to her husband to be admiring 'the grandeur of the surrounding scenery' when she is actually plotting his slow death by poison. Yet, as in Radcliffe, the abandonment of the sublime leads to horror, so that the magnificent Zofloya is transformed into a hideous monster and this recognition of him as a false sublime, and Victoria's submission to him, leads to her being flung headlong down a precipice to death and damnation.

Increasingly, just as the sublime in Milton comes to be associated with Satan himself rather than his portrayal, so the rhetorical sublime, which, like Satan, takes the natural sublime into its oratorical web, becomes crucial in the Gothic Novel, especially in *Things As They Are; or, the Adventures of Caleb Williams* (1794), in which the model of chivalry, Falkland, pursues his servant relentlessly to silence his knowledge of a murder, and nearly conquers the persecuted Williams as well as his peers by the force of his oratory. In a final revision, Williams overcomes this Longinian rhetorical sublime of social equals by a Burkean self-dramatisation of his own subjected position that undoes Falkland's power and also transforms the aristocrat back into the moral exemplar that Williams had believed him: 'Williams, said he, you have conquered! I see too late the greatness and elevation of your mind' (Postscript).

Falkland, denying Williams the moral and aesthetic discrimination of the circle of his equals, had denied him the sublime and presented him instead with the horror of guilty knowledge and oppression.

The employment of the sublime as social critique, which owes much to Rousseau's novels, is common to Godwin and Mary Wollstonecraft. The latter locates the sublime in 'the outcast of fortune, rising superior to passion and discontent', and the moral function of suffering humanity rising superior over difficulty and injustice underlies her and Godwin's daughter, **MARY SHELLEY**'s *Frankenstein; or, the Modern Prometheus* (1818), which again articulates the liberatory and moral force of the natural sublime over against the uncanny effect of horror in which the hero, Victor Frankenstein, turns in disgust from the creature of his own demonic making. In giving himself over to the assumed role of divine creation, Victor eschews the Alpine sublime that his fiancée enjoys in Radcliffean transports.

In the graveyard poets, Rousseau and Radcliffe, the sublime is a social experience that creates communion in a fallen and dislocated world, and, taught by Milton's *Paradise Lost*, it is sought by the monster, who haunts the very glacier where Radcliffe's Adeline in *The Romance of the Forest* (1791) had meditated, seeking the same Miltonic 'conversation' that Adeline and the La Lucs enjoyed. For Frankenstein the natural sublime of the glacier becomes horrible, as it brings him no imaginative expansion but the icy recognition of the demands of his monster, a horror made literally frozen in the final scenes of their encounter at the North Pole, which is as much a landscape of the horrible as the Alps are of the sublime.

The natural sublime in the period after the 1820s moves into the millenarian discourse of apocalyptic in which the paintings of John Martin and the epics of Bickersteth anticipate the abrupt ending of the world in fire and judgement. The preacher **CHARLES MATURIN**'s remarkable novels belong in this apocalyptic world of damnation and separation. The eponymous hero of *Melmoth the Wanderer* (1820), as the title of the novel suggests, bears no allegiance to place or to the natural world but damned, travels the world seeking those so unhappy they would exchange places with him. He uses the rhetorical sublime in tale after tale, century after century, to obtain release, and he also employs the natural sublime where he can to trick or manoeuvre innocents such as the isolated Imalee by his godlike powers. However, again in the post-Radcliffean Gothic, the false rhetorical sublime fails and all Melmoth's victims resist, choosing the terrors of isolation or the sufferings of the Inquisition rather than the horror of damnation.

In the Victorian period elements of the Gothic are present in much of the fiction of the time, but the natural sublime disappears and **HORROR**, in the form of **THE UNCANNY**, takes its place. Characters are faced with their double, with guilty shadow-sides of their personality, with half-recognition of the familiar, and with ghosts, which famously, are so often rationally explained in the earlier Gothic. In an influential early essay, 'On the Uncanny' (1919), Freud explains the uncanny as the return to consciousness of material hitherto repressed. When it surfaces this material or memory trace appears alien and uncanny because it is only half recognised. No **SUPERNATURAL** or transcendent is necessary in the **SENSATION** novels of the 1860s but the uncanny effects come, as for example in Collins's *The Woman in White* (1860), from false names, disguises, and unacknowledged sexual relations.

In recent critical writing on the Gothic the Freudian uncanny has been a dominant tool of interpretation. David Morris's article 'Gothic Sublimity' distinguishes (in contradistinction to the argument of this essay, which views the earlier model as dialectical, and the Gothic as a site for the playing out of the terrible and the horrible) between the eighteenth-century sublime, which in a totally unproblematic way allowed imaginative expansion, and the Gothic. Gothic tropes of repetition, whether of plot or description, evoke the uncanny, and the fear of non-differentiation. Feminist critics have also attended more to the uncanny, and Claire Kahane locates what is close to a Kristevan *abîme* in the Gothic struggle to establish a sense of identity between the abyss of maternal oneness and non-differentiation from the mother, and annihilation or possession by the father. But the loss, the gap of signification in the sublime, while emphasised often in **ROMANTICISM**, is neglected in Gothic criticism.

There is a muted psychological Gothic aesthetic in Wordsworth's 1798 'Lines Written above Tintern Abbey' in which the poet records a loss of immediacy, of the child's appetite for nature. But the loss becomes gain since in its place come the pleasures of the sublime: 'a sense sublime / Of something far more deeply interfused' that links humanity and nature and repairs their separation with a deeper unity. As in Radcliffe, the scene is shared, with a sister, but the poet's vision of an underlying presence is not yet shared by her, who is still at the stage of 'wild ecstasies', although it is the identification of his sister as his younger self that makes possible the reactivation of interpretation. Here Wordsworth softens the Gothic sublime since there is no horror but the failure of memory, no terrible that is outside the self. And yet, despite Wordsworth's immanentism, it is still the loss, the separation between poet and the landscape he describes, that restores the sublime, just as in the Gothic Novel only melancholy and the awareness of a fallen and oppressive social order can activate its consolations. Moreover, just as in Wordsworth's poem the threat to the diachronic integrity of the subject enables the influx of the sublime, so the horror and terror engendered by the Gothic Novel put its protagonists at the extremity of psychic disturbance not merely for the circular closure of uncanny repetition but to bear on their bodies the hermeneutic fracture of a fallen world.

ALISON MILBANK

The Supernatural

The term 'the supernatural' embraces all those areas above or beyond the material realm and is the usual designation for the hierarchic planes, fantastic creatures and demonic forces which exist in cosmic and parallel dimensions and which rule and direct our physical existence. To this end supernatural forces may take physical or visible form under exceptional or fortuitous circumstances, or they may even take on permanent yet ambiguous physical properties whose amorphous nature is a bridge between the spiritual and material universes.

Belief in the supernatural realm appears to be a feature of all societies and although the meaning and significance may differ from one community to another there appears to be a certain consensus in the view that creatures and forces of the supernatural have the specific abilities to transcend both time and space, cross the divide between life and death, move between the invisible and the visible and travel freely within both the spiritual and material. Supernatural forces and beings are therefore understood to be of immense power and able to manifest themselves to human beings either at their own will or through invocation. Although (usually) immaterial, the supernatural planes are deemed to be superior to the visible and material and are feared and held in awe accordingly. This is so in all the major religions, in occult practice, in folk belief as well as (at a much more banal level) in modern newspaper horoscopes.

All supernatural systems include more or less complex cosmographies or mappings and often offer themselves as suitable subjects for increasingly arcane and involved investigations (cosmologies). The relationship these investigations have had with religious belief and practice has an extremely long, complex and confused history which is beyond the scope of this article. In the West, Judaism, Christianity and Islam all have elaborate belief systems which nevertheless deny or seek to exclude certain areas of belief, which are relegated to the realm of the irrelevant or, at worst, heretical.

These excluded areas, which often retain a strong peripheral or inverted relationship with orthodox religion (such as Cabbalistic numerology), embrace the practices usually termed **THE OCCULT**. In such systems there is a much more direct relationship with the invisible realms and an overt attempt to harness the power of demonic forces (see **THE DEMONIC**) or interact with other (astral) planes of experience in order to bring about transubstantiations, metamorphoses, or other acts of direct control over the material and invisible environment. To achieve this one must combine belief with technique and a mastery over process.

Western religions see all such activities as suspect or evil whilst occult practice itself has developed its own morality and its own versions of good and evil which, may not necessarily be related to more common-place orthodoxies. In this respect religion would see occultism as trafficking with the forces of chaos, which occultists would view as forces of cosmic order in a cosmos whose explication is only dimly or perversely grasped by the religious establishment. Occultism, therefore, is not merely the mirror image of religion but rather, analogous to it.

Before looking at the progress of supernatural belief in recent times we can conclude that the term will always refer to superior invisible forces which can intervene in human affairs either for reasons of their own or because they have been invoked through prayer, ritual or some form of sorcery. These forces break into the human plane and the world of the everyday in the form either of the miraculous or of the horrific. Such forces range from the benevolence of angels and spirit guides to terrifying satanic (but not necessarily evil) entities called up from planes of existence sometimes higher and sometimes lower than the human. These entities exist in a spectrum that can embrace Celtic gods as well as extraterrestrials.

Occultists and spiritualists believe that the supernatural exists both as a physical reality and as a subjective truth but that unlike rationalist science there can be no enlightenment within the supernatural without inner or subjective illumination. This alone would serve to distance any system of occultism (spiritualism included) from any materialist enquiry proper, including that of science. For occultists, Nature (including human nature but, rather problematically, excluding free will) contains and is also directed by hierarchic sources of energy as real as (indeed in control of) physical existence itself; time and distance are annulled. The visible and tangible (including what is known of the solar system etc.) serves as confirmation of a higher cosmic order which is essentially static, 'planned' and determined by the properties of a pantheistic force which consists of the energy of 'mind'. Spiritual and yet able to manifest itself through matter, 'mind' is the original diffused godhead, which is nevertheless detached from the common notion of a directing intelligence or god. The concept retains a sense of purpose.

Although about the properties of the eternal, supernaturalism has a long history. A decisive break came in that history in 1848 when the Fox family of Hydesville in New York State became the centre of a series of strange tappings associated with John Fox's daughters, Margaret and Kate. It might be expected that these events would have been forgotten but this is not the case, for their own brand of mysticism was steeped in the peculiarism and apocalyptic imagination of America at the time, which included such visionaries as Andrew Davies Jackson, 'The Seer of Poughkeepsie.'

By the 1850s, mediums had sprung up across the United States and Great Britain, including Emma Britten, the Bang Sisters of Lily Dale near Buffalo, and Daniel Dunglas Home, whose feats of levitation, etc., helped inspire Henry Sidgwick and Frederic Myers amongst others to found the Society for Psychical Research in 1882. From a quite different starting point, Mary Baker Eddy had, in 1879, founded the first 'Church of Christian Scientists' and by the twentieth century, Lily Dale had become **SPIRITUALISM**'s largest summer camp with its focal point the re-erected Fox cottage. It was, however, with the advent of Theosophy that spiritism and the occult gained a fully comprehensible and internally logical basis.

Helen Petrovna Blavatsky, usually refered to as Madame Blavatsky, began her rise to fame in the mid-1870s. With some psychic ability and much personal charm, she joined up with Colonel Olcott and together they formed a 'Miracle Club' followed by 'The Theosophical Society' in 1875. Claiming inspiration from mysterious entities first from Egypt and then from Tibet, Blavatsky went on to complete two highly influential works, *Isis Unveiled* (1877) and *The Secret Doctrine* (1888), and to create a spiritual centre in India. In keeping with spiritualism's origins Blavatsky later became an American citizen.

All forms of occultism and spiritualism grew rapidly after the First World War, encouraged by the formation of a variety of lodges, fraternities, and opening of bookshops, the most famous of which was owned by Sir **ARTHUR CONAN DOYLE**, who was also Britain's leading advocate of spiritualistic doctrine. Aleister Crowley, self-styled 'Great Beast 666', remains the best known practitioner of the occult and (disputably) responsible for the revival of magical practice.

The term 'the supernatural' now embraces a bewildering variety of sub-branches which include orthodox mediumship, the study of earth energies and lines of power, magical and pagan practices, eco- and feminist occultism, extra-terrestrialism and ufology, and much else besides, although common threads give continuity between branches.

CLIVE BLOOM

Terror

At the time when the classic texts of Gothic fiction were being written, a number of attempts were made to define, or at least describe, terror, particularly in relation to a distinction from horror. These debates perhaps seem less important to us now, but they have left us a specific legacy, which is the valorising of terror at the expense of horror. In part this is because 'terror', through its emotional and spatial ties with the field of the 'terrific', had connections with the realm of the sublime; whereas horror was seen as an altogether less transcending form.

Looking both back on this distinction, and also across at contemporary assumptions about terror and horror, it is important to register that terror had, and continues to have, direct connections with the socio-political realm. It is, of course, no accident that the roots of Gothic fiction in a time of European revolution, one of whose manifestations was the French 'reign of terror', established 'terror' as a term which could look outward as well as inward; perhaps the emblem of horror, on the other hand, is the claustrophobic fiction of **POE**, where the individual is alone with the insupportable. Horror, we might say, is crudely terminal; it has to do with what frightens, or disgusts, us to death. Terror, on the other hand, has the hallmark of a regime; it is both deeper and less total than horror, offering us the dual possibilities of submersion in a condition of political abjection and at the same time the thought of an escape into a realm where terror has ceased and we can re-emerge from our hiding-place. Horror, we might say, induces, or capitalises upon, impotence; from terror we can gain a certain sense of ourselves, and return to the world no doubt sadder but also potentially wiser.

Early Gothic writers of the school of **MATTHEW LEWIS** were known as terror-writers; they were also occasionally referred to as 'terrorists', and the elision is important. In so far as Lewis had, or professed, roots in the earlier German tradition of terror-writing, and those writings were seen in particular as socially and politically subversive, then the question of the relation between the terrorist and the terror-writer remains an open one, to which I shall return below.

These considerations, however, pertain to the location of the text in the wider world; what has also to be considered is the deeper question of how and indeed whether a text can 'terrorise'. We might take a broad line on this and assert that all texts are instruments of terror. The justification for such a claim would be derived from such thinkers as Heidegger, Blanchot and Derrida, and their arguments about the ways in which text, or 'literature' in their various formulations, represents absence and negativity. In other words, although language may appear to 'represent', in fact its major effect is to 'stand in for' its absent other; so that when we confront a text we are inevitably confronted in turn by absence, by a sense of loss with which the words we read have a complex relation. Literature, on these readings, would be that which pre-eminently exposes us to the terrors of loss and absence, which threatens our illusions of a fullness of being.

Gothic fiction would, on this paradigm, be a model for all literature; precisely because its very subject matter is haunting, which is in the end the station of all writing. In so far as Gothic is a literature of **THE SUPERNATURAL**, it would serve mainly to render apparent the element of the supernatural – the other of nature – which is at the basis of all language and thus of all literature. Although these theorists would claim to be working in a way which transcends the psychological, it none the less remains open to us to think the issue in a psychological way, and to contemplate the roots of terror in disembodied textuality.

Horror, we might say, is a stark transfixed staring; terror has more to do with trembling, the liminal, the sense of waiting so fully adumbrated by Blanchot and by Beckett; horror, to use contemporary idiom, is 'in your face', whereas terror consorts with a certain withholding of the *occasion* of fear. We can see here one specific trajectory through later Gothic fiction, which would include **HENRY JAMES**'s 'The Turn of the Screw', the multiple hesitations of Walter de la Mare's supernatural fictions, and the contemporary writings of M. John Harrison, involved as they are with issues of ambivalence, undecidability and above all, to use Harrison's own preferred term, the equivocal.

The question of terror, then, inevitably touches upon the parallel question of explicitness. It is generally held that film has surpassed literature in its presentation of the terrifying; but it would be open to the reader to query this assumption. For example, there are literary texts – *American Psycho* might be one – which could not accurately be filmed; the terrors which occur in its pages could not be brought under the imaginative control of a medium which withholds nothing of the visual image. The very aptness of film to produce horror, which relies upon its linear timescale, or in simpler terms upon its relative unstoppability, might make it less apt for the conveyance of terror, which has its lingering aspect, the moment when the book is put aside while the sweats subside; and it is interesting that some films which aspire to this condition of terror – Polanski's *Repulsion* might be an example – seek in their very form to replicate the lengthiness and indeterminacy of the literary text.

In order to get a little further with these arguments I would like briefly to consider five texts: **JAMES HOGG**'s *The Private Memoirs and Confessions of a Justifield Sinner* (1824); **C. R. MATURIN**'s *Melmoth the Wanderer* (1820); **DICKENS**'s *The Old Curiosity Shop* (1841); Conrad's *The Secret Agent* (1907) and Doris Lessing's *The Good Terrorist* (1985). In the

Private Memoirs and Confessions of a Justified Sinner, Hogg, I would say, exposes us to terror. This terror consists in a limitless implication of the self in a series of actions which persuade us of their inexorability. Horror provides us with shock and surprise: it would, however, be vain to pretend that Hogg surprises us in the *Private Memoirs and Confessions*. On the contrary: from the moment when we realise that something is amiss in our hero's perceptions, we are drawn into a process of action which, we already know, will unavoidably take us towards a dreaded conclusion. We are already, we might say, in the Ghost Train; we are there because we have been told it will not be frightening, but it is, and we have, we shall later be told, only ourselves to blame.

The terror of the *Private Memoirs and Confessions* has to do with doubling and splitting: our hero, Wringhim, encounters a diabolic figure, Gil-Martin, who persuades him of various courses of action. Our position as readers consists in being suspended over a curious literary space; on the one hand, we are perfectly well aware that this Gil-Martin can be nothing other than a projection of Wringhim's own repressed desires, while on the other we are transfixed by the author/editor and all the panoply which surrounds these positions in the text, and their consistent attempt to make us believe that we are really here in the presence of an incarnation of the devil.

We might fairly say on this basis that one of the roots of terror is incarnation; or rather, the terror of incarnation, the fear that bits and pieces of our own psyche – or body, in the case of *Frankenstein* (1818) – will receive the gift of 'organisation' and be returned to us as a fantasised organic whole. We might want to refer this terror back to the terror of textuality in general; the fear that these words on the page might spring to life. Such a fear has two emblematic exemplars: one is the general production of fake manuscripts and similar devices in the original Gothic, which serves to remind us that the very words of the past (and **LOVECRAFT**'s *Necronomicon* and its descendants are further examples here) may rise up against us; and the other is neatly symbolised in **M. R. JAMES**'s short story 'Oh Whistle and I'll Come to You, My Lad', where the sheets of the other bed in the protagonist's hotel room rise up in the shape of a ghost. We do not even need to know that M. R. James was himself an antiquarian, an investigator of ancient sheets – of paper – to sense that this evidences the uprising of the word (the song, the whistle, the text) against the intruder; and perhaps this leads us to another root of terror, which is the fear that as observers, readers, viewers, we are ourselves intruders into a work of language which has been already achieved before our advent, and which has now only to unravel its snaky coils to involve us totally in a narrative of which, in the so-called real world, we should have no part.

Something of the same effect is achieved in Maturin's *Melmoth the Wanderer*, which works by afflicting us with the terror of proximity and involvement. *Melmoth* is a web, a highly convoluted web; it is layered by story upon story, and the inevitable concomitant is that we do not know where we are as readers, on which 'storey' of the fantastic building. As with Hogg, it would hardly be fair to say that we are surprised by Maturin's text; after all, all we need to know is that when a beautiful maiden appears she will be menaced, and when a monk appears we should say 'Boo'.

Yet this does not summarise the space – or even the spaciousness – of Maturin's fiction. For here we are drawn into what we might fairly call an 'unspeakable intimacy'; we are left beyond words, for we are all but deluged in the author's own manic fluency. We might pause here for a moment to explore a thought about the relations between Romanticism, fluency and hypomania; but time, as Maturin repeatedly tells us, will not allow. And time, indeed, is relevant to the operation of terror in *Melmoth* in another way; for through the looping convulsions of the text, we are shaken loose from our moorings in a temporal spectrum. Events and situations repeat themselves down through the generations, but always with a slight difference; as in the story of the bottle imp, time, while limitless, is simultaneously always on the brink of running out; the spaciousness of life is haunted by the shadow of death, by the sense of an ending. Behind this we may glimpse the contours of Freud's repetition principle, and also the apparently endless chain of rememorations which accompany trauma. In Maturin, it is as though the primal trauma is writ large and has continually to be re-enacted. Melmoth wants, above all, to buy a soul; but we may choose to put this in simpler terms, and say that what he wants is another life in exchange for the one he has. Thus we are confronted with a text which is about the sense of living the wrong life, where the hovering notion of a fantasised return to origins, the possibility of beginning again, receives an objective correlative in Melmoth's endless searching – which is, of course, also the substance of the tales of the Wandering Jew, of the Ancient Mariner.

In *The Old Curiosity Shop*, Dickens explicitly claims to be exploring what it is like to set a figure of the utmost vulnerability – Little Nell – amid figures of terror, and here he picks up on one of the principal structures of Gothic fiction, which is the exploitation of impotence, the placing of an undefended and usually female figure amid terrors which she cannot understand, and above whose head the narrator and the reader share a greater, but still always incomplete, understanding of what threatens. The problem with terror as thus conceived also takes us back to the fictions of **ANN RADCLIFFE**: namely, that we are confronted with a structure in which the heroine has always to maintain an impossible innocence. If we were to refer this back to a psychological root, we might say that the real fear here, despite its immediate and complex manifestations, is of contamination; that, unknown to ourselves, we take on the contours of that which terrifies us, and thus that we ourselves, in the extremity of our terror, become the very monsters from which we flee.

No doubt it is the fear of this occurring which drives Radcliffe and Dickens, among many others, to effect such a clear distinction between the persecuting and the persecuted; yet the result of this clear separation of innocence and experience is always to risk falling into sentimentality, into an over-valorisation of the self's powers of resistance to such contamination. This is a profound human wish; it is also the wish to effect a clear distinction between daytime and night-time worlds, the wish to exile the dream, the shadow, to render it 'merely objective', as though it has no place in our inner world.

Yet terror cannot be thus easily kept at bay. In *The Secret Agent* Conrad presents us with, as it were, the internal workings of a terrorist group. Admittedly we might not wish to refer to *The Secret Agent* as a 'terrorist text', in the sense originally enshrined in the series of such stories in *Blackwood's Magazine* and elsewhere; none the less, there is terror at work in this text, in at least two ways.

First, there is the terror of an arbitrary connection between fantasy and the real, between internal planning and external execution. The actual – and, in a sense, accidental – death which is at the heart of *The Secret Agent* represents the violent externalisation of that which should have been kept hidden, and thus serves to represent our own terror when our inmost, hidden thoughts and desires take on external shape, without, apparently, our active will. Secondly, there is the figure of the Professor; whereas all the other members of the terrorist group are shown to act from motives which are hypocritical and muddled, the Professor, the walking bomb, represents the extreme edge of this configuration, for he has moved beyond all care for his own actions, and thus stands as a representative of dehumanisation. For the Professor, all has ceased to matter, and he carries his own death and the death of others around with him permanently, strapped to his own body.

In *The Good Terrorist*, Doris Lessing turns the screw one stage further by showing how the self can be drawn entirely into the machinations of others. Our gradual introduction to the central character is freighted with sympathy and understanding; we see her clearly, her desires and motivations, a whole aetiology of character, and yet we also see, returning to the crucial motif of inexorability, how she is effortlessly drawn into a web of intrigue which is so complex that we can no longer say to what extent she is a willed collaborator or a passive and exploited element in the 'plot', in both senses of that word. This replicates, I suggest, another aspect of primal fear, which is of forgetting, of no longer being certain where things began or where they might end, the sense of being in a limitless flow where questions about responsibility and meaning have disappeared and where all the defences around our sense of a central self are endangered.

The meanings of terror, then, as I have tried to adumbrate them, will always hover undecidably between the psychological and the political, between the inner and the outer, between the sense of a free, humanised self and the countervailing sense of being deselfed, being 'at the mercy' of forces beyond our control. And this returns us again to the condition of all textuality, where the free will of the characters is an illusion but one in which we are more then happy to share until the point where we sense that our own freedom as readers is being demonstrably assailed and that we are being led to conclusions which involve death and destruction.

The forms, then, in which textual terror occurs will always have an element of the unvarying, as they reflect and represent deep-seated anxieties of birth and death; at the same time they will always vary according to the externalisations and projections available in the current historical and discursive field. Perhaps we might go further and say that terror is precisely the mark, the trace or residue, of this undecidability; it raises the question of whether we can sensibly see ourselves as historically responsive beings for whom understanding, enlightenment, can potentially bring about the resolution of all mystery, or whether we have to see ourselves as embedded in strata of the psyche which we are conditioned to regard as long past. In the work of terror, history and memory are no longer stable; or rather, they are stripped of the illusion of stability and continuity, and we find ourselves in a darker world where we can no longer control the boundary between inner and outer.

DAVID PUNTER

The Uncanny *see Unheimlich*

Vampire

It is probably not an exaggeration to suggest that the modern, non-scholarly, conception of the vampire is both primarily visual and, in consequence, indebted to cinematic adaptations of **BRAM STOKER**'s 1897 novel *Dracula*. The stylistic consistency of film portrayals of the vampire Count, by actors from Bela Lugosi to Christopher Lee, Frank Langella and Gary Oldman, has concretised a cultural image of the vampire as saturnine, noble, sophisticated, mesmeric and, above all, erotic. The prevalence and popularity of this perception effectively restricts access to the literary vampire, in that the acceleration of Count Dracula into an archetype has been at the expense of characterisations located elsewhere in literature and folk culture. The eroticisation of the vampire, similarly, has effectively almost eclipsed the alternative significations invested in the trope. In consequence, the vampire has become arguably no more than a subject for popular fiction and soft-core pornography, a focus for ephemeral 'Goth' subcultures, an expression of meanings apparently beneath the serious consideration of the critical establishment.

The vampire, however, has a long history, both as a literary device and as a signifier in culture. Much of the power of the trope is derived from the intimate relationship between vampires and blood. As Foucault asserts in *The History of Sexuality*, blood has traditionally operated as 'a reality with a symbolic function', a substance which is simultaneously both a literal and figurative source of power. Blood is, culturally as well as textually, an item of multidiscursive significance, a fluid which may signify at various times notions of family, race, religion, and gender. The fluid nature of blood makes both the substance and its meanings peculiarly vulnerable. It is, as Foucault suggests, easily spilled, mixed or diluted. Unmingled, it is the guarantor of purity, and thus of strength – a strength which may be desired by others beyond the circle (or circulation) of one's 'own' blood. Diluted or depleted it may signify simultaneously personal lassitude alongside racial, familial, or moral decline and degeneration. Transferred or transfused by medical, occult or sexual means (where the shedding of hymenal blood initiates a sexual encounter), it may either revive or prostrate. The individual may thus function as a synecdoche of a greater community united by encodings invested within a common blood. The vampire in this context constitutes a node at which significations both meet and are modified following their contact with their place of conjunction, the vampire itself.

The subscript of these encodings is the subtle cultural equation of blood and semen – the figurative and literal carriers of racial and individual qualities. Both fluids have been historically encompassed by religious and cultural taboos restricting their dispersal beyond the internal circulation of the body. Medicine in mid- to late-Victorian Britain in particular linked the two reciprocally in the so-called 'spermatic economy', where the excessive or unnecessary 'spending' of semen brought in consequence a decline in the vitality of the sanguine fluid. Unmentionable in normal communication beyond restricted cultural arenas such as medicine, religion and education, the seminal fluid is thus conflated with an acceptable and associated bodily secretion. This conflation is, for both writers and critics of vampire fiction, an opportunity to effectively eroticise the text. In the late twentieth century, however, the erotic as a constant in the portrayal or criticism of fictional vampirism has become, like the author in Foucault's 'What is an Author?', a functional principle by which the potential signification of the text may be restricted.

Many of the attributes and restrictions which today characterise the fictional vampire are derived not directly from folklore, but from eighteenth-century behavioural studies of the peoples of eastern Europe, published for a western European readership. However, these works consistently portray the vampire (variously identified as a *revenant, upir, nosferatu* or *vrykolakas*) as a peasant who preys almost exclusively upon his immediate family and near neighbours. In contrast to his cinematic counterpart, the folkloric vampire frequently exhibits a swollen, bloated body and displays a ruddy or livid face, discoloured through the posthumous accumulation of blood. The canine teeth, too, are seldom described as prominent. Though possibly inducted into vampirism through the bite of another vampire, he is as likely to have been an apostate or excommunicated Christian, the victim of a murder or sudden death, or a werewolf, during his lifetime. His vampiric condition, notably, does not appear to damn his soul, as is explicitly the case in Stoker's *Dracula*. Only the method of disposal has survived without serious modification in its modern guise. According to Dom Augustine Calmet, author of the influential though frequently sceptical *Traité sur les Apparitions des Esprits et sur les Vampires* (Paris 1746), the only sure method of ending a vampire epidemic is to 'cut off their head, impale them, burn them, or pierce their heart'.

The work of Calmet and his contemporaries is, in essence, a form of nascent anthropology, which makes stylistic use of the framing of a detached and frequently sceptical authorial or editorial voice and supports its contentions through the authority of published documents and testimonies, especially where these are further valorised by the signatures of medical or military witnesses. This rationalist and frequently legalistic framing was suppressed during the transition of the vampire from anthropology to poetry under the European Romantics of the late eighteenth century. The **STURM UND DRANG** preoccupations of German poetry in particular linked the vampire with the demon lover or the spectral bride. August Bürger's *Lenore* (1774) and **JOHANN WOLFGANG VON GOETHE**'s *Die Braut von Korinth* (1797), among other works, influenced the earliest British writings in the field, from Samuel Taylor Coleridge's *Christabel* (1816), to Robert Southey's *Thalaba the Destroyer* (1801), John Stagg's 'The Vampyre' (in *The Minstrel of the North*) and John Keats's *Lamia* (1819), (see **ROMANTICISM**).

The British Romantic conception of the vampire is, however, indebted in particular to the writings of George Gordon, Lord Byron, and to the cult of the Byronic Hero which the poet actively fostered around his own behaviour. Byron's published contribution to the development of the literary vampire comes surprisingly late in the evolution of the myth. *The Giaour* (1813) scripts the vampire as a Gothic **HERO-VILLAIN**, cursed to wander forever without hope of forgiveness, loathing the very sustenance which prolongs his existence, and doomed to drain the blood of his female relations. Though other authors did not respond readily to Byron's recoding of vampirism as a form of incest, the suggestion of the vampire as sexual predator was by this time already well established.

Drawing on his experiences with Byron and his associates at the Villa Diodati three years earlier, the poet's former physician, Dr John Polidori, published a novella, *The Vampyre*, in the *New Monthly Magazine* for April 1819. Polidori's vampire, Lord Ruthven, bore the name with which Byron's former lover Lady Caroline Lamb lampooned the poet in her novel *Glenarvon*. Significantly, Ruthven pursued a conventional sexual career as a seducer parallel to his occult thirst for blood. Mistakenly attributed to Byron, *The Vampyre* was rapidly translated into French. This translation in turn inspired an anonymous two-volume sequel, *Lord Ruthwen, ou Les Vampires*, published in France in 1820. This latter work, by Cyprien Bérard, was in turn often mistakenly attributed to Charles Nodier, whose play *Le Vampire* opened in Paris later the same year. The melodramatic vampire dramas of Nodier, James Planché, Dion Boucicault, and Alexandre Dumas among others, made the literary vampire accessible to a non-literate audience, and, it may be argued, facilitated the final eclipse of the folkloric equivalent.

The popularity of the literary vampire in this period generated, in the first instance, short rather than novelistic fiction, with the works of E. T. A. **HOFFMANN** (*The Serapion Brethren*, 1820), Prosper Mérimé (*La Guzla*, 1827) and **EDGAR ALLAN POE** (*Berenice*, 1833) receiving in particular popular acclaim. Already an established component of the '**PENNY DREADFUL**' school of London journalism, the vampire became in the 1840s the subject of a remarkable 109-part serial, *Varney the Vampyre; or, The Feast of Blood*, subsequently reprinted as an 800-page novel. Attributed in the twentieth century to James Malcolm Rymer, the novel constructed the vampire, Sir Francis Varney, as a dissolute and cursed aristocrat with a penchant for attractive young women. *Varney the Vampyre* makes frequent use of Romantic devices, including isolated houses, thunderstorms, and swooning heroines. The vampire himself is skeletal and pale, with bestial fangs and metallic, though hypnotic, eyes. Before his self-inflicted destruction in the crater of Vesuvius, Varney expresses a sense of repulsion at his dependence upon human blood, a gesture which links him to Byron's giaour rather than to Polidori's Lord Ruthven.

The Romantic domination of the stylistics of vampire fiction was arguably challenged in 1871 by the serial publication of 'Carmilla', a vampire novella by JOSEPH SHERIDAN LE FANU. Modern critical studies have directed attention primarily to the undercurrents of lesbianism that may be traced in the relationship between the vampire, Carmilla, and the narrator, Laura. However, it is equally notable that the republication of the work in Le Fanu's 1872 anthology, *In A Glass Darkly*, made full use of a framing of medical case work, and of a series of prologues penned by the fictional editor. Significantly, the framing fails adequately to contain or comprehend the occult nature of the narratives it encloses. Though the vampire has become subject to the discourses of medicine and psychopathology, it remains apparent that science holds but part of the explanation, and even less of the cure.

Similar sentiments, of course, punctuate *Dracula*, although the testimonial structure of Stoker's 1897 novel recalls, in addition, the value of documentation as well as testimony in legal discourse. Count Dracula, it might be added, makes his initial approaches to England through legal means, utilising the services of a solicitor and the technology of a carrier and shipping agent. The vampire is thus not merely draining the blood of a series of individuals, but drawing on the gaps left by the discourses of modern society, the greed of certain classes or races, and the general incredulity of a secular age. A social message is thus encoded within the implicit medical script of depletion and transfusion which arguably rationalises the vampire's actions in the novel. The vampiric process is not merely one of drainage, but of osmosis also. As sustenance is taken out, degeneration is injected in, and the widening circle of vampires represents the gradual decline of the host race. In an age of pogroms and mass-immigration into Britain, the potential racist connotations of the vampire metaphor become seemingly unavoidable.

The popularity of the vampire as a motif peculiarly adapted to the decadent preoccupations of the *fin de siècle* ensured its survival in literature generally to the outbreak of the First World War. Rudyard Kipling adapted the motif to an era of growing female militancy in his 1897 poem 'The Vampire', a work which generated much of the cultural concept of the cinematic Vamp of the immediately pre- and post-war years. Reginald Hodder's 1913 novel *The Vampire* inserted a literal vampire into a plot again based upon a powerful female, this time an initiate in an occult organisation. Though the aftermath of the War did not halt the output of vampire fiction, a perceptible decrease in quantity was noted as the periodical press contracted. Much of the vampire fiction published in the inter-war years, by authors such as Manly Wade

Wellman, Catherine L. Moore, and August Derleth, appeared first in the United States, often in popular journals such as *Weird Tales,* and frequently with themes drawn from science fiction. Much of this material was anthologised in Britain and the United States throughout the 1950s and 1960s, frequently in conjunction with newer works by writers such as the British author Ronald Chetwynd-Hayes.

The vampire fiction of the closing three decades of the twentieth century has, to a great extent, been shaped by the development of novels arranged in series based on the adventures of a single vampire character – for example, le Comte de Saint-Germain, in the cycle of novels by Chelsea Quinn Yarbro, or Lestat de Lioncourt, in ANNE RICE's series *The Vampire Chronicles.* In most cycles based on this theme, a chronological sequence is followed, the vampire's encounters with humanity and other vampires being charted from a period nominally near the late eighteenth century to the present day. Voyages in either direction between Europe and America frequently punctuate these narratives, and the characters often encounter the same associates or adversaries at several times during their vampiric careers. The individual novels frequently script the characters as being fully aware of the restrictions placed by fiction upon their type, only to have the vampires ridicule them as the products of superstition or fiction.

Erotic encodings and imagery, as has been suggested, now constitute an almost invariable accompaniment to any act of vampirism in contemporary fiction. Recent writings, such as 'Wanting' (1994) by Amelia G., have occasionally developed the notion of vampirism as an erotic act in conventional, mortal sexual activity, often in response to the development of 'Goth' subcultures, and particularly in the portrayal of same-sex relationships. The erotic investment in occult vampirism, however, has become increasingly problematic in contemporary fiction, largely because of changes in the cultural valorisation of blood. This problematisation is perhaps most evident in Poppy Z. Brite's 1992 novel *Lost Souls.* Brite's vampires engage in vampirism as a sado-masochistic rite to be enjoyed parallel to conventional sexual activity, although they retain a dependence on blood as food. Identified as a separate species by Brite, they reproduce sexually, rather than through the act of vampirism. Yet their victims persist in retaining notions of seduction into undeath, of an ultimate spiritual meaning coded into the draining of blood. To Brite's vampires, blood is nothing more than food. It has no spiritual or reproductive value. The trope, arguably, has turned full circle to return to the attitude adopted by Calmet's materialistic peasant-vampires in the eighteenth century.

WILLIAM HUGHES

Walpole, Horace, Earl of Orford (1717–97)

Horace Walpole is an important figure not only for Gothic fiction, but for the eighteenth-century **GOTHIC REVIVAL** in all its aspects. He is best known as the author of the first Gothic Novel, *The Castle of Otranto* (1764) and for his house at Strawberry Hill in Twickenham, which was the most complete and authentic neo-Gothic structure existing at the time. But he was also responsible for the first Gothic drama, *The Mysterious Mother* (1768), and wrote a number of scholarly but readable books on the art, letters, architecture and history of the Middle Ages, that had a considerable impact on contemporary taste. What makes Walpole distinctive among the antiquarians of the day is the fact that he did not treat the relics of the past as objects of dry curiosity. His approach was always that of an amateur in the most passionate sense. And his elevated social standing helped to increase his influence with the reading public.

He was born on 24 September 1717, the third son and sixth child of the powerful Whig politician Sir Robert Walpole. In 1721 his father was elevated to the position of prime minister, and there he remained, in defiance of fierce opposition, for the next 21 years. Horace's childhood and youth was consequently passed in an atmosphere of public dignity. At Eton he was schooled in the Classics and made a number of life-long friends. Among them was the future poet Thomas Gray, and it was with Gray that Walpole journeyed on a Grand Tour culminating in Italy, where he dutifully admired the classical ruins and began to collect Roman coins. By the time he returned to England he had already been elected an MP, representing Castle Rising near the family estate in Norfolk. Pale, slight, with a thin voice, he was not destined to cut much of a figure in Parliament. While he maintained for many years a fascination with political wheeling and dealing, and occasionally intervened in debates in an indirect way, he resolved to make his mark in other fields.

Letter-writing was the first focus for his energies. He had early felt a sense of his talents in this direction, and for the rest of his life maintained a copious correspondence with a select few, and occasional exchanges with many others. He wrote with a view to posthumous publication, and made sure that almost all his letters and most of his correspondents' were preserved. The monumental Yale edition of his correspondence, begun in 1937 and completed in 1983, runs to 48 large volumes. It is a treasure trove for any student of eighteenth-century Gothic; his exchanges with his antiquarian friends the Reverend William Cole and William Marshall deserve special attention.

Walpole's conversion to Gothic seems to have been sudden. In the summer of 1749 he made the first of many tours around the country, visiting ruins, old churches and country houses and making detailed records of their structures and contents. In autumn of the same year he announced to astonished friends his decision to reconstruct Strawberry Hill in the Gothic style. At the time, Gothic was just one of a number of exotic modes used for garden follies or indoor ornament, and Chinese was more the fashion. But Walpole persisted, and went on altering and adding over the years until the original box was transformed into an irregular edifice double the size, featuring battlements, pinnacles, arched windows, a gallery, a cloister, and two imposing towers, all executed with an authenticity till then unknown, and before long Strawberry Hill was becoming a destination for day-trippers. Eventually the stream of visitors grew so intrusive that Walpole laid down rules for entry, and prepared *A Description of Strawberry Hill* to serve as a guidebook.

His Gothic interests expanded into learned publications on early English letters, painting and architecture, and a polemical essay in defence of Richard III. But he always insisted that his researches were merely a pastime, and in 1757 established his own Strawberry Hill Press as if to emphasise his amateur status.

As a young man Walpole had written some light poetry addressed to friends, and a small selection was published at his Strawberry Hill Press. Later he wrote some short satires, which were produced as pamphlets. But nothing in his previous work anticipated his sole experiment in the novel form, *The Castle of Otranto*. It is set in a Southern Italian principality in the period of the Crusades, and concerns the fate of the family of Prince Manfred, over whom hangs a prophecy that they will lose the castle *'whenever the real owner should be grown too large to inhabit it'*. The marriage ceremony of Manfred's only son and heir unleashes a riot of supernatural occurrences. Young Conrad is crushed beneath a huge helmet, servants are terrified by glimpses of gigantic limbs, a portrait comes to life and a statue bleeds. Meanwhile Manfred grows in villainy as he attempts to restore his fortunes by divorcing his virtuous wife Hippolyta and marrying the bride intended for Conrad, and his daughter Matilda falls in love with a handsome young peasant who bears a mysterious resemblance to the last of the original line of princes. A tale of usurpation is eventually uncovered, Matilda is accidentally murdered by her father, Manfred and Hippolyta retire to convents, and the rightful heir takes possession of his inheritance.

Extravagant though the plot summary sounds, the story is in fact delivered in a light and often witty style, prompting some critics to interpret it as a burlesque. The novel was first published on Christmas Eve, 1764, in an edition of 500 copies. Walpole was nervous about the reception 'of so wild a tale', and presented it in the Preface as an antique work of Catholic propaganda, translated from Italian. But favourable reviews and good sales encouraged him, in the second edition, of April 1765, to acknowledge it as a 'new species of romance' and offer it as a model for 'men of brighter talents'. To this second edition he added the subtitle 'A Gothic Story'. Clara Reeve took up the challenge with *The Old English Baron* (1778), and in 1781 a stage version by Robert Jephson entitled *The Count of Narbonne* was produced with success, but it was not until the 1790s that the Gothic Novel was properly launched. **ANN RADCLIFFE** and **MATTHEW LEWIS** were by this time more important influences, but in 1811 Walter Scott wrote a highly appreciative Introduction to a new edition of the novel, and it has retained a reputation as the founding text of the genre.

Encouraged by the outcome of his first Gothic experiment, in 1766 Walpole began writing *The Mysterious Mother*, a tragic drama set in the period before the Reformation. But when it was eventually printed at the Strawberry Hill Press in 1768, only fifty copies were made, to be circulated among friends. The author's reticence on this occasion was apparently owing to the impropriety of the work. The *primum mobile* of the tragedy is incest. The widowed Countess of Narbonne has exiled her son Edmund for unknown reason, and leads a life of penitence for a crime which she refuses to confess to the sinister priest Benedict. Secretly Edmund returns, and with the connivance of the suspecting priest, meets and weds Adeliza, the beautiful young ward of his mother who is residing in a convent. It finally emerges that many years before, the Countess had received, on the same evening, news of her husband's death and of her son's liaison with a maidservant. She had disguised herself as the servant and, overcome by his resemblance to his father, had given way to passion; Adeliza was the consequence of their union. The Countess, on discovering the marriage of her children, kills herself, Adeliza retires once more to a nunnery, and Edmund, desolate, returns to the army.

The Mysterious Mother was the first of a genre of Gothic dramas, neither as numerous nor as well known today as their novelistic counterparts. It includes A. McDonald's *Vimonda* (1788), *The Mysterious Marriage; or, The Hermitage of Rosalva* (1798) by Harriet Lee, and Lewis's *The Castle Spectre* (1798). But in this instance Walpole's influence was limited by self-censorship. The play was never performed and had a clandestine reputation, attracting some praise and much opprobrium. Indeed, half a century later its aura was sufficiently sulphurous for Lord Byron to reprove its neglect and commend it as 'a tragedy of the highest order, and not a puling love-play' (Preface to *Marino Faliero*, 1821).

His final literary effort was *Hieroglyphic Tales* (1785), published at Strawberry Hill in an edition of just six copies, a collection of six whimsical stories somewhat in the style of the *Arabian Nights*. Free invention could go no further. While they could not be classified as Gothic by their setting, themes or mood, they do rely on effects of exaggeration and disproportion as *The Castle of Otranto* had done, and in them Walpole's taste for extreme situations is taken to ludicrous lengths. 'The King and His Three Daughters', for example, concerns a romance between the eldest princess, who 'was extremely handsome, had a great deal of wit, and spoke French to perfection' but never existed, and the Prince of Quifferiquimini, 'who would have been the most accomplished hero of the age, if he had not been dead' and sets a fashion for cadaverousness at court.

E. J. CLERY

Wandering Jew (Ahasuerus)

The Legend of the Wandering Jew has as its nucleus a narrative motif which exists throughout the Western world and the Orient in almost all ethnic communities. It deals with a person who has committed a serious transgression against the basic and sacred values (of a simpler, rudimentary type) of human society, i.e. an outrageous murder and/or an act of blasphemy. His punishment is restless exile for an almost infinite time. He has to wander on earth at least for several human life spans or centuries until his crime is atoned for or someone has taken the burden on him/herself. Under a similar predicament are the figures of the 'Wild Huntsman', the 'Flying Dutchman' and Cain with Grendel, his monstrous descendant in Old English mythology.

The Legend of the Wandering Jew went through several modifications and variations. The starting point was given in the gospels of St Matthew (xvi:28) and of St John (xxi:22–3) in the reports of Christ's condemnation, torture and crucifixion. Both evangelists write that an officer hit Jesus with his hand. The stories derived from that, depict this man either as a boundless violator of God's majesty, or as a poor sinner, or as a wicked heathen, or even as a Jew. His name is 'Cartaphilus' or 'Buttadeus'/'Botadeo', i.e. the God-striker. After his baptism he carries the name Joseph. In the High Middle Ages this narrative reaches Italy (1223). In the year 1228 the story reappears in the Anglo-Latin chronicle entitled *Flores Historiarum* written by Roger of Wendover, a monk in St Albans. Here Jesus is said to have answered to Cartaphilus: 'I am going, and you will wait till I return.' An echo of this version seems to be the old man in Chaucer's *Pardoner's Tale*, who implores the earth in vain to let him in. French, Spanish and Italian sources of the following centuries then emphasise and elaborate on the psychological and physical tortures of the Wandering Jew's existence, thus preparing it for the Gothic inventory.

In the Reformation Age, the subsequent religious wars and in the context of the military threat to Europe by the Turks, new aspects are developed. A German pamphlet (1602) speaks of the *'Eternal* Jew' [der *ewige* Jude]. He is described as being 60 years old, with wild hair, a long grey beard, badly torn clothes, and he is now called Ahasherus – a name typifying Jews in general. This notion entered into the *Volksbuch* (popular story-book for the just literate) of *Ahasuerus* and found wide acceptance so that it also turned up in ballads and songs not only in Germany but all over Europe. In England, for example, it took the form of a ballad, *The Wandering Jew; or The Shoemaker of Jerusalem* (1625), or a comedy by Andrew Franklin, *The Wandering Jew; or, Love's Masquerade* (1797).

Probably the most significant factor behind the Renaissance and the Reformation is the discovery of the 'individual'. Around the middle of the eighteenth century then – the time when the Industrial Revolution had its take-off – this process had gone so far as to effect a restructuring of the Western societies under the aspect of *individual* needs and abilities while the traditional religious beliefs were still holding on. The intellectual and psychological consequences of this are thematised in what is called the Age of Romanticism. Here, then, the Legend of the Wandering/Eternal Jew, as well as the similar story of Dr Faustus, made it possible to express the situation of a suffering, homeless individual of high moral and social responsibility, who has to live without the support of transcendental beliefs. The 'lyrical rhapsody' *Der ewige Jude* (1783), written by the German pre-Romantic (**'STURM UND DRANG'**) poet Christian Schubart, shows all the elements which are later attributed to the homeless, loveless, intellectually and aesthetically highly aware, guilt-ridden and suicidal individual of Lord Byron's works, such as *Childe Harold* and *Don Juan* ('Byronic Hero').

In **M. G. LEWIS**'s Gothic novel *The Monk* (1795) the Wandering Jew appears in the sub-story of 'Raymond and Agnes'. A new feature is the Jew's compulsive, magnetic eye. St Leon, the hero of William Godwin's novel of the same name, is a combination of Faustus, Ahasuerus and Cagliostro, a notorious eighteenth-century adventurer. **SHELLEY** makes Ahasuerus complain about God's tyranny in *Queen Mab* (1813). He also deals with that figure in *Hellas* (1822) and in *The Wandering Jew's Soliloquy* (published posthumously in 1887). Wordsworth wrote the poem *The Wandering Jew*. A widely known embodiment and surely the most Gothic version of the Wandering Jew motif seems to be **MATURIN**'s hero in *Melmoth the Wanderer* (1820), who combines Dr Faustus, Mephisto/ Lucifer, and Ahasuerus. In France we find Caigniez's melodrama *Le Juif errant* (1812). In 1844–5 there was Eugène Sue's very popular novel of the same title, and then came Halévy's opera *Le Juif errant* (1852), which is based on a libretto by Eugène Scribe. Even Leopold Bloom, the Jewish hero of James Joyce's *Ulysses*, is part of the Wandering Jew tradition.

Edwin Arlington Robinson's poem *The Wandering Jew* offers a summing up of all the aspects attributed to that character. The Wandering Jew stands for a mind depressed by human suffering, also for the suffering inflicted by society, for the search for an absconded God, and for the immense difficulties of striving for self-realisation, in an individual or in a group-specific sense. In order to thematise further aspects of such an existence, the nineteenth century began to attribute a female companion to the Wandering Jew: Herodias (Eugène Sue) or Salomé (George S. Viereck: *Salomé: The Wandering Jewess*, 1930).

The motif of the Wandering Jew and its perpetuating as well as its changing implications bear witness to most of the major intellectual developments of the last two thousand years. The disappearance of that motif in our present age may result from the emergence of a more concrete and factual picture of the Jewish people and from a weakening of the traditional religious and ethnic stereotypes. It may also be due to the impact of the modern media, and of course to the images and experience presented by an internationally significant Jewish (especially Jewish-American) literature.

HANS-ULRICH MOHR

Welsh Gothic

In the *Mabinogi* (the four great chronicles of the lives of mythical Welsh wizards and princes), collected and scribed in the early Middle Ages, there are grotesqueries and transmogrifications galore. Men and women turn into owls, eagles, wolves, deer and wild boars, and in one tale a giant taloned claw reaches in through a castle window to steal the baby prince Pryderi from his mother's chamber.

With such a store of weird and darkly inventive folklore, one might imagine that Wales would have gone on to contribute something to the later Gothic literature of Britain. But by the eighteenth and nineteenth centuries when the new Gothic Novels were in vogue in England, Wales was in the thrall of Nonconformist religious fervour, which repressed much of its people's natural passion for drama and storytelling. Indeed the only Welsh writer to contribute works of note to the Gothic tradition, **ARTHUR MACHEN** left his native Monmouthshire for London before penning his tales of **THE OCCULT** and **THE SUPERNATURAL**.

In parts of South Wales in the nineteenth century tales were recorded of vampire beds and chairs which attacked and drew blood from their occupiers. Interestingly, and perhaps appositely enough, the favoured victims of these furnitures were visiting ministers and vicars.

SION EIRIAN

Werewolf *see* Lycanthropy

Wilde, Oscar (1854–1900)

Wilde's most characteristic mode is playful and anti-serious, what Susan Sontag has described as 'camp', and nowhere is this better exemplified than in his best known and most successful work, *The Importance of Being Earnest* (1895). Nevertheless, the text which first made Wilde's literary reputation (during the late 1880s Wilde was famous simply for being famous), the novel *The Picture of Dorian Gray* (1891), is a sustained exercise in portentousness which combines the conventions of Gothic fiction with melodrama and Wilde's distinctive wit.

In effect, *Dorian Gray* is a late Victorian version of '**CONTEMPORARY GOTHIC**'. Wilde had already parodied the well-used devices of Gothic fiction in his comic short story 'The Canterville Ghost' (1891); in *Dorian Gray*, however, the super-sophisticated surfaces of life in the imperial metropolis at the century's end are interrogated by the Gothic narrative. Dorian enters into a Faustian bargain: as he remains perpetually young, so his portrait ages. Wilde delivers here his own idiosyncratic reworking of the *DOPPELGÄNGER* motif and it is interesting to note that one of the literary analogues for the novel is **EDGAR ALLAN POE**'s story of 'doubling', *William Wilson*. Dorian is Wilde's version of the Gothic over-reacher exemplified by Drs Frankenstein and Jekyll (see **MARY SHELLEY** and **ROBERT LOUIS STEVENSON**) and his fate is to fall prey to retributive justice as the past visits judgement on the present. (Dorian is pursued by a modern Fury in the shape of James Vane, and dies by his own hand.) In this respect, Wilde manipulates the narrative in much the same way as his fellow Irishman **J. SHERIDAN LE FANU** in his stories of the supernatural, one of which, 'Strange Event in the Life of Schalken the Painter', may well have had a formative influence on Wilde's novel. The generally sensationalist atmosphere of the book is maintained by Wilde's lurid, and frequently overwritten, descriptions of

Dorian's mounting terror in front of his portrait, and of London (in particular the East End and its denizens) as menacing and murderous.

In lectures, reviews and articles written during the 1880s Wilde outlined an aesthetic theory which was fundamentally anti-naturalistic; it was also Janus-faced, anticipating in its awareness of the self-referentiality of language and art some of the central tenets of the cultural criticism of our own time, and simultaneously looking back to progenitors such as Gautier, Baudelaire, Poe and Whistler. Wilde's use of the Gothic in *Dorian Gray* is clearly part of his anti-naturalistic project, matching fictive practice to aesthetic theory: it sanctions Wilde's desire to write about 'modern life' (and modish notions of cultural and ethical decadence) without simply 'mirroring' it. (In the Preface to *Dorian Gray* he claims that it is the spectator and not life that art really mirrors.) Indeed, the relationship between the portrait and its subject provides a Gothic and supernatural twist to the central theoretical paradox in Wilde's essay 'The Decay of Lying' (1891): that art is more 'life-like' (the portrait is process, it grows old) than nature, 'the real thing' (Dorian seems to enjoy the immutable beauty of the art-object).

Wilde's interest in, and manipulation of, **THE SUPERNATURAL** may have derived from the Irish oral story-telling tradition of which he was a part: many contemporaries noted the brilliance of his conversation, which sometimes improvised versions of what were to become his fairy-tales. On his release from prison in 1897, after two years of hard labour, Wilde fled England for Europe under the apparently unlikely alias of Sebastian Melmoth. This combined a reference to his favourite saint with a typically theatrical and paradoxical statement of both his exile and his national roots. **CHARLES MATURIN** was a distant relative of Wilde's and by adopting the name of the wandering 'hero' of Maturin's novel, thus casting himself to Gothic type, Wilde acknowledged both his outcast status and, obliquely, his Irishness. His connection with the **IRISH GOTHIC** tradition is completed circumstantially: as a young man he had courted Florence Balcombe, who later married **BRAM STOKER**. It has been suggested that the London prostitutes who danced in provocative celebration at Wilde's conviction provided Stoker with the inspiration for his representation of female vampires.

Clearly, Wilde's use of Gothic convention in *Dorian Gray* acquires a particular frisson in the light of his own dangerous personal circumstances: the thrills and terrors of the homosexual double life, which he likened to 'feasting with panthers', are both indulged and objectified – in effect, *aestheticised* – by the Gothic manner as Wilde flirts with his readers and the possibility of confessional disclosure. (With Lord Henry Wotton and Basil Hallward, the 'artists' who bring him to consciousness of his beauty, Dorian makes up a thinly concealed love-triangle.) Wilde's preface to the novel, with its central contention that ethical judgements should not be applied to art-objects in general, and novels in particular, is in many ways an amoral corrective to the narrative trajectory of his tale. Nevertheless, the punishment which Dorian incurs has an undeniable prophetic piquancy for Wilde, who claimed that men pay for their mistakes, and then they pay again.

NEIL SAMMELLS

Witches and Witchcraft

From about 1400 to 1700, the belief in and persecution of witches in Western Europe and America brought Gothic themes to horrific life. Innocent people, predominantly women, were accused of pacts with Satan then immured, tortured, and burned. The transcripts of their confessions tell of hauntings, omens, dreams, family curses, conspiracies, and betrayals. Yet the witch belief was not central to the first Gothic revival, nor are witches common protagonists in modern horror. Still, witches – mainly female, imagined and historical – have played the following roles in Gothic literature: divination; communing with spirits of the dead; maleficia and heresy; sexual magic; healing and white magic. More recently, fantastic literature and life have seen the advent of the 'Neo-Pagan' or Goddess-worshipping witch. All these functions, while usually represented as medieval in origin, can be found in the archetypes of Classical witchcraft, Circe and Medea.

Divination, foretelling future events, is the province of the seeress or sibyl (and of *Macbeth*'s Weird Sisters). In Salem Village, Massachusetts, in 1692, the girls' desire to divine the identity of their future husbands seems to have been at the root of the witchcraft outbreak. Fortune-telling is as useful a plot device for the Gothic as it was for Greek tragedy. This function is often assigned to Gypsies, as in **LEWIS**'s *The Monk* (1796), where a Gypsy predicts Antonia's fate and the outcome of the novel.

In the female tradition, the medium's communion with spirits seems to be instinctive rather than studied, as was the male practice of **NECRO-MANCY** (see **WIZARDS**). The Biblical Witch of Endor was a spirit medium, producing apparitions of the Prophet Samuel. In the nineteenth century, earlier witch beliefs were ascribed to mediums, after the advent of the Fox Sisters and the rise of a religion of **SPIRITUALISM**. Spiritualist literature, however, tended to be anti-Gothic, benignly viewing spectres and death; heaven looked like New England in Elizabeth Stuart Phelps's mid-century *The Gates Ajar*.

The commonest function of the witch in Western literature is *maleficia* or black magic. The plot device of the 'witch's curse' became a Gothic cliché, satirised by Gilbert and Sullivan in *Ruddigore* (1887). **HAWTHORNE** in *The House of the Seven Gables* (1851) ascribed the ancestral curse on the Pyncheons to a male: Wizard Maule. The words were actually recorded in 1692 from the condemned Salem witch Sarah Good, 'If you take my life away, God will give you blood to drink.' Witches of this type were considered heretics, deriving their powers from Satan. They were said to worship in orgiastic sabbats such as the one on the Brocken in Goethe's *Faust*.

If the cursing witch is pictured as an ancient crone, the other incarnation of malefic witchcraft is an alluring young woman, the temptress or *'belle dame sans merci'*. A common accusation during Renaissance witch-hunts was that witches caused impotence in godly men, and used their sexuality to recruit the less godly. Matilda, the lustful nun of *The Monk*, is a subordinate devil or succubus. The witch as sexual temptress may also be envisioned as the lamia, with her serpent associations, or the vampire, a literal or spiritual life-drinker. Coleridge's Geraldine, Keats's *Belle Dame*, and **LE FANU**'s Carmilla exemplify these types (see **LAMIA, RO-MANTICISM, VAMPIRE**).

In most cultures, the folkloric witch or wise woman performs white magic. Functions include healing the sick with herbs, acting as midwife, and performing abortions. In Europe, these village healers were targets of Renaissance witch-hunts. Such relatively benign images are less common in Gothic literature. Witches from non-Western cultures demonstrate these powers in stories about the Lapps by Isak Dinesen and Jonas Lie, and in tales with African or West Indian settings.

In the twentieth century, Margaret Murray's theory that ancient paganism survived in Western Europe in the form of witch cults led to the founding of modern *wicca* or Neo-Paganism. While Murray's world-view is most evident in fantasy, such as Marion Zimmer Bradley's recasting of Arthurian legend in *The Mists of Avalon* (1982), modern Gothic literature shows the changing image of witchcraft in works such as Fritz Leiber's *Conjure Wife* (1953), the occult novels of Dion Fortune, Kathryn Kurtz's *Lammas Night*, and **ANNE RICE**'s series on the Mayfair Witches.

Though the persecution of witches has often been rationalised in historical fiction, there are Gothic treatments of the subject: for the English witch trials, Harrison Ainsworth's *The Lancashire Witches*, and for the Continent, Wilhelm Meinhold's *The Amber Witch* (Lady Duff Gordon's translation, 1846). In the United States, most treatments of the Salem outbreak of 1692–3 have been resolutely anti-Gothic, but exceptions include Hawthorne's 'Young Goodman Brown' (1835), H. P. Lovecraft's 'Dreams in the Witch House' (1932), and the French Caribbean Maryse Condé's *I, Tituba, Black Witch of Salem* (1992).

FAYE RINGEL

Wizards

In archetypal theory, the wizard Merlin represents Jung's Wise Old Man. Gothic tradition favours the Shadow of this archetype: Faust. In Gothic, wizards are scholarly, amoral, power-hungry – Promethean. They derive their power equally from Satan and from Science.

For the Middle Ages and Renaissance, magic and science were one: mathematician was synonymous with wizard. Popular imagination and established religion, however, attributed such knowledge to one source: Satan. Like Faust, Gothic wizards were assumed to have bartered their souls for knowledge and power. They were not the only ones: in folklore, witches, New England Yankees, and Scots have been accused of the Satanic bargain.

Faust and Victor Frankenstein, however, were Gothic heroes (see **HERO-VILLAIN**). Nurtured on the Renaissance science of Paracelsus and Albertus Magnus, their quests were the same: eternal life and un-bounded knowledge of nature's secrets. Thus the archetypal wizard is also the 'mad scientist'. The later Promethean experimenters – **HAWTHORNE**'s Rappaccini, **STEVENSON**'s Dr Jekyll, H. G. Wells's Moreau – form the link between Gothic tradition and science fiction (see **GOTHIC SCIENCE FICTION**).

Wizards and mad scientists sought to create willing servants or protec-tors, as in the Jewish legends of Rabbi Loew and the **GOLEM** of Prague. The oldest version of this tale may be 'The Sorcerer's Apprentice', first recorded by Lucian in ancient Greece, more familiar to us through Mickey Mouse's adventure in Disney's *Fantasia*. Victor Frankenstein's creation was originally intended as a servant to mankind. Failing a magical creation, wizards usually have human helpers who are not much smarter than their robot-like counterparts. The twisted, dwarfed, or morally-twisted helper has a long lineage in Gothic, from Faust's *famulus* Wagner, through Dracula's mad Renfield, to the 'Igors' of modern horror film.

Wizards wrote their secrets in *grimoires*, books of black magic like the one in which **LEWIS**'s Ambrosio fumbled over the right page to call up Lucifer. Such books of secret lore, lost and rediscovered manuscripts, are a Gothic staple used by many authors including **EDGAR ALLAN POE**,

Robert Chambers, and **M. R. JAMES. H. P. LOVECRAFT**'s invented *Necronomicon* has acquired a life and history of its own.

In addition to mad scientific experimenters, post-medieval wizards can be found in the shape of conjurers, jugglers, hypnotists, and ventriloquists, like the 'biloquist' Carwin of *Wieland; or, The Transformation* (1798) (see **CHARLES BROCKDEN BROWN**). Mingling science with rumours of Satanism, the hypnotist Mesmer enthralled Paris during the Revolution, and inspired many Gothic hero-villains, notably George Du Maurier's Svengali. Also arising from the Revolutionary period were fears of secret societies such as the **ILLUMINATI** and the **ROSICRUCIANS** as embodied in the **NORTHANGER NOVEL** *Horrid Mysteries* (1796) and **BULWER-LYTTON**'s *Zanoni* (1842).

The greatest achievements of medieval and Renaissance wizards were divination or prophecy and necromancy, conjuring up the spirits of the dead (see **WITCHES**). John Dee, the real Dr Faustus, and Nostradamus, still famous for these deeds, lived in fear of heresy charges from civil authorities or the Inquisition, as did Ambrosio of *The Monk* (1796). Kahlert's *The Necromancer* (1794), a *Northanger* novel, details German medieval traditions. The **WANDERING JEW** (who appears in *The Monk*) and Maturin's *Melmoth the Wanderer* (1820) were wizards of this type.

In the nineteenth century, necromancy became almost respectable through the religion of spiritualism. The medium, though usually a woman, could be a man who combined the hypnotic powers of a Svengali with those of the medieval necromancer. He could summon spirits, rather than becoming passively possessed by them. In real life, the greatest nineteenth-century 'physical medium' was the American Daniel Dunglas Home (or Hume). He captivated women in the highest circles of England and France, while in Russia his influence foreshadowed that of Rasputin. For a time, Elizabeth Barrett Browning was an ardent Home disciple, thus inspiring Robert Browning's viciously anti-Gothic 'Mr. Sludge, "the Medium"' (1864).

A final role for the wizard in life and in art was to become a witch-finder, just as the convert Torquemada became a Grand Inquisitor. In Great Britain and New England until the twentieth century, self-titled 'cunning men' claimed they could identify witches and remove the curses placed on their victims. Such 'unbewitchers' are known as 'witch doctors' in Africa and the New World. In the Gothic, Van Helsing, a wise man learned in the occult sciences, exemplifies this tradition (see **STOKER**). This 'white wizard', Dracula's double, also employs hypnotic powers: only this outsider can recognise the threat of the vampire. Other psychic or occult detectives such as **ALGERNON BLACKWOOD**'s John Silence and **SHERIDAN LE FANU**'s Dr Hesselius appear in the supernatural fiction of nineteenth-century Britain. Even Sherlock Holmes may owe something to the archetype of the Gothic wizard (see **CONAN DOYLE**).

FAYE RINGEL

Zerrissenheit

The term derives from *zerreissen*, 'to tear, rend, lacerate, dismember, disconnect', 'dismemberment', 'disjointedness', 'fragmentation', 'disintegration', 'laceration', 'self-estrangement', 'alienation'; other words in this field are: *Entzweiung*, 'bifurcation', 'disunion'; *Zwiespalt*, 'discord', 'conflict', 'discrepancy'; *Trennung*, 'separation'.

Zerrissenheit describes a feeling of self-estrangement between the 'rent/lacerated consciousness' (Hegel), caused by the tensions between the individual's desires and the limitations of experience, the fragmentation of man's perception in the empirical sciences and the disintegration of his social substance. This stage of alienation or disunion, which emerges from a simple unity (in primitive or archaic cultures; childhood), is eventually reconciled in the higher unity of the absolute, characterising the stage at the end of a series of cognitive and practical activities.

The philosophic theme of the self-estranged consciousness reflects the state of mind in the Europe of Enlightenment, the period after which the ethical and religious unity of medievalism and feudalism had been fragmented. It is motivated by the growing sense of specialisation and limitation in industrialised societies. The rent consciousness sets itself in opposition to the natural and social world in which it had its origin and tries to make whole again in thought what would need a social solution. In his *Phenomenology of Spirit* (1807) Hegel first described the feeling of *Zerrissenheit* in such a way as to unify systematically the various philosophical and literary manifestations of this type of consciousness.

In literature *Zerrissenheit* advanced to a fashionable concept in Germany in the early nineteenth century, mainly in the works of Büchner and Heine. The metaphor of the rent or breach that goes through the world can be found in Büchner's dramas and his novel *Lenz*. Heine, the German Byron, uses Hegel's term *Zerrissenheit* in his essay *'Die Nordsee'* ('The North Sea') to complain about the discord within himself that shows the *Zerrissenheit* of the thinking in his days and the 'sick, rent, romantic feelings that have been collected from all countries and ages'.

In English literature William Blake and Lord Byron are entangled with the rent consciousness. Blake tries to escape from Bacon's mechanistic construct. He develops the most powerful type of division-imagery in *The Four Zoas* (1797–1804), showing the Spectres of Urthona's organs of generation as distorted. According to David Punter, both Blake and Hegel believe that 'alongside actual fragmentation, there exists in the world, and in the individual mind, a principle of unity which constitutes the hope of the future'. Consequently, reunification is the realisation of a desire created by a society that strives to liberate the whole man. This process of humanisation is opposed to the division of activities according to concepts of autonomy (of poetry) and division (of labour).

Byron's adventurous life and the heroic qualities of his literary characters shaped the ideal of Byronism and Byronic disintegration on the Continent, merging with Hegel's idealism and a feeling of political disillusionment among the opponents of the Restoration after 1815. In opposition to the organic – historicist – idealist tradition, however, Byron (and Shelley) did not believe in the unifying force of a transcendent 'idea' as the first generation of English Romantics had done. Byron's dominant feeling was that of a rootless isolation and an inability to integrate himself into any social or political order. 'I was born for opposition', says Byron's Don Juan (xv. 22). Byronic disintegration of a different kind can be found in *Childe Harold* and in *Cain: A Mystery*. With the help of Lucifer, Cain tries to overcome the torturing feelings of self-estrangement caused by his resistance towards God's limitations. Childe Harold is alienated both from society and from himself. Torn between his ideals and desires and reality, he is condemned to permanent pilgrimage. The Byronic heroes suffer from a hell inside, most of them show similarities to Prometheus.

It is far more problematic to apply Hegel's term *Zerrissenheit* to the **GOTHIC NOVEL**. However, the various appearances of the lacerated consciousness in the Gothic Novel, such as the Faustian scientist, the wanderer, or the split personality of schizophrenic **MADNESS** or the **DOPPELGÄNGER**, find a common root in the Hegelian analysis of the spirit's condition in modern culture. *Melmoth the Wanderer* describes a state of disintegration that is close to Hegel's *Zerrissenheit*. **MARY SHELLEY**'s modern Prometheus is Frankenstein. It is difficult, however, to tell who suffers more of *Zerrissenheit*, the heretical scientist who desires to transcend his knowledge, or his unhappy creature. Romantic monsters are almost human and yet lack the sensibility to become whole, thus personifying a sublime notion of man's *Zerrissenheit*. Characters who are in a league with the devil fail to unify their rent consciousness. **LEWIS**'s monk, for instance, not only suffers from a fragmentation of his self-consciousness, but is eventually physically shattered by the devil.

The hopelessness and unavoidable wretchedness of man in the Gothic novel is usually regarded as a result of his fallen condition. As the inheritor of the Romantic period, Hegel provides a set of terms to analyse the profound cultural scepticism that is conveyed in the Gothic Novel. The lacerated consciousness is the consciousness of perversion that gathers together thoughts and words which are far apart. In the Gothic Novel, however, man usually remains without hope for redemption and does *not* advance to another world of faith and pure intellection, thus gaining a still higher consciousness as suggested in Hegel's *Phenomenology of Spirit*.

CHRISTOPH HOUSWITSCHKA

Gothic Specialisms

Cabbalism

Cabbalism has been explained in even more ways than the name has been spelt. The Latin spelling, from which we get 'cabal', is a convenient reminder that most Gothic writers know about 'the Cabbala' at second hand. In *Ivanhoe*, Walter Scott reports 'a general belief ... that the Jewish rabbins were acquainted with the occult sciences, and particularly with the cabalistical art, which had its name and origin in the studies of the sages of Israel'. He says the rabbis get respect because they have power to wreak havoc. In the most famous story of havoc, the Great Rabbi of Prague creates an avenger by uttering the secret names he knows as a student of Hebrew, the language of creation; the story is retold in Gustav Meyrink's *The Golem* and echoed in *Frankenstein* (see **GOLEM**).

Cabbalism is an oral tradition attached to a written one, a secret law ostensibly revealed to Moses and handed down by word of mouth until books of sayings appeared in Spain in the late Middle Ages. Christian scholars translated the word cabbala as *traditio* or *receptio*, knowledge handed down, received. Hebrew tracts were translated into Latin and the vernacular languages, and influenced alchemists, Freemasons, and others. They provided a continuity across time to the first day of creation and across space from earth to the mind of God as revealed by the ten emanations or 'sephiroth'. For Walter Benjamin, a childhood friend of the eminent Jewish scholar Gershom Scholem, the storyteller is a cabbalist in as much as he is linked with a tradition of storytelling and with a world of stories about all worlds of **OCCULTISM**.

THOMAS WILLARD

Colonial Gothic

Colonial Gothic literature can be divided into two broad strands, one which takes Britain as its setting and the other dealing with the experience of the coloniser abroad. The former type frequently represents the fear of the incursion of the foreign 'other' into Britain, either as a single disturbing figure or as an invading force. In Charlotte Bronte's *Jane Eyre* (1847) the return of the colonial repressed is represented by Bertha Mason; demonised and confined to the attic, she retaliates by attempting to destroy her oppressors (see **THE BRONTËS**). **BRAM STOKER's** *Dracula* (1897) can also be read as a colonial text, expressing anxieties about racial purity and the loss of imperial power.

A narrative which bridges the two types is Joseph Conrad's *Heart of Darkness* (1902). It opens in London, which is described as the decaying heart of Empire, and moves to the Congo and the journey which both confronts and evades the horror of the colonial enterprise. The experience of otherness is central to colonial Gothic and in the second type is frequently manifested in attempts to control or domesticate the native peoples. In H. G. Wells's *The Island of Dr Moreau* (1896) this project is metaphorically described in the scientific efforts to make animals human.

In colonial Gothic both landscape and people are seen as uncanny, beyond the possibilities of explanation in European terms. Rudyard Kipling's short stories are an example of the way in which local superstitions are regarded sceptically, yet prove to be more powerful than the beliefs of the colonisers.

ALEXANDRA WARWICK

Counterfeit

To refer to the 'Gothic' in fiction, drama, or neo-Gothic architecture as 'counterfeit' is to point, initially, at its fake reworking of older styles and patterns now divorced from many of the social grounds and religious meanings underlying their original uses. It is to note, for example, the fraudulent 'authenticity' of the first edition of **HORACE WALPOLE's** *The Castle of Otranto* (1764), presented as a translation of an Italian Renaissance text that is itself a falsehood, and the equally 'true falseness' of mock-Gothic ruins on eighteenth-century estates that seemed to have, as Walpole said, 'the true rust of the Barons' wars' as if they were built when they were not.

This combination of playful fakery for current social and economic effect with a dim nostalgia for the earlier times recalled by symbolic forms, all epitomised by Walpole's toy-Gothic house at Strawberry Hill, makes the eighteenth-century 'Gothic' and its progeny resemble Jean Baudrillard's definition of 'the counterfeit' in *L'Échange symbolique et le mort* (1976). There 'counterfeit' describes the dominant sense of how signifiers relate to signifieds in Western thought from the Renaissance through the dawn of the industrial revolution.

The counterfeit, by this definition, is pulled in two directions at once: on the one hand, it includes a spectral longing for a fading 'natural' correspondence between sign and social status (the medieval 'bound sign'); on the other hand, that nostalgia is countered by the tendency to break signs of older status away from their earlier connections and to transfer them from one person to another – where they become counterfeits of status – at a time that allows increased social climbing depending on economic success. The neo-'Gothic' extension of this Renaissance tug-of-war visible in, say, Shakespeare (one of Walpole's main sources) begins at a greater distance from really authentic 'bound signs'. As a result, it is actually 'the *ghost* of the counterfeit' harkening back towards, yet pulling away from, the Renaissance counterfeit of the medieval in the name of a newer free enterprise.

JERROLD E. HOGLE

Cyberpunk

The term *Cyberpunk* was first applied, by author Gardiner Dozois in 1985, to exponents of a self-styled avant-garde of **SCIENCE FICTION** writers, including William Gibson, Bruce Sterling, Pat Cadigan and John Shirley. Thereafter, cyberpunk snowballed as a generally 'hot' cultural item, propelled by Sterling's own manifestoes (see his Preface to *Mirrorshades*, London, 1988). Although the writers grouped under this banner have since deserted it, cyberpunk images of a near future dominated by emergent 'corporate' artificial intelligence, both legal and outlawed, sticky, subdermal computer technologies, decaying social fabric, black-market elective surgery and free-market social and biotechnological experimentation, continue to proliferate and haunt contemporary culture. In such works as Gibson's *Neuromancer* (1984), the figure of the cyborg, a creature of the information economy and a hybrid of 'us' (humans) and 'them' (machines, computers, aliens, synthetic persons, etc.), is no longer the creation of driven and dangerous men of science, meddling with the forces of nature (see **MARY SHELLEY**); rather, the future is monstrous, nature cybernetically coalescing with machinic evolution. Thus, with the cyborg, as Donna Haraway suggests in her 'Cyborg Manifesto' (*Simians, Cyborgs and Women*, London, 1991), economics, nature, machines and women enter into a hybrid orgy, ending the reign of pure 'man'.

IAIN HAMILTON GRANT

Doppelgänger

A term coined by the German writer Jean Paul (*Siebenkäs*, 1796). The *Doppelgänger* or 'Double' constitutes a recurrent motif in Gothic and horror literature, mostly in the nineteenth century, ultimately coming from the anthropological belief in an innate duality in man. The presence of this second self or *alter ego*, an archetype of otherness and narcissistic specularity indissolubly linked to the individual, haunts innumerable literary works of Gothic and fantasy, from **E. T. A. HOFFMANN** through Dostoevsky (*Dvojnik/The Double*, 1846), to postmodern representations of Gothic, although the motif tends to lose its referential power in the early decades of the twentieth century, after the discoveries of psychoanalytical theory, which reveal man's complex subconscious.

Appearing early in Gothic fiction properly – with the climactic example of **JAMES HOGG**'s *The Private Memoirs and Confessions of a Justified Sinner* (1824) – the most fruitful evolution of this motif departs from the 1831 edition of **MARY SHELLEY**'s *Frankenstein* and provides, among others, such studies of uncanny duality as **EDGAR ALLAN POE**'s *William Wilson* (1839), Emily Brontë's *Wuthering Heights* (1847), Charlotte's Brontë's *Jane Eyre* (1849) (see **THE BRONTËS**), **STEVENSON**'s *The Strange Case of Dr Jekyll and Mr Hyde* (1875), Guy de Maupassant's *Le Horla* (1854), **OSCAR WILDE**'s *The Picture of Dorian Gray* (1891), **BRAM STOKER**'s *Dracula* (1897), H. G. Wells's *The Invisible Man* (1897) and H. H. Ewers's *The Student from Prague* (1900).

ANTONIO BALLESTEROS GONZÁLEZ

The Fantastic

The Fantastic (as opposed to the far broader category of 'fantasy') is a mode of fiction in which the possible and the impossible (or frequently 'reality' and **THE SUPERNATURAL**) are confounded, so as to leave the reader (and usually the narrator or protagonist) with no satisfying explanation for the strange events which have occurred. This theoretical stance derives from the argument of Tzvetan Todorov (1973) that fantastic fiction involves an unresolved hesitation between a supernatural (or impossible) solution and a psychological (or realistic) one; this approach to fantastic narrative has been refined and developed by Brooke-Rose and Jackson (both 1981) and Cornwell (1990). The pure, or unresolved, fantastic thrived in the high Gothic period of the late eighteenth and early nineteenth centuries in various European literatures, a prime example being Pushkin's *The Queen of Spades* (1834: see **RUSSIAN GOTHIC**), resurfacing from time to time and reaching another high point towards the *fin de siècle*: for instance *The Turn of the Screw* (1898) by **HENRY JAMES**. In the twentieth century the Fantastic has re-emerged: in the recent revival of Gothic and **HORROR** fiction and within the increasingly dominant contribution of fantasy (in its broader sense) to the mixture of modes and breakdown of genres now constituting Postmodernism and such related styles as **MAGICAL REALISM**. An excellent contemporary example of the pure fantastic revived is Toni Morrison's novel *Beloved*.

NEIL CORNWELL

Golem

The Golem is the humanoid creature of Jewish lore conjured into existence by esoteric means, usually including the invocation of the Divine Name. The symbolic resonances of the Golem featured in both Talmudic and Cabbalistic literature, vary through the ages and may have incorporated elements from Jewish Gnosticism. But from the sixteenth century in Central Europe, the Golem becomes associated with Chasidic mysticism, in particular with the Polish Rabbi Elijah Balshem of Chelm and his immediate successors. The Golem during this period also becomes increasingly associated with alchemical and especially Paracelsian ideas. This occult connection, along with the legend's dissemination into non-Jewish circles, ultimately assured the Golem a place in German Romantic thought. In 1808, for example, the legend was documented by Jacob Grimm, in his *Journal for Hermits*. By then, the Golem was closely identified with the celebrated Rabbi Jehuda ben Bezalele, more popularly known as Rabbi Loew (the Lion) of Prague, a sixteenth-century historical figure famed for his erudition and benevolence. Endowed by legend with magical powers, Loew was said to have created a Golem in order to protect Prague's Jews from a wave of Christian fanaticism.

Although made from clay and unable to speak, the Golem does seem to anticipate Frankenstein's monster in several important respects (see **MARY SHELLEY**). Huge, unwieldy, and possessed of superhuman strength, the power of the creature is unpredictable, and though not inherently evil, it becomes impossible to control and increasingly destructive. The volatile nature of such 'unnatural' creations, and the hybris dangerously implicit in such endeavours, are enduring motifs of both the Golem legend and the Frankenstein story. Both Loew and Dr Victor

Frankenstein were credited with an intense love of scientific learning – Loew was reputed to know Tycho Brahe and Johann Kepler. Both Loew and Frankenstein are invested with Faustian attributes, though Loew's piety saves him from any satanic dealings.

MADGE DRESSER

Goth, Gothic

Originally a simple racial term, referring to a Germanic tribe (possibly originally from Sweden). In the third to fifth centuries the tribe invaded the Eastern (Ostrogoths) and Western (Visigoths) Empire, and founded kingdoms in Italy, southern France and Spain. Our knowledge of their language, Gothic (see **GOTHIC LANGUAGE**), derives from the translation of the Bible by Bishop Ulfilas (Gothic name is Wulfila) (died 383) for the Goths on the lower Danube. All that remain are various fragments of an epistle, most of the gospels and part of the Old Testament book of Nehemiah, but this still gives us the most archaic Teutonic language to survive. Gothic spread over most of Europe and North Africa in the fourth and fifth centuries, then disappeared. Two much later writers gave the word an odd semantic twist. Vasari (1511–74), like most Renaissance thinkers, preferred classical to medieval architecture, and popularised the term 'Gothic' for non-Roman and Greek buildings of the twelfth to the sixteenth century, characterised by the pointed arch. The crucial formulation of **HORACE WALPOLE**, in *The Castle of Otranto, a Gothic Story*, though of course pointing the way to Gothic uses of the word, seems in itself to be merely the historical sense: characteristic of the Dark Ages. Gothick architecture is an eighteenth- and nineteenth-century imitation of the original Gothic style, and Goth punk (1980s) shows there is plenty of life in the old word yet.

U. A. FANTHORPE

Gothic Art

To know the nature of its art we must consider the two main strands of late eighteenth-century 'Gothicism' and its evolution into high Romanticism during the first three-quarters of the nineteenth-century. First, I suggest, where its dark theatricality is an emotive response, dictated not by any particular stylistic mannerism, but as a spiritual state. A reaction, if you will, to the extreme rationality of the Enlightenment and its subsequent impoverishment of poetical ideals.

Johann Heinrich Fuseli (1741–1825), who makes concrete our nightmares, leads us in one direction; the culmination of which is the supreme psychological penetration of Francisco Jose-Goya y Lucietes (1746–1828). Both, though by different means, reveal the haunted soul as a darkness through which menace is held to the edge of sight. The second strand leads to a prismatic radiance, culminating in the ecstatic works of Caspar David Friedrich (1774–1840), where the architecture of geological and vegetable nature – through man's worship – become unified in a celebration of God's works.

The former strand, if you will, is the exploration of negative fears which lie ready to pounce and fragment our fragile materialism. The latter, a positive conformation of our Pantheism where nature is the fecund, organic cathedral in which we worship. Fuseli's art may be seen as the expulsion from Eden, whereas Friedrich holds his mirror to nature and the glass remains clear.

The ascendance of the 'prismatic' during the nineteenth century led to Pre-Raphaelitism, Impressionism, and finally the roots of Post-Impressionism. However, the 'dark' tradition was not entirely neglected and in particular was evoked by the 'Fairy' painters such as Richard Dadd (1817–87) in England and the Austrian Moritz von Schwind (1804–71). In our own twentieth century darkness now holds almost complete sway. The vaulting light of spirituality seems no longer to be in fashion.

GRAHAM OVENDEN

Gothic Body

Emphasising **ANN RADCLIFFE**'s designation of **HORROR** rather than 'terror', the Gothic graphically renders the body as violently attacked and in excessive pain. Whereas sentimentalism had envisioned the pained body through a decorous, private, and emotionally poignant lens, the Gothic body is publicly displayed as the victim of social, religious, or political tyranny. Such depictions are often formulaic, and in the case of the rivalry between **M. G. LEWIS** and Radcliffe, proceed from the desire to outdo one's predecessors in the degree of violence depicted. But given the Gothic's psychological concerns, the Gothic body returns to a consciousness of the limitation and corporeal impotence that is underplayed by sentimentalism's 'selfless' morality and Romanticism's transcendent imagination. What most often returns is a body painfully and violently out of control, a body 'uncanny' in Freud's sense that it should have remained repressed, or a body like that of Frankenstein's monster, hideously cobbled together out of beautiful parts that result in a grotesque whole. Politically, the Gothic's excessive violence codes a dual, ambiguous directive for reading: on the one hand, the Gothic body envisions public justice against the tyrant (as in the people's destruction of Lewis's Prioress), and thus engages revolutionary sympathy to the restitution of the body politic; but on the other hand, such violence uses the body to depict public barbarism, to voice a fear of the body politic and to promote a more conservative, reactionary ethic. Thus the Gothic body problematically engages sympathies that it at the same time resists.

STEVEN BRUHM

Gothic Fairy-Tale

At first glance, the possibility of an inter-relational reading of fairy-tale and Gothic modes may appear anomalous. After all, instead of the sinister ambivalence of the Gothic narrative, the seemingly playful fantasies of the formulaic fairy-tale appear to refute the possibility of reader disturbance in prioritising consolation. As Bettelheim observes, it is often through reading fairy-tales that children learn to resolve real-life dilemmas. Freud, also adhering to such demarcations, maintains that despite the **UNHEIMLICH** (uncanny) qualities of literary depictions of the supernatural and the re-animation of the dead, our consolatory expectations of the fairy-tale form are so strong that they overcome such disturbing elements: 'Who would be so bold as to call it uncanny, for instance, when Snow-White opens her eyes once more?'

Via the impact of a number of deconstructive readings, however, we see precisely how uncanny so many of these narratives are. Gilbert and Gubar's re-reading of 'Snow White', for example, situates the tale within a discourse of female enclosure that quite evidently recontextualises it as **FEMALE GOTHIC**. One has only to consider the imaginative impact of the house of sweets in 'Hansel and Gretel' or Granny's cottage in 'Little Red Riding Hood' to recognise the abiding presence of Gothic motifs. Here too we find fascinated readers identifying fearfully but pleasurably with vulnerable interlopers. Here too we find the alluring façade of hearth and home gradually shifting into an imprisoning structure containing *unheimlich* secrets and the textual encoding of latent desires.

It is predominantly through the discourses of feminism and psychoanalysis that our understanding of the Gothic fairy-tale emerges. It is also in the field of contemporary women's writing that some of the most interesting recent literary explorations of this sub-genre are to be found. See especially Anne Sexton's *Transformations*, **ANGELA CARTER**'s *The Bloody Chamber*, and Lucie Armitt's *Theorising the Fantastic*.

LUCIE ARMITT

Gothic Language

The only connection between Gothic Literature and the Gothic language is the term 'Gothic' itself.

Gothic, along with Burgundian, Vandal, Rugian, and Gepidian, formed the now extinct East Germanic group of the Indo-European family. It is the only language of this group for which we have substantial attestation, in the form of the translation of the Bible undertaken by Bishop Wulfila in the fourth century AD, fragments of which are preserved in sixth-century manuscripts. Apart from a handful of Runic inscriptions, these texts constitute the earliest written record of any Germanic language.

The Goths who invaded large parts of the Roman Empire in the fifth century (see **GOTH, GOTHIC**) rapidly became romanised, and their language had disappeared by about the seventh century. However, traces persist in toponyms (possibly including *Catalonia*, from (unattested) GOTHALANIA), personal names (such as Spanish *Fernando*, from (unattested) FRITHENANDUS, 'bold in peace'), and loan words in Romance (for instance, Italian *albergo*, 'inn, hotel', from HARIBERGO, 'military camp'). The name of the Polish city of *Gdańsk*, from GOTHISCANDZA, allegedly marks the Goths' earlier landfall on the southern shore of the Baltic. Gothic-speakers also settled in the Crimea, where the language is recorded as late as the sixteenth century and may have survived for another 200 years.

For his Bible translation, Wulfila adapted and amplified the Greek alphabet. Gothic has three numbers (singular, dual, plural), three genders (masculine, feminine, neuter), and five cases (nominative, accusative, genitive, and dative, together with a vocative in some nouns). Adjectives have a strong and a weak declension. Strong verbs form their preterite by ablaut, reduplication, or a combination of the two; weak verbs by suffixation. The passive-voice forms are synthetic in the present tense, but analytic in the preterite. The syntax of Wulfila's Bible seems too heavily influenced by the Greek original to permit any valid generalisations about Gothic word order.

JOHN CHARLES SMITH

Gothic Manservant

The Gothic manservant of the late eighteenth and early nineteenth centuries forms part of the fantasy of the **GOTHIC NOVEL**. In a complex, subtly decadent and shiftingly hierarchical age, the fantasy welded together noble birth and worth and made presumption and baseness synonymous. In reality, the late eighteenth century had a 'servant problem' evidenced by much writing about the antagonism of classes and the impudent ways of the expanding and increasingly female servant population. The Gothic novel, however, creates a fantastic context in which hierarchies are clear and Defoe's 'Great Law of Subordination' holds firm. Consequently the master and the servant can, at different times, play female and childlike roles and approach close to each other. In **ANN RADCLIFFE**'s novels in particular, male servants are what middle-class society wished servants of both sexes to be, endlessly devoted, never thinking of pay-day, and gratifying all their masters' wishes, being fond and familiar when required and subservient when not. At the end of *The Italian* the servant is offered a reward; he refuses, for it has been his glory to serve and, since there is no economic basis of his servitude, he has no need of independence.

JANET TODD

Gothic Parody

Self-parody is a relatively common element in Gothic fiction. Certain Gothic texts, such as Lewis's *The Monk* (1796) (see **MATTHEW LEWIS**) or Eliza Fenwick's Jacobin Gothic *Secresy, or the Ruin on the Rock* (1795) contain strong elements of generic parody. Texts explicitly parodying the Gothic are, however, a comparative rarity.

Indisputably the best known is Jane Austen's *Northanger Abbey* (1818) (see also **NORTHANGER NOVELS**), although this, too, is a text situated problematically with regard to Gothic discourses. Conventional readings posit its heroine, Catherine Morland, as misled by her avid reading of **RADCLIFFE's** *The Mysteries of Udolpho* (1794), unable to distinguish fantasy from reality until guided by her lover–mentor, Henry Tilney. While Austen adopts standard Gothic machinery – an abbey, secret closets, mysterious manuscripts (all clearly drawn from Radcliffe's *The Romance of the Forest*) – only to undercut their significance in her dénouement, the text nevertheless offers itself as a realist interpretation of the Gothic. The novel's villain, General Tilney, may not be, as Catherine suspects, a wife-murderer, but he *is* a mercenary and uncaring father. Austen, while discarding that which she considers risible or potentially dangerous, recognises that the fears of patriarchal authority which Radcliffe's novels articulate are, ultimately, genuine.

Thomas Love Peacock's *Nightmare Abbey* (1818) contains a parodic version of the brooding **HERO-VILLAIN** in the person of Scythrop Glowry (closely modelled on **P. B. SHELLEY**), residing in a ruined tower and drinking Madeira from a human skull.

Gothic parody survives into the twentieth century by way of the related technique of metafiction. Writers such as Jorge Luis Borges and Umberto Eco habitually deploy, self-consciously and ironically, the narrative devices of the Gothic.

DARRYL JONES

Gothic Photography

Photography embodies a deceptive dualism: on the one hand, the photograph is rightly perceived as the useful artefact from which we may find out things about the world. On the other, it is a messenger from that other place, the realm of dark things where different causalities rule and events signify in ways that do not match the meanings we see so clearly by daylight. That this is due to a failure in our own perceptual strategies, whereby we do not take account of the brevity of photographic time as compared with the time needed to perceive an event's unfolding in the world, and then proceed to make up the lack by fictions from our own inner minds; is in no way to deny its significance. Neither does our knowledge allow us to escape from this perception.

We thus have in photography, or rather in the back of the photograph perceiver's mind, exactly that shifting, uncertain subversion of the mundane that is the very stuff of Gothic. The potential is always there, for any photograph; when it is recognised and exploited, through staging, manipulation, or by the simple – but so subtle – choices of photographic syntax, then the way is clear for terrible delights and ecstatic horripilations.

As exemplar in photography of the entropic Gothic of physical pathology, I would indicate Joel-Peter Witkin's images; for the secret Gothic of personal sexualities I propose a study of Jan Saudek, and the Gothic of ancient forces will be found in the photographs of Mario Giacomelli. There are many more.

PHILIP STOKES

Gothic Science Fiction

In his *Trillion Year Spree* Brian Aldiss argues that science fiction grows out of the Gothic, not the utopian mould, in that the 'need to find a secret, an identity, a relationship, accompanied the questing traveller to other worlds or futures'. He substantiated this argument in his time-travel novel *Frankenstein Unbound*. Aldiss's argument has been rejected by a number of critics, including Thomas H. Keeling who proposes (in *Bridges to Science Fiction*, ed. Slusser) that demonic agency, a pandeterministic universe and the perception of the alien as evil are all necessary characteristics of the Gothic but might or might not appear in science fiction. Keeling presupposes a homogeneity and stability in literary genres which the novels do not necessarily support, and *Frankenstein* has been read by many critics as a prototype of the science-fiction genre.

In fact Gothic motifs and narrative procedures have continued to appear in science fiction to articulate the reverse possibility to mankind's gradual expansion of knowledge through science. From countless possible examples, Wells's *Island of Dr Moreau* started out as a Gothic fantasy; the novels of Philip K. Dick repeatedly return to the fear that reality itself can be shaped by malign agencies; and arbitrary imprisonment – a staple Gothic ingredient – lies at the centre of Thomas M. Disch's *Camp Concentration*. More recently feminist science-fiction writers like Tanith Lee have rediscovered vampirism, which is now presented as the transgression of a restrictive social order.

DAVID SEED

The Grotesque

The grotesque is frequently found as an accompanying or subsidiary feature to such literary forms as the Gothic and **THE FANTASTIC**. The term 'grotesque' (Italian: *grottesco, la grottesca*, from *grotta*, a grotto or cave) originates from the fifteenth-century discovery of bizarre and monstrous wall ornamentation in ancient Roman dwellings (or grottoes). As a form of artistic representation it may be characterised as a deformation of the real-life, with verisimilitude yielding to caricature, often of human features (e.g. gargoyles), and of plant and animal forms. The word gained literary currency from its use in Victor Hugo's Preface to *Cromwell* (1827), in which it is applied to artistic images of the 'ugly', linking it with the aesthetically monstrous and extremes of the comic, or preferably both in combination. In literature it often involves freakish appearance or behaviour (see the novels of **DICKENS**) and it is to be found in a tradition stretching from Swift through Kafka to Mervyn Peake. The term 'a grotesque' may also be applied to a disturbingly eccentric fictional character. In the work of, for instance, Gogol (see **RUSSIAN GOTHIC**), the combination of the comic and the serious may be realised, often satirically, in the form of unexpected transitions: from forced elevated rhetoric to abrupt comic dénouement. It is in the abruptness of such contrasts or incongruities, in conjunction with distorted imagery, that the essence of the comic grotesque is often to be found. The standard study is by Wolfgang Kayser (1963).

NEIL CORNWELL

Hermetism

Hermetism gets its name from Hermes, especially the Egyptian Hermes, Theuth, who is distinguished from Greek Hermes and Latin Mercury as the Thrice-Great Hermes. The best known of all Hermetic texts, the *Emerald Tablet*, states, 'I am called Hermes Trismegistus because I hold the three parts of the universal philosophy.' Whether these are body, soul, spirit or earth, sky, mind or another combination, this Hermes has been treated as the inventor of all sciences, notably writing. In the Middle Ages, he was regarded as a precursor of Moses. In the Renaissance, the *Hermetic Corpus* was edited and dated to the early Christian era, but the dating had little effect on the legend. All occult philosophers were 'sons of Hermes', especially alchemists. To attribute a text to Hermes was to identify its tradition. Moreover, since the tradition was closed to outsiders, the very act of recording sacred Egyptian sayings in Greek script had to be a late effort, comparable to an anthropologist's record of legends in an endangered culture. And here we find the appropriateness in the tie of Theuth to Hermes, the god of borders and interpretation.

Renaissance Hermetism, as filtered through the work of Agrippa and Paracelsus, dominated the studies of young Frankenstein in **MARY SHELLEY**'s novel. It seemed to have more than a little of the Renaissance 'over-reacher', fated to fall in the end because trying to seize the power of God, the power over life. Another aspect of Hermetism, the trickster element in the Greek Hermes, has become important in twentieth-century novels about occultism – for example in David Foster's revisionary fiction *The Adventures of Christian Rosy Cross* (1986).

THOMAS WILLARD

Historico-Gothic

This is a subdivision of the category **GOTHIC NOVEL** which shares many of its characteristics but is more historically specific, with invented or fictionalised historical characters participating to some degree in actual historical events. Related to French historical romance, it began to appear in English in the 1760s. For example, Thomas Leland's *Longsword: William, Earl of Salisbury* (1762) has as its central character a natural son of Henry II and is set in the reign of Henry III during and after the recovery of Gascony for the English crown in 1225. It is a story of mysterious abductions, imprisonments, and miraculous escapes; treacherous noblemen, wily monks and a resourceful maidservant give it the true Gothic flavour. Sophia Lee, in *The Recess* (1783–5), invents two daughters of Mary, Queen of Scots, brought up in secrecy and a prey to the machinations of Elizabeth I when they grow up. Rosetta Ballin, in *The Statue Room* (1790), invents a child born to Catherine of Aragon after her divorce from Henry VIII and weaves a tale of intrigue round real events. Clara Reeve's *Sir Roger de Clarendon* (1793) has as its hero an authentic natural son of the Black Prince but gives him an entirely fictitious personal life. Devendra P. Varma gives attention to these works in chapter IV of *The Gothic Flame*, and Avrom Fleishman, in chapter 1 of *The English Historical Novel*, discusses their influence on Scott.

MARY WALDRON

Illuminati Novels

Illuminati, 'the enlightened', refers to the historical movement of the eighteenth century in Germany and one of the many secret societies, like the Rosicrucians and Freemasons, that appealed to the Gothic **IMAGINATION**. The Order of Illuminati was founded by Adam Weishaupt in Ingolstadt (Bavarian Illuminati) in 1776 aiming at the reformation of church and society according to the principles of rational enlightenment. In conflict with the Jesuit Order and Rosicrucians, the Illuminati were allied with the Freemasons. Members, among others, were: J. G. Herder, J. W. V. Goethe (both from 1783) and A. V. Knigge (1779–84). Prohibited and crushed by the Bavarian Elector Carl Theodore in 1785, the secret society lived on as a legend until it was renewed by Leopold Engel in 1896, as the World Order of Illuminati, which was refounded in 1926, in Berlin. Similar movements in eighteenth-century Spain were the Alumbrados, and in France, the Guérients.

The Gothic imagination, as in **P. B. SHELLEY**'s *St Irvyne, or, The Rosicrucian*, is stimulated less by the reforming intentions of the Illuminati and other secret societies than by their subversive and mysterious character. Whereas **GOETHE**'s *Turmgesellschaft* (Society of the Tower) in his *Wilhelm Meister* has much in common with the enlightened aims of the Illuminati Order and the Freemasons, Gothic treatment tends to emphasise eerie paraphernalia, political subversion, and repression. The Illuminati novel belongs to conspiracy fictions drawing on popular mythologies of secret societies that threaten the established order. Contemporary Gothic associates Illuminati with Satanism and Occultism.

PASCAL NICKLAS

Jacobean Tragedy

> Webster was much possessed by death
> And saw the skull beneath the skin
>
> (*Whispers of Immortality*, ll. 1–2)

T. S. Eliot's observation underlines the proto-Gothic preoccupations of much Jacobean tragedy. Death, sin, exotic vices in exotic settings, vengeful ghosts, torture and imprisonment, madness, murder, and a not-so-sweet excess in all things: these are regular features of a drama whose most prominent practitioners include John Webster himself (*c.* 1578–1632), Thomas Middleton (*c.* 1580–1627), Cyril Tourneur (*c.* 1575–1626) and John Ford (fl. 1630s).

Webster's *The Duchess of Malfi* (*c.* 1614) exemplifies many of these traits. Set in Italy, it depicts an excitingly unfamiliar and decadent world, replete with machiavels and hypocrite Cardinals. The Duchess, imprisoned at her brother Ferdinand's command, witnesses a series of grotesqueries worthy of that other master of immurement, **POE**: waxworks of her murdered husband and children; a troupe of madmen; a charnel-house catechism from her murderer. The play also foreshadows (the Gothic preoccupation with the bizarre consequences of a heightened or morbid sexuality.) Ferdinand's obsession with the Duchess leads him, after her death, to become a corpse-digging lycanthrope (see **LYCANTHROPY**):

> In those that are possess'd with't there o'erflows
> Such melancholy humour, they imagine
> Themselves to be transformed to wolves ...
>   ... only the difference
> [Is], a wolf's skin [is] hairy on the outside,
> His on the inside...

(The Duchess of Malfi, V.ii.8–18)

Reading this, it comes as no surprise to learn that **ANGELA CARTER** spent her teenage years engrossed in Jacobean tragedy. In fact the dark luxuriance of its imagination has informed Gothic writing from **WALPOLE** onwards.

C<small>HARLES</small> B<small>UTLER</small>

The Lamia

Most famously represented in Keats's poem *Lamia* (1820), the lamia is a mythical monster of classical origin with the face and breasts of a woman and a serpent's body. According to Lemprière's *Bibliothica Classica* (1788), the lamia was a creature that could not speak, but beguiled men and children with its pleasing hissing, whereupon it would devour them. Keats's Lamia is not so anatomically complex, but a metamorphosed figure in the Ovidian tradition, transformed into a human shape because she has fallen in love with a mortal. Keats's poem works metaphorically, to oppose the eroticism and beauty of the Lamia against the masculine world of sterile thought and philosophy. The mythical figure of the lamia has clear connections with the figurative representations of fatal women (harpies, sirens, gorgons etc.), and such creatures have a significant presence in Gothic novels such as **BRAM STOKER**'s *Dracula* as well as in Romantic poetry, where the most notable examples are Coleridge's 'Christabel' (1816), Peacock's 'Rhododaphne' (1818), and, of course, Keats's *La Belle Dame Sans Merci* (1820).

PHILIP W. MARTIN

Lycanthropy

The term 'lycanthropy' (from the Greek words for wolf, *lykos*, and man, *anthropos*) covers both the medical condition, a morbid delusion that the sufferer becomes an animal, and the belief that such a change actually takes place. Werewolf stories recur throughout history, through Greek and Norse myths, Latin literature, medieval lays, and sixteenth-century trials where the belief in the actual transformation was taken very seriously indeed, so seriously that the accused could be executed for crimes committed while he (and sometimes she) was in wolf form. Even in England, where wolves were hunted to extinction early, the figure of the man–wolf lurks behind folk tales like 'Mr Fox', the story of a murderous bridegroom, and songs about 'sly bold Reynardine', an outlaw, or perhaps something worse, who leads his innocent victim off into the forest to his 'green castle', or under the jolly trappings of the pantomime story of Little Red Riding Hood (was the wolf really Grandmother all the while?). Ireland is surprisingly rich in werewolf legends. Films gave the werewolf a whole new lease of life, and a new image as a furry anthropoid, caught in mid-transformation.

TINA RATH

Magical Realism

The term 'magical realism' was coined in 1925 by the German art critic Franz Roh, who applied it to post-expressionist painting. Since the 1950s, the term has been extensively applied to certain kinds of non-realist fiction, mainly in Latin America, but also increasingly in other countries. It has been defined in various ways, especially by Latin American critics, and a general consensus has never been reached. Uslar Pietri (1948) defined it as a poetic negation of reality, Angel Flores (1955) as an 'amalgamation of realism and fantasy', Luis Leal (1967) as 'the discovery of the mysterious relation that exists between man and his circumstance', and Miguel Angel Asturias as the portrayal of the 'original mentality of the Indians'. Several critics have considered it as the authentic expression of Latin America, others believe it is characteristic of non-Western fiction in general, while some see it as a narrative form existing in most countries. Magical realism is generally considered as a twentieth-century literary mode in which the **SUPERNATURAL** is presented not as a threat to the individual or to the laws of nature, but as a normal part of experience. Contrary to fairy-tales or science fiction (see **GOTHIC FAIRY-TALE and GOTHIC SCIENCE FICTION**) magical realist narratives do not depict fictional worlds radically different from our own, but integrate the supernatural within relatively believable worlds.

AMARYLL BEATRICE GHANADY

Necromancy

This means gaining power or knowledge through spirits of the dead. In I Samuel 28:11–19, the Witch of Endor raised the prophet Samuel's spirit. (Later, controversy raged: was the apparition genuine, or a human or diabolical illusion?) In Homer's *Odyssey* XI, Odysseus summoned his mother's ghost; in Virgil's *Aeneid* VI, Aeneas visited the underworld to seek his late father's advice. 'Necromancy' has been confused with 'nigromancy', black magic: according to James I's *Daemonology* (1597), 'Witches ar servants onelie, and slaves to the Devil; but the Necromanciers are his maisters and commanders.' The fullest Gothic treatment is *Der Geisterbanner* (1792) by Lawrence Flammenberg, alias Karl Friedrich Kahlert and Bernard Stein. Translated into English by Peter Teuthold as *The Necromancer; or, The Tale of the Black Forest* (1794), it was immortalised as one of the 'horrid' novels mentioned in Jane Austen's *Northanger Abbey* (1818), and was reprinted by Devendra Varma (1968). Volkert, the necromancer of the title, is a charlatan, unable to create truly supernatural effects. Subsequent eerie manipulations of dead matter and spirit, authentic or faked, include **MARY SHELLEY**'s *Frankenstein* (1818), Rudyard Kipling's 'They' (1904) and 'En-Dor' (1919), **ARTHUR CONAN DOYLE**'s *Professor Challenger Stories*, Agatha Christie's 'The Last Seance', in *The Hound of Death* (1933), Noël Coward's *Blithe Spirit* (1941) and Michael Crichton's *Jurassic Park* (1990).

CAROLYN D. WILLIAMS

Northanger Novels

The seven Gothic novels recommended to Catherine by Isabella in chapter 6 of the first volume of *Northanger Abbey* (1818) are *The Castle of Wolfenbach* (1793), by Eliza Parsons; *Clermont* (1798), by Regina Maria Roche; *The Mysterious Warning* (1796) (misnamed *Mysterious Warnings* by Isabella), also by Eliza Parsons; *The Necromancer; or, The Tale of The Black Forest* (1794), by Peter Teutold from the German of Lawrence Flammenburg; *The Midnight Bell* (1798), by Francis Lathom; *The Orphan of the Rhine* (1798), by Eleanor Sleath; and *Horrid Mysteries* (1796), by P. Will from the German of Karl Grosse.

Most of these titles were thought to have been invented by Austen until December 1912, when a correspondence in *Notes and Queries* revealed the existence of some of them and stimulated a search for the rest. In 1927 the research was brought together by Michael Sadleir in an address to the English Association and printed as English Association pamphlet no. 68: 'The *Northanger* Novels: A Footnote to Jane Austen'.

Reprints were brought out together by the Folio Press in London in 1968, under the editorship of Devendra P. Varma. His Preface to *The Castle of Wolfenbach* contains a detailed account of the search and some discussion of the reasons for Austen's choice; each reprinted novel has a critical Introduction.

MARY WALDRON

Paranoid Gothic

From the beginnings of the form, Gothic has been concerned with uncertainties of character positioning and instabilities of knowledge. Far from knowing everything, characters frequently know little or nothing about the worlds through which they move or about the structures of power which envelop them. We can point to three classic works, William Godwin's *Caleb Williams* (1794), **C. R. MATURIN**'s *Melmoth the Wanderer* (1820) and **JAMES HOGG**'s *Confessions of a Justified Sinner* (1824), as representations of the persecuted victim, subject to violence and pursuit for incomprehensible reasons. These types of fiction can be referred to as paranoid in that they enact a classic psychology of paranoia whereby the self is threatened and pursued by its own unaccommodated residues. We can further extend the usefulness of this description if we think of some more recent fictions, for example those of Thomas Pynchon, as again representing the individual as helpless in the grip of powerful forces – in this case military and international; in the case of other fictions like, for example, those of William Gibson or Will Self, technological and cybernetic – which represent the self as dissolved in a web of uncomprehended power structures; Gothic has proved fertile in adapting its descriptions as the historical represent-ations of power have themselves altered and developed and as the dis-courses through which power is transmitted have shifted terrain according to a logic of scientific and economic development within which the self experiences itself as at the mercy of forces beyond its control.

DAVID PUNTER

The Phantom

The French post-Freudian psychoanalysts Nicolas Abraham and Maria Torok developed the concept of transgenerational haunting, in which a family secret may be passed on unknowingly by parents or other close relatives to a child, who is then affected by this encrypted secret, without being conscious of what it is. Abraham and Torok argue that the devel-opment is not universal, as in Freudian or Lacanian models, but is partic-ular to each individual's experience and may involve a legacy from the mother's unspoken communications. Their analysis of such encrypted secrets depends upon close attention to words, especially those sug-gested by association but avoided in the patient's discourse. Using their technique of 'cryptonymy', Abraham and Torok revisited Freud's famous 'Wolfman' case, and concluded that an avoided word 'tieret' (meaning 'to rub') held a clue to the neurosis. Abraham also reviewed *Hamlet*, to argue that Hamlet's indecision was generated by the en-crypted knowledge that his father had killed Laertes' father by using a poisoned sword in a duel. This work has been extended, notably by Nicholas Rand, their translator, and Esther Rashkin, whose book *Family Secrets* applies their ideas to Conrad and **HENRY JAMES**, among others. An intriguing possibility is to read the sense of 'secrets' more widely, to include secrets handed on by non-family members, such as between the children and the governess in *The Turn of the Screw*, or cultural secrets, the unspoken encrypted knowledges of history, as seen in Toni Morrison's *Beloved*.

ALLAN LLOYD SMITH

Politico-Gothic

This is a small sub-division of **HISTORICO-GOTHIC** in which the historical narrative and familiar Gothic atmosphere of mystery and danger are used to identify the author's attitude to contemporary national and international events. For instance, in her Preface to *Sir Roger de Clarendon* (1793), at the time of the outbreak of war with Revolutionary France, Clara Reeve declares her Conservative political stance – her hero is intended to embody anti-Jacobin views. James White makes parodic reference in two of his three historical romances to political events and personalities of his time; *Earl Strongbow; or, The History of Richard de Clare and the Beautiful Geralda* (1789) contains an anachronistic parliamentary debate in which Fox, Sheridan and Pitt are caricatured; and *The Adventures of Richard Cœur de Lion* (1791) has a corrupt character who is a recognisable parallel to Warren Hastings, then going through his protracted trial. Ann Yearsley's *The Royal Captives* (1795) explores the political situation in seventeenth-century France under Louis XIV, seeing in his tyranny and religious intolerance the seeds of the next century's Revolution. Some of Scott's novels belong in this category, particularly *Redgauntlet* (1824) and *The Bride of Lammermoor* (1819), both of which refer to nineteenth-century political scenarios through a fictionalised version of past events.

MARY WALDRON

Popular Horror Fiction

Popular horror fiction derives mainly from Gothic traditions in writing, cinema and comics. Horror frequently expresses fears that middle-class security has been bought with some terrible pact or achieved through immense repression. Nemesis comes with the emergence of a long-repressed, malignant other. The best-known contemporary practitioner, Stephen King, uses characteristic themes and motifs. *Carrie* (1974) and *Misery* (1987) express masculine fears of women and sexuality. *Salem's Lot* (1975) features vampires. *The Shining* (1977) deploys haunting, telepathy and possession. *The Stand* (1978) is an apocalyptic novel about new viruses leaking from military laboratories. *It* (1986) deals with violence in the urban underworld. *Pet Sematary* (1988) demonises a repressed racial other, located (as often) in a Native American burial ground. Similar motifs appear in American writers such as Poppy Z. Brite, Dean Koontz,

Graham Masterton, Anne Rice, John Saul and Peter Straub, and British writers such as Clive Barker, Ramsay Campbell and James Herbert. Horror suggests that rationalist, consumerist modernity produces alienation from the body and denial of desires and terrors. Usually, the remedies proposed are conservative, depending not on new attitudes towards the repressed or abject, but on violent confrontation, ritual cleansing, rediscovery of lost heroism and authenticity, and reimposition of order.

RICHARD KERRIDGE

Porphyria

Porphyria is an extremely rare condition with a number of unpleasant symptoms, the most startling being the purple urine giving the disease its name. Others can include extreme sensitivity to light, so that the skin blisters in ordinary day-light, excessive facial hair, and teeth which become red-stained and fang-like. Every so often the disease is hailed as the real origin of the legends of the **VAMPIRE** and **WEREWOLF** (see **LYCANTHROPY**): medieval peasants afflicted with porphyria, only able to come out at night because of their acute reaction to sunlight. Hairy, and snaggle-toothed, they were mistaken for monsters. They might even be blood drinkers, it has been suggested, because porphyria symptoms can be alleviated by blood transfusion, and, while this was not available to the peasant sufferers, desperation might drive them to seek relief by attacking others and drinking their blood. The disease is largely genetic, and attacks can be triggered by stress, so the idea of the infectious bite could arise if someone succumbed to porphyria after an attack by a relative already exhibiting the more florid symptoms. But traditional vampires could endure daylight, and had no fangs or excessive hair, and werewolves manifested either as wolves or men, not as hairy men with sharp teeth. Only in films and fiction do the monsters show any of the characteristics attributed to the unfortunate sufferers of porphyria.

TINA RATH

Rosicrucian Fiction

Since the original Rosicrucians, or Brotherhood of the Rosy Cross, and their literary counterparts were reputed to be in possession of the secrets of perpetual youth, and invisibility, it is not surprising that they have remained elusive. Even Descartes joined the search for them. Their existence had been announced to the world through two hoax manifestoes, *Fama Fraternitatis* (1614) and *Confessio Fraternitatis* (1615), which voiced a Protestant resistance to Habsburg Catholic hegemony. These spoofs were parodied by Jonathan Swift in *A Tale of a Tub* (1704) and *Gulliver's Travels* (1726) and appear to have provided Alexander Pope with his Rosicrucian 'machinery' for the second edition of *The Rape of the Lock* (1714). The ludibrium is believed to have been engineered by Johann Valentine Andreae, who is also the author of the Rosicrucian allegory *The Chemical Wedding* (1616). Through alchemical and Hermetic means (see **HERMETISM**), the Rosicrucians were alleged to be in possession of the philosopher's stone and the elixir of life, through which they could prolong their existence.

This legend generated a sub-genre of Gothic literature, whose hero is a wandering immortal. Branching out from William Godwin's *St Leon* (1799), are **PERCY BYSSHE SHELLEY**'s *St Irvyne, or, The Rosicrucian* (1811) and **MARY SHELLEY**'s tale 'The Mortal Immortal', which was first published in 1833. Later examples are **CHARLES MATURIN**'s *Melmoth the Wanderer* (1820) and **EDWARD BULWER-LYTTON**'s *Zanoni* (1842) and *A Strange Story* (1862).

Modern texts that draw upon Rosicrucianism include G. W. Surya, *Moderne Rosenkreuzer* (Modern Rosicrucians, 1907), Temple Thurston, *The Rosicrucians* (1930) and David Foster, *The Adventures of Christian Rosy Cross* (1986). That the Cartesian search for the Brothers of the Rosy Cross has been continued more recently, is evident from Umberto Eco's *Foucault's Pendulum* (1989). Here the inebriated hero sets out to decipher an engraving of the Rosicrucians' Invisible College in the belief that it contains cryptic messages from the Brotherhood.

MARIE MULVEY-ROBERTS

Schauerroman

Meaning 'shudder' or 'quiver novel', this term is often used to refer to the German Gothic Novel in general (see **GERMAN GOTHIC**). A sub-category is the *Räuberroman* (Robber Romance), of which Schiller's *Die Räuber* (*The Robbers*) was the Romantic prototype. Its effect on Coleridge was to make him 'tremble like an aspen leaf', whereas **PERCY BYSSHE SHELLEY** proved to be more intrepid (see **ROMANTICISM**). Peacock in *Nightmare Abbey* (1818) (see **GOTHIC PARODY**) parodies Shelley's enthusiasm for the *Schauerromantik* when he describes Scythrop sleeping with a copy of the Marquis of Grosse's *Horrid Mysteries* (1796) under his pillow in order to induce nightmares.

Vintage *Schauerroman* is a bloodbath of horrors and supernatural excesses. According to Carlyle, it was a 'bowl and dagger' extravaganza, often set in the Black Forest, which was peopled with spectral nuns, and outlaws with huge whiskers. More nameless terrors, often of a sadistic nature, were unleashed upon the reader, who could be forced to contend with ambulatory cadavers and marauding bandits. The leading exponent of the *Schauerromantik* was Joseph Alois Gleich (1772–1841), who wrote under the pseudonym 'Dellarosa' and penned such unspeakable horrors as *Die Totenfackel; Oder, die Höhle der Siebenschläfer* (*The Torch of Death; or, The Cave of the Seven Sleepers*) and *Udo der Stählerne; Oder, die Ruinen von Drudenstein* (*Udo the Man of Steel; or, The Ruins of Drudenstein*).

MARIE MULVEY-ROBERTS

Sensation Fiction

The heyday of the Sensation Novel was the 1860s. Particularly popular were *The Woman in White* (1860) by Wilkie Collins and *Lady Audley's Secret* (1862) by Mary Elizabeth Braddon. Other Sensation authors include Charles Reade and Ellen Wood. The subject matter of Sensation Fiction was mystery and crime, and the main narrative method, suspense. Like the Gothic Novel of the late eighteenth and early nineteenth centuries, the Sensation Novel sought to induce fear, excitement and curiosity (see **GOTHIC NOVEL**). It was regarded as a reaction against realism in its mixing of the incredible and the documentary and in its refusal to stay within the 'proper' sphere of acceptable character types in domestic settings.

The manner in which the heroines of Sensation Fiction challenged Victorian ideals of femininity marked it as a distinctly subversive genre. Many of the reviewers' anxieties derived from the perception that it was a form generally written by, about and for women; it was regarded as a 'feminine' literary genre, irrespective of the particular Sensation author. The guardians of high culture in the mid-Victorian years condemned the popularity of Sensation Fiction, regarding its mass-market appeal as a deplorable 'feminisation' (and debasement) of literature.

SALLY LEDGER

Sensibility

The Cult of Sensibility was an eighteenth-century phenomenon which emphasised a sensitive response to the pathetic or affecting in life and art. Virtue from good feelings came to be preferred to rationally inspired goodness, and physical manifestations such as tears, blushes and palpitations became signs of virtuous sympathy. Although associated with major male writers such as Richardson and Sterne, the mode of sensibility was much favoured by women, who entered literature in large numbers realising they could for the first time write and publish without losing their modesty. When, towards the end of the century, women came to write Gothic novels, these tended also to be in the sentimental mode, although it was by this time fashionable to denounce sensibility as self-indulgent. **ANN RADCLIFFE** used her works such as *The Mysteries of Udolpho* (1794) both to present sensitive heroines and sentimental ideals of semi-feudal communities and to deliver lectures on the dangers of excessive sensibility for women.

JANET TODD

Spiritualism

The main tenet of spiritualism is that it is possible for the living to contact and communicate with the spirits of the dead. This belief has an ancient history, one often associated with fortune-telling and magic. Certain mediumistic phenomena are reported in the witch trials of the Middle Ages, and many of those persecuted for the practice of witchcraft were probably what would now be called mediums (see **WITCHCRAFT**).

Modern spiritualism was introduced to England by an American, 'Mrs Hayden', who began to advertise her services as a spiritual medium in 1852. Nineteenth-century spiritualism in Britain had a distinctly 'progressive' flavour, partly because of its implicit challenge to Christian revelation (it became associated with the Victorian 'Crisis of Faith'). By the 1870s, when the most successful metropolitan séances obtained a certain glamour and cachet, women constituted some of the most popular mediums of the day. The most famous of them could produce spectacular, theatrical séances during which invisible spirits played upon musical instruments, rapped out messages and occasionally quite literally materialised. Séances also became a popular pastime in Victorian drawing rooms. Whilst the heyday of Victorian spiritualism began to wane in the mid-1880s, 'feminist spirituality' began to emerge in the 1970s, one of its objects being the rediscovery of Goddess worship and witchcraft as powerful, nurturing and humane forces.

Spiritualism is by no means only – or even originally – a Western phenomenon. Practices very like those of a modern spiritualist séance have been reported in various parts of the world – for example Haiti and among the North American Indians – and the traditions of African Spiritualism are made manifest in Toni Morrison's novel from 1988, *Beloved*.

SALLY LEDGER

Sturm und Drang (Storm and Stress)

A precursor of **ROMANTICISM**, this literary movement represented a reaction against the literature of the Enlightenment. Beginning in Germany during the 1770s, it lasted little more than a decade. Named after the title of a play by F. M. Klinger (1752–1831), *Sturm und Drang* emerged mainly through drama, as in the plays of J. M. R. Lenz (1751–92), H. L. Wagner (1747–79) and F. M. Klinger (1752–1831), where the conventions of the Aristotelean unities were swept aside. An exception can be found in **GOETHE**, whose novel *Die Leiden des jungen Werthers* (1774) (*The Sorrows of Young Werther*) was a key text and became an international best-seller. The suicide of its hero, whose tormented self is projected onto the natural world, sets the key-note for the heightened subjectivity of Goethe's early poetry. Another well-known exponent is Johann Christoph Friedrich von Schiller, whose drama *Die Räuber* (1781) (*The Robbers*) expressed the rebelliousness and identification with nature associated with the movement. Its theoretical anchor was Johann Gottfried Herder whose essays, particularly the one on Shakespeare in *Von deutscher Art und Kunst* (*Of German Art*) (1773), proved to be the manifesto of *Sturm und Drang*. Other influences included Jean-Jacques Rousseau, James Macpherson, the Ossian forger and the graveyard poet Edward Young (see **GRAVEYARD SCHOOL**).

MARIE MULVEY-ROBERTS

Transgression

Gothic writing has been associated with transgression in several ways. As a sub-genre of romance, it has been seen as seducing readers away from the proprieties and responsibilities of daily life in a manner which transgresses the notion of civil order. In relation to content, Gothic romances (which often include elements such as murder, rape or incest) have in the past been castigated as morally corrupting, since their plots incorporate deeds which transgress normal social codes of morality. These deeds may themselves often be read as symbolic of transgression against a larger social or political order: for example, the murder of a father may indicate a desire for overthrow of Church or government; an incestuous relationship may be read as subversive of the ideological role played by the family within a patriarchal culture. For these reasons Gothic romance is often associated with insurrection and cultural dissent. Further, Gothic writing frequently challenges literary and aesthetic conventions in so far as it dissolves the differences between Romanticism and realism, history and romance, high and low culture; in so doing it appears to transgress generic boundaries.

AVRIL HORNER

Unheimlich (The Uncanny)

The German word *unheimlich*, meaning 'uncanny', is one much used in criticism of Gothic writing. Its use in this manner derives from Sigmund Freud's famous essay 'The "Uncanny"', published in 1919. In this essay, Freud distinguishes between *heimlich*, meaning 'familiar' or 'belonging to the home', and *unheimlich*, meaning all that is 'unhomely', or 'uncanny', and is frightening precisely because it is *not* known and *not* familiar. However, he points out that *heimlich*, in so far as it is associated with the domestic or the private, can also mean that which is concealed and kept out of sight. From these lexical ambivalencies, he deduces that in some senses *unheimlich* coincides with its opposite, *heimlich*. Analysing E. T. A. HOFFMANN's story of 'The Sand Man', Freud suggests that the uncanny nature of the Sand Man in Hoffman's story bespeaks a morbid anxiety about the loss of sight, which is indicative of the fear of castration. The projection of such fears upon others results in a DOPPELGÄNGER effect which unites the known with the uncanny, or the *heimlich* with the *unheimlich*. Freud claims, therefore, that Hoffmann's tale gains its power by making use of unresolved forms of disturbance which occur in the ego during primary narcissism: his story is thus seen as inviting regression to a time when the ego is not sharply differentiated from the external world and from other persons.

Using the idea of repetition and recurrence as a link, Freud then proceeds to analyse the fear which derives from the helplessness experienced by one who continually finds himself confronting that from which he desires escape, or the anxiety generated through the repetition of harmless events (for example, coming across the number 62 several times in a single day). Such *repetition-compulsion*, Freud argues, is based upon early instinctual activity and lends a 'daemonic character' to certain aspects of mind; things which remind us of this repetition-compulsion are therefore associated with the uncanny. The uncanny itself, therefore, is linked with both the infantile and the neurotic in so far as it is connected with what Freud calls 'the over-accentuation of psychical reality in comparison with physical reality'. Freud's final example of how the *unheimlich* conflates with the *heimlich* derives from observation of male patients who, he claims, often declare that they feel there is something uncanny about the female genital organs. Freud points out that 'this *unheimlich* place, however, is the entrance to the former *heim* (home) of all human beings'. Once again the prefix 'un' is the token of repression, a repression which generates fear and anxiety, which are, in turn, projected upon something or someone in the environment.

Freud's essay and terminology have been adopted by critics of the Gothic who thereby read texts as codified forms of instinctual drives and mechanisms of repression. The more sophisticated of these, such as Mary Jacobus in her essay on Charlotte Brontë's *Villette* (see **THE BRONTËS**), develop the cultural implications of his work. See also Hélène Cixous's article 'Fiction and Its Phantoms: A Reading of Freud's *Das Unheimliche* (The "uncanny")', which attempts to deconstruct Freud's essay.

AVRIL HORNER

Urban Gothic

Urban gothic has its roots in the close connection between architectural structure and the psychological experience of characters in the earliest Gothic literature. In *The Castle of Otranto* (1764) for example, the paranoia and persecution of the characters is figured with reference to the rooms, tunnels and dungeons of the castle itself. In the nineteenth century the increasing concern about the relationship of the individual to urban surroundings to be found in many discourses leads to a rich representation of the city, particularly London, in *fin de siècle* Gothic literature.

The city is seen as uncanny, constructed by people yet unknowable by the individual. **EDGAR ALLAN POE**'s detective stories show the attempts of the individual to know the Gothic city, and **CHARLES DICKENS**'s unfinished *The Mystery of Edwin Drood* (1870) is a similar fragment. The city is also a place of ruins, paradoxically always new but always decaying, a state of death-in-life exploited fully in **BRAM STOKER**'s *Dracula* (1897).

The alienation of the urban subject, leading to paranoia, fragmentation and loss of identity, is another important theme, to be found in a number of works, including Thomas de Quincey's *Confessions of an English Opium Eater* (1822), **R. L. STEVENSON**'s *The Strange Case of Dr Jekyll and Mr Hyde* (1886), **OSCAR WILDE**'s *The Picture of Dorian Gray* (1891) and **ARTHUR MACHEN**'s *The Hill of Dreams* (1907).

Contemporary texts continue to deal with the issues of urban Gothic, notably in the work of Iain Sinclair, *Downriver* (1991) and *Radon Daughters* (1995), and the Gothic city of the future has been the setting for a number of films, such as Ridley Scott's *Blade Runner* (1982).

ALEXANDRA WARWICK

Selected Reading

General

Armitt, Lucie, *Theorising the Fantastic* (London: Arnold, 1996).

Birkhead, Edith, *The Tale of Terror: A Study of the Gothic Romance* (London: Constable, 1921).

Botting, Fred, *Gothic* (London: Routledge, 1996).

Bruhm, Steven, *Gothic Bodies: The Politics of Pain in Romantic Fiction* (Philadelphia, PA: University of Pennsylvania Press, 1994).

Castle, Terry, *The Female Thermometer: Eighteenth-Century Culture and the Invention of the Uncanny* (Oxford: Oxford University Press, 1995).

Cavaliero, Glen, *The Supernatural and English Fiction* (Oxford: Oxford University Press, 1995).

Clery, E. J., *The Rise of Supernatural Fiction, 1762–1800* (Cambridge: Cambridge University Press, 1995).

Cornwell, Neil, *The Literary Fantastic: From Gothic to Postmodern* (London: Harvester Wheatsheaf, 1990).

Cottom, Daniel, *The Civilized Imagination: A Study of Ann Radcliffe, Jane Austen, and Sir Walter Scott* (Cambridge: Cambridge University Press, 1985).

Day, William Patrick, *In the Circles of Fear and Desire: A Study of Gothic Fantasy* (London: University of Chicago Press, 1985).

Fiedler, Leslie, *Love and Death in the American Novel* (New York: Criterion Books, 1960).

Fisher, Benjamin F., *The Gothic's Gothic: Study Aids to the Tradition of the Tale of Terror* (London: Garland, 1988).

Frank, Frederick S., *Gothic Fiction: A Master List of Twentieth-Century Criticism and Research* (London: Meckler, 1988).

——, *The First Gothics: A Critical Guide to the English Gothic Novel* (London: Garland, 1987).

Geary, Robert F., *The Supernatural in Gothic Fiction: Horror, Belief, and Literary Change* (Lewiston, NY: The Edwin Mellen Press, 1992).

Graham, Kenneth W. (ed.), *Gothic Fictions: Prohibition/Transgression* (New York: AMS Press, 1989).

Grixti, Joseph, *Terrors of Uncertainty: The Cultural Contexts of Horror Fiction* (London: Routledge, 1989).

Howard, Jacqueline, *Reading Gothic Fiction: A Bakhtinian Approach* (Oxford: Clarendon Press, 1994).

Howells, Coral Ann, *Love, Mystery and Misery: Feeling in Gothic Fiction* (London: Athlone Press, 1978).

Jackson, Rosemary, *Fantasy: The Literature of Subversion* (London: Methuen, 1981).

Kelly, Gary, *The English Jacobin Novel, 1780–1805* (Oxford: Clarendon Press, 1976).

Kiely, Robert, *The Romantic Novel in England* (Cambridge, MA: Harvard University Press, 1973).

Kilgour, Maggie, *The Rise of the Gothic Novel* (London: Routledge, 1995).

Kliger, Samuel, *The Goths in England: A Study in Seventeenth and Eighteenth Century Thought* (Cambridge, MA: Harvard University Press, 1952).

Kristeva, Julia, *Powers of Horror*, trans. Leon Roudiez (New York: Columbia University Press, 1982).

Lloyd Smith, Alan, and Sage, Victor (eds), *Gothick: Origins and Innovations* (Amsterdam: Rodopi, 1994).

MacAndrew, Elizabeth, *The Gothic Tradition in Fiction* (New York: Columbia University Press, 1979).

Malin, Irving, *New American Gothic* (Carbondale: Southern Illinois University Press, 1962).

McNutt, Dan, *The Eighteenth-Century Gothic Novel: An Annotated Bibliography of Criticism and Selected Texts* (Folkestone, England: Dawson, 1975).

Morretti, Franco, *Signs Taken for Wonders* (London: Verso, 1983).

Napier, Elizabeth R., *The Failure of Gothic: Problems of Disjunction in an Eighteenth-Century Literary Form* (Oxford: Clarendon Press, 1987)

Punter, David, *The Literature of Terror: A History of Gothic Fictions from 1765 to the Present Day* (London: Longman, 1980); revised edn, Volume 1: *The Gothic Tradition* (London: Longman, 1996).

Railo, Eino, *The Haunted Castle: A Study of the Elements of English Romanticism* (London: George Routledge and Sons, 1927).

Roberts, Marie [Mulvey-], *Gothic Immortals: The Fiction of the Brotherhood of the Rosy Cross* (London: Routledge, 1990).

—— and Hugh Ormsby-Lennon, *Secret Texts: The Literature of Secret Societies* (New York: AMS Press, 1995).

Sage, Victor, *Horror Fiction in the Protestant Tradition* (London: Macmillan, 1988).

—— (ed.), *The Gothick Novel: A Casebook* (Macmillan: London, 1990).

—— and Allan Lloyd-Smith (eds), *Modern Gothic: A Reader* (Manchester: Manchester University Press, 1996).

Scarborough, Dorothy, *The Supernatural in Modern Fiction* (New York: Putnam, 1917).

Sedgwick, Eve Kosofsky, *The Coherence of Gothic Conventions* (London: Methuen, 1986).

Simpson, Mark S., *The Russian Gothic Novel and its British Antecedents* (Columbus, Ohio: Slavica, 1986).

Tompkins, J. M. S., *The Popular Novel in England, 1770–1800* (Lincoln: University of Nebraska Press, 1961).

Tracy, Anne B., *Patterns of Fear in the Gothic Novel, 1790–1830* (New York: Arno Press, 1980).

Varma, Devendra Prasad, *The Gothic Flame: Being a History of the Gothic Novel in England: Its Origins, Efflorescence, Disintegration, and Residuary Influences* (New York: Russell and Russell, 1966; London: A. Barker, 1957).

Voller, Jack G., *The Supernatural Sublime: The Metaphysics of Terror in Anglo-American Romanticism* (DeKalb, IL: Northern Illinois University Press, 1994).

Female Gothic

Bronfen, Elisabeth, *Over Her Dead Body: Death, Femininity and the Aesthetic* (Manchester: Manchester University Press, 1992).

Delamotte, Eugenia C., *Perils of the Night: A Feminist Study of Nineteenth-Century Gothic* (Oxford: Oxford University Press, 1990).

Doody, Margaret, 'Deserts, Ruins, Troubled Waters: Female Dreams in Fiction and the Development of the Gothic Novel', *Genre*, 10 (1977), 529–72.

Ellis, Kate Ferguson, *The Contested Castle: Gothic Novels and the Subversion of Domestic Ideology* (Urbana and Chicago: University of Illinois Press, 1989).

Fleenor, Juliann E. (ed.), *Female Gothic* (Montreal: Eden Press, 1983).

Gilbert, Sandra, and Gubar, Susan, *The Madwoman in the Attic* (New Haven, CT: Yale University Press, 1979).

Heller, Wendy Tamar, *Dead Secrets: Wilkie Collins and the Female Gothic* (New Haven, CT: Yale University Press, 1992).

Holland, Norman, and Sherman, Leona, 'Gothic Possibilities', *New Literary History*, 8 (1977), 278–94.

Hume, Robert, 'Gothic versus Romantic: A Revaluation of the Gothic Novel', *PMLA*, 84 (1969), 282–90.

Kahane, Claire, 'The Gothic Mirror', in Shirley Nelson Gardener, Claire Kahane and Madelon Sprengnether (eds), *The (M)other Tongue: Essays in Feminist Psychoanalytic Interpretation* (Ithaca: Cornell University Press, 1985), pp. 334–51.

Massé, Michelle A., *In the Name of Love: Women, Masochism and the Gothic* (Ithaca, NY: Cornell University Press, 1992).

Milbank, Alison, *Daughters of the House: Modes of the Gothic in Victorian Fiction* (Basingstoke: Macmillan; 1992).

Miles, Robert (ed.), 'Female Gothic Writing', *Women's Writing*, 1, no. 2 (1994).

——, *Gothic Writing 1750–1820: A Genealogy* (London: Routledge, 1993).

Moers, Ellen, *Literary Women* (London: W. H. Allen, 1977).

Restuccio, Frances L., 'Female Gothic Writing: Under Cover to Alice', *Genre*, 18 (1986), 245–66.

Small, Helen, *Love's Madness: Medicine, the Novel, and Female Insanity, 1800–1865* (Oxford: Clarendon Press, 1996).

Angela Carter

Anwell, Maggie, 'Lolita Meets the Werewolf: *The Company of Wolves*', in Lorraine Gamman and Margaret Marshment (eds), *The Female Gaze: Women as Viewers of Popular Culture* (London: The Women's Press, 1988), pp. 76–85.

Gamble, Sarah, *Angela Carter: Writing from the Front Line* (Edinburgh: Edinburgh University Press, 1997).

Jordan, Elaine, 'The Dangers of Angela Carter', in Isobel Armstrong (ed.), *New Feminist Discourses* (London: Routledge, 1992), pp. 119–31.

Neumeier, Beatie, 'Postmodern Gothic: Desire and Reality in Angela Carter's Writing', in *Modern Gothic: A Reader*, ed. Victor Sage and Allan Lloyd-Smith (Manchester: Manchester University Press, 1996), pp. 141–51.

Sage, Lorna, *Angela Carter* (Plymouth: Northcote House, 1994).

—— (ed.), *Flesh and the Mirror: Essays on the Art of Angela Carter* (London: Virago, 1994).

Edgar Allan Poe

Allen, Michael, *Poe and the British Magazine Tradition* (New York: Oxford University Press, 1969).

Budd, Louis J., and Cady, Edwin H. (eds), *On Poe: The Best from 'American Literature'* (London: Duke University Press, 1993).

Burdock, Michael L., *Grim Phantasms: Fear in Poe's Short Fiction* (London: Garland, 1992).

Fisher, Benjamin F., *The Very Spirit of Cordiality: The Literary Uses of Alcohol and Alcoholism in the Tales of Edgar Allan Poe* (Baltimore: Enoch Pratt Free Library and the Edgar Allan Poe Society, 1978).

Mooney, Stephen, 'Poe's Gothic Wasteland', *Sewanee Review*, 70 (1962), 261–83.

Thompson, G. R., *Poe's Fiction: Romantic Irony in the Gothic Tales* (Madison: University of Wisconsin Press, 1973).

Ann Radcliffe

Butler, Marilyn, 'The Woman at the Window: Ann Radcliffe in the Novels of Mary Wollstonecraft and Jane Austen', *Women and Literature*, 1 (1980), 128–48.

Castle, Terry, 'The Spectralization of the Other in *The Mysteries of Udolpho*', in Laura Brown and Felicity Nussbaum (eds), *The New Eighteenth Century: Theory, Politics, English Literature* (London: Methuen, 1987), pp. 237–53.

Clery, E. J., 'The Politics of the Gothic Heroine in the 1790s', in *Reviewing Romanticism*, ed. Philip Martin and Robin Jarvis (Basingstoke: Macmillan, 1992), pp. 69–85.

Miles, Robert, *Ann Radcliffe, The Great Enchantress* (Manchester: Manchester University Press, 1995).

Murrah, Charles C., 'Mrs Radcliffe's Landscapes: The Eye and the Fancy', *University of Windsor Review*, 18 (1984), 7–23.

Poovey, Mary, 'Ideology in *The Mysteries of Udolpho*', *Criticism*, 21, 307–30.

Tompkins, J. M. S., *The Work of Mrs Radcliffe and its Influence on Later Writers* (1921; rpt New York: Arno Press, 1980).

Mary Shelley

Baldick, Chris, *In Frankenstein's Shadow: Myth, Monstrosity, and Nineteenth-Century Writing* (Oxford: Clarendon Press, 1987).

Bann, Stephen (ed.), *Frankenstein, Creation and Monstrosity* (London: Reaktion Books, 1994).

Botting, Fred, *Making Monstrous: 'Frankenstein', Criticism, Theory* (Manchester: Manchester University Press, 1991).

Marshall, Tim, *Murdering to Dissect: Grave-Robbing, Frankenstein and the Anatomy Literature* (Manchester: Manchester University Press, 1995).

Mellor, Anne K., *Mary Shelley: Her Life, Her Fiction, Her Monsters* (London: Routledge, 1988).

Sunstein, Emily W., *Mary Shelley: Romance and Reality* (Baltimore: The Johns Hopkins University Press, 1989).

Veeder, William, *Mary Shelley and Frankenstein: The Fate of Androgyny* (London: University of Chicago Press, 1986).

Bram Stoker

Arata, S. D., 'The Occidental Tourist: *Dracula* and the Anxiety of Reverse Colonization', *Victorian Studies*, 33 (1990), 621–45.

Bentley, C. F., 'The Monster in the Bedroom: Sexual Symbolism in Bram Stoker's *Dracula*', *Literature and Psychology*, 22 (1972), 27–34.

Frayling, Christopher (ed.), *Vampyres: Lord Byron to Count Dracula* (London: Faber and Faber, 1991).

Gelder, Ken, *Reading the Vampire* (London: Routledge, 1994).

Hughes, William, *Bram Stoker: A Bibliography* (Brisbane: University of Queensland, 1997).

Pick, D., 'Terrors of the Night: *Dracula* and 'Degeneration' in the Late Nineteenth Century', *Critical Quarterly*, 30 (1989), 71–87.

Smith, Andy, *Dracula and the Critics* (Sheffield: Pavic Publications, 1996).

Horace Walpole

Harfst, Betsy Perteit, *Horace Walpole and the Unconscious: An Experiment in Freudian Analysis* (New York: Arno Press, 1980).

Hogle, Jerrold E., 'The Ghost of the Counterfeit in the Genesis of the Gothic', in *Gothick: Origins and Innovations*, ed. Allan Lloyd Smith and Victor Sage (Amsterdam: Rodopi, 1994), pp. 23–33.

Kallich, Martin, *Horace Walpole* (New York: Twayne's English Authors Series, 1971).

Ketton-Cremer, R. W., *Horace Walpole: A Bibliography* (London: Methuen, 1964).

Sabor, Peter (ed.), *Horace Walpole: The Critical Heritage* (London: Routledge & Kegan Paul, 1987).

Watt, Ian, 'Time and the Family in the Gothic Novel: *The Castle of Otranto*', *Eighteenth Century Life*, 10:3 (1986), 159–71.